HISTORICAL
ASPECTS OF
NEWMILNS

WEAVE·TRUTH·WITH·TRUST

*Dedicated to
all citizens of Newmilns,
past, present or future.*

*Ha'e ye mind lang, lang syne,
When the summer days were fine,
An' the sun shone brighter far
Than he's ever dune since syne.*

DR. GEORGE LAWRIE

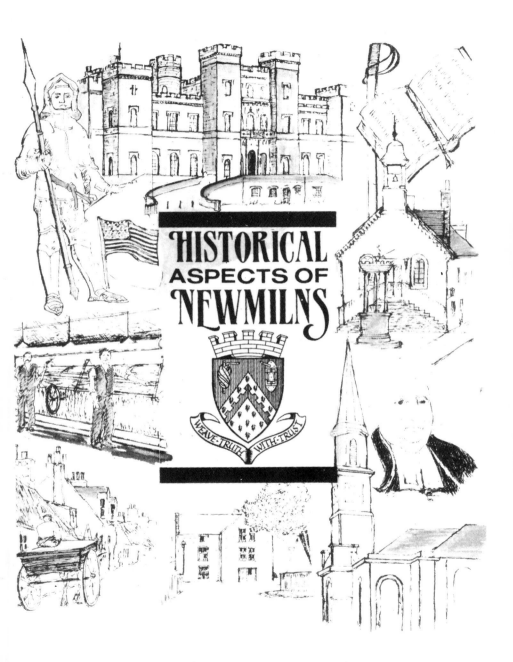

HISTORICAL
ASPECTS OF
NEWMILNS

WEAVE·TRUTH·WITH·TRUST

© Newmilns and Greenholm
Community Council

First Published in 1990

Printed in Scotland
by
Walker & Connell Ltd.,
Hastings Square, Darvel,
Ayrshire.

ISBN 0-907526-44-6

Preface

As part of the Quincentenary celebrations of the Burgh of Newmilns in 1990 it was decided to publish a history of the town. A committee of townspeople began the task in 1988 of bringing together into this single volume many of the recorded writings as well as some recently researched articles pertaining to the burgh's history and heritage.

In view of the format adopted, with different aspects of the town's history being contributed by different authors, some overlapping of the subjects covered was unavoidable so that each article could remain complete in itself.

The committee wish to thank Bobby McBride for his invaluable assistance in editing the manuscript, adding much original research, and designing the format of the book and the book jacket. Thanks also to Dr. Simpson and David Brown for photographs and to John Hood of Newmilns and Viviene Enemoser of Glasgow University for their co-operation.

The Newmilns Quincentenary Committee would like to thank the following for their contribution to this publication which records yet another chapter in the history and heritage of Scotland.

BURMAH PETROLEUM FUELS LTD.

BRITISH GAS plc (Scotland)

GRAMPIAN HOLDINGS plc

HEWDEN STUART plc

JAMES HOWDEN & CO LTD

NEWMILNS & GREENHOLM COMMUNITY COUNCIL

THE MARQUIS OF BUTE

SHANKS & McEWAN (Contractors) LTD.

JOHN MENZIES plc

ROYAL BANK OF SCOTLAND

STRATHCLYDE REGIONAL COUNCIL

TILCON LTD.

LORD WEIR

WALKER & CONNELL LTD.

INDEX

Charter
upon the creation of the Town of Newmyllis into a Free Burgh of Barony (1490)

James IV., by the Grace of God, King of Scots, to all good men in the whole Kingdom, clergy and laity, greeting, know ye that for the particular favour which we bear towards our Lovite George Campbell of Loudoun, our Sheriff of Ayr, and for the advantage and utility of our lieges the inhabitants of the town of Newmyllis and other places adjacent, with the advice and counsel of the Lords of our Council, we have established, created, and made, and by the tenor of this our present Charter, establish, create, and make the said town of Newmyllis, lying in the Barony of Loudoun, within our Sheriffdom of Ayr, into a free Burgh of Barony forever. We have also granted, and by this our present Charter grant to the inhabitants of the said Burgh and future inhabitants thereof, full power and free liberty of buying and selling in the said Burgh, wines, wax, woollen and linen cloths broad and narrow, and other lawful merchandise whatever, with power and liberty of having and keeping Bakers, Brewers, Fleshers, and sellers as well of Flesh as of Fish, and other craftsmen anyways pertaining and belonging to the freedom of a Burgh of Barony, and we have granted, and by the tenor of this our present Charter grant, that in said Burgh there be Burgesses, and that they have power in all time coming of electing Bailies and other officers necessary for the Government of said Borough, and in like manner we have granted, and by the tenor of this our present Charter grant, that the Burgesses and inhabitants of the said Burgh may have, hold and possess forever a Cross and Market on Sunday weekly, and public Fairs on every year forever upon the feast day of Saint Dionisius in Autumn, and for four immediately following said feast, with customs and all other liberties pertaining or which can justly be said to pertain to Fairs of the same kind in future. Having and holding the said town of Newmyllis in all time to come in a mere and free Burgh in Barony with the aforesaid privileges, liberties and concessions, and all and singular other privileges, profits, advantages, and easements and just pertinents whatsomever, as well not naimed as naimed pertaining or which may be justly held to pertain to a Burgh in Barony in future. And these as freely, quietly, amply, fully, honourably well and in peace in all and by all things as any Burgh in Barony in our Kingdom in whatever times by past has been more freely invested or held without any revocation whatever, wherefore we strictly order and command all and singular whom it concerns or may concern, that no one presume to act in opposition to this our Grant or any of the premises in any manner of way under every pain which may be competent in such case. In testimony whereof we have ordered our Great Seal to be appended to this our Charter before these witnesses, the Reverend Fathers in Christ, Robert, Bishop of Glasgow, William, Bishop of Aberdeen, our beloved cousins, Colin, Earl of Argyle, Lord Campbell and Lorne, our Chancellor, Patrick, Earl of Bothville, Lord Halis, Alexander Hume of that ilk, our Great Chamberlain, William, Lord Saint John, Master of our Household and our Treasury, John, Lord Glamings, John, Lord Drummond, our Justiciaries, the Venerable Father in Christ, John, Prior of St. Andrews, Keeper of our Private Seal, Andrew, Lord Gray Lawerence, Lord Oliphant, and our beloved Clergymen masters, Richard Murehead, Dean of Glasgow, Clerk of our Council Register and Rolls, and Archibald Whitelaw, Sub-Dean of Glasgow, our Secretary. At Linlithgow, the ninth day of January, in the year of our Lord one thousand four hundred and ninety, and of our reign the third year.

A History of Newmilns, Ayrshire

FRED WOODWARD

The burgh of Newmilns is situated at the narrowest part of the Irvine Valley and occupies the site of a suitable fording place across the River Irvine on the major route from Ayrshire into Avondale, Clydesdale and Central Scotland. In former times Newmilns provided a welcome respite to travellers on the trade routes from Edinburgh to the West Coast.

The area was already inhabited by 2000 BC as indicated by the site of a neolithic stone circle east of the Gowf course whilst a Neolithic Barrow at Henryton contained stone axes which dated from 1500 BC.

This Henryton site was still occupied in Bronze Age times circa 1000 BC since the site also contained a Cairn with cists which are reputed to have contained bronze implements.

By Roman times the route was well established and considered of strategic importance as evidenced by the development of a Roman camp at Loudoun Hill circa 200 AD coupled with the development of characteristic Roman straight roads passing down the Valley to Ayr.

Following the Roman withdrawal the Valley continued to provide a trade route as well as an easy access to potential invaders and it has been suggested that King Arthur fought a battle in the area about 542.

In 575 a further battle is thought to have been at the mouth of the Glen Water between the local tribe of Domnonii and the invading Scots who originated from Ireland. In time this lead to the establishment of farms in the area with Gaelic names e.g., Pobaith, meaning Pool of the Birches; and Wraes, meaning The Neuk.

Between 800 and 1200 the area was under Viking occupation resulting in the introduction of Nordic words to the Scots language. During this period forts were established on virtually every burn in the parish hence the presence of Medieval earthworks and possible motte north of Loudoun Kirk as well as Castle Hill, Alton Farm; Judge's Hill south of East Newton together with the remains of a medieval Castle west of Woodhead Farm with adjacent lime-kilns.

Christianity became the accepted religion, although pagan ceremonies were still being practised, Loudoun Kirk was established in 1451.

The earliest part of Loudoun Castle, a square tower with battlements, is reputed to have been built in the 12th or 13th century and was partially destroyed when besieged by General Monk in the 17th century.

The lands forming the Loudoun estates were established circa 1190 under a charter from David I (1084-1153) to James de Loudoun. His daughter, Margaret de Loudoun, married Sir Reginald de Crawfurd, heritable Sheriff of the County of Ayr, an office the Loudoun family held almost without interruption for over 500 years until the post was abolished in 1747.

Sir Reginald's eldest son, Hugh de Loudoun, succeeded his father and a daughter of his, Margaret, became the wife of Sir Malcolm Wallace of Elderslie and mother of Sir William Wallace, Scotland's national hero. In 1296 the region was again the scene of battle; the Scots under William Wallace defeating the English at the Battle of Loudoun Hill. At this period Galston was a Wallace stronghold, being also known as Wallacetoon.

In 1303 the fifth Crawfurd of Loudoun died for the Scottish cause, the estate passing to the Campbells through his only daughter, Susannah who married Sir Duncan Campbell, the grandson of Sir Colin More Campbell, the ancestor of the Duke of Argyll. Her son, Sir Andrew Campbell of Loudoun, heritable Sheriff of Ayr is mentioned in a charter of 1307.

In 1307 Robert Bruce also defeated the English at the Battle of Loudoun Hill to provide his first victory in the quest for a free Scotland. The grave from this battle can still be seen to this day.

On Bruce's death his heart is reputed to have been brought back to Scotland for burial by Sir James Keith, a Galston Knight.

In the early fifteenth century building work took place at Loudoun Castle with the erection of the Towerhouse which raised the battlements above the surrounding mass of buildings thus providing a commanding view across the Irvine Valley.

At the close of that century King James IV made the town of Newmyllis into a Free Burgh of Barony in 1490.

The sixteenth century began violently. In 1525 the Kennedy's of Culzean set fire to Loudoun Castle resulting in the deaths of Sir Hugh Campbell's wife, his nine children and a nurse maid in the flames. The Loudoun Charter, however, was saved from the fire by the two sons of a Mr. Jamieson from Whatrigs.

It was presumably as a result of this catastrophe that the 16th Century Tower was erected in Castle Street, Newmilns. This castle was occupied by members of the Loudoun family till at least 1615.

In 1566 Newmilns is reputed to have received a further Charter from Mary, Queen of Scots to Sir Matthew Campbell of Loudoun, confirming the right of 'holding courts and applying the issues thereof to common uses'. This extension also permitted Newmilns to hold Fairs, and Markets, to buy and sell wines and wax and woollen and linen cloths.

On the 30th June, 1601, James VI bestowed the title of Lord Campbell of Loudoun upon Sir Hugh Campbell, the First Lord Loudoun, Sheriff of Ayr and Scottish privy councillor and further extensions to Loudoun Castle took place.

This century proved a violent one for the Newmilns area and was a stronghold for the Covenanting cause. John Nisbet of Hardhill, gave his life in the cause being executed at the Grassmarket, Edinburgh on the 4th December 1685.

Other martyrs included Matthew Paton, a Newmilns shoemaker who was taken at Pentland and executed at Glasgow on the 19th December 1666.

David Findlay, of Newmilns who, in 1666 foolishly mentioned to his fellow townsmen that he had seen the Covenanting army pass through Lanark, this indiscretion was brought to the notice of Dalziel, and since Findlay refused to disclose further details he was shot.

James Wood, captured at the battle of Bothwell Bridge, who was hanged at Magus-Muir on 25th November 1679 because he refused to call the Bothwell rising a rebellion or accept Bishop Sharp's death as murder.

John Nisbet, who was executed on the 14th of April 1683 at Kilmarnock because he refused to give information as to the whereabouts of his friends during the Bothwell rising.

James Nisbet of Highside was sentenced to death at Glasgow on the 11th of June 1684 as a result of attending the funeral of John Richmond of Knowe who had been executed at Glasgow for his adherence to the Covenanters work for Reformation.

The new Loudoun Old Parish Manse, situated on St. Margaret's Hill, was built about 1700 to replace its predecessor which stood in the glebe. This new manse is locally associated with Scotland's National Bard, Robert Burns, through his friendship with its minister Dr. Lawrie. It is also of interest that a lintel in the manse, dated 1768, is inscribed with the initials 'G.L.' and 'M.C.' together with the Hebrew 'Jehovah Jireh'. These initials stand for George Lawrie and his wife Margaret Cunningham.

Hugh, 3rd Earl of Loudoun subscribed the notorious articles of the Union which, in 1707, unified the Parliaments of Scotland and England. It is reputed that this historic document was signed beneath the Loudoun Yew which stands to this day immediately in front of the Castle but it is more probable that only the drafting of it took place here.

Looking west along Main Street early this century. On the left is the old Council House of the ancient burgh of barony, built in 1739. The bell which greatly predates the building is engraved with the date 1547. Upstairs is the Council chamber with the tollbooth or jail on the ground floor. The construction of such a prestigious building at that time marked the growing importance of the burgh as a textile centre. In front, at the Cross, is a drinking fountain presented by Miss Martha Brown of Lanfine at the installation of gravitation water in 1890. Further along at the Brigend public house is another provided by Joseph Hood, Provost of the town.

By 1725 roads were beginning to be developed in the area, the only wheeled cart belonging to the Castle, local farmers and gentry using horse-drawn sledges, at that time known as caurs, for transport, ploughing being by use of oxen.

It was about this period that John, the 4th Earl of Loudoun, introduced the brown and white cattle from Teeswater which were to provide the ancestors of the famous Ayrshire breed of cattle.

1738 saw the opening of Loudoun Old Parish Church on the site of a previous Church judging by the tombstones to the Covenanters.

At this time the principal occupation in the town was weaving, virtually every house having a loom; the other chief occupation was peat cutting, the price being four modern pence for a cartload.

The Old Council House, prominently sited in the town square, was built in 1739 through the co-operation of the Earl of Loudoun and the Town Council. Its upper room was originally used as a court and council chamber whilst the lower floor acted as a Tolbooth for the 'imprisonment and warding of delinquents and other vagrants'.

The council accounts indicate that the Tolbooth was also used for the confinement of 'pressed men' since an entry for 1757 reads–'Archibald Browning 2 loads of coals for the Prest Men in the Tolbooth. 13 shillings'.

In addition the Old Council House steps have provided a perfect platform for orators and reformists to address the assembled townspeople in the square below.

Adjacent to this are the premises today occupied by Todds. This building bearing a plaque to the effect that it was rebuilt in 1883 on the site of a former building, the carved coat of arms of which were incorporated in the front chimney of the new building.

The year, 1750 heralded the forestation of the Loudoun estates by John, 4th Earl of Loudoun, coupled with the provision of improved drainage, enclosed fields with planted hedges and windbreaks, which has formed the landscape as we know it today. It is estimated that he planted in the region of one million trees during this project, including Elm, Ash and Oak.

At this date his farm workers would expect to receive a fair remuneration and it is recorded that a male domestic servant who was able to plough, thatch, mow, bind, cart, sledge, harrow, do all husband work, axe-man, would receive two pounds fifty yearly or two pounds twenty-five pence plus two pairs of shoes. At the same time a young girl, able to spin in winter and herd in summer–at this time there were few hedges in Scotland–would receive eighty-three pence per year or sixty-seven pence and two pairs of shoes.

In 1756 the Earl of Loudoun was appointed Governor of Virginia and as a result found himself in the enviable position of being able to obtain exotic shrubs from America and other parts of the world visited during his travels. In this way he was able to introduce virtually all the known willows in cultivation in England, Ireland, Holland, Flanders, Germany, America and Portugal to the Loudoun estates.

Coupled with this introduction of trees the Earl also established several lime kilns in the area due to the need to improve the condition of the soil on his estate.

1773 saw the opening of the United Presbyterian Church in High Street, the members who formed the congregation having previously travelled to Kilmaurs each Sunday in order to attend a Church in accordance with their beliefs. The first minister, the Reverend James Gray had a stipend of £40 and was there for 40 years, but two subsequent ministers remained even longer, the Reverend James W. Dalgleish, M.A., for 46 years whilst the Reverend John Bruce, D.D., remained for 56 years. This United Church was replaced by a larger one, Newmilns West Church, situated immediately behind it in 1833, serving the congregation until it closed in 1961.

About this time the celebrated Scottish poet, Allan Ramsay, father of the artist of the same name, visited Loudoun Castle presumably for patronage. During this visit he took a walk by the river and, on seeing a girl working in the fields wrote his song, *'The lass o' Patie's Mill, Sae bonnie, blythe and gay'*. Sadly Pate's Mill was demolished in 1977.

John, 4th Earl of Loudoun, affectionately known as 'The Farming Earl' died in 1782.

Robert Burns visited the valley on several occasions in the 1780's to see his friend the Reverend Dr. Lawrie, minister at the Loudoun Old Parish Church. It was during one such visit to the manse that Burns inscribed on the window of his room–

'Lovely Mrs. Lawrie she is all charms'

This window has been greatly treasured by the successive ministers of Loudoun and is preserved to this day being currently in the possession of the present minister, the Reverend Ian Hamilton.

Burns also wrote *'A Prayer left by the Author at a Reverend Friend's House'*

The Paisley weaver and packman, Alexander Wilson, visited Newmilns about 1790 in an attempt to gain patronage from the Loudouns for the publication of his book of poems which were much in the style of his contemporary, Robert Burns.

1811 saw the completion of the major portion of Loudoun Castle which by this time was often referred to as the 'Windsor of Scotland'.

From 1816 to 1832 there was a resurgence of support for social reform in the Valley, the Old Reform Flag of Newmilns being unfurled amidst great agitation and threatened riots. With the rise of industry in Europe the demand for goods lessened with the result that weavers who had been making fifty pence per day were working sixteen hours per day for a six day week in order to earn twenty five pence per week by 1840.

Thomas Brown, of Langside, Glasgow, and acting Professor of Botany of Glasgow University from about 1796 to 1807, took up residence at Lanfine in the 1820's and set to work planting trees and shrubs throughout the estate. It is to his foresight that we owe our present views of the picturesque wooded valley and the Brown's Road connecting Newmilns to the neighbouring town of Darvel. Thomas was also an active collector and amassed fine collections of minerals and fossils including an important collection of fossil vertebrates from the Siwalik Hills, India. Due to these collections coupled with his academic background Lanfine became a centre for Natural historians and was visited in 1855 by the Reverend David Landsborough, senior, of Saltcoats, a leading figure in the Disruption as well as the Scientific community of that time. Landsborough, a keen marine biologist, wrote the natural history of Arran, and was known affectionately as the Gilbert White of Ayrshire. His son, David Landsborough, junior, was a Minister in Kilmarnock, and a founder member of the Glenfield and Kilmarnock Ramblers who have spent many happy excursions to Lanfine. On Thomas's death his collections passed to the Royal Scottish Museum in Edinburgh and Glasgow University.

1831 saw the commencement of the feud between the Loudoun family and the 'troublesome' folk of Newmilns in their long running dispute over a right-of-way through Loudoun policies known as the Lime Road. In 1831 barricades were erected in an attempt to close the road but these were immediately removed by a body of Newmilns men. Subsequently in 1870 the barricades were again erected on three separate occasions only to be removed by the townsfolk. Then, in 1878, wooden gates were erected to be immediately demolished. In September 1886, the road was again closed, but the following week the radicals marched down and again demolished the barricades. A few weeks later the same thing occurred and again the barriers proved fruitless. This course of action was repeated the following summer and yet again in 1891 when for the ninth time they were removed by the Newmilns men. In desperation the Loudouns set to digging up the road whereupon the townspeople set up a committee to take legal action. The case was taken to the Court of Session in Edinburgh, and after two trials the verdict was returned in favour of the people of Newmilns so that in 1893 the last remains of the offensive barriers were removed and the road left for free access to the townspeople.

By 1844 the population of Newmilns had increased considerably and the 1738 Loudoun Old Parish Church proved too small for its congregation so that it was demolished and the present Loudoun Old Parish Church was erected on the same site.

Gas was first introduced to the town in 1845, a second private company being established in 1870. Both of these companies were taken over by the town council in 1902.

Loudoun East Church, known as the Free Kirk was founded after the Disruption of 1843, its first services being held in the Sun Inn from 1845 until the Church opened in 1847. It was built at a cost of £844 and was demolished in 1986, the congregation being amalgamated with that of the Parish Church in 1980.

During 1864 the Newmilns Anti-Slavery Society, which met at the Black Bull Hall, the building opposite the Browns Institute now occupied by the Clydesdale Bank, sent resolutions of sympathy and support to President Lincoln and his Government, in spite of the fact that the local weavers were being hit hard by the loss of cotton from the southern states. As an expression of appreciation, Abraham Lincoln eventually sent an American Flag to the town at the hands of a Mr. John Brooks, a coloured gentleman.

The flag in question was presented to John Donald, a local leader in the Chartist movement, and driving force of the Newmilns Anti-Slavery Society. He was born in 1804 and died in his 89th year.

For many years afterwards the *Lincoln Flag* was brought forth and paraded in company with the *Blue Blanket* which had been carried at Drumclog, on all major Ceremonial occasions in the Burgh, such as the Trade Races.

An innovation to the weaving industry came in 1867 with the erection of the first power-loom factory on an open site at Greenholm. Built by Joseph Hood, the noted loom builder and Hugh Morton, a weaving agent, the Wincey Mill was the first factory in the valley to use a steam engine for manufacturing the cloth, with a cotton warp and a woollen weft, known as wincey.

In 1870 the Brown's Institute, in memory of Thomas Brown, of Lanfine, was gifted to the town and contained a library and reading room together with a recreation room, and acted in company with the Temperance Hall as a social centre for the town for lectures, concerts and weddings. It is perhaps fitting therefore, that it is presently the headquarters of Newmilns Silver Band.

In 1872 the Police Burgh boundaries were extended across the River Irvine into Galston parish to create the larger burgh of

Newmilns and Greenholm.

The decline of handloom weaving in the Irvine Valley was offset in 1876 by the foresight of a Darvel cotton agent, Alexander Morton, with the introduction of a power loom from Nottingham to establish a new type of cotton manufacture, namely the factory production of lace curtains. This was followed by others in Darvel and Newmilns. in the 1880s the introduction of madras power looms strengthened the Valley's hold on the industry, but also resulted in the demise of traditional handloom weaving.

This new industry at one time boasted nineteen factories in Darvel and thirteen in Newmilns, the Irvine Valley becoming world-famous as a centre for the production of lace and madras furnishings ousting the parent centre of Nottingham.

The year 1877 witnessed the opening of Lady Flora's Institute as a school for young girls, erected by Lady Sophia Hastings as a memorial to her sister, Lady Flora Hastings, who was the subject of calumny at the Court of Queen Victoria. Lady Flora's poem's were published by her sister and raised £700; this sum being supplemented by a further bequest of £12,000 by Lady Sophia. The resultant funds providing for the erection of the school and an endowment for its upkeep. On the abolition of School Boards in 1921 the school was converted into a Women's Institute administered by the County and provided the community with a variety of activities until its closure in 1981 when the building was deemed unsafe. The grounds in front of Lady Flora's, which include the town's War Memorial, were laid out by the Civic Week Committee in 1949 to improve the appearance of the town, were transferred to the town council who undertook their continued upkeep. This responsibility was transferred to Kilmarnock and Loudoun District Council following the reorganisation of Scottish Local Government in 1976.

In 1894 a further educational advance in the town took place, with the opening of Newmilns School. Situated in High Street, it overlooked the River Irvine across to the Lanfine woods. Designed by a local architect and literateur, John Macintosh, it replaced an older school in Union Street which had to be demolished to make way for an extension to the railway to Darvel. For many years the school was affectionately called 'Hood's School' after Mr. Archibald Hood who was its headmaster for 40 years. The School continued until 1960·when it was irretrievably damaged by fire.

The Morton Hall opened in 1896 and originally seated 750 people. It was gifted to the town by William Morton who left Newmilns for Birmingham where he made his fortune and is reputed to have been built on the site of his childhood home. The hall has recently been refurbished and once more is playing an active role in the community nearly one hundred years after its establishment.

During the First World War the town of Newmilns suffered the loss of 138 young men killed in the conflict. They are commemorated by the War Memorial erected by the townspeople in front of Lady Flora's. Their sacrifice, together with that of those killed in the Second World War of 1939-1945 is still recalled each year by the Armistice Day parade and service.

The Cinema came to Newmilns in 1913, courtesy of the Young family, with the building of the Cine at the top end of the town in the area now occupied by the Townhead Garage.

The original silent pictures were soon replaced by talkies. Wireless arrived too, with the simple crystal sets, followed by radios and the gramophone.

The year 1920 is often remembered as the year of the flood, much of the lower parts of the town suffered severe damage when the Irvine overflowed its banks to such an extent that Greenside resembled a lake. A large part of river banking at Kilnholm Street was washed away completely. This section has since been replaced and today is often referred to as the Red Wall.

The depression of the late twenties and early thirties had considerable impact on the town with mass unemployment and the introduction of a Means Test. As a result a branch of the National Unemployed Workers' Movement was formed in the town and its members regularly joined the hunger marches.

As the depression abated the town started to prosper once more with the development of new housing schemes, improved street lighting and sanitation.

The Old Men's Cabin, adjacent to the river on Browns Road, was opened in 1930. Built by public subscription it has provided a tranquil setting for the town's elder citizens and, as a result of the increased population and life expectancy, has been extended as recently as 1985.

September 1939 saw the outbreak of World War Two, and also the opening of The Rex Cinema, in Main Street, on the site of the old Cross Keys Inn. This purpose-built theatre was considered a model of comfort and opened with the film 'Alexander's Ragtime Band'. This new venture looked doomed when, together with the Cine, it was ordered to close due to the Government's concern for the safety of patrons in case of enemy bombing. Fortunately common sense prevailed so that both were soon playing to packed audiences with Saturday matinees for children. Sadly the availability of T.V. hastened the demise of the cinema and the Rex finally closed in 1986.

Loudoun Castle, was destroyed by fire in 1941 and the Countess of Loudoun, mother of Lady Jean Campbell of Loudoun, took up

1975 – THE LAST TOWN COUNCIL

BACK ROW:
Trevor Whale; Jim Lindsay, Town Chamberlain; Jim Pollock, Burgh Surveyor; Maureen Morris;
Bert Brown; John Young; Guy Mair, Town Clerk.

FRONT ROW:
Wm. Morton; Baillie Jim Leitch; Provost John White; Baillie Alex Muir; Treasurer Tom Hamilton.

residence in the Dower House nearby.

The townsfolk set up a committee in 1949 to organise a week of celebrations, 'Newmilns Civic Week', which took place from the 28th May until June 4th. The festivities included a gala day pageant, five a side football, country dancing displays, Newmilns Burgh Band concerts etc. It was during this week that the U.S. Consul General Mr. D.C. McDonough presented the town with the American Flag, which is now in the Parish Church, to replace the original one given to the Newmilns handloom weavers by Abraham Lincoln in 1864 in recognition of their support by the formation of an Anti-Slavery Society.

The year 1954 is often referred to as the year of the mud flood and was caused by the town coup at Isles Public Park being washed into the Norrell Burn and from there being carried into Darvel Road, Main Street, Union Street and Burn Road, the coup refuse being accompanied by additional uprooted trees and dead live stock. The situation deteriorated further following further rain resulting in the accumulating debris being washed into the Irvine, a sea of mud and uprooted trees accompanying the flood water into Campbell Street, Isles Street as well as down Main Street as far as East Strand.

The year 1960 will be remembered as the year the school burnt down, the largely timber building producing a spectacular blaze, being fanned by a strong breeze blowing along the valley. The joy of the pupils was short lived, with classes being held in makeshift classrooms in local halls, until the school was replaced by the Primary School at Gilfoot in 1964. The secondary pupils subsequently moving further west to the Loudoun Academy which opened in 1971.

Reorganisation of Scottish Local Government in 1975 saw the demise of the Newmilns Burgh Council. From this date Newmilns has been administered by the newly created Kilmarnock and Loudoun District Council whose headquarters are in Kilmarnock.

Lady Flora's closed in 1981, due to the building being considered unsafe. Coincidently this was the year in which Lady Jean Campbell died. Lady Jean was succeeded at the Dower House by her daughter, Mrs. Sheena Williams, husband Donald and their daughter.

The Burgh's motto, 'WEAVE TRUTH WITH TRUST' has stood the community in good stead for the past five hundred years.

Murdoch Nisbet and the New Testament in Scots

By REV. ADAM GIRVAN

The 14th century Yorkshireman and theologian, John Wyclif, became towards the end of his life progressively more radical in his views. In furtherance of his convictions, he had the Bible translated from Latin into the English vernacular of his day to make it more accessible to ordinary people. And, to give wide currency to the Gospel, he sent out travelling preachers to preach whenever they could gain a hearing. His writings and the translated Bible and the work of his itinerant preachers won a large number of adherents. They were known as Lollards. This group attacked the social abuses of the day as well as being outspoken in denouncing the corruptions at that time in the church and of the clergy.

Wyclif died in 1384. Despite continued persecution Lollardy persisted and had something of a revival 100 years later. In time it became one of the contributory sources of English Protestantism.

Through contact with England, Lollardy had some influence in Scotland and certainly in South-west Scotland. At the beginning of the 16th century Murdoch Nisbet owned a farm called Hardhill in our parish of Loudoun. There is a rubble of stones at the back of Loudoun Manse, between the manse and Claremont Farm which is all that remains of this Hardhill. Like many of his fellow countrymen he became acquainted with the work of John Wyclif. What Wyclif had done for England Murdoch Nisbet determined to do for Scotland. He decided to copy a revision of Wyclif's New Testament but to alter the English words and phrases into Scots wherever he thought this might be of help to his fellow countryfolk. No one knows exactly when he began to write by hand a copy of the New Testament in Scots, although the main text appears to have been completed around 1520.

One wonders how a small time farmer found time for such a demanding task but Murdoch Nisbet soon had plenty of time. Having joined the Lollards of Kyle–the name given to the Ayrshire followers of Wyclif–he was in danger of being brought to trial as a heretic. As a result he had to quit his farm and flee the country. It is not known exactly where he went but there is evidence to suggest that he went first to England and then to Germany. While abroad he completed his

New Testament in Scots. Although it was still an offence punishable by death to own such a book, he braved the journey back to Scotland with his precious manuscript. He had to go into hiding and literally went underground. He built a shelter under his farmhouse and hid there to avoid capture. Men, women and children went there to visit him and to see his precious book which included lessons from the Old Testament as well as a complete copy of the New Testament.

In time, through popular demand for changes in the ordering of Church affairs, Murdoch Nisbet, by then an old man, was lucky enough to be able to come out of hiding and share in the events which ultimately led to the Reformation in Scotland in 1560.

When he died his book passed on to his son, Alexander, then to his grandson, James, and to his great-grandson, John, the famous Covenanter whose memorial stands in front of Loudoun Church.

John Nisbet is another story, part of the Covenanting story of our parish. He fought at Drumclog and Bothwell Bridge.

When John was executed Murdoch Nisbet's book passed to his son, James, who had kept a diary until the age of 21, providing a compelling insight into the lives of John and Margaret Nisbet and of their struggles during their 4 years on the run. This diary is now preserved in the Signet Library in Edinburgh under the title 'Private life of the persecuted or memoirs of the first years of James Nisbet, one of the Scottish Covenanters.'

As James and his wife had no children when he died, his widow entrusted Murdoch Nisbet's book to Sir Alexander Boswell, an Edinburgh advocate, thinking James's nephew might not appreciate the value of the book. Boswell, however, in due time returned the book to the nephew who sold it to a certain Gavin Hamilton. It was on Hamilton's bookshelves that Boswell found it quite by chance in 1745, the year of the Jacobite Rebellion. And so it was that the first New Testament in Scots came into the possession of the Boswells of Auchinleck, in whose library it remained until 1893. Then, after passing through the hands of a bookseller the manuscript was purchased for his collection of rare and interesting Bibles by Lord Amherst of Hackney, a noted book-lover and collector who lent it to the British Text Society.

Where is the original manuscript now? It is in the British Library at the British Museum, having been purchased from the Amherst family in 1909.

Murdoch Nisbet's intention was that it should be possessed by the ordinary people of Scotland. Should this original manuscript not be on display in a place of honour in his native land for all to admire?

I Byde my Tyme

Loudoun

The Loudoun Family

By FLORA THOMPSON

The history of Newmilns and the Loudouns go hand in hand throughout the centuries. The origins of the family go back to the reign of David I (1084-1153) when Richard de Morville was Constable of Scotland. It was from him that James de Loudoun, son of Lambinus obtained the charter to the lands of Loudoun.

James's heir was a daughter, Margaret, who married Sir Reginald de Crawfurd, heritable Sheriff of the County of Ayr. Their eldest son Hugh de Crawfurd de Loudoun succeeded his father and a daughter of his, Margaret married Sir Malcolm Wallace of Elderslie. Their son was Sir William Wallace, Scotland's national hero, one of whose swords hung in Loudoun Castle until it was sold by auction in the 1920s. The castle was destroyed by fire on 1st December 1941.

The fifth Crawfurd of Loudoun, Sir Reginald fell fighting for his country in 1303. He left an only daughter, Susannah who married Sir Duncan Campbell, an ancestor of the Dukes of Argyle.

A grandson of theirs Sir Hugh Campbell was appointed to meet James I at Durham in 1423 and one of his sons, John was one of the hostages for the ransom of the king the following year. Sir John also accompanied Margaret, daughter of James II to France for her marriage to the dauphin. He died in 1450.

In 1451 his widow gave money to the monks of Fail to establish the first church in the district at Loudoun Kirk.

In 1490 on the application of George Campbell a charter was granted by James IV making Newmilns the first inland Burgh of Barony in Ayrshire and fifth oldest in the county.

In 1527 a party led by Sir Hugh Campbell assassinated Gilbert, Earl of Cassillis at Prestwick. According to tradition the men from Carrick in retaliation besieged the keep of Auchruglen which was situated near Crosstree Farm. They set fire to it, killing the Lady Loudoun and her nine children.

Sir Hugh died in 1552 and was succeeded by Sir Matthew Campbell, Sheriff of Ayr who added to the Loudoun Estate the lands of Darvel from Gavin, Commendator of Kilwinning on January 1564.

The first of the Campbells to attain nobility was Sir Hugh–First Lord Loudoun–created Lord of Parliament in 1601 by James VI. He died in 1622 and was succeeded by his granddaughter Margaret who married Sir John Campbell of Lawers in 1629. He was created First Earl of Loudoun, Baron Terrinyean and Baron Mauchline in May 1633.

In 1640 he was sent as commissioner to parliament and was committed to the Tower of London and sentenced to be executed by Charles I but was saved by the Marquis of Hamilton's intervention.

Supporting the royalist cause he was made Chancellor of Scotland in 1641 and took part in the coronation of Charles II at Scone in 1650. He fought at the Battle of Dunbar in the same year.

After Charles's defeat by Cromwell at Worcester 1651 he retreated to the Highlands where he spent the rest of his days. He died in Edinburgh in 1663 and is buried at Loudoun Kirk.

His son James became Second Earl and being a supporter of the Covenanting cause, he was a wanted man and spent most of his life abroad until he died at Leyden in Holland in 1684. When writing home to his wife, to avoid interception, he addressed his letters

To: The guidwife at Auldton,
At the old yew tree of Loudoun,
Scotland.

The Third Earl was Hugh who succeeded his father. He was privy councillor to both George I and Queen Anne, Knight of the Thistle and joint Secretary of State for Scotland. He was one of the commissioners to discuss the Act of Union in 1707 and in the following year became keeper of the Great Seal.

In 1715 he became Lord Lieutenant of Ayrshire and fought at Sheriffmuir under the Duke of Argyle.

In the general election after the union he was elected one of the sixteen representative peers from Scotland and was re-elected at each election until his death in 1731. He was also Lord High Commissioner of the Church of Scotland on six different occasions.

After his death his wife lived at Sorn Castle and died five months short of her 100th birthday in 1779.

John, the Fourth Earl was born in 1705 and succeeded his father in 1731. He was an elected representative peer from 1734 till his death at Loudoun Castle in 1782. In April 1741 he was appointed governor of Stirling Castle and in 1743 Aide-de-Camp to King George II. During the Jacobite Rebellion of 1745, he was commander-in-chief in Scotland under Sir John Cope, but most of his regiment were killed or taken prisoner at the Battle of Prestonpans. He was then sent north with money and arms to raise an army and his force of two thousand men relieved the garrison at Fort Augustas. When the Jacobite army returned to Inverness in 1746 he tried to trap Prince Charles at Moy Castle, the seat of the Macintoshes, but was driven off by a collection

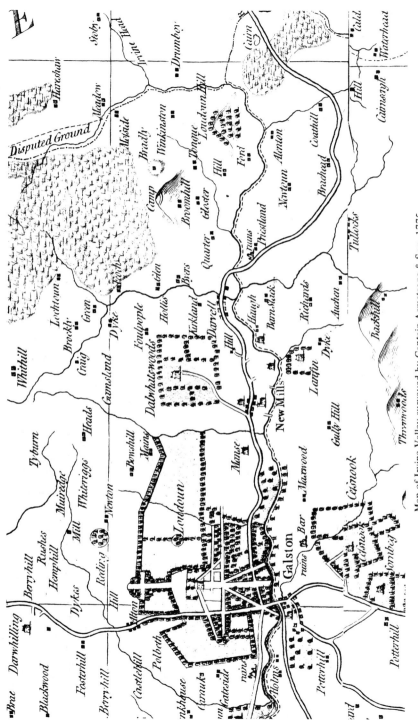

Map of Irvine Valley surveyed by Captain Armstrong & Son, 1775

of farm workers and servants led by the lady of the castle, afterwards nicknamed 'Colonel Anne.' He retreated to Skye, not taking part at the Battle of Culloden . In 1756 he was appointed commander-in-chief of His Majesty's forces in America but was later recalled, in 1762, to become second in command of the British troops in Portugal fighting against Spain. His last post was that of governor of Edinburgh Castle which he took over in 1770.

At Loudoun he was responsible for planting what has been estimated at a million trees which created 'Loudoun's bonnie woods and braes.' As well as modernising farming, he built the first made-up road in Ayrshire–from the castle to Newmilns–predating any others by thirty years.

James Mure Campbell born 1726 assumed the name Mure after succeeding his mother to the estates of Rowallan–his grandmother was the Countess of Glasgow. He was a soldier and a member of parliament, reaching the rank of Major General. He succeeded his cousin as Fifth Earl of Loudoun in 1782 and died at Loudoun Castle in 1786 leaving an only child Flora Mure.

James's father, Sir James Campbell was awarded the Order of the Bath from George II for his gallant conduct at the Battle of Dettingen 1743 against the French.

The Sixth holder of the title was Flora Mure Campbell, born 1780, who succeeded at the age of 6 and was brought up by the Earl and Countess of Dumfries with whom she stayed till 1803. When she married Francis Rawdon Hastings, Second Earl of Moira in Ireland in 1804–the bride was given away by the Prince Regent.

Lord Moira was one of the most notable men of his time. He entered the army in 1771, fought in the American War of Independence and was wounded at Bunker Hill in 1775. Afterwards he became Commander of the army in Scotland in 1803 and a Knight of the Garter in 1812. In 1816 he was holder of the titles:- Marquis of Hastings, Earl of Rawdon and Viscount Loudoun.

Appointed Governor General of India in 1812 he made vast territorial gains for the East India Company. A statue to his memory stands in the Dalhouse Institute, Calcutta. In 1824 he was given the post of Governor General of Malta but, in failing health, he died two years later aboard H.M.S. Revenge and was buried in Malta. He gave instructions that on his death his hand should be cut off, preserved and buried with his wife.

Throughout his life Lord Moira spent a huge amount of money on Loudoun Estate including £100,000 on the castle in 1811 making it one of the most attractive castles in the country and earning it the title 'The Windsor of Scotland.' The castle had ninety rooms and was built round the 17th century keep. The Countess and Lord Moira had

five children. The first, George succeeded both his mother's and
father's titles. The second child was the ill-fated Lady Flora
Hastings. The third Sophia Frederica Christina was married to the
2nd Marquis of Bute and provided the money for the-building of Lady
Flora's Institute.

The Hastings came to Britain with William the Conqueror the
founder of the family being Paulyn Roydon who received a grant of
land in Yorkshire on which at present stands Rawdon Hall. They
gradually migrated to Scotland and received lands from William the
Lion which were held under this curious poetical title deed:-

CONCESSUM AD PAULYM ROYDON

I William the King, the thire yere of my reign
Givee to Paulyn Roydon, hope and hopetoune
With all the bounds both up and downe
From heaven to yerthe, from yerthe to hel
For thee and thine there to dwel
As truly as this king right is myn
For a cross bowel and an arrow
When I sal cum to hunt in yarrow
And in token that this thing is sooth
I bit the whyt wax with my tooth
Before Meg, Maud and Margery
And my third sonne Henry.

The 7th Earl of Loudoun and 2nd Marquis of Hastings was George
Augustus Francis. Born in London 1808, he succeeded his father in
1826 and his mother in 1840. He was a Lord of the Bedchamber from
1830 to 1837. He died at Southampton in 1844 and was succeeded by
his brother Paulyn Reginald Serlo the 8th Earl of Loudoun. Born in
1832 he was an officer in the army and died unmarried in Dublin in
1851.

He, in turn, was followed by his brother Henry Weysford Charles
Plantagenet, 4th Marquis of Hastings and 9th Earl of Loudoun. The
Ninth Earl's claim to fame was his extraordinary inability to predict
winners of the turf and because of this the family was brought to near
bankruptcy. He left no children and was succeeded by his sister Edith
Maud Abney Hastings. Her husband, Charles Frederick Clifton, was
created 1st Lord Donington in 1880. He died in 1895 and was
succeeded by his son Charles Edward Hastings who was already 11th
Earl of Loudoun, succeeding his mother in 1874. He died in 1920 and
was succeeded by his niece.

The twelfth holder of the peerage was Edith Maud Abney-
Hastings. Born May 13th 1883, daughter of Paulyn Rawdon Hastings

(brother of 11th Earl) and Lady Maud Grimstone (daughter of the Earl of Verulam), she married Major Reginald Mowbray Chichester Huddleston in 1916 and succeeded to the Scottish titles, Loudoun and Tarrinzean in 1920. Both changed their name by Royal licence in 1918 to Abney-Hastings.

The abeyances existing in the Baronies of Botreaux, Stanley and Hastings in England were determined in favour of the Countess of Loudoun by letters patent in 1921.

The Countess had six children:-

Ian Huddleston–Lord Mauchline, born 23rd March 1918. Killed on active service in Italy, 11th July, 1944.

Barbara Huddleston–The present Countess, born 3rd July, 1919.

Jean Huddleston Campbell of Loudoun–Born 3rd October, 1920, succeeded to the estate by deed of gift from her mother.

Iona Mary Huddleston–Born 17th March, 1922.

Fiona Huddleston–Born 26th February, 1923. Married to the Baron de Fresnes, staying at Cessnock Castle.

Edith Huddleston–Born 19th January, 1925.

The Countess died 24th February 1960 and is buried in Loudoun Kirk.

The present holder of the title (the thirteenth) is Barbara Huddleston Abney Hastings. She carries the same titles as her mother. Her son Michael Edward (Lord Mauchline) was born 1942 and is resident in Australia. The Countess has five other children, Frederick James born 1949, Selina Mary born 1946, Margaret Maud born 1956, Mary Joy born 1957 and Clare Luise born 1958.

Lady Jean Campbell has two daughters, the estate and castle being held in trust for them: Sheena and her husband Donald Williams who live in the Dower House and Madeleine and her husband John Kerr residing at Waterside Farm, Galston.

As can be seen from the preceding chapter, the Loudouns have played a very large part in the history of both Scotland and the United Kingdom throughout the centuries. Without their efforts the country's history and heritage would be much the poorer.

Loudon's bonnie woods and braes.

Words by ROBERT TANNAHILL.

Lou-don's bon-nie woods and braes, I maun lea them a'—, las-sie,
Hark! the swelling bug - le sings, Yielding joy to thee, lad-die;
O, resume thy won - ted smile, O, su-press thy fears, las-sie;

Wha can thole when Bri - ton's faes Wad gi'e Bri - ton's law, las - sie?
But the dole - ful bug - le brings Wae - fu' thochts to me, lad - die.
Glor - ious hon - our crowns the toil That the sol - dier shares, las - sie.

Wha wad shun the field o' dan - ger? Wha frae fame wad live a stran-ger?
Lane - ly I maun climb the moun-tain, Lane - ly stray be - side the foun-tain,
Heav'n will shield thy faith - ful lov - er Till the venge-ful strife is ov - er;

Now when free-dom bids a-venge her, Wha wad shun her ca', las-sie?
Still the wea-ry mo-ments coun-tin' Far frae love and thee, lad-die.
Then we'll meet, nae mair to se-ver Till the day we dee, las-sie.

Lou-don's bon-nie woods and braes, Ha'e seen our hap-py bri-dal day's, And
On the go-ry fields of war Where ven-geance drives his crim-son car, Thou'lt
'Midst our bon-nie woods and braes We'll spend our peace-fu' hap-py day's As

D.C.

gen-tle hope shall soothe thy waes, When I am far a-wa', las-sie.
may-be fa', frae me a-far, And nane to close thy e'e, lad-die.
blythe's yon licht-some lamb that plays On Lou-don's floo-'ry lea, las-sie.

Loudoun Castle

Loudoun Kirk

The Covenanters

By DAVID DUMIGAN JNR.

When Charles I came to the throne in 1625 he had lived most of his life in England. Son of James VI of Scotland who also became James I of England, Charles had left Scotland when he was three and did not return there until the eighth year of his reign. He thus had little knowledge of, or indeed much interest in, Scottish affairs.

Charles had been brought up a devout Episcopalian like his father and disliked what little he knew of the Kirk and the Scottish Presbyterians.

In the years since the Reformation marked differences were now apparent in the manner in which the two countries had adopted the new religion.

In England, at the instigation of Henry VIII, and for his own reasons, Protestantism had been adopted nationally, complete with a system of church government by bishops and archbishops appointed by the Crown.

The Reformed Church in Scotland had a vastly different tradition. It had come into being not with the help of the Crown but despite it. The Reformation in Scotland was also much more radical and there was no place in the Kirk for a hierarchy of bishops—church government was in the hands of lay elders and latterly presbyteries.

There is little doubt that Charles considered it his duty to bring the Scottish Kirk into line with the Anglican Church and passed a number of measures to this end. These included introducing the use of an English-type Prayer Book into the Scottish church service.

This Prayer Book was read for the first time in St. Giles Church in Edinburgh on 23rd July 1637 and provoked scenes of violence, urged on we are told by Jenny Geddes throwing her stool at the Dean, and which developed into rioting in the streets.

The following year 1638 on a flood tide of national protest the National Covenant was signed in Greyfriars Kirkyard and then throughout the country. A committee called the Tables which had been formed at the outset of the troubles became in effect the government of Scotland.

The king responded by sending an army to Scotland. This was easily defeated by a superior Scottish army at Berwick and a threatened attack by a second army was pre-empted by the Scots who crossed into England and took Newcastle.

Charles was obliged to negotiate and conceded all the Covenanters demands. Charles recalled his Westminster parliament but with the king weakened by these defeats, the parliamentarians rose up against the king and civil war ensued.

Early on in the war the parliamentarians asked for and received help from the Covenanters who signed an alliance with the parliamentarians–the Solemn League and Covenant–in which presbyterianism was to be fostered in England.

The support of the Scottish army tipped the balance in favour of the parliamentarians and the royalists were defeated. King Charles I was executed by beheading two years later. The Scots protested at the execution and proclaimed the young Charles II king.

Cromwell now seeing the Scots as a threat to the commonwealth invaded Scotland, defeated the Scottish armies and occupied the country.

When Cromwell died in 1658 his son Richard succeeded him, but unlike his father Richard was weak and within two years the commonwealth had collapsed.

The monarchy was restored and Charles II crowned king in 1660.

On ascending the throne Charles II took up where his father Charles I had left off in persecution of the Scottish presbyterian faith in a further attempt to extend the Anglican church and to introduce the episcopalian system of church government to Scotland.

Under his new regulations ministers were required to give up their charges and receive them again from their bishops. This met with considerable opposition particularly in the South West of Scotland and over 300 ministers walked out of their churches and manses rather than submit. This was a move supported by the people and soon 'illegal' open air services or conventicles were being held in isolated areas throughout the country.

Newmilns was a staunch Covenanting town and many gave their lives for the cause.

Under the command of John, 1st Earl of Loudoun many local men had served in the army which invaded England in 1640. On the accession of Charles II, John the 2nd Earl of Loudoun was forced into exile until his death in Holland in 1684 and the parish minister of Loudoun, John Nevay was banished.

The most famous Covenanter from Newmilns was John Nisbet of the farm of Hardhill. He was born in 1627 and like many Scots, fought abroad under Gustavus Adolphus in the religious wars on the continent. He returned to the family at Hardhill in 1648, and later married Margaret Law.

At the battle of Pentland, he was wounded and left for dead, but recovered and escaped during the night. At the battle of Drumclog, he arrived in time to take his place in the ranks of the Covenanters who routed Claverhouse and his dragoons.

But John Nisbet was a rebel to the authorities, who put a price on his head and threw his wife and children out of their home, to wander over the country and find shelter wherever they could. Four years later, his wife died after an illness. Nisbet was summoned and when he finally arrived, his wife had been buried for several days. His daughter too died a few hours before his arrival and two of his sons were unconscious with a fever. His daughter's body was laid to rest alongside his wife under the cover of darkness in Stonehouse Churchyard. A search was made for him the next day by the authorities, but he managed to escape.

One Saturday in November 1685 at the farm of Midland between Waterside and Fenwick, John Nisbet, met with Peter Gemmel, George Woodburn and John Fergushill for a service of prayer. They had been there for a short time when they learned that Lieutenant Nisbet, who was a cousin of John Nisbet, and a party of dragoons were searching for them. The soldiers arrived and proceeded to search the house but found nothing. They left Midland, and on the way they met two men, and one told them 'they were good seekers but ill finders'. When the soldiers returned to the farm to look again, they eventually found the four fugitives who defended themselves but surrendered when the soldiers threatened to set fire to the farm. John Nisbet was wounded six times, the other three were seized and shot dead.

John Nisbet was taken to Edinburgh, where he was sentenced to be executed in the Grassmarket on the 4th December.

At the front of the Church in Newmilns stands a memorial stone to John Nisbet.

During the reigns of the Stewart kings Charles II and his son James VII of Scotland and II of England the people of Newmilns and district were subjected to military repression and troops were garrisoned at the Newmilns Keep which was also used as a prison. The troops were under the command of the notorious Captain Inglis.

One evening in April 1685 at the farmhouse of Little Blackwood near Moscow twelve men met for prayer and worship when the farmhouse was raided by Peter Inglis, son of Captain Inglis, and a party of soldiers who were stationed at the Newmilns Keep.

James White picked up a gun in self defence, but when he pulled the trigger it misfired and the soldiers shot White dead. Three of the party managed to escape, but the rest were taken to Newmilns and put in prison at the Keep. One of the soldiers cut off the head of James White and took it to Newmilns, where the soldiers played

Painting of The Battle of Drumclog by Sir George Harvey,
reproduced by kind permission of Kelvingrove Art Gallery, Glasgow
with close-up section below.

football with it on the burgh green.

Epitaph to James White in Fenwick Churchyard.

This martyr was by Peter Inglis Shot
By birth a tiger rather than a Scot
Who, that his monstrous extract might be seen
Cut off his head then kicked it o'er the green
Thus was the head that was to wear a crown
A football made by a profane dragoon.

The next day Captain Inglis brought the eight prisoners out and was about to execute them, but the bailies of the burgh managed to persuade Inglis, that it was contrary to the law and justice. Inglis conceded and sent a request for an order of execution from the Council in Edinburgh, which he knew he would easily obtain. In the interval John Law and other friends of the prisoners decided to make an attempt to free them. They agreed on a night to attempt the rescue, and as providence would have it Inglis had on his person an order to shoot the eight prisoners the next day. The friends succeeded in the attack, in which they shot the guard and smashed the gates with forehammers, taken from a nearby smithy. With hardly any resistance against them, they managed to escape with only one loss of life. This was John Law who was shot dead by a soldier in the tower.

A monument to John Law can be found in the lane behind the central shop of the Co-op Society in Main Street with the following, now badly weathered inscription.

HERE LIES JOHN LAW

Who was shot at NEWMILNS, At
The relieving of 8 of CHRIST'S–
Prisoners, Who were taken at A meet[g]
For Prayer at Little Blackwood, in the
Parish of KILM[k] in April 1685, by CAPT
INGLIS and his PARTY, For Their
Adherence to the Word of GOD
And Scotland's Covenanted Work
of Reformation.

Cause I CHRIST'S Prisoners reliev'd
I of my Life was soon beriev'd.
By cruel Enemies with rage
In that Recounter did engage.
The Martyr's honour and his Crown
Bestow'd on me, O high Renown,
That I Should not only believe,
But for CHRIST'S cause my life Should give

Renewed in 1820 and in 1930.

In the churchyard of Newmilns there is a stone with the inscription:

Erected September 1829 by the Parishioners of Loudoun in testimony of their deep admiration of the noble struggle in defence of the civil and religious liberties of their country against the despotic and persecuting measures of the house of Stuart, maintained by the undernamed martyrs belonging to this parish, who suffered and died for their devotedness to the Covenanted work of Reformation:

Matthew Paton, shoemaker in Newmilns, who was taken at Pentland, and executed at Glasgow, December 19th, 1666.

David Findlay, who was shot at Newmilns, by order of Dalziel, 1666.

James Wood, taken at the battle of Bothwell Bridge, and executed at Magus-Muir. Nov 25th, 1679.

James Nisbet, in Highside, executed at Glasgow, June 11th 1684.

John Nisbet, in Glen, executed in Kilmarnock, April 14th, 1683.

'These are they who came out of great tribulation.' Rev. vii, II.

Matthew Paton and three others were taken prisoners, and were all put to death in spite of every plea set up on their behalf. Woodrow says 'They were executed that day. The men were most cheerful and had much of a sense of the Divine Love upon them, and a great deal of peace in their suffering.'

David Findlay from Newmilns, had been in Lanark when the Covenanter army passed through the town. He foolishly told of all that he had seen when he returned home, and Dalziel got to hear of it and had Findlay brought to him. When Findlay could not answer certain questions that were put to him, Dalziel ordered him to be shot. Findlay pleaded to have one night to prepare for eternity, but this was denied him. Dalziel had heard of his request and told the officer to obey without scruple, and so the man was shot dead, then stripped naked, then left where he had fallen.

When James Wood was taken prisoner he carried no arms, but because he would not call the rising at Bothwell, rebellion and Bishop Sharp's death, murder, he was sentenced to be hanged.

James Nisbet was taken prisoner while attending the funeral of the Covenanter John Richmond of Knowe who was executed in Glasgow for his adherence to the Covenant.

John Nisbet was executed at the Cross in Kilmarnock.

A stone marks the spot in the churchyard where the body of John Gebbie lies. Gebbie had fought at Drumclog and was carried off the field mortally wounded, and later died with the shouts of victory ringing in his ears.

Nearby is the stone raised to John Morton, a tenant of Broomhill, a farm in the parish of Loudoun, who was shot by Claverhouse at Drumclog.

All through the Covenanting period Newmilns was a centre of unrest, and of religious upheaval and protest. As can be seen Newmilns had its share of heroes and martyrs, who through their determination and sacrifice helped to establish the religious freedom we enjoy in Scotland today.

--------------------------- INTERESTING SNIPPETS ---------------------------

One of the most outstanding buildings in the town is the Royal Bank building in Brown Street.

Built originally for the Mitchell family of Johnstone Shields, Ltd., around 1890 the building was modelled both inside and outside on Brodick Castle.

The staircase has five stained glass windows with likenesses of the Scottish poets, Robert Burns, Sir Walter Scott, Alan Ramsay, Robert Tannahill and James Hogg.

Armourial Bearings of the Former
Burgh of Newmilns and Greenholm 1490-1975

Newmilns was created a Burgh of Barony in 1490 by a Charter from King James IV in favour of George Campbell of Loudoun and this Charter was confirmed by Sir Matthew Campbell of Loudoun in 1556. Newmilns was raised to a Burgh of Regality in favour of Hugh Campbell, 3rd Earl of Loudoun, in 1707. There is no doubt that a seal would have been in use from 1490, but its whereabouts or description is unknown.

Newmilns, along with its neighbouring suburb of Greenholm, from which it is separated by the River Irvine, adopted the Lindsay Act in 1872, and under the Burgh Police Act of 1892, took for its Common Seal the following:-

A shield, the upper part of which contains a sword supporting a pair of scales representing the sword and scales of Justice. On either side is a distaff and a shuttle. In the space beneath is a representation of the old Council House with its stair, in old records called the Tolbooth which was erected about 1739. Above the shield is a bee-hive representing Industry, and beneath is the motto 'Weave Truth with Trust' which is also the Motto of the Guild of Weavers.

It would appear that the Burgh of Newmilns & Greenholm adopted the details of the Seal as Armourial Bearings and this coat of arms was used from 1892 to 1951 without authority and indeed the Burgh was committing a Statutory Offence for all of this time.

After the Civic Week, when it was discovered that the Burgh had no legal Armourial Bearings, a petition was sent to the Lord Lyon, King at Arms and a Matriculation was granted for the following Arms on 28th January, 1951.

'Per chevron Gules and Ermine, a Chevronel embattled on its upper edge of the First in base and in chief a spinning rock and shuttle Or. Below the Shield which is surmounted of a coronet proper to a Burgh is place on an Escrol this Motto 'Weave Truth with Trust'.
(Lyon register, xxxviii, 47: 28 January 1951)

The arms have for their field the red and ermine colours of Campbell of Loudoun. The red embattled chevronel recalls the old Tolbooth and thus the Lordship of the Regality of Loudoun; a

representation of the building appeared on the seal adopted by the
Burgh in 1892, as did the Spinning rock and shuttle which represent
the weaving industry of the town. This is thought to have sprung
from Dutch and Huguenot refugees, who settled in Ayrshire in the
seventeenth century.

The Armourial Bearings of the Former Burgh of Newmilns and
Greenholm granted in 1951, were registered in the names of the
Provost, Magistrates and Councillors of the Burgh of Newmilns &
Greenholm. All local areas of Government ceased to exist from 16th
May, 1975, and the local councils also ceased to exist. There was,
therefore, no one in charge of the Armourial Bearings whom the
Lord Lyon could look to for implementation of the obligations and
duties involved and the arms being in vacuum reverted to the Crown
in the Lord Lyons hands. This, like many more things during the
transition stage of the Local Government (Scotland) Act 1973, was
overlooked. It could be argued that the local councils ceased to exist,
but the communities did not. The interpretation of the Act is that the
Local Government (Council) of the former Burgh ceased to exist, but
their duties were taken over by District and Regional Councils,
therefore the District Council should have taken over these duties
from the Lord Lyon.

Old versions of the 'illegal' Coat of Arms can be seen at the library
and the Morton Hall; the new approved Coat of Arms is on the sign at
the east entrance to the burgh and on the provost's lamp.

Agriculture around Newmilns

By KAREN A. WOODWARD B.Sc.

When considering aspects of agriculture in a given area, it is important first to establish the geological and physical constraints set.

The first aspect is the genetic soil group. Newmilns is situated on surface water gleys, and gleyed brown forest soils. Gleying is characteristic of fine textured soils which are poorly drained and is essentially the removing of the element iron, leaving the soil with a grey tinge. There is poor soil drainage. However this is improved by the fact that most of the land lies on a slope. The soils are mainly of the clay loam and clay classifications, giving rise to soils which waterlog readily and are therefore heavy to work. The annual rainfall is high, more than 60' (1500mm) which means that most years the soil will be moist all year round. The potential evaporation for the area is only 14' (350mm) which means there will be 46' (1150mm) of water which must be removed from the soil by run-off e.g. streams and rivers, or by percolation down through the soil, then eventually into the rivers.

The other important restraint when considering an appropriate farming system is the average annual accumulated temperature. This is calculated by taking base temperature, and on each day that the temperature is greater than the base adding the difference to the accumulating temperature. The normal temperature used as a base is 6°C (42°F) as this is the temperature at which grass (and most other temperate crops) start to grow at. The Annual Accumulated Temperature around Newmilns is between 1000 and 1500 day degrees, which is an indication of the short growing season and cool climate.

Due to these geological and physical factors the land in the Newmilns area is best suited to the growing of grass as a crop, and this has been the case throughout history.

Farming nowadays shows little resemblance to the farming of the centuries gone by. In the early 1700s, farming was based on the Infield/Outfield system. All the land belonged to the local landlord and the inhabitants would live in groups of farms or crofts called ferm-touns with the surrounding land shared for cultivation or grazing. Rent and also part of each person's harvest was paid in obligations to the landlord. Although the land was shared, the tenants were not co-operative farmers. The land close to the ferm-toun the 'Infield', was divided into strips and each tenant got a share of the strips. These strips were reallocated regularly. The infield was under constant cropping, therefore it received all the manure produced. The tenants also practiced a crude form of crop rotation. The outfield was mainly common grazing, although a small area would have been cultivated for a few years at a time. There were no permanent enclosures, just temporary barriers erected to protect crops from wandering livestock. The major crops of the time would be oats, followed by peas, beans, turnips and some bere, a type of barley. In this way the rural community of all of Scotland lived until nearly 1800.

The years between 1750 and 1800 have commonly been called the Agricultural Revolution. Running parallel to farming developments of these times, there was a move from feudalism to capitalism occurring in Scotland.

Newmilns is situated in the top parts of the Irvine River Valley. At one time all the surrounding lands belonged to estates, Loudoun Estate and Lanfine Estate, although through the years most of these pieces of land have been sold. During the 'Agricultural Revolution' it was radical-thinking estates that carried out improvements and it is well documented that Ayrshire was one of the first regions to erect permanent fences. Another of the estates' improvements, which is easily witnessed today, was the planting of trees, both to provide cover for hunts and shoots and for shelter from wind for stock. A good example of this is to be seen in Downiesburn Park, where the field is sheltered from all sides, and contains further single trees to provide shade.

These improvements were common throughout Scotland but there was one improvement of major importance that occurred in Newmilns and its surrounding areas and that was the evolution of the Ayrshire Dairy Cow. Up until then Beef and Dairy cattle were not distinct from each other, although there was the Dairy Shorthorn. However with careful studying of animal breeding a new breed of cow was born. It was well suited to the lush grass grown in Ayrshire, and although relatively small and dainty it was able to produce vast quantities of milk of the highest quality.

Upon the appearance of the Ayrshire, a nice reddish brown and white cow, in areas where it was possible, milk production became the main way of life. For many years all milking was done by hand, a long arduous task. However, early this century a major break-through was the invention of the milking machine. Not only did this reduce the workload of the farmer, it also increased the rate of milking, which meant farmers could keep more than half a dozen milking cows. The estates had already been split into small parcels of land surrounding individual farm steadings with the advent of fencing, rather than the old Infield Outfield system, but now the tenants decided they needed larger patches of land, and so depopulation of the countryside started, with larger but fewer farms. In Ayrshire the tenants liked the farm steadings to be built such that the buildings were parallel to one another.

During the 1930's there was a long period of depression mainly due to cheap agricultural imports from Europe. To help to counteract this the Milk Marketing Boards were set up. However this ended the sale of the South of Scotlands surplus milk to the North East of England.

Many changes have taken place over the years in dairy farming. The milking machine started with one single machine being used, however after the 2nd World War the byre system became popular. In this system the cows would be chained by the neck in a cubicle, the whole herd at once, and the dairyman would milk these cows using a number of milking machines, six on average. Once one cow was milked the milking machine was removed and used to milk the next. In this way the dairyman could easily milk around 30 cows in an hour.

With the advent of still bigger herds and a new breed of cow, the black and white Friesian, the byre system was no longer able to cope. This led to the advent of the most popular system today, that of the parlour. There are numerous variations of the parlour, including Herringbone parlours and Rotary parlours, but they all have the same basic concept in that the dairyman remains relatively stationary with the machines, and the cows come to him. With this advancement it is now possible for one man to milk over 60 cows in one hour, using a six by six Herringbone parlour, that is with six cows on either side of the milking pit. The cows enter in batches of six, have their udders washed and the machines attached, and then if the system contains automatic cluster removers the dairyman can forget about them.

The fact that dairy herd sizes increased due to mechanisation and the fact of the increased milk yield of the Friesian over the Ayrshire led to rapidly increasing quantities of milk being produced. This, in turn, lead to the introduction of milk quotas, which now limit the amount of milk individual farmers can produce.

Milk quotas have had the biggest effect on Ayrshire farming since the invention of the milking machine. Now instead of farmers striving to increase milk production, all are cutting back, and many have had to opt out altogether. This has led to a diversifying of the farming systems around Newmilns in the past five years, as farmers go out of milk production and into beef or sheep. There is little other option as the land around the Newmilns area is best suited for the growing of grass.

So in the past 500 years Newmilns and its surrounding lands have evolved from the Feudal past of Scotland and have been actively involved in the improvement of Scottish milk production. However this has had to be somewhat curtailed in the past five years due to milk quotas.

History has shown that the area is adaptive and willing to embrace new ideas which may now be necessary to maintain the farming community as we know it.

Pate's Mill which was demolished in 1977 was a corn mill which served generations of local farmers. It is remembered in Allan Ramsay's song "The Lass of Patie's Mill". Further upriver the buildings of another corn mill — Loudoun Mill are still standing. This mill which was in the possession of the Loudoun family for over 300 years, was probably, together with the adjacent waulk mills, responsible for giving Newmilns its name 500 years ago — 'New Mylls'.

The Lass o' Patie's Mill.

Words by ALLAN RAMSAY.

Key B♭.

Andante espressivo.

* spreading.

D. C.

Newmilns and Robert Burns

By JOHN R. HARRIS

To write about Newmilns and Robert Burns, we have to start in the district town of Kilmarnock. The Kilmarnock that Burns knew was a community of only 3,000. It was a thriving manufacturing centre and during Burns's lifetime doubled in size. It was a compact place clustered around the cross, where the weekly markets were held. The new thoroughfares, however have swept away most of the 'Streets and Neuks o' Killie'. Something of the atmosphere of the past may be recaptured if you leave the cross and go to the Laigh Kirk. There in it's graveyard lie Tam Samson and the ministers satirized by Burns in 'The Ordination', which celebrated the installation of the Rev. James McKinley by the Earl of Glencairn, patron of Robert Burns.

Kilmarnock though is probably more famous for the printing of the Kilmarnock Edition of Burns poems which he entitled 'Poems Chiefly in the Scottish Dialect'. It was printed in John Wilson's printing shop in the Star Inn Close, now the Burns Precinct shopping centre, at three shillings a copy.

Kilmarnock, did more for Burns than print the first edition of his poems, for the town and many of its citizens were Burns's principal contacts in social and intellectual affairs and he was a welcome guest and friend in their homes. The Kilmarnock friends, Robert Muir, John Goldie, Tam Samson, Sandy Patrick, would gather to hear Burns reading his poems and were among those who subscribed for copies of his book.

While it can be said that Kilmarnock was the means of Robert Burns becoming known as the Ayrshire Poet, it was however Newmilns which was instrumental in ensuring that he remained in Scotland to become our national poet.

Prior to the printing of the Kilmarnock Edition Burns's morale was at its lowest, due mainly to the failure of his farm at Mossgiel, and the confrontation with James Armour who was against Burns's relationship with his daughter, Jean. Even after Burns gave Jean Armour a written acknowledgement of their marriage, which was legal in Scotland at that time, James Armour, still did not acknowledge Burns as his son-in-law, believing him to be unworthy of his daughter and in fact he started legal proceedings against Burns.

As a result of all this Burns was considering the possibility of finding better fortune abroad in the West Indies.

To avoid arrest, Burns had to go into hiding. The poet stayed at his aunt, Jean Brown's house, at Old Rome Forest which had the advantage of being near John Wilson's printing shop in Kilmarnock so that he could put the final touches to his book.

When his poems were finally published in July 1786, they went immediately to the heart of the country-folk, young and old reading it with equal avidity and delight. As a result of the success of his book Burns became for the first time in his life 'the master of £20' and he booked passage to the West Indies in a vessel which was to sail from Greenock in September.

For some time Burns had become a frequent visitor to Newmilns and in particular had enjoyed the hospitality of Rev. George Lawrie at Loudoun Manse on many occasions.

Dr. George Lawrie came of a long line of ministers. His father, grandfather, great-grandfather, and great-great-grandfather as well as his son and grandson were all ministers. Of the seven, five lived and laboured in Ayrshire. Born in 1729 George Lawrie was presented to the parish of Loudoun by John 4th Earl of Loudoun in 1763. In the following year, he married a daughter of Dr. Archibald Campbell, professor of Church History in the New College of St. Andrews. Dr. Lawrie himself was no mean scholar. He was well read, an eloquent speaker and preacher, had a fine sense of humour, was a racy conversationalist, and his word was not without considerable influence in the Church Courts. His special study was the early poetry and music of the Celts in Scotland and Ireland. Amongst his friends, he numbered men eminent in the world of letters, and Loudoun Manse extended its hospitality to the literary society of his day.

Dr. Lawrie took a keen interest in the young farmer poet and recognised in his work and through his conversation, during their social evenings at the manse, the budding genius of Burns who was delighted by the hospitality of Loudoun Manse—the ideal of a moderate Minister's dwelling: there were the poet, the pleasant lady, a young son, a daughter, beautiful and accomplished, who could play on the spinnet, an instrument new to Burns, another daughter in her teens, and the children. In the manse there was on occasions, after supper, a dance. His brother Gilbert Burns wrote 'This was a delightful family scene for our poet, then lately introduced to the world. His mind was roused to a poetic enthusiasm, and the stanzas were left in the room where he slept.'

The stanzas referred to are 'A Prayer left by the Author at a Reverend Friend's House'.

One morning Burns was late for breakfast and young Archibald Lawrie was sent to enquire of Burns what had detained him. The boy met Burns on the stairs. 'Good morning, Mr. Burns', he said, 'I hope you slept well last night'. 'Sleep, my young friend, I scarcely slept at all. I have been praying all night. If you go to my room you will find my prayers upon the table', replied the poet. The manuscript is still preserved with pride in the family of Dr. Lawrie's descendants.

O thou dread Power, who reign'st above,
    I know thou wilt me hear,
When for this scene of peace and love
    I make my prayer sincere.

The hoary Sire–the mortal stroke,
    Long, long be pleas'd to spare:
To bless his little filial flock,
    And show what good men are.

She, who her lovely offspring eyes
    With tender hopes and fears–
O, bless her with a mother's joys,
    But spare a mother's tears!

Their hope, their stay, their darling youth,
    In manhood's dawning blush,
Bless him, Thou God of love and truth,
    Up to a parent's wish.

The beauteous, seraph sister-band–
    With earnest tears I pray–
Thou know'st the snares on every hand,
    Guide Thou their steps always.

When, soon or late, they reach that coast,
    O'er Life's rough ocean driven,
May they rejoice, no wand'rer lost,
    A family in Heaven!

These lines were not the only memento of his visits to Loudoun Manse. On one of the window panes in the room he occupied, he scratched with his diamond–'Lovely Mrs. Lawrie, she is all charms'. Known locally as the 'Burns Window', the window frame has since been removed for safe keeping but can still be seen at Loudoun Manse.

The following verses were penned by Burns and presented to the daughters of Dr. Lawrie as a descriptive sketch of a visit to Loudoun Manse.

> 'The night was still, and o'er the hill
> The moon shone on the castle wa',
> The mavis sang, while dew-drops hang
> Around her on the castle wa':
>
> Sae merrily they danc'd the ring
> Frae eenin till the cock did craw,
> And ay the o'erword o the spring
> Was:–'Irvine's bairns are bonie a'!'

It was on his way back to Mossgiel, after paying what he thought was his last visit to Loudoun Manse, that Burns composed his poem 'The Gloomy Night is Gath'ring Fast' which reflected his foreboding and which ends with his farewell.

> 'Farewell, my friends! Farewell my foes!
> My peace with these, my love with those-
> The bursting tears my heart declare,
> Farewell, my bonie banks of Ayr!

Fully realising Burns's dilema Dr. Lawrie sent a copy of The Kilmarnock Edition 'Poems Chiefly in the Scottish Dialect' to his friend, Dr. Blacklock, the celebrated blind poet in Edinburgh, acquainting him with the poet's circumstances and warmly commending him to his favour. Dr. Blacklock was a man of considerable influence in Edinburgh and in time a letter came back from Blacklock via Dr. Lawrie, full of encouragement and good cheer, praising his poetry and urging him to issue a second edition of his poems without delay.

The timely intervention of Dr. Lawrie tipped the balance in favour of Burns's remaining and he abandoned his plans to emigrate, and arranged to go to Edinburgh.

The rest is legion–Burns remained to spend his brilliant but all-too-short life span in his native land furnishing us, from his prolific pen, with a wealth of literature–of poems, songs and letters–at which we can only marvel and for which we can be proud that the influence of Dr. Lawrie of Newmilns in some way played a part.

Dr. George Lawrie

Loudoun Manse

Lang, Lang Syne

By DR. GEORGE LAWRIE 1797-1878
(Tune: John Peel)

Ha'e ye mind lang, lang syne,
When the summer days were fine,
An' the sun shone brighter far
Than he's ever dune since syne;
Do ye mind the Hag Brig turn,
Whaur we guddled in the burn,
And were late for schule in the mornin?

Do you mind the sunny braes,
Whaur we gathered hips and slaes,
And fell amang the bramble bushes,
Tearin a' oor claes;
And for fear they wad be seen
We gaed slippin hame at e'en,
But were lickit for oor pains in the mornin'?

Do ye mind the miller's dam,
When the frosty winter cam',
Hoo we slade alang the curlers' rinks,
And made their game a sham;
When they chased us through the snaw,
We took leg-bail ane an' a',
But we did it o'er again in the mornin'?

What famous fun was there,
Wi' our games at houn' and hare,
When we played the truant frae the schule,
Because it was the fair;
And we ran frae Patie's Mill
To the woods at Windy Hill,
But were fear'd for the tawse in the mornin'.

Where are those bright hearts noo,
That were then sae leal and true?
Oh! some ha'e left life's troubled scene;
Some still are struggling through;
And some ha'e risen high
In life's changeful destiny,
For they rise wi' the lark in the mornin',

Now life's sweet Spring is past,
And our Autumn's come at last;
Oor Summer day has passed away;
Life's Winter's comin fast;
But though lang its night may seem,
We shall sleep without a dream,
Till we wauken on yon bright sabbath mornin'.

Newmilns Weavers and the American Civil War

By STEVE BROWN

At the time of the American Civil War the people of Newmilns suffered badly because of a shortage of cotton from America due to the blockade of the Southern cotton ports. This resulted in a severe fall in the output from their looms and the consequent hardship affected nearly everyone. Despite this, Lincoln and his policy of the abolition of slavery were staunchly supported.

At that time influential opinion in this country either favoured the South or proclaimed a policy of neutrality. But throughout the country, groups, ranging in size from the 'London Emancipation Society' to what the *Glasgow Herald* called 'her small sister at Newmilns,' were vocal in their support of Lincoln and the emancipation of the slaves.

In Newmilns there existed an Anti-Slavery Society which met at intervals in the Black Bull Hall, and sent resolutions of sympathy and support to Lincoln and his Government. The French Huguenot refugee strain and the Covenanting tradition of their forefathers probably contributed to an independence of judgement by the Valley weavers. Unfortunately the Minute Book of the Society has been lost, but we are indebted to Mr. R.M. Paterson, headmaster of Newmilns School for his work and research, carried out in 1949 for the Newmilns Civic Week, which brought to light much of the information which is related here.

The following message was found in the National Archives, Washington D.C.

Minute of Meeting of NEWMILNS ANTI-SLAVERY SOCIETY forwarded to the American Ambassador, London, for transmission to Abraham Lincoln, President of America.

According to the Previous Arrangements a Meeting of this Society took place in Black Bull Hall upon Friday, 25th November, 1864, for the purpose of receiving two volumes of correspondence between the American Government and all the other Governments from October, 1862, till August, 1864, presented to them by Mr. Underwood, late American Consul in Glasgow, for the manly, humane and sympathising manner in which the Society had expressed its feelings on behalf of the downtrodden slaves and for the restoration of the American Union...

The Chair was occupied by the President, Mr. Matthew Pollock, who opened the proceedings by stating that the meeting had two objects in view, one for receiving Mr. Underwood's handsome testimonial, the other to express our gratitude to the true Republicans of America for the triumphant manner in which they had once again placed Abraham Lincoln upon the most honorable, and the most exalted pinnacle of political glory in the world. How mortifying must it be to the aristocracy of this country to see a man from the working class raised to such a position!–an aristocracy which has viewed the American Republic with the same eye as Milton's devil viewed the Garden of Eden when he scanned this world in its infancy, causing his fallen and worthless angels to cry 'Break the Blockade of Heaven, and crush this newly formed Republic on earth.' Yes, ever since the days of Billie Pitt down to the present day, they have all along been viewing the American Republic with the same feelings as Satan did, with envy and malice causing the 'Times' Newspaper and the worthless Satellites who moved around it to cry 'Break the Blockade, recognise and support a power which declares the Head Corner Stone of their building to be human Slavery.' But alas, how futile the hopes and wishes have been, in not finding Abraham Lincoln an Adam to eat the apple. No, he is not an Adam, but Abraham, the Father of the Faithful, whose name will be handed down to posterity by the echoes of one generation after another, until the oppressors of Mankind shall vanish from the face of the earth, amidst the execration of a Noble and patriotic people.

Mr. John Brooks to whom Mr. Underwood entrusted the two volumes for presentation rose and after delivering an able address presented One Volume to the Members of the Society and the other to the President...

Mr. John Donald then rose and returned thanks to Mr. Underwood for his handsome testimonial bestowed as a token of his esteem for our sympathy on behalf of the slaves and the restoration of the American Union, and after a short and suitable address moved the following resolution... 'That we, the members of this Society, tender our sincere thanks to Mr. Underwood, late American Consul in Glasgow, for his condescension in noticing our humble efforts on behalf of his bleeding country, struggling for the freedom of the slaves, and in returning to his native home may he enjoy the blessings of peace, the restoration of the union, with universal Liberty is our earnest prayer.'

Mr. Alex Pollock, Teacher, Stewarton, gave a very impressive address contrasting Slavery with Christianity...

Mr. Daniel McArthur followed with a number of very touching and entertaining anecdotes connected with Slavery...

Mr. Andrew Wallace next in a very interesting manner enumerated the different measures adopted by President Lincoln for the extinction of Slavery and the Preservation of the Union.

The Chairman then proposed the following resolution 'That this meeting, being deeply impressed with the importance of the late Presidential election in America cannot allow their exultations to pass without giving vent to their feelings by congratulating the true Republicans of America for the splendid victory they have achieved for the whole human race by re-electing Abraham Lincoln–the man from the people, with the people, and for the people–whose honesty of purpose, uprightness in judgement, unflinching performance of his duty, aided by the new stream of Republican life that has flowed into both Senate and Congress from the late elections, will enable him to bring this unjust and unholy war to an honorable, a just, and a lasting Peace...'

Resolved 'That the foregoing be signed by the President and a copy be forwarded to the Honorable Charles Francis Adams, American Ambassador, London, and to be transmitted to Abraham Lincoln, President of America, and another to Mr. Underwood, late American Consulate, Glasgow...'

The business of the meeting being over, a vote of thanks was given to the President for his conduct in the chair...

The meeting being composed of both sexes, they agreeably refreshed themselves, after which Mr. Thomas Campbell, jun., opened the after-programme by singing 'Callum O' Glen,' the rest of the evening being spent in song and sentiment from both sexes, giving to all great satisfaction.

(Sgd.) MATTHEW POLLOCK, *President.*

Newmilns Anti-Slavery Society, December 12th, 1864.

THE NATIONAL ARCHIVES, WASHINGTON, D.C. RECORD GROUP NO. 59, GENERAL RECORDS OF THE DEPARTMENT OF STATE. Diplomatic Despatches, Great Britain, Volume 88, November 25, 1864–March 23, 1865.

As we should expect, Lincoln's assassination was not allowed to pass unremarked. Mr. Dayle C. McDonough, American Consul in Glasgow, traced the following resolution in the American Diplomatic Correspondence.

Text of resolution passed at a meeting held by the Newmilns Anti-Slavery Society, Newmilns, May 5, 1865.

In public meeting assembled it was unanimously resolved to present the following unto the honorable Andrew Johnson, President of the United States of America:

'Honoured Sir: We, the members of the Newmilns Anti-Slavery Society, having early espoused the side of humanity in the great struggle going on in your beloved country for the emancipation of mankind from bondage–a bondage which made the humane of every land shudder to contemplate–proud as we were over him who undertook the task to grapple with this gigantic evil, what are we to think, or how can we express our feelings, when we know that he who was the appointed instrument to erase from the land of America the accursed blot which had so long stained your honoured and will-be respected flag, and he who with calmness, fortitude, and dignified mercy, held in the one hand the palm of victory, in the other the olive-branch, crying peace! peace! being struck down and deprived of life by the assassin's hand, when on the very verge of seeing his long-wished-for desire successfully consummated; and, honoured sir, in our lamentations over the sad event, may we be permitted to congratulate you, upon the knowledge we have, through the honorable Mr. Adams, the American Ambassador, London, and Mr. Stodart, Glasgow, of the high attainments you possess for the important office you have been so unexpectedly called upon to fill. We therefore tender unto you, and along with you our sincere sympathy for the bereaved widow of the late honoured and respected President, Abraham Lincoln, acknowledging our gratitude to God for the miraculous preservation of the honorable Mr. Seward and family; and while we mourn, along with every true friend of humanity, the unparalleled event that has befallen your country, and although the horizon seemed dark for a time after such a calamity, we are again hopeful when we see the sun emerging from behind the cloud in your own likeness, supported by General Grant and the gallant army–Farragut and the navy–the patriotic people of America, and all who stood forward so nobly in time of need in defence of those institutions for the good of mankind contained in the glorious republic of America, all deserving and receiving our best thanks.

'Signed in behalf of the meeting:

MATTHEW POLLOCK, *President.*

ALEXANDER DYKES, *Secretary*

'Resolved, that the foregoing be forwarded to the honorable Charles Francis Adam, American Ambassador, London, for transmission to the honorable Andrew Johnson, President United States of America.

M.P.
A.D.'

Oral tradition holds that, as an expression of appreciation, Abraham Lincoln himself sent an American Flag to Newmilns but there is no doubt whatever that an American flag arrived in the community during the Civil War, at the hands of a Mr. John Brooks, a coloured gentleman.

The *Glasgow Herald,* whose policy was neutrality, had some fun at the expense of the Society on the receipt of the flag. Here are some comments from one of its leaders in December, 1864:–'If our readers should not happen to know what Newmilns is or where it is, we do not mind confiding to them that Newmilns is one of the most remarkable villages in Ayrshire... The Newmilns Anti-Slavery Society had a great gala day a few months ago, on the occasion of its being presented with an American Flag; and when the stars and stripes were unfurled, the flow of oratory and the shouts of enthusiasm would have done Mr. Lincoln's heart good to have heard. The Society rose up as one man, or perhaps as half-a-dozen altogether, and planted the Yankee banner either on the church steeple or on the lock-up house–we forget which–where it fluttered in the breeze for a few hours, and might well have given rise to the supposition that the village had just sworn allegiance to the Federal President and the Federal Constitution...' The *Glasgow Herald,* however, on this issue was not on the side of the angels.

On all ceremonial occasions in the Burgh, such as the Trades Races, this Lincoln flag was brought forth in company with the Covenanting flag, the 'Blue Blanket,' that had seen service at Drumclog.

Twenty years after the Civil War, the *Kilmarnock Standard* recorded a great franchise demonstration at Kilmarnock in 1884. It mentions the creditable muster of 600 men from Newmilns, 'Beside a flag of '31,' says the Standard, 'with the words 'Reform, good.laws, cheap government', 'there was another that attracted more attention although few may have known its history. It was a national flag of the United States, presented to a townsman during the American Civil War by President Lincoln.'

This townsman, John Donald, was a remarkable character who was born in 1804 and died in his 89th year. He took a leading part in the 1832 agitation for reform, he signed the address of Newmilns men inviting William Cobbett to what the latter described as 'this little and most beautifully situated manufacturing town.' He was a friend of the unfortunate Lady Flora Hastings, and found in Norman Macleod, in his first charge at Loudoun, not only an ardent controversialist but also an admirable lecturer on geology. He was a local leader in the Chartist agitation and, with Cobden, he believed the Crimean War was a 'crime.' But his finest hour was during the American Civil War when he was the driving force of the Newmilns Anti-Slavery Society, and to him is reputed to have come the famous flag. Unfortunately, in spite of enquiries in every direction, all efforts to trace this flag have failed.

A link with the Burgh and the United States of America was again forged at the Civic Week celebrations in 1949 when Mr. Dayle C. McDonough acting for the American Ambassador, handed over a flag to the Newmilns Civic Week Committee. This was passed to the Town Council for safe keeping and the flag took pride of place in the Morton Hall from 1949 to 1975, until the Town Council was disbanded and the administration of the town was taken over by Kilmarnock and Loudoun District. At the date of hand over, it was placed in Loudoun Parish Church, where it remains with the other colours of the town.

During the Civic Week of 1949 the U.S. Consul General Mr. D.C. McDonough (left) presented to Mr. R.M. Paterson, chairman of the Civic Week Committee a new flag to replace the original "stars and stripes" given to Newmilns by Abraham Lincoln in 1864.

--------------------- INTERESTING SNIPPETS ---------------------

The Scottish Lace & Textiles Workers' Union, although no longer independent, will be one hundred years old in 1990.

It served the members in the local industry independently from 1890 until transferring engagements to the powerful General Municipal Boilermakers & Allied Trades Union (now the GMB), in October 1983. It still retains its local office in Main Street, Newmilns, and although the General Secretary, Jim McChristie, travels on a much wider field geographically and industrially, both still serve the membership in the Irvine Valley.

The Puzzling of Jinny Willock

It is said by a Loudoun Valley lady who had the tale from her grandmother, that there lived in a top garret in Newmilns a worthy citizen of that weaving and lace-making town. His life work was to collect the snippings from the undersides of stuffs on the loom and take them away in his horse drawn cart.

He was says the story teller, what in those supposedly prim and mealy-mouth days, was called a Jinny Willock. 'A queer person', she whispers, 'with skin like a flower-petal, no stubble, never even down, and a high pitched voice.' But in spite of all these gentle characteristics Jinny Willock had apparently the manly habit of getting drunk as a lord at Nannie's ale-house most Saturday evenings after work. The halflin drinkers who had known him all their young lives as a harmless village eccentric, mocked him without malice and always led him gently home to his garret after his weekly topping had left him incapable of finding it himself.

But there came a time when his over-fancy for a dram seemed like to do him mischief and young Doctor Stirrat, who patronised the same ale-house, minded him again and again that he was liquoring himself into an early morkist. He had spoken quite seriously to the snippings-man once more on the Saturday night of this story but the old man was beyond taking in the warning. His head was on his arms on the table and as usual the two Cooper lads and the giant callant Hew Dandie emptied their own pint stoups, sighed, and while two oxtered him outside, the third unhitched the old man's horse and cart and the little procession creaked and clopped and trailed along the road to Jinny Willock's entry.

The usual procedure was to take the horse out of the shafts, take her through the small back yard and leave the cart tipped up against the wall at the front. Then they would carry the helpless Jinny up the narrow spiral of stone stairs to the bare little attic with its wall-bed, chair and small square, barred window.

That night Jinny was laid safely on his bed senseless as usual, to sleep off the effects of his night out and be ready for the Kirk in the morning. However Geordie Cooper had a brainwave. The three tiptoed down the stair and brought the horse back through the entry from the yard and with much stifled laughter coaxed her protesting up the garret stair. The horse whinnied and clattered but nothing wakened Jinny Willock and eventually they had the animal in the tiny room, tethered to the window bars, with her head beside her master's bed.

Then they crept downstairs again and spent a cheerful and busy half-hour dismantling the cart, wheels, shafts, sides and bottom of which they carried carefully into the entry and up the stairs. Another happy half-hour was spent putting the things together again so, that when they left Jinny Willock snoring unsuspectingly in the wall-bed, in the room keeping him company, was his horse and cart.

He was a puzzled man, nay a frightened man, at his own cleverness when he woke up next morning to find Betsy's head on the pillow beside him. He spent some time of the sermon that day wondering, not only how he got the horse and cart up the winding stair, but how on earth would he get it down again.

No one can say just how he did it, nor whether Jinny Willock risked his health and reason by going back to the ale-house, ever again.

A picture of Newmilns taken at the beginning of the century from the Macintosh Collection.

The Tragic Story of Lady Flora Hastings

By WYLIE CUNNINGHAM

Reproduced by kind permission of Kilmarnock Standard

At 4.30 in the morning, of Wednesday, July 10th, 1839, a funeral procession moved slowly through the eerily-silent streets of London. A strange hour for a funeral; but stranger still were the coaches in that mournful line. An empty coach, bearing the arms of the Royal Family, followed the hearse and it, in turn, was followed by a line of empty coaches representing some of the noblest houses in Britain!

Even at that early hour crowds lined the streets, standing silent with bared heads as the hearse passed. But when these same crowds saw Queen Victoria's vehicle, the presence of a large guard of policemen could not prevent ugly scenes. Shouts of 'Murderer!' were heard and at one point a volley of stones smashed into the Royal coach.

This was, for the young Victoria, the culmination of many weeks of intense unpopularity. Abuse and vituperation had been hurled at her at Ascot; she had been hissed while driving in Hyde Park; state occasions in the grandeur of Drury Lane had been spoiled by shouted insults and, perhaps worst of all, she had driven through the streets of her capital city in complete silence while crowds expressed nothing but contempt for their young queen.

A TERRIBLE MISTAKE

What was the cause of these amazing outbursts against Victoria who later was to become the revered mother-figure of the omnipotent British Empire, the empire on which the sun never set? The answer lay in the poor corpse which was being carried through London that July morning, the corpse of Lady Flora Hastings of Loudoun Castle. The answer lay with her, and in a terrible mistake by a member of the medical profession.

Lady Flora Hastings was born in 1806, the eldest daughter of Francis Rawdon-Hastings, who was created first Marquis of Hastings in 1817, and his wife, the former Lady Flora Mure Campbell, in her own right Countess of Loudoun. Lady Flora was brought up in the beautiful Loudoun Castle, known as the 'Windsor of Scotland'. When her father died in 1826, Lady Flora was a beautiful young woman with a slim and elegant figure, fine eyes, a straight nose and delicate mouth.

Eight years later, in 1834, she became lady-in-waiting to the Duchess of Kent, mother of the Princess Victoria, heiress-presumptive to the throne, and entered a family split by the difference between mother and daughter. The Duchess was impetuous, charming and emotional, while her daughter was something of a 'cold fish'. Their only common characteristic was a stubbornness which showed itself especially in an insistence on being given their proper place.

UNOFFICIAL ADVISER

Victoria became queen in 1837 and her former governess, Fraulein Lehzen, became the Baroness Lehzen, unofficial adviser to the Queen, taking the place of the Duchess in Victoria's affections. Correspondingly, the Duchess of Kent began to look on Lady Flora more as a daughter than anything else.

On January 10th, 1839 Lady Flora returned to Buckingham Palace after a holiday in Scotland and immediately consulted Sir James Clark, the Queen's physician, about abdominal trouble which was affecting her.

Sir James was a Scotsman who had studied in his native country and in London. He had served as a naval surgeon during the Napoleonic Wars and was to work with Florence Nightingale in the Crimea. In 1820 Sir James was the doctor who treated the poet John Keats during his fatal illness in Rome. How much Clark's diagnosis of stomach trouble contributed towards Keats's death, from tuberculosis, only a medical expert can say, but the mistake seemed to have little effect on Clark's career, for he was physician to the King of the Belgians before becoming Queen Victoria's personal doctor.

Lady Flora's symptoms were a bilious sickness, pain low on the left side, derangement of the bowels and considerable swelling of the abdomen. This last effect of her illness was being noted by the spiteful eyes of Palace society, ever-eager to seize on some new, choice morsel of gossip to spread. They, naturally, put the most obvious assumption on Lady Flora's appearance.

THE RUMOUR BEGINS

It is not certain who actually started the rumour that Lady Flora was pregnant but it was generally accepted that Baroness Lehzen was the originator, helped by Lady Portman and Lady Tavistock. Wherever it started, by the beginning of February, Lord Melbourne, the Prime Minister, summoned Clark and told him that Lady Flora's appearance had given rise to the rumour that she was privately married.

Clark, although he had been attending her for a month, admitted that he did not know the exact nature of Lady Flora's condition.

Prompted by Melbourne, Clark tried to get Lady Flora to undergo an examination which would clear up the matter but she refused. Exasperated, Clark told her about the rumours which were circulating in the Palace and when she again refused said that 'no one could look at her and doubt it.'

By this time the story was common knowledge in 'Society' and, although the Duchess of Kent refused to believe anything harmful to Lady Flora's character, her daughter, Queen Victoria, accepted the word of others and, according to sources within the Palace, refused to admit Lady Flora to her presence. By this time there was open speculation about the identity of Lady Flora's partner.

JOINT STATEMENT

Finally, persuaded by the Duchess, Lady Flora submitted to a medical examination by Clark and by another doctor, Sir Charles Manfield Clarke. They issued a joint statement that, although there was an enlargement of the stomach, there were no grounds for the suspicions that Lady Flora was pregnant.

Separately Sir Charles wrote: 'The subject was inviolate thus putting out of the question every possible suspicion.'

Indignant at the slanders put on Lady Flora, the Duchess of Kent refused to dine or spend the evening with the Queen or to allow Lady Flora to do so. She also dismissed Clark and ordered Lady Portman not to enter her presence.

Lord Hastings, Lady Flora's brother, despite illness, hurried from his estate in Donington, Leicestershire, in an effort to find out who had started the rumour, only to find that he was beating his head against a wall of silence and Palace protocol. After being fobbed off many times, he retired, baffled, to 'nurse his wrath,' vowing vengeance on all concerned. Victoria summoned Lady Flora, expressed sorrow and dismissed the subject at that!

But the malicious gossips of the Palace refused to accept the medical statement and continued to believe the 'evidence' of their own spiteful eyes. The talk of Lady Flora's pregnancy went on, not in the slightest diminished by the proof of her innocence.

PRESS COMMENT

So far the matter had been kept within Palace walls but the 'Morning Post' of March 5th contained the story, without using names. It spoke of jealousy in Court circles, saying: 'It is added that this malevolence, which has produced much family difference, has assumed within a few days a more decided and virulent form; that an imputation of an odious description was raised against the honour of the noble maiden.'

Five days afterwards another publication added the names of the parties involved. Other newspapers followed, and soon the case was known and being discussed in every corner of the Kingdom. Most papers angrily denounced the behaviour of the 'Palace set' although a few, staunchly Royalist, claimed feebly that it was all a plot to discredit the Queen and the Establishment.

Many of Clark's aristocratic patients dismissed him and other doctors refused to meet him in consultation. The public, too, supported Lady Flora and she was cheered whenever her carriage appeared.

Meanwhile, Lord Hastings, who had been impotently fuming at Donington, attacked along another line. He had been advised to take either duelling pistols or a horsewhip to his sister's detractors but Hastings adopted the less spectacular but more sensible policy of trying to take the case before a court of law. He was told, however, probably correctly, that he would have little chance of prosecuting the Establishment and reluctantly had to abandon his plan.

PUBLIC IS SHOCKED

At this stage, Lady Flora's uncle, Captain Hamilton Fitzgerald, came into the picture. He took his niece's case to the open court of public opinion, publishing a clear, accurate and detailed account in the 'Examiner'. The public, although branding the Captain as a gossip and a busybody for confiding all the intimate details, were shocked and amazed by his story. Said Sir Charles Greville: 'The Palatians behaved monstrously ill in the first instance. There seems to have been a continued series of blunders and of sins against delicacy, justice, propriety and good taste.'

The newspapers, particularly the Tory press, took the opportunity of fanning the attacks against the Queen and Lord Melbourne, demanding the removal of Sir James Clark and most of the ladies-in-waiting.

At the theatre the Queen was greeted with shouts of 'Dismiss Lady Portman'. In Hyde Park she was hissed and at Ascot the Tory aristocracy greeted her with mocking cries as 'Mrs. Melbourne'; when the Duchess of Kent entered the course with Lady Flora, the cry 'One cheer more for Lady Flora' was heard many times. The growing bitterness was shown by this newspaper comment: 'The continuance in office of Sir J. Clark gives some colour to the rumour that her Majesty, and not the physician, was the original author of the slander.'

SCENE AT THEATRE

Queen Victoria, faced with such overwhelming disapproval, made an unsuccessful attempt to redeem her reputation. She took Lady Flora with her on every possible public occasion, to dinner parties, to church, for carriage drives, showing friendliness and favour to her in public. But privately, she refused to speak to Lady Flora or even to acknowledge her existence.

This trick, however, did not fool many people. At Drury Lane theatre, on one occasion early in April which the Duchess of Kent had refused to attend because Lady Tavistock was with the Queen, the audience greeted Victoria with the gibe 'Where's your mother?' In her drawing room she was hissed; the crowds which watched her pass in her carriage were silent and, quoting from a letter of Lady Flora's to her sister, 'an officer on duty heard a respectable man say to the crowd "Don't take off your hats–she does not deserve it" ': cries of 'Mrs. Melbourne,' 'Dismiss your doctor' and 'Go home to your mother' were also frequent.

Victoria adopted an attitude of schoolgirl priggishness to the whole affair, amazing in a monarch. She treated Lady Flora with the sarcastic, puerile, cruelty of a thirteen-year-old. In his biography of her, Lord David Cecil wrote of an entry in Victoria's journal. After a party at the Palace, she wrote: 'Mama is here with her amiable and virtuous lady.'

Lady Flora was still fulfilling her duties, constantly being thrust into the company of those who had injured her most, but her health was failing rapidly. The illness which had caused all the trouble and so baffled Clark was beginning to take its toll. Her last public appearance was on June 10th when she attended the Chapel Royal with the Queen and the Duchess. Appropriately, the sermon that day was taken from the Ecclesiastes text 'Be not rash with thy mouth, and let not thine heart be hasty to utter any thing before God.' Whether this jogged Victoria's conscience no one knows but later that day she broke her silence and sent a note to Lady Flora, enquiring after her health. But it was too late for reconciliation!

QUEEN'S LAST VISIT

Within a week the Court Circular was carrying bulletins of Lady Flora's illness, and by the 19th it was accepted that she was dying. Dr. Chambers, who was in attendance called for some of her family to stay with her in the Palace until her death. Lady Sophia, her sister, did so but refused to sleep on a bed belonging to the Queen. Instead she slept on a couch in Lady Flora's room. The Duchess of Kent cancelled her public appearances so as to stay with Lady Flora. But, it was with great difficulty that Lord Melbourne persuaded Victoria to cancel the state ball arranged for the 28th. It took all Melbourne's persuasiveness and influence to convince the Queen that in the name of common decency, she could not allow the ball to go on.

Finally, Victoria, forced by opinion and on the advice of her ministers, asked to see Lady Flora. There was no third person present at the meeting but reports said that the Queen came into the bedchamber, said: 'Lady Flora, I am sorry you are still ill,' and left again.

On Saturday, June 29th, the Bishop of London brought Holy Communion to Lady Flora. On July 3rd, Lady Flora, fully aware of her condition, made her family promise that a post mortem would be held to clear her name. The following day she was so weak that the Queen had to cancel a dinner party at the Palace and early on the morning of July 5th, Lady Flora Hastings died quietly in her sleep.

PROOF OF INNOCENCE

That same evening, Sir Benjamin Brodie, Dr. Chambers and three other doctors examined the body and issued a joint statement that Lady Flora Hastings had died of an enlarged liver which had caused among other symptoms, her stomach to be swollen.

With the final proof of Lady Flora's innocence. Tories, the Press and the public launched a series of bitter attacks and accusations against the Court. Victoria tried to make amends by giving gifts to the Hastings family, who returned them immediately and pointedly, and by paying the medical expenses. Said one newspaper: 'It would have been better if her Majesty had closed her ear to the slanders to whom the death that now clouds the palace, is attributable, and closed her doors against the 'fingering slave' who acted as the dirty tool of the dirty party in the dirty calumny, of which we now see the deplorable result.'

Feelings as high as this caused the night journey which took Lady Flora's body to St. Katherine's Wharf to be put aboard ship for Edinburgh from where it was brought home to Loudoun Castle where it lay in state for a weekend before being buried on Monday, July 15th, in the family vault in Loudoun Kirk, amid scenes of great mourning and sorrow by thousands of Scots who came to pay a last tribute to a victim of Court intrigue and jealousy.

UNBELIEVABLE SEQUEL

For the next few months, Victoria was faced with jeering, catcalling crowds but time passed and memory, ever fickle, forgot the scandal. Her marriage to the German prince Albert, and the subsequent Royal children brought the English public back to their customary reverence of Royalty and, under Albert's influence, the ladies of the court became more subdued, and some, including Lehzen, were retired. Soon the whole affair was nothing but a dim memory.

But 'Revenge triumphs over death' and the almost unbelievable avenging of Lady Flora was to come 22 years after her death.

Victoria had retained Sir James Clark as her personal physician, showing remarkable loyalty to her doctor. In December, 1861, Prince Albert fell ill. Clark diagnosed a 'feverish sort of influenza' and treated him accordingly. When the Prince grew worse, William Jenner was called in. He found that Albert was, in fact, suffering from typhoid fever, but, by that time, treatment was too late and on December 14th, 1861, Prince Albert, Victoria's 'beloved Albert', died–as the result of another mistake by Sir James Clark!

Lady Flora Hastings

Lady Flora's Institute

EDUCATION

By IAN POLLOCK

The first formal educational establishment in the town was the parish school which began in 1781 in a building on the site of the present church hall in Greenhead. A plaque on the wall reads:

Here stood
Loudoun Parish School
in Memory of whose schoolmasters
Andrew Campbell
John Lyon Campbell
their descendants gifted this site
1781 1934

In 1791 the school was described as *'One of the best in the west country with always over sixty often ninety scholars.'* At that time the population of the town was approximately one thousand.

By 1820 George Robertson's topographical description of Cunninghame lists the curriculum of the pupils in Loudoun Parish's two schools, the Newmilns Parish School and the new Darvel School built by the Loudoun family in 1815, as follows:-

Read only	172
Read and Write	96
Read Write and Count	52
Latin or Greek	12
Maths etc. French	14
Total Pupils	325

The first schoolmaster was Mr. Murdoch followed by Andrew Campbell and then John Lyon Campbell. The parish school continued till 1872. It was unable to cater for the demand and as a result it was quite usual for people midway through the century to be unable to write their name.

A new school, sometimes called Victoria School set up by Miss Brown of Lanfine, was opened in 1860 in Union Street. Its most famous headmaster was Archibald Hood who became head in 1874. A very progressive man, he started primary classes for 3 to 7 year olds at 2d per month in 1881 and continuation or night school classes in 1882. The school roll by that time was 294.

Mr. Hood remained headmaster till 1894 when the Loudoun School Board built a new public school at High Street, and such was his importance in the town that the new school was affectionately referred to as Hood's School. At the opening, the town's school roles were as follows:

Public School — Boys 381, Girls 106. Lady Flora's — Girls 200.

The public school was designed by another famous local man–John Macintosh of Strath Cottage. As well as being an architect he was also a poet and author, publishing books such as 'Irvinedale Chimes', 'Ayrshire Nights Entertainments' and 'Historical Review of Galston and Loudoun Parishes'. His photographic plates remain the most comprehensive record in existence of the period.

By this time Lady Flora's School for girls was playing an important role in the educational progress of the town. Building was started in 1875 and the school opened on the 14th September 1877 providing much needed education for girls as well as giving the town one of its most beautiful buildings. The school had only three headmistresses; Elizabeth Gemmell, Christina McGillivray and Miss Pearson M.A.

Lady Flora's School continued until 1919 when pupils were transferred to the public school. The building later re-opened as a women's institute on the 3rd September 1921 and remained an important social centre until its closure in 1981.

Now in a state of disrepair, the loss of the building is causing great concern in the community.

Archibald Hood continued as Headmaster of the public school till 1914. His letter of resignation to the Loudoun School Board read as follows:

Gentlemen,

I beg to give notice that under the regulations of the superamatic scheme for teachers I have to retire from service on 1st May 1914. In view of this the following items may be of some interest to the Board:-

I began my educational career in 1863 as pupil teacher. I am in my 45th year as a certificated teacher. Forty of these years I have spent as Headmaster (twenty in the old school and twenty in the new).

I was appointed in May 1879 by the first School Board of Loudoun–so that I have served under all the School Boards (14 in all).

In Newmilns Public School I have enrolled 5,200 children–I have trained 38 pupil teachers and have had the service of 37 female assistants and 34 male assistants while the last grants to the school were the highest we have had.

Since 1881/2 I have been almost continually engaged in

evening schoolwork.

While thus resigning my situation as at 1st May I beg to thank the members of the Board for their courtesy, kindness and consideration during the past years and I remain, gentlemen, yours respectfully–A. Hood, F.E.I.S.

His place was taken by Hugh McArthur B.A. who continued until forced to retire on health grounds in 1923.

In September of that year the Ayrshire Educational Authority confirmed the appointment of R.M. Paterson as headmaster of the public school. R.M. as he was known had been acting headmaster for some time and was the youngest teacher to hold such a position in Ayrshire. His appointment heralded the start of a period of sustained progress in education. Newmilns School was considered by both pupils and teachers to be the finest in the country–'Big Boab', as he was nicknamed by the generations of pupils, pushed staff and children to the peak of performance and many have him to thank for their eventual success. R.M. retired in 1954.

Mr. William Johnson continued the good work until disaster struck on Monday 1st February, 1960 when all but three classes in the main school building were destroyed by fire. The school continued to function for some time using various halls throughout the town. Later wooden huts were added and this for a time kept the school on one site.

On the 18th November 1964 the new primary school was opened at the west end of the town. The site had caused much controversy and was against the wishes of the majority of the townsfolk, but the Ayrshire Education Authority had its way.

The school was also too small and 11 classes were squeezed into 8 rooms, some classes had 50 pupils. Wooden huts were added but Mr. Johnson's job was still difficult, with the two parts of the school a mile apart.

Loudoun Academy was officially opened in 26th February 1971 and took all the secondary pupils from the 4 valley towns–prior to that pupils in Newmilns were sent to Kilmarnock Academy, Galston Higher Grade or remained at Newmilns according to their ability. Eventually on prize giving day 30th June 1970 an entry in the log book read 'Today Newmilns Junior Secondary School ceased to exist'.

Mr. Johnson retired in January 1970 and his place taken by Hugh Gillespie B.Sc. who guided the primary school through the many changes in education in the seventies, including regionalisation when all schools came under the control of Strathclyde Regional Authority.

Mr. Gillespie retired in 1980 and in keeping with modern trends the first lady headmaster, Mrs. Ruth Nicol was appointed. She too had to guide the pupils and teachers through many changes including the introduction of computers, word processors and calculators. One wonders what the pupils back in 1781 would have made of the complexities of today's education system.

DAVID BORLAND

In 1914 a Trust Fund was set up by David Borland to provide prizes for excellence in education and athletics. Most prestigious of these was the dux prize awarded annually to the best scholar in the school.

David Borland born on 7th April 1868 and brought up in Newmilns became a successful sugar broker and entrepreneur in Glasgow. Held in high esteem by his contemparies, he was elected collector of the Trades House of Glasgow in 1920 but died on 9th October, 1921 before being made Deacon Convener. A golf cup bearing his name is still played for annually by the Trades House.

During his last few years he opened the first picture house in Glasgow, the La Scala in Sauchiehall Street, as well as the first garage in Ayrshire, at Troon. He was also a director of Morton, Young & Borland, lace manufacturers, Newmilns.

He and his family returned many times to attend sports day and prize givings. He is buried in Newmilns cemetery, his impressive tombstone standing opposite the main entrance.

DAVID BORLAND DUX WINNERS

Roll of Honour

1914	James Reid Young	1934	Jean Dunn
1915	John McIvor Young	1935	Jenny Allan
1916	Andrew McPherson	1936	Alexander Young
1917	William Steel	1937	Lorna Denny
1918	Robert Gordon	1938	William Allan
1919	Jessie Coubrough	1939	Netta Young
1920	Lizzie Wyper	1940	Margaret Bulger
1921	Alexander Cochrane	1941	Mary Thomson
1922	Jenny Hamilton	1942	Isobel Young
1923	Mary Neil	1943	Jean Bell
1924	Margaret Young	1944	Margaret Thompson
1925	Isa Wilson	1945	Margaret McCartney
1926	Isa Wilson	1946	Margaret Paterson
1927	Jessie Welden	1947	Helen Richmond
1928	Andrew McLuckie	1948	John Campbell
1929	Helen Mair	1949	Hilda Pollock
1930	James Morton Muir	1950	Stuart Wilson
1931	Lewis Dunlop	1951	Ronald Crichton
1932	Jean Hood	1952	Margaret Grier
1933	James Allan	1953	George Hamilton

1954	Elizabeth Campbell	1963	Lilian Parker
1955	James Mitchell	1964	Christine McEwan
1956	Olive Mitchell	1965	Ada Dunn
1957	Jean Aird — Frances Walker	1966	Stewart Morton
1958	Jill Simpson	1967	Elizabeth Gillespie — Ian Kerr
1959	Anne Lawson	1968	Colin Allan
1960	Brian Griffin	1969	Susan Allan
1961	Jean Neil	1970	John Dempster
1962	Sheila McGibbon		

From 1914 to 1926 gold and silver medals were awarded and from 1927 to 1940 gold and silver watches, from 1941 onwards the winners were given books.

List of Cup Winners

DAVID BORLAND SENIOR BOYS CUP–Champions

J. Scoular	1916	John M. Howie	1947
T. Campbell	1917	John M. Howie	1948
J. Lawson	1918	Robert J.J. Brown	1948
J.K. Melville	1919	Thomas Blane	1949
M. Young	1920	Wm. Campbell Wilson	1950
H. Brown	1921	Robert Taylor	1951
David Hamilton	1922	Hugh Morton	1952
Hugh Mair Young	1923	Hugh Morton	1953
Hugh Mair Young	1924	Alexander C. Glass	1954
John C. Inglis	1925	Ian Pollock	1955
Wm. McCartney	1926	Alexander Chisholm	1955
Archibald Mair	1927	Owen J.M. Leitch	1956
Jack Kerr	1928	Tom Young	1957
Thomas Morton	1929	Mitchell Julyan	1958
George C. Jamieson	1930	Robert Mitchell	1959
John B. Crichton	1931	Wm. R. Oliver	1960
Robert Galloway	1932	Hugh Allan	1961
Hugh Quinn	1933	Joe Murray	1962
John B. Crichton	1934	Sydney Smith	1963
John H. Pollock	1935	James Dykes	1964
Jas T. Young	1936	Derrick Julyan	1965
Jas. T. Young	1937	Derrick Julyan	1966
William Allan	1938	Robert McC. Frame	1967
Thomas G. Bryden	1939	Robert McC. Frame	1968
Robert Gebbie	1940	Ian Hood	1969
James A. Shedden	1941	H. Collins	1970
John M. Wood	1942	Iain Smith	1971
Samuel C. Watson	1942	Iain Smith	1972
John M. Hood	1943	Iain Smith	1973
John W. Smith	1944	B. Glover	1974
William King	1945	B. Glover	1975
William Wright	1946	S. Warnock	1976

Alan Duncan	1977	David Rooney	1983
Robert Hunter	1978	John Cairns	1984
Stephen Greer	1979	Kevin Spence	1985
Alan Kirk	1980	Neil Gibson	1986
James Alexander	1981	Billy Phillips	1987
Roland McCallum	1982	Gary McGee	1988
Stuart Holt	1982	Gavin Luna	1989

IAN BORLAND JUNIOR BOYS TROPHY–Runners-up

Thomas Ross	1953	James Bryson	1971
Andrew McKinlay	1954	Tommy Brown	1972
Angus McP. Hood	1955	Tommy Brown	1973
Mitchell Julyan	1956	S. Menzies	1974
Ian Spence	1957	Ian Crerar	1975
Brian Griffin	1958	A. Morris	1976
Stuart J. Gibson	1959	John Hughes	1977
Duncan Ryburn	1959	Michael Scott	1978
Duncan Ryburn	1960	David Campbell	1979
Bryce C. Whiteford	1961	G. Caldwell	1980
Derrick Julyan	1962	Alan Baird	1981
Derrick Julyan	1963	Stephen Hampshire	1981
James F. Finnie	1964	Steven Bell	1983
James F. Finnie	1965	Robert Frater	1984
Robert McC. Frame	1966	Stuart Bell	1985
Andrew Mair	1967	Martin Spence	1986
Richard A. Martin	1968	Graeme Russell	1987
Andrew B. McMillan	1968	Donald Deans	1988
David Dougan	1969	Kirk Lyon	1989
A. Murray	1970		

WINIFRED BORLAND ROSE BOWL–Champions

Mary Johnston	1927	Jenny W. Woodburn	1943
Jean Steel	1928	Margaret M. Thomson	1944
Jenny S. Campbell	1929	Nan D. Young	1945
Mary R. Smith	1930	Jean S. Mair	1946
Mary A. Kerr	1931	Margaret M. Fleming	1947
Evelyn D. Burnie	1932	Margaret O'P. Frater	1948
Jean P. Smith	1933	Mary K. McDowall	1948
Jenny McCallan	1934	Lily C. Henderson	1949
May Hamilton	1935	Helen Y. Luke	1950
Ella M. Morton	1936	Myra K. Borland	1951
Lorna D. M. Dennie	1937	Joan Cairns	1952
Irene M. Morton	1938	Elsie C. Julyan	1953
Mary Frater	1939	A. Margaret Campbell	1954
Nan L. Crichton	1940	Bessie Beveridge	1955
Helen M. Browning	1940	Olive Mitchell	1956
Mary B. Thomson	1941	Jean M. Young	1957
Annie B. Mann	1942	Elizabeth Wardrop	1958

Jean Hunter	1959	K. Gemmell	1974
Elizabeth F. Campbell	1960	S.A. McVey	1975
Kathleen Whitelaw	1961	H. Little	1976
I. Dorothy Mason	1962	Elaine Moore	1977
Moira Lindsay	1963	Lesley Tulip	1978
Lyn Worn	1963	Helen Aird	1979
Margaret Quinn	1964	S. McKibbin	1980
Elizabeth Julyan	1965	Laura Hunter	1981
Anne Watson	1966	Gwen Kirk	1982
Isobel Fraser	1967	Sharon McGregor	1983
Catherine Smith	1968	Shona Alexander	1984
Susan O. Allan	1969	Deborah Frater	1985
R. McCrindle	1970	Lorna Ballantyne	1986
L. Young	1971	Emma McManus	1987
I. McColl	1971	Emma Bone	1988
S. Taylor	1973	Emma Jensen	1989

JAMES SCOULAR JUNIOR GIRLS TROPHY–Runners-up

Christine Gordon	1953	A. Julyan	1972
Bessie McC. Dean	1954	K. Gemmell	1973
Margaret Hunter	1955	E. Ferrie	1974
Elizabeth Wardrop	1956	M. Hodge	1974
Rena Hill	1957	E. Bryson	1975
Kathryn Ross	1958	S.A. McVey	1976
Kathryn Ross	1959	Margaret Duncan	1977
Anne Woodburn	1960	Jane Clark	1978
Dorothy Mason	1960	Valerie Paterson	1979
Dorothy Mason	1961	G. Kay	1980
Margaret Quinn	1962	H. Coleman	1980
Jessie Henderson	1963	Lynn Warnock	1981
Andrena Loudoun	1964	Sharon Dykes	1982
Andrena Loudoun	1965	Rosemary Mainds	1983
Isobel Fraser	1966	Fiona Cook	1984
Catherine Smith	1967	Angela Phillips	1985
Susan O. Allan	1968	Claire Pollock	1986
Norma Stewart	1969	Kirstie Russell	1987
A. Connell	1970	Eilidh Harper	1988
I. Glover	1971	Kati Lawrence	1989

Willie Deans

Like most places Newmilns had its share of worthies who are either eccentrics or are different from 'the common run'. Willie Deans was one such. A tailor by trade, he was one of the best-known worthies in the Irvine Valley.

Opposing the First World War Willie as a conscientious objector was imprisoned for his beliefs in Ayr Gaol. After the war when the Communist Party was set up in 1920 he joined and was a member for the rest of his life. Typically, though, he always interpreted the party line in his own individual way.

Spare of build, he had a lean look that concealed outstanding native humour, compassion and a genuine gentleness which endeared him to all who knew him. Willie gave and never counted the cost. On Fridays he would go round the town to collect payments for his tailoring but hard-luck stories affected him so much that he often finished up with less in his pocket than when he started. Latterly he gave up his own business to become an employee with the local Co-op and when he brought home his first pay packet his wife, Lizzie, could hardly believe it was all theirs.

In his spare time he sometimes, with his fiddle, joined a few cronies to form a concert party entertaining the old folk. He himself was always in demand as a speaker at Burns Suppers and Golden Weddings.

But Willie Deans will best be remembered for his fund of original stories which could range from the ribald to the poignant and for his pawky comments on current events. Typical was his telling of how during World War II when all the lace production in the Valley was directed to help the war effort by weaving mosquito netting that 'they had woven that much mosquito netting that every mosquito had a net tae itsell.'

He died on the 2nd of August, 1966, aged 80.

INTERESTING SNIPPETS

Dr. Johnston visited Loudoun from 30th October to 8th November, 1773.

Keir Hardie M.P. gave a lecture in the Temperance Hall on 27th September, 1894.

Willie Deans

Lanfine

By ALAN P. PARK & ALEX BARRIE

Not much is known about the early history of Lanfine. The origin of the name is obscure though it is possible that it is derived from Lann Fionn, meaning 'sacred enclosure.'

In 1471 a chapel was established in the grounds of Cessnock Castle, known in the Middle Ages as the Tower of Galliestoun. At this time Cessnock belonged to a family of Campbells who were probably related to the Campbells of Loudoun; the families were certainly later connected by marriage. The clergyman appointed to the chapel which presumably was designed for private worship by the Campbell family, was granted as a source of income, the 'Lands of Lenfene' for life.

The lands of Lanfine may have returned to the Campbells of Cessnock either at the Reformation in 1560, or on the death of the incumbent chaplain. In 1573 the estate passed to John Lockhart of Barr, in Galston. He was a supporter of the Protestant cause, as were the Campbells of Cessnock. There probably were close connections between the two families and both Barr Castle and the Lockhart estates seem to have passed to the Campbells of Cessnock about 1670.

The male line of Campbells died out early in the 18th century and the estate passed through marriage to a Sir Alexander Hume.

The Hume's Cessnock lands were sold off in 1769 and Lanfine estate was bought by John Brown of the Glasgow banking firm Carrick, Brown & Co., at or around the same time as he acquired Waterhaughs.

THE BROWNS OF LANFINE

The person regarded by the members of the Brown family themselves as founder of the family was Nicol Brown, a young officer of Dragoons who was billeted in Newmilns in 1638. In this year all over Scotland men were defying the government of King Charles I in London by signing a National Covenant to defend the Presbyterian system of church government against the attempts of the king to force a system of government by bishops on the church in Scotland. In Galston Parish alone over three hundred signatures were added to the National Covenant. Those signing were mainly the heads of households, so the support for the National Covenant was much greater numerically than the number of signatures alone suggests. The families living in the collection of crofts which made up the fermtoun of Lanfine at this time are on record as being signatories. They were 'Thomas Patersoune in Lenfeine, Robert and John Patersonne in Lenfeine and George Ritchmont and Thomas Ritchmont, younger in Lenfeine'. The Covenant represented a rebellion against the authority of the king so it is not surprising that troops were billeted in the Valley.

Nicol Brown apparently settled in Newmilns either before or after meeting and marrying a local girl who was a daughter of the miller at Ranoldcoup and whose surname was also Brown.

A son of this marriage, James Brown became a minister of the Gospel and was for a time chaplain to the Laird of Cessnock. In 1685 during 'the Killing Time' when Covenanters from all over the south-west of Scotland were being hunted down by the forces of the Crown he was forced to flee and seek refuge in the Boston area, of North America. However he returned to Scotland in 1687 and in 1688 managed to convince the Court of Justiciary in Edinburgh of his innocence of any offence against the Crown. Following the 'Glorious Revolution' of 1688 the Presbyterian Church became the established Church of Scotland and James Brown went on to become minister of the High Church in Glasgow. He died in 1714. Many of his sermons, prayers and letters were later presented to the University of Glasgow by Miss Martha Brown.

The Rev. James Brown had a sister, Margaret, who married a Newmilns man called Thomas Brown and he was the direct ancestor in the male line of the Browns of Lanfine. He and Margaret had a son, John, who was born about 1650. He was a surgeon in Newmilns and was a bailie in Newmilns Town Council in 1705.

John Brown had at least two sons who survived to have children of their own.

Nicholas (1697-1739) was the younger of the two and we shall deal with him first since it is from him and not his elder brother, James, that the Browns of Lanfine were directly descended. However the line established by this elder brother, James is of interest as well and we shall return to James later.

Like his father, Nicholas was a surgeon in Newmilns and a bailie in Newmilns Town Council in 1726. He married Marian Campbell, daughter of the Laird of Waterhaughs who was related to the Campbells of Loudoun and possibly also to the Campbells of Cessnock. He had two sons who survived into adulthood and again the younger provides the direct line to ownership of Lanfine and again we shall revert to the elder brother later.

John (1729-1802) the younger son, became a successful textile manufacturer and banker. He was also a bailie in the city of Glasgow and became wealthy enough to buy Waterhaughs, the property of his maternal grandfather. He also acquired 400 acres at Lanfine presumably when Cessnock estate was sold by the Hume family in 1769 and immediately set about the construction of a new mansion house. The building work was undertaken by James Armour of Mauchline who was to become the father-in-law of Robert Burns. Lanfine House was completed in 1772.

FAMILY TREE OF THE BROWNS OF LANFINE

Nicol Brown — dragoon and surgeon
married a daughter of Brown the miller of Randlecoup

Rev. James Brown

Margaret
married Thomas Brown

John Brown
Surgeon and Town
Bailie 1705

James (born 1680)

NICHOLAS (1697 - 1739) married Marion Campbell

Thomas 1.
bought Langside
died 1782

JOHN Banker (1729 - 1802)
Bought Lanfine

THOMAS 2. (1775 - 1853). Professor of Botany at Glasgow University. Inherited Lanfine on death of cousin Nicol.

NICOL (1769 - 1829)
Greatly improved Lanfine.

Harriet

THOMAS 3.
(1802 - 1873)
Laird from
1853 - 1873

MARTHA
(1808 - 1897)
last of Browns
of Lanfine died
1897.

Marion

(This family tree does not show in full female descendants and their descendants)

Thomas (1) the older brother of the John who bought Waterhaughs and Lanfine, was a ship's surgeon and apothecary who went to India and made a fortune. On his return to Britain he lived for a time in London before settling in Glasgow where he bought the estate of Langside and acquired another estate, Daldowie, through marrying an heiress.

Thomas (2) son of Thomas (1) was a physician in Glasgow and for a time became Professor of Botany at Glasgow University. In 1829, on the death of his cousin, Nicol, Laird of Waterhaughs and Lanfine, he inherited these estates.

Fortunately for future generations he indulged his interest in botany by planting many exotic trees and shrubs and large areas of woodlands. These are now mature specimen trees or are to be seen today in the beauty of the tree-clad landscape extending from Newmilns to Darvel on the south of the river. He also cultivated less hardy species in the large greenhouses within the walled garden

Thomas (3) his son, inherited the estates on the death of his father in 1853. He was an advocate and had some reputation as a classical scholar. He was Laird of Waterhaughs and Lanfine till his death in 1873.

The estate of Lanfine had by now grown from the original 400 acres acquired by John Brown in 1769 to over 10,000 acres. With the successive lairds adding their own improvements it was now a magnificent country estate with woodlands and tree-lined avenues leading to the three gatehouses, one at Darvel and two at Newmilns. Brown's Road was built as a riverside walk between Newmilns and Darvel and bridges at Ranoldcoup Road and Craigview Road provided access to the estate. Within the policies there were numerous path ways, pleasant walks with small bridges, follies, rustic seats, and ornamental gardens, all maintained in the style of last century by estate workers, gardeners and foresters.

Martha, sister of Thomas (3) was the last of the Browns to hold the estates.

A keen supporter of the Liberal Party and a devout member of the Free Church, she took a great interest in the welfare of the inhabitants of the Valley towns, privately through giving help to individuals in need, and at a public level as well. In 1872, 1873 and 1875, she established the Brown's Institutes in Newmilns, Darvel and Galston respectively. When a gravitational supply of water was provided for the Valley towns, she donated a public drinking fountain to each of the three towns. Miss Martha Brown died in 1897 in her 90th year leaving an estate valued in her will at £30,422.

Newmilns Churchyard has tombstones raised to the memory of these various branches of the Brown family. The oldest 'The

Nicholas Stone' contains the remains of Nicholas Brown (1697-1739) and his four children. This stone is badly weathered. Then there is 'The Waterhaughs Stone' the last resting place of seven members of the family including John Brown who bought Lanfine.

The last of the Browns of Lanfine, Thomas, advocate and scholar and his sister Martha are buried in Darvel Old Cemetery beside the east gate.

One stone at least to the 'Browns of Newmilns,' the vastly more prolific branch of the family is in Newmilns Churchyard. The Family Tree of James Brown, elder son of John Brown (1) and elder brother of Nicholas is given here.

THE FAMILY TREE OF JAMES BROWN,
son of John Brown 1
and elder brother of Nicholas

James Brown (born 1680)
Merchant in Newmilns

Charles
Town Measurer,
1796

James married
Margaret Louden
of the Louden
family who were
hereditary millers
in Louden Mill.

James, married
Jean Morton, 1735
of Darvel Mill.

Margaret

Hugh married—Agnes Findlay
Town Treasurer   descendant
in 1787.   of Peden
                  the Prophet.

James married
Margaret Pollock
of Shewalton,
1835.

Nicol married
(1777 - 1858)
Banker in
Newmilns.

Jean Paton
(1781 - 1850)
descendant of
Covenanter,
Captain John
Paton.

John married
Elizabeth Steel
1785. Bailie
1836.

Over 392 descendants of the two brothers James and Nicholas had been traced in 1942. This number, no doubt, will have increased greatly since then. Naturally not all of these bear the surname, Brown. Names listed as having passed to descendants of Browns in the female side include Findlay, Hutcheson, Howie, Wyllie, Meason and Mason, but there are undoubtedly many more in the Valley as well as elsewhere. This information was collated in 1942 by

Lanfine House

Alexander Taylor Brown a direct descendant of Nicol Brown banker in Newmilns.

Moreover the descendants of the three brothers James, Nicol and John are scattered over many parts of Britain, America, Australia, New Zealand and South Africa, many having distinguished themselves in one or other of a wide variety of professions and callings.

THE SUBSEQUENT HISTORY OF LANFINE

After the death of Miss Brown in 1897 the estate passed into the possession of Thomas Neil McKinnon in 1902 but who was forced to dispose of the estate when he became bankrupt in 1910.

Sir Charles William Cayzer purchased the entire estate in 1911 as a wedding gift for his son Herbert Robin Cayzer who was later elevated to the peerage and became the first Lord Rotherwick. Sir Charles was the owner of the Clan shipping line and the first Lord Rotherwick acquired the Union Castle and a number of lesser shipping companies. At one time his companies had over 130 ships at sea. Many of these were mail boats with regular sailings to South Africa from Southampton. The Union Castle line was later taken over by the South African government.

Over the years the grounds and gardens were frequently made available for fetes, garden parties or band concerts and locals were welcome to enjoy the fine and sheltered walks through the estate. One regular group of visitors, the Glenfield Ramblers are on record of making a visit and confirming the continuing excellent condition of the estate 'Its trees and shrubs were artistically planted and included many interesting specimens such as Weeping Ash, Weeping Elm, Beech, Dogwood, Redwood, Araucarias, Spanish chestnuts and beautiful Silver pines ... gardens and hothouses were visited, in the latter were two plants of banana ...'

An annual event for many years was the arrival at 'the big hoose' of shooting parties for the grouse season. This required the enlistment of numbers of boys and young men from Newmilns and Darvel as beaters.

A report in the Kilmarnock Standard of March 1938 states 'On the 12th the party shot over the moor of Burnhead, Lanfine and had 131½ brace grouse, on the 13th over Greenfield, Lanfine and had a bag of 152½ brace grouse, and on the 15th over Auchmannoch with a record bag of 102 brace. With the addition of Auchmannoch the total area of the estate was now in excess of 24,000 acres. This subsequently rose to 37,000 acres when the Duke of Hamilton's Avondale lands including 11 farms were acquired.

The present Lord Rotherwick succeeded to the lands on the death of his father in 1958. In 1967 the joint estates of Lanfine and Avondale were put up for auction in the Station Hotel, Ayr and bought by Ashdale Land Property, a holding company of Eagle Star Insurance Company. Auchmannoch estate had earlier been sold to Lord Sorn.

Later Lanfine House and policies were bought back by Lord Rotherwick in 1969 and resold in 1971 to Mrs. Holt of Lanford Lodge Holdings. Mrs. Holt was connected to a well-known firm of that name which still produces car accessories such as brake fluid and de-icer.

In 1982 much of the estate was sold off to tenant farmers and others and the remaining 2,200 acres and Lanfine House were sold to the German millionaire, Herr Roesner, in whose possession it still is at this time of writing.

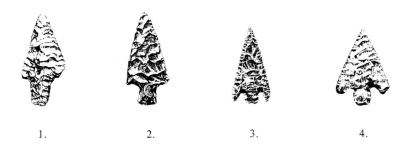

1.   2.   3.   4.

Evidence of the existence of early man in the area is to be seen in these four flint arrowheads found on Lanfine Estate in the middle of last century when draining large areas of peat bog. The two older arrowheads (Nos. 1 and 2) are from the late Neolithic period around 5,000 years ago. The two barbed arrowheads (Nos. 3 and 4) are much younger, being early Bronze Age but still about 4,000 years old. These arrowheads are only part of a considerable number of archaeological finds, which together with other antiquities and many fine examples of fossils made up the collection of Miss Martha Brown of Lanfine. These are now preserved in serveral of Scotland's national museums.

Religion in Newmilns

By REV. ADAM GIRVAN

The first ministers of religion in the parish of Loudoun were almost certainly Druid priests. When the Romans came to Britain they practically exterminated the Druids. There is evidence enough that the Roman legionaries were in the area–the fort at Loudounhill for example–and it is probable that a few of the soldiers were at least acquainted with Christianity. When the Romans finally left Scotland in the 4th century almost nothing can be taken for certain about the state of religion in our parish until we come to Loudoun Kirk, the old Church of the parish, lying about 2 miles west of Newmilns. Erected with money donated by the lady of Sir John Campbell of Loudoun in 1451, it was, from the beginning, dependent on the monastery of Kilwinning until 1619, when Archbishop Spottiswoode of Kilwinning resigned to the king the Church of Loudoun, with its tithes and revenues, its manse and glebe, in order that the king might grant them the following year to the Campbells of Loudoun.

With the passage of time Newmilns became the centre of activity and of population, and although we cannot say with any certainty just when the original Loudoun Kirk fell into disuse, we know for a fact that in 1738 a church was erected on the present site in Main Street and the place of worship transferred to Newmilns. (It seems almost certain that there had been a meeting place or church in Newmilns prior to that date but known authentic records give 1738 as the date of transfer). The Church erected in 1738 was in time found to be inadequate to meet the needs of the parish and the present building was erected in 1844, as tradition has it, around the fabric of the old, and the old church thrown out of the present windows.

The foundation stone of the present church was laid on the 3rd of May 1844. There was a procession from the glebe, with the magistrates and Town Council in front, followed by the local Masonic Lodge, the Kirk Session and Heritors of Loudoun Parish, the Oddfellows' Lodge, the Squiresmen, Lodge St. Peter's, Galston, Lodge St. James of Kilmarnock and a strong guard of the Constables. They proceeded to the Kirkyard, where they halted and opened right and left to allow James Patrick of Drumbue, factor of Loudoun Estates and Master of Lodge Loudoun-Kilwinning-Newmilns to go to the platform. The Master then instructed the Secretary to prepare a bottle to be placed inside the foundation stone. This bottle still contains the sum of £1. 7s.6ød. in coin presented by the Magistrates of the Burgh, together with a copy of the 'Ayrshire Advertiser,' a copy of the 'Kilmarnock Journal,' a copy of the 'Glasgow Herald,' 2/6d in silver from the Kirk Session, a roll containing the names of the Magistrates and Town Councillors, the Heritors, the Kirk Session, the contractors for the building, the last three ministers of Loudoun and the population of the Parish of Loudoun. Into the bottle was also placed a copy of the bye-laws of Loudoun-Kilwinning-Newmilns with the following roll written in parchment:-

'This church was erected in the year of Masonry 5844 and of our Lord 1844, on the 3rd day of May and in the seventh year of the reign of Her Majesty Queen Victoria the First of Great Britain and Ireland, the foundation stone was laid in true masonic style by James Patrick Esq. of Drumbue.'

The bottle was sealed with the stamp of the Lodge, the Master put it into the stone and the stone was laid in its place. Thereafter a very eloquent address was given by Dr. George Laurie, Minister of Monkton and chaplain to the Lodge. The procession then reformed and walked off through the town and the Greenholm; when they came to the Black Bull (now the Clydesdale Bank) they parted and all went to their respective house of meeting.

The new church was opened for public worship on Sunday, September 14th, 1845 (the congregation was accommodated in Newmilns West Church from 1844 to 1845). Fifty years after this the whole church was renovated and the decision taken to introduce an organ at the congregation's expense.

We must turn, however, to other church history in the parish as well. We begin with Loudoun East Church. The congregation of Loudoun East was founded after the Disruption of 1843. To explain, briefly, the Disruption, we must go back to the Reformation. In the year 1560 the Church in Scotland ceased to be Roman Catholic and became Presbyterian. It insisted on several things–on the value of every human soul, on the right of each one to direct communion with God, on the Bible as the only authority on God possessed by man, and on all being taught to read and understand the Scriptures. It was a natural result of these principles that the very first General Assembly of the Church of Scotland should meet in Edinburgh on its own authority, without permission of either Queen or Parliament. One of the important statements of the 'First Book of Discipline' was 'It appertaineth to the people and to every several congregation to elect their minister.' Thus at the beginning of the reformed Church of Scotland, the General Assembly was entirely independent of any court or power and the people had the right to choose their own ministers.

That freedom won by the Reformation was not long unchallenged. The Stuart kings of the U.K. did their best to take it away and so we have the story of the Covenanters. It cost Scotland 50 years of persecution and bloodshed to regain even the appearance of her religious liberty. In 1689 the Church of Scotland was again declared to be Presbyterian by the law of the land, when William and Mary came to the throne. But it was not complete freedom, for the Patronage System, by which the local landowner virtually appointed the minister to his parish, came back after a brief 22 years. Within another 20 years the Session Church was formed by Erskine of Stirling when he was censured by the General Assembly for preaching against the Patronage System. (The history of Newmilns West Church is tied up with this as we shall see).

Towards the end of the 18th century the Established Church of Scotland was certainly in need of revival and evangelical preaching began to make itself heard. Church Extension began under the organising genius of Dr. Chalmers. Within 6 years over 200 new churches were built. By Act of General Assembly, 1834, these new churches were to be given a parish area. In the same year it decided that the time had come for congregations to have the power to say who were to be their ministers, so the Veto Act was passed to ensure that if a majority of male heads of families, being communicants, objected to the Patron's presentee, the Presbytery should not proceed with his induction. Thus the right to refuse, if not actually to choose a minister was established.

Both these Acts of 1834 were declared illegal by the Court of Session. The State had interfered in the affairs of the Church of Scotland.

In 1842 the Claim of Right was sent to the Queen and to the Government and a Convocation of Ministers was held to decide what was to be done if the appeal for spiritual freedom was unheeded. 474 ministers met, not knowing what their position would be if they actually left the Established Church. Their congregations did not appear to be enthusiastic.

However, 3 days before the opening of the General Assembly of 1843, a Protest was signed by 400 members, declaring that the freedom of the Church had been taken away, and that the Protesters were to withdraw from the Assembly and meet as the Church of Scotland Free. And so the Free Church came into being with 480 ministers demitting their charges. Within 4 years it had built 650 churches.

What was the effect of all this in Loudoun Parish? The minister of Loudoun Parish was the Rev. Norman Macleod, a strong

Dr. Norman Macleod minister of Loudoun Old Parish Church from
1838-1845 went on to become chaplain to Queen Victoria and was
Moderator of the Church of Scotland in 1869. When Norman Macleod
died in 1871, Queen Victoria placed two stained glass windows in
Crathie Church in his memory inscribed "In memory of Rev. Norman
Macleod, D.D., Dean of the Most Noble and Most Ancient Order of
the Thistle, Dean of the Chapel Royal, and One of Her Majesty's
Chaplains, a man eminent in the Church, honoured in the State, and
in many lands greatly beloved."

personality who was active in the parish and to whom his parishioners were loyal. In 1843, however, he moved to Dalkeith and his successor the Rev. James Allan was of a difficult stamp, so much so, that the local Presbytery had to discuss the case for his induction for 18 months. Some parishioners objected to him because, it was alleged, he had been seen leaving the stage coach at Perth in a state of intoxication!

It was after this that a strong move was set afoot to gather together all those interested in setting up a Free Church. The very first Free Kirk service was held in the hall of the Sun Inn on 30th June 1845 and thereafter services were held regularly. On 10th March 1846 the foundation stone of the Free Church in King Street was laid by Mr. Crauford of Craufordland Castle. The first minister was the Rev. Andrew Noble and the first Communion Roll contained 209 names.

As we have seen, the Church of Scotland has a history of 'splits' and we have to refer again to secession. In 1733 Ebenezer Erskine led what was known as the Secession, which, believing that the Union of Parliaments of 1707 which made the Parliament at Westminster the only one for Great Britain and the ensuing Act of Patronage of 1712 were infringements on pledges given at the time of the reign of William and Mary and had been followed by inroads of rationalism in the ministry, broke with the Established Church. In 1761 Thomas Gillespie founded the Relief Church from a protest against forcing on unwilling congregations, patrons' nominees of moderate or rationalistic views. In 1847 the Secession and Relief Churches became one in the United Presbyterian Church. (In 1900 the Free Church and the United Presbyterian Church formed the United Free Church of Scotland: and in 1929 this body and the Established Church of Scotland joined together to form the present-day Church of Scotland).

The hand-loom weavers in our parish in the 18th century were decided in their opinions and loyal to their standards. They were not slow to sacrifice themselves or their comforts, if principles were at stake. Thus it was that some who adhered to the principles of the Secession Church found that Kilmaurs was the nearest centre where a church could be found which would satisfy their religious scruples. And so to Kilmaurs some of them would travel Sunday after Sunday over indifferent roads to the first Secession Church in the west of Scotland. The number of Seceders in Newmilns grew until in 1767 a definite attempt was made by those who had been travelling to Kilmaurs to band themselves together and in 1773 a Secession Church was formed in Newmilns. A Meeting House, as it was called, was built in front of the High Street site of Newmilns West Church

Loudoun Old Parish Church pictured during World War II

(the church is now demolished but became the home of the Seceders and so, subsequently, the United Presbyterians. It was built in 1833). In 1863 the United Presbyterian Church in Newmilns had 384 members. A fair number of this church came from Darvel and in due course a United Presbyterian Church was built in Darvel (1884). This left the membership in Newmilns at 301.

As has been stated there was a union between the Free Church and the United Presbyterian Churches in 1900. So Newmilns United Free Church came into being until 1929 when with the union with the Established Church of Scotland the Church became known as Newmilns West Church. In the centenary year of the church building–1933–the membership of Newmilns West Church stood at 434.

Thus, in our parish we have had three mainstream churches over the centuries since the Reformation in Scotland in 1560, giving us Loudoun Old, Loudoun East and Newmilns West. There were also small Christian denominations in the parish in the 20th century:-the Christian Union, the Plymouth Brethren and the Salvation Army, all contributing to the Christian influence over the life of the community.

The congregation of Newmilns West Church, at the conclusion of the ministry of the Rev. Jonathan M. Fletcher in 1961 agreed after considerable negotiation to dissolve. The membership of the congregation attached themselves to either Loudoun Old or Loudoun East.

When the Rev. Eric J. Alexander moved from Loudoun East Church in August 1977, the members of both Loudoun East and Loudoun Old selected the Rev. Ian Hamilton to be initially inducted to Loudoun East Church and, on the retiral of the Rev. E.T. Hewitt from Loudoun Old on 30th September 1980, to become minister of a united charge to be known as Loudoun Church.

And so Loudoun Church of Scotland remains worshipping in the Main Street Church building built in 1844. The Church building of Loudoun West was pulled down shortly after 1961 and the Church building of Loudoun East pulled down in 1986.

Presbyterian government in the shape of the Church of Scotland, and the churches in Scotland, has stood in our midst now for well over 400 years. Because of this the Roman Catholic tradition has never been strong in the parish, the few Roman Catholics worshipping in Galston Parish from the inception of the Roman Catholic Church there (though there is now a small Roman Catholic Church in Darvel). There is great talk today of the Ecumenical Movement. In Scotland the Reformed Churches and the Roman Catholic Church are friendlier than they have ever been. Given the decline of the Churches in this secular, consumerist age it is difficult to forecast from a Christian point of view what the 21st century may bring. One thing is certain. Man cannot live by bread alone.

Loudoun Old

LIST OF MINISTERS

1567	Ranken Davidson
1574	Robert Wilkie
1594	James Landless
1597	James Greig
1637	John Nevay
1664	William Hume
1673	Hugh Campbell M.A.
1674	Anthony Shaw M.A.
1685	John Campbell
1695	Hugh Fawsyde
1753	Andrew Ross
1763	George Lawrie D.D.
1793	Archibald Lawrie D.D.
1838	Norman Macleod
1845	James Allan
1865	John Robertson
1891	Hamilton Moore M.A.
1927	J.G. McLeod Thomson B.D.
1940	Edward T. Hewitt M.A.

Rev. E.T. Hewitt, Minister of Loudoun Old 1940-1980

Loudoun East

LIST OF MINISTERS

1847	Andrew Noble M.A.
1880	Thomas Fowler
1891	Thomas Marshall M.A.
1896	R. Bruce Taylor B.D.
1900	John Fulton B.D.
1906	Graham Park M.A.
1916	Hector MacPherson M.A. F.R.S.E. F.R.A.S.
1922	William M. Reid M.A.
1926	Roderick Bethune M.A.
1936	William Fitch B.D. Ph.D.
1944	Robert C. Lennie M.A. B.D.
1952	James M. Thomson B.A.
1962	Eric J. Alexander M.A. B.D.
1979-1980	Rev. Ian Hamilton B.A. B.D. M.Phil.

Loudoun East

Newmilns West

LIST OF MINISTERS

1773	James Greig
1816	John Bruce
1863	Andrew Alston
1877	John T. Burton M.A.
1885	James W. Dalgleish M.A.
1931	George McI. Allison M.A.
1939	George S. Campbell
1946	James Martin M.A. B.D.
1955-1960	Jonathan M. Fletcher

Newmilns West

The Lace Industry

By ALEX MUIR

At the end of the sixteenth century, long before handloom weaving was the main occupation of Newmilns, Protestant refugees from France and Flanders arrived in Scotland bringing with them the skills and technique of pattern weaving. They settled in three main areas and in each developed specialised types of cloth; in Strathaven they made silks, in Kilmarnock they were engaged in cloth weaving which latterly went into Kilmarnock bunnets and in Newmilns and district they made lace.

Cotton came to Britain at the end of the eighteenth century and by this time there was a sufficient tradition of weaving craftsmanship in Newmilns and Darvel for the Irvine Valley to become prominent as one of the main handloom centres in the country. Newmilns was so suitable a place for the trade that the town increased in population from approximately 500 in 1750 to 2,000 in 1850.

The following table shows the numbers employed in textiles in 1841:-

Male Weavers	460
Female Weavers	90
Clippers (Females from 8 years)	230
Winders of Pirns	154
Weavers Wrights	8
Warpers and Starchers	12
Mounters and Twisters	4
Agents and Manufacturers	13

Joseph Hood was born in Newmilns in 1821 and was a man who had a considerable influence on the textile trade both in his native town and elsewhere. Inspired by having seen a Jacquard weaving machine in his early youth he was driven by the idea of producing such machines as a new line of business. This he achieved to such good effect that before his 21st birthday he had already supplied a number of Jacquard machines of his own design and manufacture. He also introduced a number of other important weaving improvements which are now in common use.

He patented a twining and pirn-filling machine of his own invention which worked to considerable advantage in chenille manufacturing.

Joseph Hood, Newmilns loom builder and inventor engaged in a number of textile business ventures and became Provost of the burgh on several occasions. He gifted to the town the drinking fountain which stood at the Brigend.

He was also successfully engaged in various businesses connected with his native district and was one of the prime movers in introducing the Nottingham lace curtain machine to the Valley at the time when handloom weaving seemed on the point of extinction.

Mr. Hood took an active part in the public life of the burgh and was chosen as Provost several times.

With the introduction of the power loom, by 1877 only one third of the former number of handlooms were still working. In the 1880s, the introduction of madras-making power-looms further hastened the decline of the handloom weaver.

Young men began to leave the town, many of them to seek secure employment in the forces or the police force and many more went further afield.

Meantime the power looms were working night and day but the new industries called for so few workhands that this alone was unable for a time to stop the tide of emigration.

In the 1890s the United States introduced the McKinley tariff to protect their own lace industry. This tariff was first levelled at 40% and then increased to 60%. For a time this caused serious concern till new markets were found.

By 1907 new businesses were developing and many weavers who had left their native town began to return. This point marked the beginning of the golden years of the lace industry.

The First World War ended this great period as effectively as earlier crises such as the American Civil War and the Crimean War had done others by destroying markets and sources of raw materials.

The 1920's saw small boom periods of a year or two at a time but foreign competition increased especially from France, Germany and Italy. The government introduced a 33⅓% tariff to protect home markets in 1925.

The 1930's was a very difficult decade for the industry owing to the world recession and in 1931 a dispute between manufacturers and employees ended in a 4½% cut in wages.

The Lanfine bleaching and finishing works (known locally as 'The Bleachfield') was opened at the Strath in 1883 but following wage disagreements between bleachfield workers and the owners the plant was closed in 1932. The buildings were destroyed by fire in 1945.

In 1939 the Second World War was to mark the start of what was probably the greatest decline in the industry's history.

During World War II the lace industry underwent a change in structure, products and numbers employed. There was a disappearance of individuality, a characteristic which meant a great deal to the mainly family businesses.

All lace and madras producing units were formed into the British

A typical lace loom with Jacquard overhead.

Lace workers including weavers, spoolers, shuttlers and cardmen

Lace Federation under government control. All orders were allocated from the B.L.F. offices. The Scottish office was in a part of Morton, Young & Borland's premises.

Much of the production was switched to the manufacture of mosquito netting for the Far East and bomb blast protective netting.

When war ended in 1945 the industry gradually returned to peace-time production and business boomed for a time in spite of labour shortage which continued to worsen with men finding employment in the new post-war factories in Kilmarnock such as the Massey-Harris tractor factory, and the Glacier Metal Company.

The lace industry declined seriously from the 1960's to the present time. In 1945, at the end of the war, there were twelve lace and madras factories in Newmilns, today there are only six.

The late 1950's and early sixties saw the introduction of Raschel knitting machines which, weaving polyester yarns, revolutionised the window furnishing trade. Most of the local factories installed these machines which although smaller than the Nottingham lace machines were much faster, required fewer people to mind them and were much cleaner. The finished products were also easier to launder.

Another new machine came along in the 1970s. This was the Jacquard Raschel which produced a fabric which has the appearance of Nottingham lace and is woven in polyester or acrylic.

During the 1960's there was great demand for dress lace which produced a short-lived boom for the industry. Most of the leading fashion houses, both in Britain and the United States, were using locally woven lace in their creations.

At the present time there appears to be a trend to return to cotton fabrics both in this country and abroad. This is something which the old lace machines can weave satisfactorily and which, at present, the Raschels and Jacquard Raschels cannot, as the fluff from the cotton clogs the needles.

Lace, as we know it, has been produced in the Irvine Valley for over 120 years and some of the lace machines installed at the turn of the century are still in perfect working order with little variation from the machines installed much later.

Although the industry has diminished much in capacity over the last 40 years, there is still a world wide demand for lace and with proper marketing and the right product this unique fabric will still be produced in Newmilns for many years to come.

Loudoun Gowf Club

Loudoun Gowf Club takes its name from the Gowf Field of Loudoun Castle named as such as far back as records are available. This was the private Gowf field of the Loudoun family and had been in existence from the early sixteenth century. Gowf has been played on these fields for over 400 years. It is believed that this ground has never at any time been under the plough in all of these years. One can therefore, appreciate why the turf at Loudoun is unique and probably among the finest of any inland course. Hampden Park was returfed from the rough along the road side of the 14th hole around 1920 and this was only renewed in 1982.

On 10th November, 1908, twelve Galston gentlemen met in the library room of the Brown's Institute with a view to resuscitating the, by then, extinct Galston Golf Club. This former club of 9 holes was situated on the Sorn Road roughly west of Cessnock Castle and had been in existence for only a few years, around the turn of the century.

The meeting agreed to approach Charles Edward Hastings the 11th Earl of Loudoun with reference to ground at the Gowf Field in order to form the new Club. The Earl agreed to rent the ground.

The expenditure envisaged would require subscriptions from 44 Gentlemen of ten shillings and sixpence, 44 Ladies, subscriptions of seven shillings and sixpence and 10 Juveniles, subscriptions of five shillings with a similar number of subscriptions in each category from Newmilns.

Newmilns responded to the appeal and a Joint Committee was formed, empowered to rent the Gowf field and to summon the first Annual General Meeting to which a new Constitution and Local Rules were submitted for the new club to be called Loudoun Gowf Club. The committee were further instructed (with the assistance of Mr. Hydes of Barassie) to survey the Gowf Field with a view to laying out a nine hole course and to subsequently survey the 'Hag Park' from the point of view of forming an 18 hole course.

Terms were agreed with the Earl of Loudoun and rents were fixed at £70 for the Gowf Field and £35 for the Hag Park. One of the conditions of the rent was that should the Club cease to use the ground all fences should be replaced as they had been when it took over and that all bunkers, tees etc., should be levelled off.

This clause is probably one reason why the course exists today as never at any time till 1947 did the club have enough money to replace the fences and return the course to its original condition. It was in fact cheaper to carry on–even at a loss. Mr Hydes was engaged to lay out the 18 holes, for which he was subsequently granted an honorarium of £1.1/-. Mr. Robertson of Troon was appointed the first Greenkeeper at a wage of £1 weekly with liberty 'to make and mend clubs and to sell clubs and balls in his spare time.'

It was decided that the fees for members be Gentlemen; one guinea, Ladies; fifteen shillings, *('who may play Mondays, Wednesdays, Fridays at all times but on Tuesday and Thursday till 5 p.m. and Saturday till 3 p.m.')* Juveniles; five shillings, subject to the same rules as ladies. Caddies came under the jurisdiction of the Greenkeeper; Fee: 1 Round, 6d.

Many were the trials and tribulations which beset the Club Committees but the members continued to enjoy their golf, always putting pressure on committee and green staff for better playing conditions.

A 'shelter' for Ladies and Gentlemen was erected late in 1910 and from this grew the 'White House of Loudoun' which continued in use till 1967. One of the first mention of facilities in this shelter is contained in a committee minute; *'The committee agreed to purchase 1 brush and comb and 1 clothes brush for the Gents and the Ladies room.'* Such were the finances in these days. By this time the club was being financially embarrassed by unpaid subscriptions.

The balance sheet for 1911 shows income of £255 with outgoings of £262 and an overdraught of £107.

The question of laying out a putting green first arose in 1914 and it was agreed to proceed. Then came World War I and like many small clubs at this time they were in deep trouble financially.

This financial trouble was not eased by a patriotic decision to waive the fees of all members serving in the armed forces, though many of these would not have been in a position to pay their fees anyway. There were 30 unpaid subscriptions, an overdraught of £10 with £50 rent due for the past half year and £15 Income Tax also due. Various suggestions were discussed such as reducing to 9 holes, allowing cattle to graze, etc., but when a suggestion was made by the agricultural committee of the day that the course should be ploughed, some senior members guaranteed an overdraught of £100 and it was agreed to carry on for the time being.

However, by 1916 the course was let for cattle grazing to save it from the plough and reduced to 9 holes with fenced greens. Little golf was played but the club survived.

By 1919 interest in golf was beginning to revive. Thanks to the fact that the rent received from grazing was now twice that paid out to Loudoun Estate the Club was restored to an 18 hole course and reverted to the grazing of sheep only. Between the wars, the Club struggled on, never quite clear of debt and never with much money to spend.

Despite this, improvements were made in the condition of the course. Around 1926 with the closure of Loudounhill Golf Course there was an influx of Darvel members which helped to bring more life and money to the club and which ensured its continuity. This was the position until the advent of World War II and once again the troubles of the previous generation were repeated.

The course was in fact in very serious danger of being ploughed up. This was averted largely through the efforts of Mr. Wm. Steel, the then Town Chamberlain of Galston. He went to the commanding officer of an army unit which was quartered in Nissen huts in the old Loudoun Castle Avenue to the west of the course and he persuaded him to tell the authorities that the course was needed as a recreation area for his troops.

However only the first twelve holes remained in play. Cattle were grazed on the course and the twelve greens in play had wire fences round them to keep the cattle off.

After the war, sheep replaced cattle, the fences were removed and the last six holes were again brought into play.

Again the course survived thanks to several big-hearted members who cut fairways and greens. In 1947 a sale of work and gala was held which raised £700 (the most money the club had ever had to date). The bulk of this was spent on a corrugated asbestos hut built behind the clubhouse and used as a refreshment hut and committee room.

In 1948 the factor of Loudoun Estate not unreasonably took exception to the fact that the club's income from grazing was considerably more than the rent paid by the club to the estate, and doubled the rent.

There was once again a real danger that the club might cease to exist, but it was saved by two decisions taken at a very heated A.G.M. One was that annual subscriptions should be raised from £2.10s. to £4. A second was that Sunday golf should be introduced. Sunday play was not to begin before 1 p.m. and members had to pay a shilling every Sunday they played.

In fact no real effort was made to keep the course closed until 1 p.m. on Sundays and although several people resigned because it was against their principles to play golf on a Sunday, Sunday was soon the busiest day on the course.

There were various reasons for this. One was that most members could not play on a Saturday morning because they worked on a

Saturday morning, so Sunday for most members was the only day of the week when they could play in the morning.

Also because of the need for income, the course was open to visitors on Sundays, and since in other parts of Ayrshire and in Glasgow it could take up to ten years on a waiting list to secure entry into a private club, Loudoun was inundated with visitors on Sundays–to the considerable annoyance of members.

A second result of the situation was that the club took in a large number of members from Glasgow. These members from outwith the local area undoubtedly played a major role in keeping the club in existence throughout the 1950's. Their presence, however, helped create a fear, unfounded as it turned out, that some well-to-do group from Glasgow might take over the course and make it a Glasgow club. This fear stimulated the committee to continuous efforts throughout the 1950's to gain greater security for the club by buying the ground on which the course stood, but the Countess of Loudoun would not sell.

In 1960 the Countess of Loudoun died and with only a year-to-year lease of the course the club faced a crisis. Death duties would require to be paid and the course was potentially the most suitable land for development. Lady Jean Campbell verbally assured the club that if the land had to be sold it would only be sold as a golf course. In order to start a fund to buy the course, should it ever go up for sale, a levy of £10 per member, £5 per associate member, payable over 2 years was agreed at an extra-ordinary A.G.M. 60 members and 20 associate members immediately resigned leaving some 190 members only.

Fortunately with increasing leisure time the popularity of golf continued to grow. New members came from Glasgow, East Kilbride and increasingly from Kilmarnock. In addition quite a few of the members who had resigned rejoined. Thus when the course came up for sale in 1964 the club was in funds to the tune of approx. £5,000. An offer was made by the club to purchase but this was rejected. However a year later the course was purchased for £20,000.

Plans were drawn up for a new clubhouse and further expenditure of around £15,000 was envisaged. £6,000 was raised by interest free loans from members and other sources made money available. By 1966 the clubhouse was started, shouldering a debt of around £20,000. In 1967 the new building was opened but within 5 years the premises were found to be inadequate for the 400 members and 100 associates who were now using the course. An extension involving incorporating the Clubmaster's house into the lounge and changing room and building a new Clubmaster's house was put in hand at a cost of £25,000. This was formally opened in 1972.

Since 1974 most expenditure has been on the course itself. There is now a building for the machinery, tools and fertilisers used by the greenkeepers. A number of large tees, particularly at the short holes have been constructed, several new bunkers have been made and the planting of trees is now well under way. To date 2,500 trees have been planted.

Loudoun Gowf Club is beginning to take on a new appearance with clumps of trees and trees lining fairways and holes which were straight now having a definite shape to them. In general the greens are larger than before with more attractive shape.

In 1988 the burn was restored to its original course across the 3rd and 4th fairways and now add further interest to these holes.

There is now a total membership of 695 made up to 475 men 120 ladies 50 juniors and 50 juvenile members.

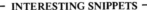

INTERESTING SNIPPETS

In 1891 textile workers from Newmilns set up a lace making firm in Gothenburg.

They were situated near the Orgryte Sports Club at Balders Hage and very soon taught the athletes how to play football.

On 22nd May 1892, the first organised soccer match in Sweden was played at Heden in Gothenburg and six of the Orgryte team were Scots—their opponents were a team called the 'Soldiers of Luck'.

When the Swedish National Championship Tournament started in 1896 the Scottish players were not allowed to participate so a second team was set up which eventually became the world famous Gothenburg Football Club.

In 1893 Johnstone Shields & Co. sent workers to Barcelona to set up a lace factory which still operates today.

The men formed a football team 'Colonia Escocesa' which in 1900 contested the first Spanish Cup Final against Barcelona—the team lost 2-0 and included in the line up were the two Black brothers and George Girvan, later a Provost of Newmilns who also played for Hispania and Barcelona before returning to his homeland in 1903.

NEWMILNS FOOTBALL CLUB

Newmilns Football Club was one of the twenty four clubs which formed the first Ayrshire Junior Football Association in 1889. There was already a senior club in the town, but the junior game was more suited to a small burgh. The team had to wait ten years for its first success, winning the Irvine and District Cup in season 1898-99. The great years for the Club opened with the new century, soon carrying off the Ayrshire Junior Challenge Cup in 1901-02, a feat repeated three times in seasons 1906-07, 1909-10 and 1910-11. They also won the Ayrshire Charity Cup in 1907-08 and 1908-09 and the Ayrshire Consolation Cup in 1908-09 and in 1926-27 their last success before disbandment in season 1930-31. The photograph shows the winning team of 1901-02 with its officials. They are the second generation of the typical Scots football players who gave the world the modern passing game, bringing style and artistry to what had previously been a general kick and rush upfield as in rugby. The new method witnessed 11 wins to 4 in Scotland-England internationals in the first twenty encounters. Among the players seen here are representatives of four well-known local, football-playing families, Cairns, Kerr, Williams and Wilson. At this period the town supplied dozens of players to famous professional clubs north and south of the border with, in one instance, three brothers Danny, Robert and Alex Steel at Tottenham Hotspur in 1910-11. Since 1931 football has continued in various forms in the town, organised in the Churches' League, Juvenile, Amateur, Schools and other minor associations in addition to the spontaneous kick-abouts and entertaining five-a-side competitions.

J.P.M

Natural History of Newmilns and district

By FRED R. WOODWARD, B.Sc. FLS.

The neighbourhood of Newmilns retains much of its natural environment due in part to the local landowners, in part to its farming community and in part to its geographical situation outwith the main Clyde Valley Industrial Belt.

Geologically it lies on principally Carboniferous rocks belonging to the Productive Coal Measures, several exposures occurring in the stream and river banks and containing Marine fossil Brachiopods. Bivalve and Gastropod Mollusks, Corals as well as occasional fish remains are found in the form of fish scales. These marine deposits are interspersed with freshwater deposits containing fossil freshwater mussel shells and plant remains.

The North of the area includes older Old Red Sandstones of Devonian age which are of considerable scientific importance since they contain some of the earliest fossil vertebrates in the form of the primitive fish Cephalaspis, examples of which are in the Hunterian Museum, The University of Glasgow, the Art Gallery & Museum, Kelvingrove, Glasgow and the Royal Museum of Scotland, Edinburgh.

This solid geology is overlain by Glacial Deposits from the Ice Age together with later alluvial clays and peat deposits, the former yielding agates known locally as Burnawn pebbles in the river deposits. These are much sought after by collectors.

The botany of the area owes much to the local landowners, in particular to the Earl of Loudoun who planted several thousand trees on his estates at the end of the eighteenth century and also to Mr. Thomas Brown of Lanfine who did likewise on his Lanfine estate in the second quarter of the nineteenth century. Both estates have since allowed these woodlands to remain in a semi-natural condition avoiding excessive forestry management practices, in this way considerably enhancing the survival and enrichment of plant and animal species in the area.

Plants of particular significance are various orchids including the Broad Leaved Helleborine. Other plant species include The Giant Bell Flower, Wood Avens, Teasel (probably introduced during the early weaving days), together with various non-flowering plants such as ferns, the Giant Horsetail, lichens etc.

The fauna is also rich. Its mammals include Badger, Fox, Stoat, Weasel, Rabbit, Hare, Roe Deer, Bank Vole, Field Vole, Mole, Hedgehog, Brown Rat, House Mouse, Long Tailed Field Mouse, Common Shrew, Water Shrew and Wild Mink because of an unfortunate escape from a former Mink farm in Newmilns, the species has become well established on the river much to the detriment of the native wildlife which it kills indiscriminately. The River affords an ideal site for Bats which roost amongst the tree roots as well as at Loudoun Castle. Otters have also been seen from time to time passing through the Valley. The area is also significantly noteworthy for its native Red Squirrel population which has survived and is still relatively safe, the species being under threat of extinction in the British Isles due to considerable competition from the Grey Squirrel introduced from America.

Birds include Swifts and Swallows which annually inhabit the town together with Blackbird, Robin, Song Thrush, Starling, House Sparrow, Wren, Hedge Sparrow, Blue Tit, Great Tit, Coal Tit, Greenfinch, Chaffinch, Bullfinch, Goldfinch, Spotted Flycatcher, various warblers, Magpie, Crow and Jackdaw (which nests throughout buildings in the town as well as forming a large colony in the ruins of Loudoun Castle). Rooks are also abundant with several Rookeries in the area, the largest being on the Loudoun estates whilst others occur at Lanfine. Herons are relatively common on the river and can often be seen in Brown's Field whilst Dippers and Pied and Grey Wagtails are often to be observed at the waters edge. If you are especially fortunate you may see the elusive Kingfisher on the river opposite Loudoun Golf Course whilst Mallard Duck, Lapwings, together with Black Backed and Black Headed Gulls occur on the marshy ground below Loudoun Castle. Birds of prey are represented by the Kestrel and Sparrowhawk together with the Tawny Owl and Barn Owl which is still present although reduced in numbers.

Amphibians are represented by the Common Frog, Toad and Smooth Newt, all three breeding in the ponds and ditches of the area, whilst Reptiles are the Adder and Common Lizard which can often be seen sunning themselves amongst the bracken near the Cairn.

Fish include Salmon, Sea Trout, Brown Trout, Minnow and Common Eel.

Invertebrates are well represented by both woodland and open farmland species. The largest group, the insects, includes the following–Butterflies the Green Veined White, Large Garden White, Small Tortoiseshell, Peacock Butterfly, Red Admiral and Painted Lady and in addition the Orange Tip was also present in Newmilns in 1986/7. Moths include the Ghost Moth, The Old Lady, The Peach

Blossom, The China Mark Moth, Yellow Underwing, The Burnished Brass, The Silver Y, The Ermine Moth, and countless others.

Beetles are also present in numbers and include Burying Beetles, Violet Ground Beetle, Ladybird, Devils Coachhorse, etc., the semi derelict woodlands of the Loudoun and Lanfine estates providing an ideal habitat for woodland species whilst the river and ponds provide suitable habitats for aquatic forms.

Other insect groups include a wealth of Mayflies, Caddis Flies and Stone Flies due to the considerable amount of water in the area which also harbours Midges, Dragonflies and Demoiselle Flies (including one species only recorded for nine localities throughout the British Isles).

Plant Bugs, Aphids, Lacewings, Craneflies, Sawflies, Bees, Wasps, Hoverflies, Ants and Bluebottles are all present in large numbers.

Mollusks include the Garden Snail, White lipped Snail, Brown Lipped Snail, Copse Snail, Amber Snail, Pond Snail, Freshwater Limpet, Great Grey Slug, Field Slug, etc., including one species which has so far only been recorded from one other Scottish locality.

Spiders are well represented and include the House Spider, Common Garden Spider, Wolf Spider, Crab Spiders and numerous others, their abundance being partly due to the large number of insects available to them for food.

Other minor invertebrate groups include Protozoa, Earthworms, Roundworms, as well as Flatworms, the latter including one species that has only been recorded once before in Scotland and that record being from Aberdeen in the last century.

From the above it will be realised that our area has much to offer the amateur naturalist and provides a potentially important natural resource for future generations for recreational pursuits and planned conservational development.

--------- INTERESTING SNIPPETS ---------

In the late 1940's the Newmilns Angling Club began a fish hatchery in the building next to the river in Craigview Road which was once part of the town's yard.

Each November adult trout would be caught to provide eggs and after careful and expert management up to 80,000 young fish were released into the River Irvine.

The hatchery finished in 1974 by which time both Darvel and Galston Angling Clubs were also taking part.

NEWMILNS BURGH BAND

Newmilns Burgh Band had its origins among the demobilised soldiers of the Napoleonic Wars and the first mention of a bandsman in old records is James Brown in Townfoot in 1819. It is not until 1833 that there is formal recognition of a town's band with a list of its first members, including bandmaster William Smith and percussion in the hands of James Wyllie, "big drummer" and John Storrie "wee drummer". At that time it is more accurately described as a wind band as it included woodwind with five clarinets, two flutes and a strange snake-like instrument called a serpent. After the mid-19th century the trend was towards a full complement of brass instruments. The high points in the Band's career were in the years before the 1st World War when outright winners in three successive years, 1909, 10, 11, of the Ayrshire Challenge Trophy for 1st Section Bands. This was followed by a long successful run under bandmaster George Hawkins between the two World Wars. He carried them to 2nd place in the Scottish Championships in 1934 and 1st place in the Glasgow Charities Contest in 1937. The picture shows the Band in that year with the trophy taken beside the old Band Hall in Greenside. With only two short breaks in 157 years it continues as a 1st Section Band carrying on a great musical tradition and aiming for additional glory for the town.   J.P.M.

The Lammas Floods

In recent years during the construction of the Galston by-pass road the engineers disregarded, to their cost, the phenomenon known locally as 'The Lammas Floods'. Had they looked at the records they would have seen that the Lammas Floods are not folk-lore but in fact a harsh recurring reality as the following reports show.

Extract from **Weekly Supplement and Advertiser** 17/8/20:—

Newmilns... In common with the West of Scotland we were on Tuesday sharers of an extraordinary rainfall, and it has been estimated that as much rain fell on that day as on the whole month of August of last year. No wonder then that so many unprecedented scenes were the outcome. On the rain showing no sign of abatement as the day wore on, Tuesday evening saw the Irvine steadily rising, and soon it developed into a mighty volume. At nightfall a sense of fear that something verging on dangerous lines would occur, kept the townsfolk on the lookout along the course of the river. During the night the river became a seething and uncontrollable current refusing to be limited to its own narrow channel and ultimately it gained an opening at all weak parts of its boundaries. Daylight revealed the results, which passed all the guessings of human intelligence. The stone wall in Main Street had been unable to stand the pressure, and the river had borne on its crest a considerable portion of the wall and roadway, leaving only as much solid ground in the street as to permit of a horse and cart to pass. The damage here is serious and what the result would have been had the torrent lasted for another hour is awful to contemplate. As it is the damage can only be repaired at a heavy cost. There is also the subsidence of a portion of the Bridge further up, the corner near the Railway Hotel having got a bad twist.

On account of the danger attached to these places, a special meeting of the Council was held on Wednesday afternoon, when it was resolved to make temporary repairs and barricade the Bridge for vehicular traffic. The factories did not escape. At Messrs. D. Ligat & Sons, the corner of the shed next to the river was completely cut off, and all its contents of bobbins etc., swept away. At the Townhead, Messrs. Henderson, Morton, Inglis & Co., also suffered badly–their factory being built over a lade, which under the pressure of water, burst its covering and flooded the interior of the shed. The water had

The floods of 1920 at their height and below the aftermath

no outlet and the machines naturally must have suffered seriously by their partial immersion. Further down it was discovered that the sewage pipe across the river had been carried off and the Sewage Bridge also met with a likewise fate. Fields in the near vicinity were covered up and had become a veritable dumping ground. Trees, sand and mud had been freely deposited and as a result much damage was done to crops belonging to Mr. Murray of Strath. As a consequence most of the factories are idle, the electric cables being interfered with. Many minor swampings could be cited, each being serious enough to cause anxiety. It can be safely said that never before has flooding to such an extent taken place, and no one who saw it will forget it readily.

The following is gleaned from the Kilmarnock Standard of 23/10/54:—
MUD TIDE HITS NEWMILNS

Persistent heavy rain throughout Scotland last week-end resulted in widespread flooding which damaged property, impaired communications and squashed hopes of ingathering a late harvest. Probably the Scottish town which suffered most was Newmilns, where the burgh refuse tip dissolved into a river of dense mud which ploughed down the Darvel Road and into the town....

In Newmilns where thousands of pounds worth of damage was done to homes and to the factory of Messrs. Henderson, Morton, Inglis & Co., lace manufacturers, no one was prepared for the sudden sweeping torrent of black debris-littered scum which careered into the Main Street late on Monday afternoon.

Dusk was drawing into the rain-filled sky about 4.30 on Monday afternoon; day shift was nearing an end at Henderson, Morton, Inglis and most of the children from Newmilns J.S. School had arrived home. Then the black mud slowly encroached on the Darvel Road. Increasing in volume the dark tide, bearing tons of debris such as uprooted trees, ashes and household refuse crashed through the home of Mr. & Mrs. John Currie, 'Lizzieville,' halfway up the hill.

Mrs. Currie and her son, a commercial traveller, ran upstairs as the filth swilled into the living room, eventually covering the ground floor to a depth of over 3 feet, destroying furniture and sending huge tree roots and rubble crashing against the walls of the house. Standing outside the house was a Standard Vanguard van belonging to Mrs. Currie's son; this was swept downhill by the flood. It ended its passage over a hundred yards away in Campbell Street, the radiator buckled and the engine filled with grit.

At this time two buses were caught in the liquid avalanche. As the mud gained momentum, tearing up bushes and hedges and demolishing garden walls, it fanned out across a field to become more than 50 yards wide and several feet deep.

The first double-decker bus jerked to a stop at the side of the road and was knocked into a garden hedge. Many of the passengers, including some children, had to jump out and wade, thigh-deep to get clear of the marooned vehicle. One man described the onrushing stream of filth as 'like a wall of molten lava pouring downhill towards us'. Then a second bus was driven back by the impetus of the flood, escaping the wall of the lace factory of Henderson, Morton, Inglis and smashing a window before coming to rest. When the double-decker bus smashed the factory window it was the first warning which the 50 or so workers of Henderson, Morton, Inglis received.

... Householders got down to the job of making their homes habitable and sweeping the mud from homes and gardens...

... An emergency Town Council meeting decided to organise a Flood Relief Fund, donations of which would be accepted by local banks and the council also wanted to know how the flood began. A team of surveyors from Baptie, Shaw and Morton visited the site of the refuse dump to inspect the contours, and to study the path of the flood and local rainfall statistics. By this method they hope to discover the cause of the black tide of ill-fortune which struck Newmilns at 4.30 on the afternoon of Monday, October 18th.

CLAIM FOR DAMAGES

Mr. James Inglis of the lace firm of Henderson, Morton, Inglis, whose factory suffered severe damage in the flood, has informed Newmilns Town Council that he intends to file a claim for damages against them, charging that the deluge of mud was the result of neglect in the siting of the burgh refuse tip. This was told to a Standard representative by Mr. Guy Mair, Town Clerk, on Wednesday morning, shortly after receiving a letter from Mr. Inglis.

The burgh coup has been situated in its present position–or pre-flood position for 18 years said Mr. Mair. 'It has never been considered dangerous in the past'.

——————————— INTERESTING SNIPPETS ———————————

Two Newmilns companies have received the Queen's Award for Industry–Vesuvius Crucible Company in 1973 and 1981 and Haddow, Aird & Crerar, Ltd., in 1979.

Memories of Civic Week 1949

By JOHN STRAWHORN

The drab years of postwar austerity were passing. Men and women were returned from military service and war work. The new Masons Holm scheme was building and people were anticipating better domestic and social standards. Everyone was ready for a jollification. And if Darvel could have a Lace Queen Day, obviously we could organise something bigger and better.

It started in the Public Library committee. After a successful arts and crafts exhibition, somebody suggested, ambitiously, a civic week like Dunfermline's. And before we knew, we had twelve committees, each spawning sub-committees, till there were about 150 committee members, twice as many more helpers, and eventually few households not involved somehow.

The modest original plans were devised by an executive committee of nine, who became the directors of the Civic Week. The Chairman was an obvious choice–R.M. Paterson who as pupil, then teacher, and ultimately headmaster of Newmilns Higher Grade School knew everyone in the town, and was known and respected by them all. Giving the town council's co-operation was Provost Jamieson 'Wee Dick' as everybody affectionately knew him. Councillor Archie Smith of Pate's Mill was in charge of publicity, produced the fine brochure and programmes, and kept all informed from Bertie Greene of the 'Valley News' to BBC World Radio Service–we had no TV then! The intricate task of contacting Newmilns folk throughout the country and abroad and organising an Exiles Reunion was done by wee Willie Morton, backed by the flourishing Men's Club. Planning of arts, crafts, historical and industrial exhibitions was in the hands of Willie Muir. Hugh Sands, the insurance agent, was Secretary (working in harmony with the Burgh Chamberlain Lewis Stewart). The present writer was given the job of producing a pageant. Joint Treasurers were the two local bankers, Tom Todd (Clydesdale) and James Campbell (Royal). The Civic Week was to be non-subsidised and while an immense amount of voluntary assistance was readily available, funds were needed. Three or four whist drives and dances were held, a drama show, a concert, a bring-and-buy sale, and a school display. About a hundred people gave their names as guarantors should there be a deficit.

I remember how things escalated. The original Pageant and Gala Day committee split into a Pageant sub committee (under big John Kennedy the teacher); a Costumes sub committee (supervised by Councillor Mrs. Jean Brown of Lady Flora's); a Processions sub committee (led by a young incomer called Trevor Whale); a Teas and Refreshments sub committee (run by Mrs. Hugh McGhee the baker's wife); a Gala and evening Carnival sub committee (with Tom Mair as convener). Then sub-sub-committees were formed with producers responsible for the twenty-five items in the pageant. And John Dunbar dropped everything to paint all the backcloths for the tableaux, on war-surplus poison gas cape fabric. Though I was responsible for the general plans, I had no idea just what the pageant would look like till the day, and some items I did not see properly till the showing of the Film the following winter.

Saturday 28th May dawned fair. The town council, private householders, and the Decorations committee (under Councillor Bobbie Munro) had bedecked the streets with flags and laid out displays of flowers. The sun broke through as the grand procession left Gilfoot. It was led by the Town Crier, Adam Ross, then the Burgh Band conducted by James Steel, supported by the B.B. Pipe Band under George Jamieson.

At Downiesburn Park the tableaux characters dismounted from their lorries and formed up on either side of the platform. Here the Provost and Magistrates were arrayed in unaccustomed splendour, in robes borrowed from Prestwick Burgh–'like penguins' to quote Bailie Geordie Girvan. After Provost Jamieson officially opened the proceedings, came the ceremony of Handing on the Newmilns Tradition. Six representative characters from local history handed symbols to Rev. E.T. Hewitt, who presented scrolls to two representatives of Newmilns youth–the Heirs of Truth and Trust–20 year-old John Stupart and 16 year old Jean Mair. A Psalm of Praise was led by the school choir under Adam Girvan. Then, in a special ceremony, the U.S. Government's representative presented to R.M. Paterson a flag to replace that which President Abraham Lincoln had sent to the Newmilns weavers. So the Stars and Stripes floated up beside St. Andrew's Saltire, unfurled under the naval expertise of Trevor Whale. Thereafter a couple of gala hours, clearing up, and Old Time Dancing in the Morton Hall brought to an end a hectic but successful first day.

Sunday (for some) a day of rest, with a Church Parade, a Community Religious Service, and an evening Festival of Music with the church and male voice choirs.

The ensuing week saw crowds of visitors to the exhibitions in Lady Flora's and Loudoun Old Church halls, and conducted tours round eleven Lace and Madras factories, and there was something every evening. Monday–drama, tableaux, and songs in the Morton Hall, Tuesday–an afternoon bus trip for the old folk, who then joined in the Exiles Reunion, which included 25 from overseas. Wednesday–evening sports in the old Public Park up the Dalwhatswood road. Thursday–Old Folk's Night, run by Miss McKenzie, Mrs. Loudoun, and their committee. Friday–Willie Leitch's Cabaret Show.

Saturday saw the revival of the local Cattle Show, held at Townhead Park, planned by Councillor William Morton the auctioneer and James Morris the grocer. Sunday 5th June brought another packed audience in Loudoun Old Church to hear local singers and musicians conducted by Matthew Morton in Handel's 'Messiah'. A fireworks display organised by Sandy Higgins' committee, and postponed by a downpour on Saturday, formed Monday's spectacular conclusion to the Civic Week.

As the lights of the fireworks died over the Store Park beyond the old school playground, what was left? First, an unexpected surplus of £400 which two years later was spent in laying out the Civic Garden in front of Lady Flora's Institute. Second, an excellent film generously financed by Provost Jamieson which shows everything except the shared work done by so many behind the scenes. And last, a feeling of exhausted satisfaction. This, we said, is something no community can do often, but Newmilns must do it again sometime!

INTERESTING SNIPPETS

In November, 1961 Marion (Mysie) Morton then Mrs. John Moffat wife of General Manager of B.P. Refineries launched the 15,000 ton tanker 'The British Merlin' from the Govan yard of Harland & Wolff. The Morton family stayed at Ashbourne, Loudoun Road.

SELECTED VERSES FROM LOCAL POETS

SCENES OF YOUTH

Fond Memory ever, with unerring truth,
Cherishes and recalls the scenes of youth,
And every day we rove or league we roam
Strengthens her hold upon our childhood's home.
I've wandered long and far, but every year
Has made that sacred spot of earth more dear,
And every distance which is placed between
That spot and me but vivifies the scene.
When at the last mine eyes must close in death
And thou would'st speed with cheer my fleeting breath,
Remember where I spent my boyhood days,
And speak of "Loudoun's bonnie woods and braes".

William Blane

THE CHARMER FROM THE HYDROPATHIC

Enamoured with a passing glance
   Bestowed I thought, so very kindly,
I asked the charming girl to dance,
   And oh, the creature danced divinely.
We tripped across the polished floor,
   Her hand in mine—'twas bliss ecstatic;
I've loved her now a week and more
   That charmer from the Hydropathic.

John H. Greene

REED NOTES

A weaver sat upon his loom
   Ae dark December day,
Sad thoughts o'ercast his face with gloom,
   An' slow he plied the lay.
Sad an' slow the shots he threw,
   An' slow he trod the treadles,
An' slow the harness-flow'rs they grew,
   As see-saw gaed the heddles.
Syne thought he on the wab o' life,
   How swift its shots are cast;
How a' its flow'rs, or scant, or rife,
   Are woven out at last.

He thought upon the warp an' woof,
   Serv'd by a righteous han'
That maun be wrought to stan' the proof
   O' mair than mortal man.
Fu' blithely now his arm he swang,
   An' fast he trod the treadles,
An' fair the curtain flow'rs they sprang,
   As lichtly danced the heddles.

Thomas Bruce

WHAT NEWMILNS FOLKS ARE SAYING

I wandered up the street yestreen,
　　Short time before the gloamin',
To ca' on clishmaclaver Jean,
　　A decent married woman.
I eased the sneck, and walkit ben,
　　As I'm accustomed daein;
"Guid night," quo' I, "I've just come in,
　　To hear what folk are sayin',
　　　　This summer night

"Sayin'," quo she, "deil clip their tongues,
　　There's nae end o' their sayings,
And fightings wi' their lusty lungs,
　　Like dogs o'er worthless banes;
Sookin' at other folks plum jam,
　　And ilka dish that's dainty;
Sittin' wi' gossips o'er a dram,
　　Till ae lee breeds its twenty,
　　　　In braid daylight."

　　　　　　　　　　John Macintosh

THE SWAN SONG

Grieve not that I die young. Is it not well
To pass away ere life hath lost its brightness?
Bind me no longer, sisters, with the spell
Of love and your kind words. List ye to me,
Here I am blesseed—but I would be more free:
I would go forth in all my spirit's lightness.
　　　　Let me depart!

　　　　　　　　Lady Flora Elizabeth Hastings

"OH, IT'S HARD TO DIE FRAE HAME"

The evening sun is shining noo
　　On bonnie Lochanside,
And to the byre are creeping doon
　　The kye, my mither's pride;
The weans are sporting on the green,
　　I see things just the same
As if amang them a' mysel'—
　　Oh, it's hard to die frae hame!

　　　　　　　　Rev. Dr. Norman Macleod

John Macintosh, civil engineer and architect designed many local buildings. He was also an author in his own right with five published books. These contain many of his poems but also a wealth of local history. Taken in conjunction with his work as an amateur photographer and the large number of glass photographic plates which he made he has left a valuable record of the period around the end of the nineteenth century. A man of many talents, in addition to his interests in poetry, music and painting he spent considerable time and effort on violin making for which he received favourable mention in the work on "British Violin Makers."

ArtScroll Tanach Series®

A traditional commentary on the Books of the Bible

Rabbis Nosson Scherman/Meir Zlotowitz
General Editors

THE BOOK OF Ruth

THE BOOK OF RUTh

MEGILLAS RUTH / A NEW TRANSLATION
WITH A COMMENTARY ANTHOLOGIZED FROM
TALMUDIC, MIDRASHIC AND RABBINIC SOURCES.

Published by

Mesorah Publications, ltd

Translated and compiled by
Rabbi Meir Zlotowitz

'An Overview/Ruth and the Seeds of Mashiach'
by:
Rabbi Nosson Scherman

FIRST EDITION
First Impression . . . April, 1976

SECOND EDITION
Revised and Corrected
Fifteen Impressions: December 1976, March 1977, January 1978,
June 1979, May 1981, May 1983, June 1985, March 1986, May 1987,
May 1988, May 1989, October 1990, January 1993, December 1994, February 1996

Published and Distributed by
MESORAH PUBLICATIONS, Ltd.
4401 Second Avenue
Brooklyn, New York 11232

Distributed in Europe by
J. LEHMANN HEBREW BOOKSELLERS
20 Cambridge Terrace
Gateshead, Tyne and Wear
England NE8 1RP

Distributed in Israel by
SIFRIATI / A. GITLER — BOOKS
4 Bilu Street
P.O.B. 14075
Tel Aviv 61140

Distributed in Australia & New Zealand by
GOLDS BOOK & GIFT CO.
36 William Street
Balaclava 3183, Vic., Australia

Distributed in South Africa by
KOLLEL BOOKSHOP
22 Muller Street
Yeoville 2198, Johannesburg, South Africa

ISBN

THE BOOK OF RUTH / MEGILLAS RUTH
0-89906-002-1 (hard cover)
0-89906-003-X (paperback)

THE FIVE MEGILLOS
(set of five volumes)
0-89906-010-2 (hard cover)
0-89906-011-0 (paperback)

Typography by CompuScribe at ArtScroll Studios, Ltd.
4401 Second Avenue / Brooklyn, N.Y. 11232 / (718) 921-9000

Printed in the United States of America by Moriah Offset
Bound by Sefercraft, Quality Bookbinders, Ltd. Brooklyn, N.Y.

לזכר נשמות

דוב שלום ב״ר ישראל משה רייכעל ע״ה

שנפטר יא שבט, תשכ״ג

דאבא לאה בת ר׳ חיים יצחק ע״ה

שנפטרה ה טבת, תשמ״ב

אהובים ונעימים, יקרי רוח

ופועלי צדק

זכו לראות בנים ובני בנים

עוסקים בתורה ובמצוות

תנצב״ה

Table of Contents

הסכמת הגאון האמיתי שר התורה ועמוד ההוראה
מורנו ורבנו מרן ר׳ משה פיינשטיין שליט״א

RABBI MOSES FEINSTEIN
455 F. D. R. DRIVE
NEW YORK, N. Y. 10002
OREGON 7-1222

משה פיינשטיין
ר״מ תפארת ירושלים
בנוא יארק

בע״ה

הנה ידידי הרב הנכבד מאד מוה״ר מאיר יעקב בן ידידי הרב הגאון ר׳
אהרן זלאטאוויץ שליט״א, אשר היה מתלמידנו החשובים בהישיבה וכל
העת מתנהג בכל הענינים כראוי לבני תורה ויראי השי״ת וכבר חבר ספר
חשוב על מגלת אסתר בשפה האנגלית המדוברת ביותר במדינה זו, אשר
קבץ דברים יקרים ופנינים נחמדים מספרי רבותינו נ״ע אשר הם מעוררים
לאהבת התורה וקיום המצות וחזוק האמונה בהשי״ת. ועתה חבר ספר
כזה גם על מגילת רות וכבר ראה אותו בני הרה״ג ר׳ דוד שליט״א ושבחו
מאד, אשר על כן דבר טוב הוא שמדפיסו ומוציאו לאור עולם להגדיל
אהבת השי״ת ותורתו הקדושה, וע״ז באתי עה״ח בכ״ז לאדר השני
תשל״ו

נאום משה פיינשטיין

בעזהשי"ת

הרב אהרן זלאטאוויץ

Rabbi Aron Zlotowitz

CONGREGATION ETZ CHAIM ANSHEI LUBIN
EXECUTIVE DIRECTOR: BOARD OF ORTHODOX RABBIS OF BROOKLYN

RESIDENCE:
1134 EAST 9 STREET
BROOKLYN, N.Y. 11230
(212) 252-9188

Preface

הַמַּתְחִיל בְּמִצְוָה אוֹמְרִים לוֹ גְּמֹר

This volume marks the second in a planned series to be presented to the Jewish public.

The overwhelming response with which the previous offering — Megillas Esther, published two months ago — has been received, has clearly indicated that the Torah audience is anxious for unadulterated traditional commentaries, lucidly, dignifiedly, and literately presented, and aesthetically and attractively packaged.

With this in mind, I approached my good friend REB NOSSON SCHERMAN and asked him again to take part in such a noble project: to make accessible to the Torah public a Chazal's-eye view of another of the twenty-four sacred Books of the Bible, a book that is deceiving in its seeming simplicity, but which holds the inscrutable secrets of Mashiach and the Kingship of the Davidic Dynasty.

I approached Reb Nosson with some trepidation, knowing how deeply involved he is in chinuch and service to k'lal and how precious little personal time he has.

But his erudition and flowing style, as well as his insights and philosophical presentation of the sublime thoughts of our Sages were indispensible to the success of this venture. He consented to put the public's needs before his own and gave freely of himself.

The resulting work is prima-facie evidence of his erudition: his association has raised its level beyond description.

SCOPE OF THE COMMENTARY

The commentary was meant to appeal to the needs of a large cross-section of people — from the early-teenage day school student to the Hebrew teacher; from the college student with a limited Hebrew background to the young Kollel scholar who has neither access to all the sources in their original nor the time to investigate them individually — therefore, a serious attempt has been made to bridge the very wide gap and fill the unique individual needs of each reader.

The Book of Ruth was more difficult than Esther in this area. The commentary on every nuance of every word is more copious and abundant; the Book of Ruth is more laden with Halachic implications; the Book is more

"compact" in its narrative — the first few verses alone condensing ten years of events into a few words — the commentators are, on the whole, more esoteric and require more elaboration and interpretation. There were many concepts such as the sin of Elimelech and his sons, the conversion of Ruth, Moabite marriage, the period of the Judges, Davidic monarchy, etc., which needed a fuller treatment in order for the reader to comprehend the Book of Ruth — not as a 'love story,' God forbid; but as a Book of the Holy Scriptures aglow with inner meaning and understandable only in the light of our Sages who expounded every word בִּקְדֻשָׁה וּבְטָהֳרָה — with sanctity and purity.

To this end a new, free-flowing translation of the main text — not literal, but true to the interpretation of our Sages — was prepared. This new translation, designed to be as readable as possible, eliminated many of the 'surface difficulties' dealt with by the Midrash, Rashi and Ibn Ezra because their interpretations were incorporated directly into the translation.

Continuing with the method used in Esther, the Gemara, Midrashim, and Zohar Chadash were then consulted and virtually every Chazal directly concerned with פְּשַׁט, — the literal and intended meaning of the text, which could be meaningfully incorporated into the framework of an English-language commentary, was included.

The classic commentaries, Rashi, Ibn Ezra, Alshich and Vilna Gaon — were then painstakingly culled for essential comments not suggested in the translation, or quoted in the Talmudic source.

Next, the major commentaries were consulted: primarily the monumental Iggeres Shmuel by Rav Shmuel de Uzeda; Meishiv Nefesh by the Bach; Akeidas Yitzchak by Rav Yitzchak Arama; Simchas haRegel and Nachal Eshkol by the Chidah; Kol Yaakov by the Dubno Maggid; and the Malbim.

What was sorely missed is the encyclopedic and erudite commentary of Me'am Loez on Ruth which is not at this time available.

[In response to many readers of Esther, an extensive bibliography — with enlarged biographical description of the authorities quoted — has been added to the back of this volume as well.]

The major problem here was limiting and condensing the vast amount of commentary on every word, into a book of meaningful and intelligible proportions that would satisfy both the scholar and the casual reader. Often, concepts briefly noted in the commentary are treated fully in the Introduction/Overview. I hope the resulting volume does justice both to these readers and to the Gaonim whose sublime writings are quoted.

HASHEM's Name

It was decided that wherever the Hebrew Four Letter Name of God appears, it would be translated in large and small caps: "HASHEM," i.e. 'The' Name — the Holy name of God. Where the Hebrew has Elokim, the more general and less 'personal' Name of the Diety — it was translated 'God.' Although the name of the Creator is generally written 'G-d' and not spelled out in its entirety, since this Book is a portion of the Holy

Scriptures and the full Four Letter Name of HASHEM appears in the Hebrew, it would have been ludicrous to abbreviate the spelling of the English word God. אֶרֶץ יִשְׂרָאֵל was translated Eretz Yisrael (Land of Israel). Where the word Israel is found, it refers to the Jewish people.

A cross between the Sephardi and Ashkenazi transliteration of Hebrew words was used: Ashkenezi consonants, so to speak, with Sephardi vowels. Thus: Yisrael, not Yisroel; Iggeres Shmuel not Iggeret Shmuel, etc. Proper names that have become generally accepted have been retained; thus: Ruth, Bethlehem, Jesse were retained and not changed to conform to our method of transliteration. Although there are several inconsistencies, the style has generally been held throughout the work.

ACKNOWLEDGEMENT'S

This work is not entirely my own. That it is in any way worthy of the reader's attention is because I have the honor of benefiting from the friendship and counsel of some of the most scholarly and intellectually gifted personalities on the contemporary Torah scene. They have graciously given of their free time and genius to read the manuscript in its evolutionary stages, saving me, in many cases, from my own ignorance. I am indebted to:

My father HARAV HAGAON ARON ZLOTOWITZ who has reviewed the work and allowed me to benefit from his hashkafa and erudition. May he and my dear mother תחי׳, be rewarded בְּכָל מִילֵי דְמֵיטַב.

A very great note of thanks is due רַבִּי אַלּוּפִי וּמְיוּדָעִי, RAV DAVID FEINSTEIN, who, seeing the importance of such a series, again made an exception to his general policy, to assist in the preparation of this work. He graciously allowed me to remain in constant communication with him, and he patiently clarified many difficult Chazals, reading the entire manuscript and offering most sensitive suggestions. He allowed me the freedom to decide what to include and what to omit — and hence is absolved from any responsibility for the final redaction — but his scholarship and בְּקִיאוּת is something I could not have done without.

RAV JOSEPH ELIAS, who kindly consented to read through the whole manuscript and who spent hours offering many concepts from the storehouse of his vast scholarship and in many ways raising up the level of the work.

My very good friend RAV DAVID COHEN, who graciously took time from his hectic schedule to read and comment upon the entire manuscript, guiding me to thoughts and interpretations, elucidating upon many of the underlying concepts and tenderly removing many stumbling blocks. He performed "constant righteousness" — עוֹשֵׂה צְדָקָה בְּכָל עֵת, by lending me many of the volumes I needed for researching this anthology. He freely gave of his time allowing me to "air out" important insights before commiting them to writing. I am grateful for his loving concern.

My long-time friend, RABBI ELI MUNK, *was good enough to meticulously read the entire manuscript. He diligently checked the comments against the original sources and pointed out several discrepancies which were corrected before publication. These tangible fruits of his long friendship are appreciated.*

MR. DAVID H. SCHWARTZ, *as always, was near at hand with his warmth and friendship. He made many practical suggestions which are gratefully acknowledged.*

RABBI RONALD GREENWALD, *a dear and devoted friend, has been kind enough to make invaluable and encouraging suggestions, many of which were incorporated into the final work. His wife,* MIRIAM תחי׳, *was kind enough to read the manuscript, and offered several suggestions.*

My dear friend and colleague, REB AVI SHULMAN, *who, along with his wife,* תחי׳, *made many very important stylistic and conceptual observations on portions of the commentary. Avi shouldered the burden at ArtScroll during my involvement with this work and, seeing the need for such a commentary, almost single-handedly ensured its dissemination on a broad scale.*

RABBI NISSON WOLPIN *has again offered much in the way of stylistic approach to the commentary. He reviewed sections of the manuscript and offered invaluable suggestions.*

The proprietors of J. BIEGELEISEN CO., *Booksellers, are to be thanked for providing me with many of the difficult to obtain volumes on Ruth from which the anthology was culled. They have always warmly responded to my needs and have gone out of their way to help.*

The efforts of my friend REB ZUNDEL BERMAN, *seforim dealer and publisher, are deeply acknowledged. He envisioned the harbatzas-Torah-value of this series and he undertook to distribute it to the broad spectrum of b'nai Yeshivah with whom he enjoys a fine reputation, and with whom he is so intimately involved. He has gone out of his way to cooperate in every way possible.*

A note of thanks is due to my friends at ARTSCROLL STUDIOS, LTD., *whose high degree of professionalism and self-sacrificing devotion and loyalty ensured a beautiful production:*

MRS. JUDY GROSSMAN *and* MISS RIVA ALPER *gave of their personal time to proofread the manuscript through the various stages of editing. They ensured a nearly error-free publication. They gave the gift of time, which is greatly appreciated.*

MISS MAZAL LANIADO, MISS MIRIAM FLAM, MISS PEARL EINHORN, *and* MISS NANCY LEFF *have followed through the technical end with great devotion and dedication. My great thanks to them.*

T*o be adequately appreciated, spirituality must be esthetically clothed, and my* חָבֵר נֶאֱמָן REB SHEA BRANDER *is the 'master-tailor.' The finished*

volume could not possibly have attained this degree of graphic excellence were it not for his efforts. He labored strenuously to assure a perfect product וּבַחוּץ בִּפְנִים, inside and out. He has my eternal gratitude for his every kindness, patience, and courtesy — both in the compilation of the anthology — which he (and his wife Henny תחי׳) were kind enough to read with a most critical eye; and the final layout and design. He let nothing stand in the way of ensuring a beautiful production. Words do not adequately express my appreciation.

My devoted wife, RACHEL, is the recipient of my most profound blessings. Her patience continues to mystify me. She creates a home for me and our children which is conducive to Torah study, and which, to her delight, has become לַחֲכָמִים וַעַד בֵּית, a gathering place for scholars. She inspires my efforts for Harbatzas Torah — in that merit may she be abundantly rewarded. ׳ה מֵעַם שְׁלֵמָה מַשְׂכָּרְתָּהּ תְּהִי.

I again end with a prayer that the work be received by the Torah world as a tool toward understanding and appreciating yet another one of the Sacred Books of the Bible as our Sages wanted us to understand and appreciate it; without recourse to so-called 'scientific' or other untraditional sources, so that the hidden depths of the Torah will become the possession also of non-Hebrew reading Jews — too many of whom have been condemned to varying degrees of spiritual pauperdom — so that 'their souls will be drawn to HASHEM and His Torah.'

Meir Zlotowitz

Brooklyn, N.Y. Rosh Chodesh Nissan, 5736

An Overview —
Ruth and the Seeds of Mashiach

Ruth and the Seeds of Mashiach

בשביל שני פרידות טובות [רות המואביה ונעמה העמונית]
חס הקב"ה על שתי אומות גדולות ולא החריבן (ב"ק לח:)

Because of two good 'doves' [pure and righteous
Ruth the Moabite and Na'amah the Ammonite], the
Holy One, blessed be He, had mercy on two great
nations [Ammon and Moab] and did not destroy
them.   (Talmud)

שתי נשים היו שמהם נבנה זרע יהודה ויצא מהם דוד המלך
שלמה המלך ומלך המשיח ... תמר ורות ... ושתיהם עשו
בכשרות כדי לעשות טובה עם המתים   (זהר)

There were two women from whom were built the
seed of Judah and from whom descended King
David, King Solomon, and the King Mashiach . . .
Tamar and Ruth . . . Both acted properly in order to
do good with the dead.   (Zohar)

שבטים היו עסוקים במכירתו של יוסף, יוסף היה עסוק
בשקו ותעניתו, ראובן היה עסוק בשקו ותעניתו, יעקב היה
עסוק בשקו ותעניתו, ויהודה היה עסוק ליקח לו אשה,
והקב"ה היה עוסק בורא אורו של מלך המשיח (בראשית רבה)

The tribes were occupied with the sale of Joseph,
Joseph was occupied with his sackcloth and fast,
Reuben was occupied with his sackcloth and fast,
Jacob was occupied with his sackcloth and fast, and
Judah was occupied with taking a wife. And the
Holy One, blessed be He, was occupied in creating
the light of the King Mashiach.   (Midrash)

I. The Period—A Moral Perspective

The Book of Ruth begins with a phrase that, at
first glance, appears designed to place the story in a
historic time frame: בִּימֵי שְׁפֹט הַשֹּׁפְטִים — *And it was*
in the days when the Judges judged. Upon closer ex-

amination, however, we see that Samuel, author of *Megillas Ruth* has, in fact, told us very little. The period of Judges began with the death of Joshua and extended until King Saul introduced monarchy to *Eretz Yisrael* — a period of roughly 350 years. By telling us that the story of Ruth occurred during the period of the judges, the prophet is hardly telling us when the events took place.

True, the Talmud says אִבְצָן זֶה בֹּעַז — the Judge Ivtzan was Boaz *(Bava Basra 91a)* in which case the marriage of Ruth and Boaz took place in the year 2792 (968 BCE), 304 years after Joshua led *B'nai Yisroel* into the Land and 259 years after the period of Judges began *(Toldos Am Olam)*. Nevertheless, *Scripture* does not declare explicitly that Boaz and Ivtzan were one and the same, a statement that would be of utmost necessity if the opening phrase of *Megillas Ruth* were indeed intended to establish the chronology of the succeeding events.

Thus it is that our Sages interpret the phrase "When the Judges judged" not as a historical, but as a moral statement (see *Commentary* 1:1). Ruth emerged during a chaotic period in Jewish history. It was a time when people did not respond to their leaders and too many of the leaders did not earn the allegiance of the people. During such a period, famine struck the land — not only physical but spiritual; when there are no leaders and no followers, the soul of Judaism hungers with pangs no less severe or lethal than those of an emaciated body *(Ohr Yohel)*.

When there was no King

Although *Megillas Ruth* is a separate book of the Twenty Four, it is strikingly similar in many ways to two of the sorriest tales in Scripture, both at the conclusion of the Book of *Judges* — פִּלֶגֶשׁ בַּגִּבְעָה, The Concubine in Giv'ah [*Judges 19*] the story of an atrocity that led to a civil war resulting in over 80,000 dead and the virtual decimation of the tribe of Benjamin; and פֶּסֶל מִיכָה, The Idol of Michah that led astray a sizeable portion of the tribe of Dan [*Judges*

18]. Those episodes, too, are placed in an indefinite time frame and the commentators disagree concerning when they occurred. But the author of the Book of Judges describes the respective periods very pithily:

בַּיָּמִים הָהֵם אֵין מֶלֶךְ בְּיִשְׂרָאֵל אִישׁ הַיָּשָׁר בְּעֵינָיו יַעֲשֶׂה

In those days there was no King in Israel, every man did what was right in his own eyes (Judges 17:6, 18:1, 19:1, 21:25).

How striking! The precise year of the event is unimportant. Even the name of the contemporary Judge matters not at all. Were we to know these historical curiosities, they would not add to our understanding of the episodes or instruct us for the future. And, in the final analysis, the Scriptures are not a history book. The narratives are often incomplete and the chronology indefinite. Any number of inspirational and miraculous tales are told only in the *Talmud* and *Midrash*. Why aren't they in Scripture? They aren't because they needn't be; the Torah is neither a history book nor a story book. God in His infinite wisdom gave us the סֵפֶר תּוֹלְדוֹת אָדָם, *the 'Book of the Generations of Man' (Genesis 5:1)* and included in it what was necessary for us to know. The Jewish people produced over a million prophets until the period of prophecy came to an end with the Babylonian Exile, but only fifty five are mentioned in the Twenty-four Books of the Torah. Only those stories and prophecies needed by posterity were recorded. The others, too, were manifestations of the mind, hand, and word of God — but, needed only in the period when they were revealed, they were not immortalized in the eternity of Torah *(Maharal)*.

But the closing tragedies of the Book of Judges: the concubine in Giv'ah and the Idol of Michah, were. They were indelibly inscribed in Jewish thought because they are more than tales. They are expressions of what can occur when *'there is no king in Israel, every man does what is right in his own*

eyes.' As such, they are timeless and eternal. The Jew in every age must know what his fate can become if he refuses to accept authority and leadership. Ruth is of a piece with those other illustrations of what can happen when there is no vested authority in Israel. *Megillas Ruth*, too, begins with a cryptic phrase *'in the days when the Judges judged.'* The prophet, in three Hebrew words captures the attitude of an era. As the Talmud interprets, it indicates that the people judged, criticized, flouted their judges. Under such conditions authority breaks down. When that happens, there is famine — physical and spiritual. When that happens, even so great a man as Elimelech — learned, honored, wealthy — can cast off his responsibility to his people and flee to the fields of Moab (see *Commentary*).

The Story of Ruth

Seen in this light, the story of Ruth as the background of מַלְכוּת בֵּית דָוִד, the kingship of the House of David takes on a new perspective. Ruth, princess of Moab, might never even have seen a Jew, much less married one, had it not been for the lapse of Elimelech and the Jewish people. Because there was relative anarchy, a family from Bethlehem went to Moab and set in motion a chain of events that resulted in a princess from Moab becoming אִמָּא שֶׁל מַלְכוּת, the mother of Jewish royalty, matriarch of the family that produced David, bearer of God's glory on earth, and will ultimately produce *Mashiach* who will lead Israel and all mankind to the spiritual splendor intended by God when He said יְהִי אוֹר, *'let there be light!'*

It is axiomatic in Jewish belief that God's hand is everywhere and that the seeds of salvation can often be planted in a greenhouse of tragedy. Joseph was sold into slavery and his righteous father grieved for twenty-two years, but meanwhile God was preparing for Joseph to become the gracious and merciful viceroy who would ease the way into an Egyptian exile that had to be. A Jewish baby was placed in a basket to die in the sea, but he became Moses, the

ward of Pharaoh's daughter and the faithful shepherd of the Jewish people. Elimelech fled his destiny and we can only imagine how mortified the tribe of Judah must have been that its most illustrious son deserted it in its time of desperate need, but God was preparing the genesis of the Davidic house which would bring to Judah at long last the glory that Jacob pledged it in his final blessing.

Elimelech fled his destiny ... but God was preparing the genesis of the Davidic house.

II. The Sins of the Ancients

A Frame of Reference

Before proceeding further, it is important to understand that the sins of the ancients cannot even be mentioned in the same breath as ours. The Torah creates no cult of hero worship; it freely and frankly discloses the transgressions and shortcomings of the Jewish people as a whole and of the most exalted figures in its history. When such greats as Moses and David fall short of the exacting standards expected of them, they are criticized in a way that can make modern-day readers smug and complacent in their own fantasies of self-righteousness. Superficial readings of Torah have resulted in the images of violence, cruelty, and lust profitably merchandized by by writers and producers who dare to cheapen history's greatest souls to turn on easy profit. Yet one of our great scholars and righteous men of recent generations expressed the Torah view succinctly and well when he said, "If only our *mitzvos* could be as holy as their *aveiros* (transgressions)." It is ingrained in our system of belief that earlier generations — because they were closer to the wellsprings of revelation and to Sinai — were infinitely more holy than ours. So much so that, even in *Halacha*, the outstanding decisors of any era can only interpret and compare, but never dispute, the findings of their predecessors

When such greats as Moses and David fall short of the exacting standards expected of them, they are criticized in a way that can make modern-day readers smug and complacent in their own fantasies of self-righteousness.

It is ingrained in our system of belief that earlier generations — because they were closer to the wellsprings of revelation and to Sinai — were infinitely more holy than ours.

of a previous period. The demarcations of periods were decreed by the leading scholars of a generation when they, themselves, realized that they did not approach the stature of the preceding greats. Thus it was that the sages of the Talmud decided that the illustrious period of the Mishnaic *Tannaim* had come to an end. In the same way, the personal conduct of the ancients — and especially the greatest among them — was measured by a standard infinitely higher and more exacting than ours.

The personal conduct of the ancients — and especially the greatest among them — was measured by a standard infinitely higher and more exacting than ours.

Such a concept should not be entirely foreign to us. We expect higher standards of conduct from people holding positions of responsibility. One might feel extreme annoyance at the sight of a drunken bicycle rider — after all he could collide with someone or something, endangering himself and others. But we would be appalled at the thought of a drunken airline pilot with hundreds of passengers, and of untold innocents below at the mercy of his inebriated mind and uncontrollable hands. Similarly, succeeding generations have learned to shrug at the corruption of leaders and magnates, but *Baruch Hashem*, we could not even conceive of such behavior on the part of our Torah giants.

Conversely, because more is expected of greater people, their lapses must be judged by a higher standard as well. The standard the Torah imposes on the holy figures of ancient times is harsh and unforgiving — and it is proof of their greatness: one does not expect big things of small people, nor should one be indulgent of "human" weakness in mighty figures.

One does not expect big things of small people, nor should one be indulgent of "human" weakness in mighty figures.

Con- demnation — But no Sin

וַיֵּלֶךְ רְאוּבֵן וַיִּשְׁכַּב אֶת־בִּלְהָה פִּילֶגֶשׁ אָבִיו
And Reuben went and slept with Bilhah, his father's concubine (Breishis 35:22).

A horrible sin! The children of Jacob had only recently exterminated the city of Shechem for a lesser abomination, and yet Reuben remained a son in good standing, a respected father of the Jewish nation. The

The Talmud
explains that Reuben
did not commit the
sin of adultery:
'whoever says
Reuben sinned is
mistaken'.

Talmud explains that Reuben did *not* commit the sin of adultery; מִי שֶׁאָמַר רְאוּבֵן חָטָא אֵינוֹ אֶלָּא טוֹעֶה, 'whoever says Reuben sinned is mistaken' (*Shabbos 55b*). After the death of Rachel who had had the status of Jacob's principal wife, Leah and her children felt that the honor of family primacy was due her. When, instead, Jacob's personal belongings were moved to the tent of Bilhah, Reuben felt that his mother had been slighted. To right the wrong, he removed Jacob's things to the tent of Leah. An understandable, even commendable, deed by most standards. But for a person of Reuben's stature to

For a person of
Reuben's stature to
tamper with his
father's privacy, to
interfere in the
personal life of the
Patriarch Jacob, was
a gross, coarse act.

tamper with his father's privacy, to interfere in the personal life of the patriarch Jacob, was a gross, coarse act. By the standard of behavior expected of a Reuben, such an indiscretion is tantamount to adultery and the Torah so labels it.

וַיְהִי לְעֵת זִקְנַת שְׁלֹמֹה נָשָׁיו הִטּוּ אֶת־לְבָבוֹ אַחֲרֵי
אֱלֹהִים אֲחֵרִים ... וְלֹא שָׁמַר אֶת אֲשֶׁר צִוָּה ה'

And it happened when Solomon was old that his wives turned his heart away to other gods . . . he kept not that which HASHEM commanded. (I Kings 11:4-10).

Scripture apparently makes it clear that the aging Solomon became an idol worshipper. Again, the Talmud says no (*Shabbos 56b*). His wives attempted to draw him after the idols, but he did not heed them. Just the same, Solomon is condemned as an idolator, the harshest approbrium the Torah can confer because, by his indulgent attitude toward the sins of his foreign wives, he allowed them to think that they could sway his heart from the service of God. This might be excusable in lesser men, but never in Solomon.

Solomon's wives
attempted to draw
him after the idols,
but he did not heed
them. Just the same,
he is condemned as
an idolator, the
harshest approbrium
the Torah can
confer.

An Exalted Nation

Similarly, higher standards are expected of the Jewish people, especially during the period of Scriptures when they were witness to miracles, audience to prophecy. The classic, indisputable case in point is the incident in *Joshua 7*, which tells of the

shocking, demoralizing defeat suffered by Israel in their attack upon the small town of Ai. After the miracle of Jericho and the Divine promises that they would conquer the land without a casualty, this setback cast a pall upon the entire people. Joshua and the elders tore their clothes, put ashes on their heads, and fell before the Holy Ark pleading with God to tell them why the tragedy happened.

God responded with a shocking and frightening litany of the transgressions of His once holy and righteous people:

חָטָא יִשְׂרָאֵל וְגַם עָבְרוּ אֶת־בְּרִיתִי ... וְגַם לָקְחוּ
מִן הַחֵרֶם וְגַם גָּנְבוּ וְגַם כִּחֲשׁוּ וְגַם שָׂמוּ בִכְלֵיהֶם

Israel has sinned and they have also transgressed my covenant ... and they have taken of the devoted property, and have also stolen, and falsified, and they have put it among their own goods.

How bold and all-encompassing a condemnation! A nation of traitors and thieves had Israel become!

Joshua investigated and it was discovered that Achan — only one man from an entire nation — had violated Joshua's prohibition against looting the spoils of Jericho. Because of one man's lapse, the nation was castigated in the sharpest terms and doomed to defeat in the wars commanded by God. Because of only one man's frailty, the Divine pledge to the patriarchs and their children was jeopardized.

Did Scripture not tell the story explicitly, we could not imagine that Achan's deed could even be considered a serious sin, much less imperil a nation. That it was considered so grievous an act points up to an inspiring and unimaginable degree how great was the nation that, because of its malfeasance in winking at his act, could be so stringently judged for the failure of one of its insignificant members. (For a fuller treatment of the above concept and further examples of it, see *Michtav Me'Eliyahu* I p. 162.)

Ruth in Perspective

It is a valid indication of the depth of ignorance and the shallowness of scholarship with which most of T'nach is studied — or, better said, read.

Megillas Ruth has been referred to ignorantly and sacrilegiously by people far from Torah as history's first love story. That such a statement makes any Torah Jew shudder with disgust and bristle with anger goes without saying. Just the same, it is a valid indication of the depth of ignorance and the shallowness of scholarship with which most of T'nach is studied — or, better said, read. True, a literal reading of much of T'nach presents a blood-and-guts, lust-and-transgression picture of the Jewish people in what should have been the most spiritual and fulfilling period of its history. To be sure, Israel fell short of the goals set for it — but let us never forget that it fell short of its goals, not of ours. Even during its period of deepest decline; Israel was far, far above the moral, ethical, scholarly, and religious standards of the twentieth century which so enjoys basking in the self-anointed status of occupant of civilization's highest rung.

Even during its period of deepest decline, Israel was far, far above the moral, ethical, scholarly, and religious standards of the twentieth century.

Our Sages make it clear that Ruth's visit to Boaz in the dark of night was, in truth, the dawn of the blazing sun of the Davidic dynasty. Far from lusting after a Moabite woman, Boaz dedicated the last day of his life and the last strength of his aging body to the holy task of preparing the source of *Mashiach* with the righteous and pure 'dove' for whose sake God spared incestuous, selfish, iniquitous Moab for over seven hundred years. Even the sins of a generation judging its judges, the shortcomings of judges unequal to their responsibilities (see *Commentary* 1:1), and the lapse of the great Elimelech and his family (*Commentary* 1:1-5) cannot be understood in terms of the corruption, cowardice and rebellion with which we have become inured in recent years.

Their sins, however real, were defined by a standard as elevated from ours as is heaven from earth.

The Book of Judges is called סֵפֶר הַיָּשָׁר, The Book of the Just, because during the three-and-a-half centuries of the judges, the Jewish people, as a rule, did what was 'upright in the eyes of God' (*Avodah Zarah* 25a). This in no way contradicts the many tales of sinfulness found in the pages of *Judges*. The years of sin were relatively few, they did not enmesh

the entire nation, and the sins, however real, were defined by a standard as elevated from ours as is heaven from earth.

III. Monarchy in Israel

A Command-ment Deferred

There is a basic difference between a king and a judge and, in order to understand the period, we must understand the difference.

As is made clear in the opening of *Megillas Ruth* and the references to the lack of a king in the chapters of the concubine in Giv'ah and the Idol of Michah, the rule of Judges was not the ideal condition of Israel, and the absence of a king was, from time to time, sorely felt. Clearly there is a basic difference between a king and a judge and, in order to understand the period, we must understand the difference. Further, if monarchy is the ideal condition of Jewish government, why was it not established as soon as Israel entered *Eretz Yisrael*? And why, when the Jews finally asked Samuel to give them a king, did he criticize them so bitterly for doing so? The Torah ordains as one of the Six Hundred Thirteen Commandments that Israel request a king (*Deuteronomy* 17:14-15) according to the halachically accepted view of Rabbi Yehudah (*Sanhedrin* 20b, *Rambam Hilchos Melachim*) that:

שלוש מצות נצטוו ישראל בכניסתם לארץ:
להעמיד להם מלך, ולהכרית זרעו של עמלק,
ולבנות להם בית הבחירה

'The Jews were charged with three commandments upon entering the Land: to appoint a king, to cut off the seed of Amalek, and to build the Bais Hamikdosh...

If so, why did God scathingly describe the request for a king as

לֹא אוֹתְךָ מָאָסוּ כִּי אוֹתִי מָאָסוּ מִמְּלֹךְ עֲלֵיהֶם,
Not you [Samuel] have they rejected, but Me have they rejected that I should not reign over them (I Samuel 8:7)?

Government in Israel

The Jewish concept of government is unique and always has been. Josephus Flavius put it this way:

> *Some nations place the sovereignty of their land in the hands of a single ruler (monarchy), some in the hands of a small number of rulers (oligarchy), and some in the hands of the people (democracy). Moses our Teacher taught us to place our faith in none of these forms of government. He taught us to obey the rule of God, for to God alone did he accord kingship and power. He commanded the people always to raise their eyes to God, for He is the source of all good for mankind in general and for each person in particular and in Him will people find help when they pray to Him in their time of suffering, for no act is hidden from His understanding and no hidden thought of man's heart is hidden from Him (Contra Appion).*

Josephus's description of Jewish government is often mistakenly described as theocracy, but it is not that at all. *Jewish government was never the province of priests, an exchange of ermine for cassock.* The Chashmonaim established a royal dynasty after their overthrow of the Syrian-Greeks, it is true, but the attempted perpetuation of that priestly monarchy was in violation of Jewish law in that it usurped the prerogative of the House of David and perverted the purpose of the priesthood. For their persistance in occupying the seat of power, the Chashmonaim were punished with extermination in a slave rebellion (*Ramban, Genesis* 49:10).

The government described by Josephus is not one of priests, but of God. It mattered not whether the throne was occupied by a king or, as in earlier days, the accepted authority was a Judge — *the true King of Israel is God; whatever human hands hold the reins of government are but His tools.*

Why, then, the commandment to install a king?

כִּי תָבֹא אֶל הָאָרֶץ אֲשֶׁר ה' אֱלֹקֶיךָ נֹתֵן לָךְ
וִירִשְׁתָּהּ וְיָשַׁבְתָּ בָּהּ וְאָמַרְתָּ אָשִׂימָה עָלַי מֶלֶךְ
כְּכָל הַגּוֹיִם אֲשֶׁר סְבִיבֹתָי

*When you come into the land which
HASHEM your God gives you and you
take possession of it and dwell in it — and
you say: I would set a king over me like all
the nations around me* (Deut. 17:14).

The commandment makes it clear that it is *not* the
purpose of a king to serve as a charismatic conqueror
uniting the nation behind him, meting out judgment
to the enemy, and conquering and securing the land
for his people (*Kiddushin* 37b). For it was only *after*
having conquered and inhabited the land that a king
was to be sought. Israel needed no mighty warlord to
win its land — for had not God Himself promised
them speedy conquest and total victory? ה' אִישׁ
מִלְחָמָה ה' שְׁמוֹ, *God is a Man of war, with His Name
HASHEM* — what need had they of a mortal conqueror? Security, prosperity, fruitfulness, happiness,
and health were to be theirs as a natural consequence
of observing the commandments, not for allegiance
to a becrowned head or awe of a bemedaled breast
(*Deut.* 28:1-14).

For Israel upon its entry into *Eretz Yisrael* to have
a king with all his royal trappings would have
cheapened itself and its king. Had Israel been a conquering army with a king at its head, the presence
and assistance of God would have been obscured by
the glitter of a crown and the plush of royal robes.
The fiction would indeed have been created that
Israel had won its land by force of arms rather than
by grace of God; that the foe had been slain by a
flesh and blood king rather than by the King of
Kings, blessed be He.

During the days of Samuel, significant stretches of
Eretz Yisrael had not yet been conquered. Indeed, it
was to the enduring shame and centuries-long discredit of Israel that it allowed such a condition to persist. Rather than take advantage of Divine assistance

*Israel needed no
mighty warlord to
win its land — for
had not God Himself
promised them
speedy conquest and
total victory?*

*Security, prosperity,
fruitfulness,
happiness, and
health were to be
theirs as a natural
consequence of
observing the
commandments, not
for allegiance to a
becrowned head or
awe of bemedaled
breast*

*Had Israel been a
conquering army
with a king at its
head, the presence
and assistance of
God would have
been obscured by the
glitter of a crown
and the plush of
royal robes.*

and heed the Divine command that it purge the Holy Land of its profane inhabitants and turn it in its entirety into the land of Abraham, Isaac, and Jacob, Israel was content to settle what had been won, retire to its vineyards and fig trees, and allow the less fortunate tribes — those whose inheritance was still in alien hands — to bemoan their fate in isolation. For not uniting as a nation and carrying out its destiny, it was condemned to endure the presence and invasions of its enemies in a centuries-long cycle of fall, punishment, repentence, and deliverance (*Judges* 2).

Rather than take advantage of Divine assistance ... Israel was content to settle what had been won and allow the less fortunate tribes to bemoan their fate in isolation.

It was a weary people fearing invasion by Ammon and seeking a defender and military leader that confronted aging Samuel and demanded a king. But it was not for defense and conquest that God ordained royalty upon Israel — for those purposes, Israel had to worry less about the weaknesses of its fortresses than about the stubbornness of its spirit; less about crumbling the defenses of its enemies than about shattering its own nature-conditioned heart.

It was not for defense and conquest that God ordained royalty upon Israel.

So it was an angry and disappointed Samuel who recited the catalog of miraculous Divine interventions in behalf of Israel, interventions that should have been more than sufficient to clarify the road of deliverance from their enemies. Samuel said:

וַתֹּאמְרוּ לִי, לֹא כִּי מֶלֶךְ יִמְלֹךְ עָלֵינוּ וַה׳ אֱלֹקֵיכֶם מַלְכְּכֶם,

'And you said to me, No; but a king shall reign over us — but HASHEM, your God is your King! (Samuel 12:12).

Yes, the Torah indeed commands Israel to request a king, but, in Samuel's day, the request was premature.

Yes, the Torah indeed commands Israel to request a king, but, in Samuel's day, the request was premature. They got their king, Saul — a great and righteous man, head and shoulders above the rest of the nation — but his monarchy ended in tragedy because the people were wrong in demanding it then.

The Role of a King

The ideal Jewish king ascends his throne in a time of tranquility. The nation is secure and prosperous because its ultimate King, God, has made it so, and its way of life is charted by the Torah. The king

The king is the living embodiment of Torah and how its statutes and holiness ennoble man.

plays a unique role. He, as first citizen of the nation, is the living embodiment of Torah and how its statutes and holiness ennoble man. Holder of immense and almost unbridled power, he submits to the laws in the *Sefer Torah* which he carries with him at all times; required by his duty to the nation to hold wealth and exhibit pomp, he acquires what he must, but shuns excess; enabled by his station to indulge his passions, he sets an example of sobriety and self-control; inhibited by no mortal restraint, he turns his energies to the selfless service of his people; able to establish the absolute dominion of his own will, he

The King does not rest until his people know the rigors of Torah study and a discipline of honesty and morality in their personal and business lives that would earn sainthood in any other nation.

does not rest until his people know the rigors of Torah study and a discipline of honesty and morality in their personal and business lives that would earn sainthood in any other nation.

When the nation sought its king, it had not yet attained the stature it needed to be worthy of that type of monarch. Nevertheless, it did possess a man suited to the role — David, an unknown shepherd who was

Had Israel been worthy, David would have become the final Mashiach and the eternal Bais Hamikdosh would have been built by him.

unappreciated even by his own family. Had Israel been worthy, David would have become the final *Mashiach* and the eternal *Bais Hamikdosh* would have been built by him. As it was, he became the father of the dynasty whose ultimate heir will one day proclaim the kingdom of heaven upon earth. (Although there are many sources for the above treatment of Jewish monarchy, it is based primarily upon *Rav S.R. Hirsch, Deut.* 17:14).

Powers of the King

It is the function of the king to safeguard the Torah and see to it that the people study it and obey its commandments. Nor is he to be considered above the Halacha — on the contrary, it is his duty to be a model of scrupulous adherence to the laws of the Torah. His office, however, carries with it a unique legal status which may be divided into two categories:

a) As the sovereign embodiment of the nation, the king is entitled to respect and reverence ex-

ceeding anyone elses. All must step aside to make way for him and even property may be destroyed for his convenience. Nor may the king voluntarily forfeit any of his prerogatives; to do so is to demean the nation he leads. He is as obligated to exercise his claim upon the awe of the nation as is each of its members to grant it.

b) The king has extra-legal powers to confiscate, punish, and condemn to execution. A Jewish court of law may not execute a murderer save under a set of extraordinarily strict rules of evidence and testimony; a king may have the murderer killed, so long as he is satisfied that sufficient proof of guilt exists, even if the evidence is circumstancial. Whoever is disrespectful or defiant of the king is liable to the death penalty upon his command and at his pleasure.

All this is to insure that he has the power to inspire the fear of, and destroy the capacity of evil-doers (*Rambam, Hilchos Melachim* 3).

In the exercise of his extra-legal powers, the king is guided by one consideration — '*to correct any situation, as required by the times*' (*ibid*).

Thus it becomes clear why Samuel, author of Judges, explains the worst aberrations of the people with the unadorned statement, *In those days there was no king in Israel, every man did what was right in his own eyes.* A king would not have permitted the barbaric city of Giv'ah to go unpunished after its act of *wantonness against a helpless concubine* innocently seeking nothing more than a place to rest her head before going on with her craven Levite husband. Nor would a king have allowed the Levite, in his grief and anger, to incite the other tribes against Benjamin. Nor would he have allowed a jurisdictional dispute between the Sanhedrin of Benjamin

A king would not have permitted the barbaric city of Giv'ah to go unpunished.

and the rest of the nation to result in such tragic bloodshed. The existing legal system at the time could not cope with the travail engendered by the atrocity of Giv'ah, but a king transcends and overrides the legal system.

Nor would a king have allowed the marauders of Dan to make off with Michah's idol and carve out a little kingdom of their own up north. His duty to maintain the spiritual standard of the nation would have forced him to act; no lack of power or jurisdiction could have stood in his way.

The defection of Elimelech, too, at the beginning of *Megillas Ruth* was a result of the 'judging of the judges' — a lack of constituted, accepted, powerful leadership. Elimelech, great and wealthy, felt a responsibility but feared its burden. He would be expected to establish some sort of order to cope with the ravages of famine and his treasury would have to be thrown open to the poor and hungry. Elimelech felt unequal to the task — and fled. Trying to conserve his fortune and peace of mind, he lost both — and his Jewish identity. Save for the sacrifice and idealism of Ruth, he would have lost his posterity, as well. Had there been a king — who knows? The responsibility upon Elimelech might not have been so overwhelming and the majesty of the throne might have been employed to prevent the flight of the erstwhile patron of Bethlehem.

The Power of a Judge

Extra-legal powers are not the province of a king alone. The Sanhedrin, too, has the power to ordain coercive measures in defense of the nation and its mission. There were such courts in the days before the monarchy. The Torah commands that judges and officers of the court be established in all cities (*Deut.* 16:18). They were, and they performed valiantly throughout the period, even under foreign occupation and terror; these were the judges whom Deborah praised several times in her song (*Judges 5*).

But the courts were loath to exercise their extra-legal powers as is shown from the formula, *In those days there was no king,* to explain how such tragedies could have happened.

For there is a basic difference between the residual power of the monarchy and the Sanhedrin:

כל אלו הרצחנים שאינם חייבים מיתת ב״ד אם ירצה מלך ישראל להורגם בדין מלכות ותקנת עולם הרשות בידו. וכן אם רצה ב״ד להורגם בהוראת שעה, אם היתה השעה צריכה לכך יש רשות להם כפי מה שיראו

All these murderers who are not liable to execution — if a Jewish king wishes to kill them using his regal powers and for the benefit of society, he may do so. So, too, if a court wishes to execute them by an extraordinary decree, if the times require it, the court has the right as it sees fit (Rambam, Hilchos Rotzeach 2:4)

Rav Tzvi Hirsh Chayes (in *Toras Nvi'im* 7) deduces from the subtle differences in Rambam's descriptions of the respective authority of king and court, that the king's powers, while identical to those of the court in the case under discussion, may be more freely exercised. Rambam (*Hilchos Sanhedrin* 18:6) differentiates between הוֹרָאַת שָׁעָה, extraordinary decree, and דִין מַלְכוּת, the law of the king. This further indicates a presumption of authority that is automatically attributed to the king purely by virtue of his office — an authority that the court cannot exercise unless it is absolutely convinced by the particular circumstances that the national interest and severity of the situation require it to act extra-legally.

Plainly, any Sanhedrin, local or national, would be most ginger in annexing such powers to itself. Only in the most serious of cases would it tamper with the laws of the Torah; it is no small matter for a court of Torah law to go beyond the strictures of Torah law.

The king is bound by no such restrictions. His very position and resultant responsibility to the nation demand and require that he exercise the powers

of his position. A weak king does the nation no good — he becomes an invitation to religious lassitude and the paralysis of leadership that results in spiritual famine, atrocity, and idolatry. Indeed, the constant obligation to respect the king's personal majesty — the neglect of which can result in the death penalty — is in order to strengthen his position as national leader so that he can better serve the nation.

The judges of old were national leaders, but their leadership was based on law and public acceptance. They did not have the power inherent in the office of the king.

The judges of old were national leaders, but their leadership was based on law and public acceptance. They did not have the power inherent in the office of the king. They could lead if the people followed and they could exercise the extra-legal powers of a Sanhedrin under such conditions as allowed a court to exercise those powers. But the ability to lead varies with many factors, and Jewish judges did not exercise extra-legal powers with impunity.

There was another circumstance conferring power on a judge. The people could accept him upon themselves with all the rights and powers of a monarch — including the right to execute the disrespectful and disobedient. Joshua was given such acceptance (*Joshua* 1:16-18) and the people were anxious to establish a Gideonic dynasty (*Judges* 8:22).

The period of the judges was one of striving imperfectly toward goals that were never achieved.

Generally, however, the period of the judges was one of striving imperfectly toward goals that were never achieved — the goal of national unity under God, sovereignty over all of *Eretz Yisrael*, the attainment of the Divine blessings of peace, prosperity, and security. Had that goal been achieved, the people could have gone on to the fulfillment of the Torah's commandment that they ask God to select a king to lead them to even greater spiritual heights. It was not achieved. The result was the turbulence of the period of judges and flawed monarchy aiming at a spiritual summit that has, for millennia, awaited the coming of *Mashiach*.

The result was the turbulence of the period of judges and flawed monarchy aiming at a spiritual summit that has, for millennia, awaited the coming of Mashiach.

IV. The Murky Roots of Monarchy

The Kingship of Judah

Jewish monarchy is
no mere political
system; when it is
ordered according to
the Divine Will, it is
an end unto itself.

Jewish monarchy is no mere political system; when it is ordered according to the Divine Will, it is an end unto itself. It is this end which is particularly represented by the kingdom of Judah. The final one of the Ten *Sefiros*, the stages through which God's will is carried out in creation, is מַלְכוּת, *malchus* (kingship.) *Malchus* represents the final revelation, the coming to fruition of His will. To the extent to which His will is obscured by the human fiction of *'my strength and the power of my hand has created for me all this accomplishment,'* His rule on earth fails to find expression in our lives.

When Leah's fourth child was born, she named him Judah saying 'הַפַּעַם אוֹדֶה אֶת ה, *now I will praise HASHEM*. Rashi explains that she gave special praise then, rather than previously with the birth of her first three sons, שנטלתי יותר על חלקי, *for I have taken more than my share*. The matriarchs knew that Jacob would have twelve sons; that should have meant three sons for each of Jacob's four wives. When Leah gave birth to her fourth son, she gave special thanks because God had given her more than her share. That is why Jews are called *Yehudim* (implying that they are descended from Judah) no matter what tribe they belong to. Even Mordechai, a Benjaminite, is referred to in *Megillas Esther* as *Mordechai haYehudi*. We are Yehudim because we always thank God for giving us more than our share, more than we deserve. The Jew is ever conscious of the graciousness and mercy of God. To him, health, prosperity — life itself — are never his by right; he thanks God for everything, for it is all an undeserved gift (*Chidushei HaRim* in *Sefer haZechus*).

The matriarchs
knew that Jacob
would have twelve
sons; that should
have meant three
sons for each of
Jacob's four wives.
When Leah gave
birth to her fourth
son, she gave special
thanks because God
had given her more
than her share.

To the Jew, health,
prosperity — life
itself — are never his
by right.

The strength of Judah lay in his readiness to be a willing receptacle of God's talent, blessing, and responsibility while ascribing nothing to himself. His very name indicates this quality. The Hebrew spelling of Judah's name, יְהוּדָה, contains the sacred four-

letter name of God — plus one more letter, a ד *dalet*. The word דַל, *dal* in Hebrew means a pauper. Judah has within himself the majesty of his Creator; his kingship is no less than the kingship, in a mortal guise, of God Himself, — in his own eyes, Judah remains דַל, a pauper. No matter how exalted his position, whatever he has is an undeserved gift of God.

David, first of the Judean kings and model for all his successors, embodies the same concept in his name. It begins with *dalet* and ends with *dalet*. For all his grandeur and achievement, for all the love his Maker bore for him and the holiness that made even the blood of his war victims seem like holy offerings before the altar of God, David, from beginning to end, considered himself a pauper, an impoverished mortal who carried only the gifts of God, but nothing of his own. The future *Mashiach* is described by Zechariah as עָנִי וְרוֹכֵב עַל חֲמוֹר, *a poor man riding a donkey*. He will finally fulfill the purpose of creation by bringing the kingdom of heaven to earth and by crowning God as King of all mankind — but he is a pauper riding the humblest of domestic beasts of burden.

For all the holiness that made even the blood of his war victims seem like holy offerings before the alter of God, David considered himself a pauper who carried only the gifts of God.

Such kings represent the final stage of revelation. They are themselves but an embodiment of God's will on earth (*Sfas Emes, Vayigash*).

Tainted Origins

It is no less than astounding that the conception of the Davidic dynasty was shrouded in mists of impropriety.

Lot's daughters, thinking they were the only people left on earth, intoxicated him, lived with him, and gave birth to Ammon and Moab.

Lot and his daughters were miraculously saved from the destruction of Sodom. His daughters thinking they were the only people left on earth, intoxicated him, lived with him, and gave birth to Ammon and Moab. Centuries later, Ruth the Moabite became the great-grandmother of David. Even later, Naamah the Ammonite became the wife of King Solomon and mother of his successor, Rechavam. True, the righteousness of Ruth and Naamah was of such magnitude that their nations were spared by God for

all the centuries spanning traditions of selfishness and cruelty, but why was it neccessary for God to defile His servant David by planting his origin in a guise of incest? And what luster could it add to the Holy Name for His מַלְכוּת, kingship, to trace its source to so ignoble a beginning?

Why was it necessary for God to defile His servant David by planting his origin in a guise of incest?

After the sale of Joseph into slavery, Judah left his brothers to found his own family. First his oldest and then his second son married Tamar. Each of the young men died because of his own sin (see *Genesis* 38). Judah, fearing that Tamar had some blame in the unusual pair of tragedies, delayed the יְבּוּם, levirate marriage of Tamar to his youngest son, Shelah. She realized that Judah would not allow her to marry Shelah but she wanted to share in building God's Kingdom, so, posing as a harlot, she lured Judah into spending a single night with her. She conceived and gave birth to twins, Peretz and Zerach. Her ambition was fulfilled — Peretz was the ancestor of David.

Tamar's ambition was fulfilled — Peretz was the ancestor of David.

> *Rabbi Yochanan said, Judah sought to pass by Tamar. The Holy One, blessed be He, dispatched the angel of lust to waylay him. The angel said to Judah, 'Where are you going? From where will kings arise, from where will great men arise?' 'Then he [Judah] turned to her by the way' — he was coerced, against his good sense (Breishis Rabbah 85:8).*

Not only did Judah father the twins in an apparently illicit manner, the shame of his action became public knowledge by his own admission in an act of moral courage that remains a shining example of honesty even under the most distasteful circumstances. But Judah's tryst with Tamar left him no less righteous and chaste than before. It was more than Divinely inspired — it was forced by the Hand of God. But why? Why did God's design require so convoluted an execution; why did His plan require such unbecoming conduct?

Judah's tryst with Tamar left him no less righteous and chaste than before. It was more than Divinely inspired — it was forced by the Hand of God.

The next episode in the strange Divine scheme was the marriage of Ruth and Boaz. (See Commentary 3)

Why a Moabite? Why a blot in the family— ... לֹא יָבֹא מוֹאָבִי בִּקְהַל ה', 'a Moabite may not come into the Assembly of HASHEM' — that took years to erase? Why a stealthy night-time visit by the Moabite woman to the field where the righteous, aged Judge slept guarding his harvest? Why so profane a method to carry out so sacred a mission?

A Bribe for the Satan

The eternal struggle between good and evil revolves essentially around man. It is not God who struggles with evil; the Satan exists only as long as he suits God's purpose. That evil exists and that it has the ability to becloud the senses of even the wisest of men is in order to create the battleground for man's free-will struggle to choose correctly. People are rewarded only for having prevailed in the struggle to choose right over wrong; if the emptiness of evil and the virtues of good are so obvious that the choice becomes automatic, then there is no justification for rewarding the righteous. One does not reward a child for not reaching into a blazing fire; the consequences of doing so are so plain that no sane person would try it. On the other hand, the child who is all alone with a tempting cookie jar and conquers his greed is amply deserving of recognition. Had there been no prophets of Ba'al with their 'miracles' and appearance of rectitude, no one would have been fool enough to reject Elijah. The forces of evil must have the power to confuse, confound, convince — otherwise man's mission would be an exercise in the obvious (Derech Hashem).

That evil exists and that it has the ability to becloud the senses of even the wisest of men is in order to create the battleground for man's free-will struggle to choose correctly.

The forces of evil must have the power to confuse, confound, convince — otherwise man's mission would be an exercise in the obvious.

A direct frontal attack on the יצר הרע, the evil inclination, is too often doomed to failure. The powers of the Satan are usually too great for mortal man. Indeed, his own flesh-and-blood drives and desires are too strong to be vanquished and sublimated without a long, complex, and devious struggle.

But there are ways. The evil inclination is far from invincible — in fact, it is eminently deceivable. The Sages have an interesting expression: שׁוֹחַד לשטן, a bribe for the Satan. All of us know the popular methods

for developing self-control. 'I won't allow myself a piece of cake until I finish forty-five minutes of study.' 'I will take a vacation if I am successful.' To a serious thinker these ploys are ridiculous — except that they work! People have an awesome capacity for self-deception — the sincere and intelligent person uses this capacity for the good; the self-indulgent and shallow person uses this same capacity to cause his own downfall. The old witticism 'it's the easiest thing in the world to stop smoking — I've done it thousands of times,' is all too true!

The strategems in the battle against evil are like one step backward and two steps forward.

The strategems in the battle against evil are like one step backward and two steps forward. They are a means of utilizing the frailities of human nature to combat, weaken, and eventually conquer the evil inclination that is part of the very humanness of man.

Man is fully capable of knowing and understanding himself well enough to cope with his urges, and to utilize rather than be defeated by them. Even base desires — like greed and vanity — can be sublimated by using money for charity or accepting honor only for worthwhile accomplishments (see *Ramban, Lev. 16:8* and *Michtav meEliyahu I p. 262*):

But it remains true that our world is a balance of good and evil with every person facing the challenge of choosing one over the other.

But it remains true that our world is a balance of good and evil with every person facing the challenge of choosing one over the other. And man seldom succeeds by directly attacking the forces of evil; in order to maintain the balance, they were given too much power to be easily defeated. They will bounce back with a counter-attack that will leave the presumed victor bloodied and disarrayed.

No greater good exists than the kingdom of God on earth and its champions, the tribe of Judah with its most distinguished son, David. Its development began with Judah's apparently inexplicable weakness in straying from the path — literally and figuratively — after Tamar in harlot's disguise. The episode illustrates that the Satan will not — cannot — permit spiritual heights to be scaled without a fierce struggle. To take the direct path would be to court failure by inviting the Satan ferociously to thwart

The Satan will not — cannot — permit spiritual heights to be scaled without a fierce struggle.

the attainment of good. The Satan must be appeased. Judah's act had the appearance of a lamentable fall as the great leader of Jacob's sons was powerless to control his lust for a stranger. Satan laughed, the Canaanites snickered, Judah was ashamed — but God was doing His work by striking the spark that would ultimately become the brilliant light of *Mashiach* (*Chafetz Chaim on Torah*).

Satan laughed, the Canaanites snickered, Judah was ashamed — but God was doing His work by striking the spark that would ultimately become the brilliant light of Mashiach.

Drawing out the Sparks

מִי יִתֵּן טָהוֹר מִטָּמֵא?
'Who can withdraw purity from impurity?' (Job 14:3)

Abraham came from Terach, Hezekiah from Achaz, Yoshiah from Omon, Mordechai from Shim'i, Israel from the nations, the world to come from this world. Who could do this? Who could command this? Who could decree this? No one but [God] the only One on earth! (Bamidbar Rabbah 19:1).

In a deeper sense, there is more to the strange and distasteful circumstances surrounding Lot, Judah, and Ruth than a bribe to the Satan. There is a constant refrain in Kabbalist and esoteric literature that this world is a mixture of good and evil symbolized by עֵץ הַדַּעַת טוֹב וָרַע, the Tree of Knowledge of Good and Evil. In all evil there is some good — otherwise it could not exist. Man's highest purpose is to extract the sparks of good from the evil. Obviously this is no simple task. It demands a high degree of self-perfection before it can even be attempted, but the mission of mankind on earth is to withdraw the spiritual good from its captivity.

Man's highest purpose is to extract the sparks of good from the evil. Obviously this is no simple task.

It is known to all who have been given understanding that the soul of David was clothed in the shell of Moab and that it was freed from Moab through Ruth. Concerning this, too, Scripture says: Who could withdraw purity from impurity [see Midrash above]. These were the intentions

An Overview/Ruth and the Seeds of Mashiach [xlii]

of the inscrutable wisdom of the Creator in guiding His world to bring every act to its proper path. Every act of God travels through byways, often in complex, crooked ones . . . For such has occured to all great souls as they go among the 'shells' of impurity to capture and extract the good (Rabbi Moshe Chaim Luzatto in Megillas Sesarim).

The sparks of goodness are scattered throughout creation. One was in Lot and remained glimmering even in the moral filth of Sodom. To salvage that spark, God sent the angel Rafael, who, after healing Abraham, went to Sodom to save Lot, bearer of the spark that would become the soul of David. It went down the generations until the time came for it to leave the impurity of Moab and enter the Jewish nation through Ruth.

There was a spark in Canaan and it was lodged in Tamar. Judah had to unite with her, but of his own free will he would never have done it.

There was a spark in Canaan and it was lodged in Tamar. Judah had to unite with her, but of his own free will he would never have done it. An angel forced Judah into the path of a harlot when God was ready to begin the creation of the Davidic dynasty.

Lot's spark travelled through his Moabite descendents for seven centuries until it reached its ultimate destination. When the proper time came, Ruth went from the field of Moab to the field of Boaz. While popular wisdom held that no Moabite could ever enter the community of God, the scion of Judah, leader of his people, unearthed the long-neglected law that a Moabitess was not forbidden to marry a Jew. One fateful night, the last one of Boaz's life, the spark of Lot and the brilliance of Judah were united as Ruth and Boaz were married. That night, Oved, the grandfather of David, was conceived.

V. The Marriage—Levirate and Moabite

The Torah's first mention of the obligation of יִבּוּם, levirate marriage, appears when Er, first-born son of Judah, died and Judah instructed his second son, Onan to marry the widow and וְהָקֵם זֶרַע לְאָחִיךָ, *raise up seed for your brother* (Gen. 38:8).

The *Holy Zohar (Vayeishev 177)* explains that the death of a person does not remove him from his eternal roots on earth because his children carry on his role in life. When someone dies without children, his mission on earth would go uncontinued and unfulfilled. To prevent this tragedy and maintain the departed's link in the chain of life, the Divine Wisdom ordained that his widow and his brother marry and produce children . . . The newborn child becomes the receptacle for the soul of the departed so that his mission in life can be completed through the children of his widow and closest relative.

Man and wife are considered like one body, one unit.

Shaar Bas Rabim (Vayeishev) explains further that man and wife are considered like one body, one unit. It is her duty to perpetuate his life through levirate marriage because, with the death of her husband, it is as if part of her own body had died. The closest relative is a brother because he and the deceased are products of the same parents. Therefore, the commandment of levirate marriage applies to the brother.

In early generations, לפני מתן תורה before the Torah was given, the wise men knew that in the absence of a brother to marry the widow, the closest blood relatives, too, could function to make "whole" the disrupted family unit.

In early generations, לִפְנֵי מַתַּן תּוֹרָה, *before the Torah was given*, the secret of levirate marriage was known to wise men of the caliber of Judah. They knew that in the absence of a brother to marry the widow, the closest blood relatives, too, could function to make "whole" the disrupted family unit. Therefore, Judah's unwitting marriage to Tamar was legal, even commendable. Only its mode — the apparent wanton act with a "harlot" and the resulting humiliation of Judah — was degrading. When the Torah was given with the statutes that most forms of family marriages were incestuous, a relationship such as Judah's and Tamar's became forbidden. Still,

levirate marriage was so holy that God continued to permit, even command, it in its highest form — that of a brother marrying his widowed, childless sister-in-law (*Ramban*).

Boaz was a "redeemer" and a potential participant in a levirate marriage with Ruth by virtue of the fact that he was a close relative — but not so close that a marriage would be forbidden as incestuous. He was second in line; the closest relative was Tov, a brother of Elimelech and an uncle of Machlon. The next relative was Boaz, a cousin of Machlon. True, the Torah does not ordain levirate marriage except for a brother of the deceased, but, as is apparent from *Megillas Ruth*, in those days, Jews acknowledged a moral obligation to provide a resting place for the soul of the departed by providing an offspring from his wife (see Commentary 3:1; 3:10).

It is apparent from Megillas Ruth that, in those days, Jews acknowledged a moral obligation to provide a resting place for the soul of the departed by providing an offspring from his wife.

Moabite But Not Moabitess

In prohibiting converts from Ammon and Moab from ever marrying into the 'congregation of God,' the Torah explains the reason why:

עַל דְּבַר אֲשֶׁר לֹא קִדְּמוּ אֶתְכֶם בַּלֶּחֶם וּבַמַּיִם
בַּדֶּרֶךְ בְּצֵאתְכֶם מִמִּצְרָיִם

Because they met you not with bread and water on the way when you came forth from Egypt (Deut. 23:5)

The Sages interpret the verse to indicate that עַמּוֹנִי וְלֹא עֲמוֹנִית, מוֹאָבִי וְלֹא מוֹאָבִית, only male Ammonite and Moabite converts may not marry into the nation (*Yevamos 76b*). This interpretation is implicit in the verse itself. The Torah gives us a reason for the prohibition: that the accused nations failed to show simple human decency in not greeting the travel-weary Jews with food and drink. It is customary for men to travel into the desert to meet travelers, point out our Sages, but it is not proper for women to do so. Therefore, women were absolved from the national guilt and hence welcome to convert and marry into the Jewish nation.

The Torah gives us a reason for the prohibition that accused nations failed to show simple human decency in not greeting the travel-weary Jews with food and drink.

Like all interpretations that modify Scriptural prohibitions, this one was transmitted to Moses by

The Sages did not
legislate; they
merely pointed out
the Scriptural basis
for an apparently
incongruous law.

God. The Sages did not legislate; they merely pointed out the Scriptural basis for an apparently incongruous law — nowhere do we find a law of this type that applies to one sex, but not to the other. Egyptian converts, male and female alike, are forbidden to enter the congregation of God until their third generation as Jews. *Mamzeirim* (people born of incestuous or adulterous unions which can never be legitimized by marriage) are forbidden to marry other Jews no matter what their sex. Why, then, should the Ammonite and Moabite nations be different? The answer — our Sages *explain*, but do not originate — is found in Scripture itself as cited above.

This law was known to Moses and his disciples. During the three centuries between Israel's entry into the Land and the time of Ruth and Boaz, the law gradually became forgotten, probably because it fell

Those were the times
when the Oral Law
was still oral — the
interpretations of
Scripture were not
committed to
writing; they passed
from teacher to
student down
through the
generations.

into disuse. Those were the times when the Oral Law was still oral — the interpretations of Scripture were not committed to writing; they passed from teacher to student down through the generations. If no Ammonites or Moabites sought to convert — a natural consequence of the long-standing hostility between them and Israel — the legal question of their marital status would never have required decision by a court. And the average Jew, even most scholars, would have assumed that the prohibition upon them was as sexless as those upon Egyptians and *mamzeirim*. Of course, had the question come before the Great Sanhedrin or any of the other distinguished courts of the Land, it is virtually certain that a decision would have been rendered in favor of Ammonite and Moabite women. Indeed, it *did* arise in the court of Boaz at that pivotal time in Jewish history and it *was*

Many legal concepts
become hazy with
disuse, however, and
this was one of them.

so decided. Many legal concepts become hazy with disuse, however, and this was one of them. So it was that it was almost universally thought, even by a minority of the greatest sages, that Ruth's marriage to a Jew was prohibited.

An analogy can be found in the prohibition against eating certain species of birds. The Torah

specifies that only twenty kinds of fowl may not be eaten. All others — the overwhelming majority of all birds on earth — are permitted. With the passing of time, successive exiles, and the increasing disuse of the Scriptural Hebrew names of the forbidden birds, the exact identities of the forbidden fowl were forgotten. Not knowing with any degree of certainty which birds are forbidden, the Jewish people have refrained from eating any fowl save for those which were in constant use down through the centuries. Those are permitted only because uninterrupted traditions guarantee that they are not among the forbidden twenty. Turkey, for example, was once of doubtful status until it was learned that in some areas such a tradition existed; that being established, the permitted status of turkey was accepted by the overwhelming majority of Jews.

Not knowing with any degree of certainty which birds are forbidden, the Jewish people have refrained from eating any fowl save for those which were in constant use down through the centuries.

Boaz's proclamation that any Jew might marry Ruth must be understood in this way. Boaz permitted nothing new; he merely popularized a law that had been forgotten by the majority of the population. That many found it difficult to accept this repudiation of the popular misconception is obvious from the reaction of Tov, the *Ploni Almoni* of *Megillas Ruth* who refused to marry Ruth on the grounds that he would be tainting his posterity by marrying a forbidden Moabitess (*Ruth* 4:6).

Boaz permitted nothing new; he merely popularized a law that had been forgotten by the majority of the population.

An ensuing tragedy lent credance to those who disputed Boaz and his court. Righteous Boaz married Ruth and lived with her for only one night — the next day he was dead. The wags of the generation were convinced they knew why: Boaz had publicly defied the Torah's prohibition by marrying a forbidden daughter of Moab — for that he was struck dead. The truth, of course, was just the opposite. God kept an aging Boaz alive and in good health so that the centuries-old design could come to fruition. The holiness lodged in the seed of Lot, the holiness lodged in the seed of Tamar and the holiness lodged in the seed of Judah joined that night to produce the grandfather of David. But the truth is not always visible.

The holiness lodged in the seed of Lot, the holiness lodged in the seed of Tamar and the holiness lodged in the seed of Judah joined that night to produce the grandfather of David.

When Ruth's baby was born, the birth was celebrated by few because, for many, it was not a blessed event at all, this product of a 'forbidden' marriage (*Ruth* 4:14-17; see Commentary).

This popular misconception died hard; it hung like a black cloud over the family until the time of David — and very nearly changed and embittered the course of Jewish history.

Marriage in Moab

The flight of Elimelech and his family to Moab in itself is enough to strain the credulity of even the casual reader. The simple text makes abundantly clear that Elimelech's was a most distinguished family. The Sages go even further in extolling Elimelech and in pointing out the enormity of his sin in deserting his people — imagine the blow to them when the great man to whom they look for encouragement, guidance, and material support during the famine defected to an antagonistic neighbor. But the marriage of Machlon and Kilion to Ruth and Orpah hurt even more. How could they intermarry with Moabites? Whatever their lack of loyalty to their people, surely there was no justification for the marriages that kept them anchored in Moab until their deaths!

Whatever their lack of loyalty to their people, surely there was no justification for the marriages that kept them anchored in Moab until their deaths!

The commonly known view is that of Rabbi Meir as expounded in the *Midrash*:

לא גיירום ולא הטבילו אותם

'They neither converted nor ritually immersed them'.

(Ruth Rabba 1:4)

In that view, the marriage is but one more unpleasant indication of how far lapsed people can sink once they cut loose from their moorings. Support is lent to this view by the Talmud (*Yevamos* 47b) which derives the laws of proselytes from the exchange between Naomi and Ruth (See *Commentary* 1:16). It would also explain why Naomi tried so hard to encourage Ruth and Orpah to return home rather than go to *Eretz Yisrael* with her. If her daughters-in-law had converted prior to their marriages, Naomi would

It would also explain why Naomi tried so hard to encourage Ruth and Orpah to return home rather than go to Eretz Yisrael with her.

have had no right to send them back to idolatry.

On the other hand, if, indeed, the Moabite brides were unconverted during their marriage, several other difficulties arise. Scripture repeatedly refers to Naomi as the mother-in-law of Ruth — had Ruth been a Moabite during her marriage to Machlon, the marriage would not have been legally binding under Jewish law, thus rendering incongruous the references to 'mother-in-law.' But the problems are more than semantic. If Ruth was never legally married to Machlon, then much of the succeeding story of Ruth is incomprehensible. Boaz was a redeemer of Ruth's property — what property? Under Jewish law she had no right to any property of Machlon. Boaz accepted a moral responsibility to enter into a levirate marriage with Ruth — but only the widow of a Jewish marriage falls within the purview of the levirate relationship. A non-Jewish Ruth would no more obligate Boaz than any other widowed Moabite.

If Ruth was never legally married to Machlon, then much of the succeeding story of Ruth is incomprehensible.

Indeed, there is a second view, that of *Zohar Chadash* that Ruth and Orpah *did*, in fact, convert to Judaism prior to their marriages:

> *Rabbi P'dos asked the son of Rav Yosi, a man from Socho: Since Ruth was a proselyte, why did they not call her by another [Jewish] name? He answered him: So have I heard — she did have another name and when she married Machlon, they renamed her Ruth and from then on she used that name. For her conversion came when she married Machlon, and not afterwards.*
>
> *He said to him: But it is written later, 'where you sleep, I will sleep and your God is my God,' etc. (Ruth 1:16). Naomi gave her many warnings [against the rigorous life of a Jew] as we have learned, and Ruth accepted them all. If she had already converted previously, why was all this necessary at that time?*

When Ruth married,
she converted and
remained under the
presumption of
אימת בעלה
"fear of her
husband."

*He replied to him: God forbid that
Machlon married her while she was still a
gentile. Rather, when she married she converted and she remained under the
presumption of אֵימָת בַּעֲלָה, fear of her
husband, she and Orpah, in this matter.
When their husbands died, Orpah
returned to her abominable ways, and
Ruth remained in her goodness, as it is
written, 'behold your sister-in-law has
returned to her nation and her god, but
Ruth clung to her' (Ruth 1:14) as she had
earlier. When her husband died [Ruth]
cleaved to her of her own free will (Zohar
Chadash Ruth 180-182).*

According to this view, how could Naomi have allowed, much less urged, the widows to return to
Moabite idolatry?

It may be that the key words in solving this serious
difficulty are אימת בעליהם, 'the fear of their husbands'. Machlon and Kilion came to Moab as very
wealthy, highly eligible young אֶפְרָתִים, 'Ephrathites' — distinguished citizens of Judah's leading
city [see *Commentary* 1:2]. So esteemed was the
family of Elimelech that the royal family of Moab
wanted two of its daughters to marry the newly ar-
In those days, the
prospective bride
had little say in such
an arrangement,
especially when it
was a marriage of
state
rived Jewish brothers. In those days, the prospective
bride had little say in such an arrangement, especially
when it was a marriage of state made for considerations transcending personal preferences. If Machlon
and Kilion had insisted that their brides convert to
Judaism as a condition of marriage, the young
women would surely have felt compelled to accede.
If Machlon and
Kilion had insisted
that their brides
convert to Judaism
as a condition of
marriage, the young
women would surely
have felt compelled
to accede.

This could well have
constituted a coerced
conversion.
This could well have constituted a coerced conversion. In the case of such a conversion, the mere fact
that the marriage took place and that the converted
woman lived as a Jewess would not in and of itself
prove that the conversion was valid. Should she have
become widowed and then — newly freed — declared
her refusal to continue her fiction of Jewishness, her

conversion would have been proven invalid from the start.

When Machlon and Kilion died, Naomi put Ruth and Orpah to the test. Was their original conversion sincere? Had they become committed Jews in the course of their marriages? Or were they accompanying her back to *Eretz Yisrael* merely out of pity? Orpah turned her back with a parting kiss thereby proving that her conversion had never been sincere. Ruth withstood the test — she demonstrated her commitment thus proving that her membership in the Jewish nation was entirely unfeigned.

The problem of conversion was not limited to Machlon and Kilion. A similar, though not identical, question was raised concerning far greater *tzaddikim* than they, Solomon and Samson, who also married non-Jewish wives. Rambam raises the question in *Hilchos Issurei Biah* 13:14-16. He states categorically that it is inconceivable that those two great men married unconverted women. Their wives were converted. Rambam explains that a convert must demonstrate that his conversion is sincerely motivated — that it is not done for money, prestige, or fear, and that it is not done for love of man or woman. If there are no ulterior motives, the rabbinical court teaches the would-be convert the responsibilities of Torah and its commandments. When the court is convinced of his sincerity, he is accepted. As an example of the sincere convert, Rambam cites Ruth.

During the reigns of David and Solomon, *Rambam* continues, converts were not accepted because the lures of conversion were too great to insure that sincerity was present. Despite this ban, many non-Jews did join Israel thanks to conversions performed by uninformed, unsophisticated, makeshift courts. Those converts were ignored by the legitimate courts — not ostracized, and not embraced — until time and experience showed whether or not they were truly sincere.

The wives of Samson and Solomon, *Rambam* con-

Ruth withstood the test — she demonstrated her commitment thus proving that her membership in the Jewish nation was entirely unfeigned.

Rambam explains that a convert must demonstrate that his conversion is sincerely motivated — that it is not done for money, prestige, or fear, and that it is not done for love of man or woman.

As an example of the sincere convert, Rambam cites Ruth.

Those converts were ignored by the legitimate courts — not ostracized, and not embraced — until time and experience showed whether or not they were truly sincere.

cludes, converted for the sake of marriage, without any true motivation for Jewishness. For this reason *Scripture* refers to them as non-Jews; in terms of the standards expected of sincere converts, they were. Their outcomes told the story — they remained idolators proving that their conversions were but a sham.

It may be that it was this knowledge that motivated Naomi's attempts to dissuade her daughters-in-law. Were they truly her daughters-in-law or were they merely the Moabite common-law widows of her sons? She performed her task well. Orpah was never truly a Jew; Ruth was one of the finest daughters — and mothers — Israel ever had.

(It should be unmistakably clear that the above discussion is not meant and must not be taken as the basis for any halachic decision. The laws of conversion, like most areas of Halacha are based on a two thousand year accumulation of Mishnaitic, Talmudic, and post-Talmudic literature. Especially in so sensitive an area as conversion, only highly qualified rabbis are competent to render decisions.)

VI. The Emergence of David*

Oved, son of Ruth and Boaz, and Jesse, son of Oved, were outstandingly righteous men, among the greatest of their age. Inevitably, people began to feel that such people could not have been
the progeny of a sinful marriage — surely God would not invest holiness so promiscuously. So Jesse's family was the most respected in Bethlehem.

God revealed to Samuel that the successor to King Saul would be a son of Jesse the Bethlehemite. The

---

* *A superlative treatment of this topic can be found in Sefer haToda'ah* by Eliyahu Ki Tov. Much of his essay is beyond the scope of this paper, but is highly recommended reading.

prophet was commanded to go to Bethlehem where God would show him the future king (*I Samuel* 16). Samuel asked Jesse to come with his sons to a feast. As we can well imagine, the great prophet's invitation was a rare privilege. Jesse came with seven of his sons; David was left behind. David — red of complexion, short of stature, tender of sheep, desert hermit — could not possibly become God's anointed. There wasn't a soul in Bethlehem, not even his father or brothers, who thought that. No one knew that he was not alone in the fields, that he was attuning his soul to his Maker; that his very being was a harp in the hands of holiness, reverberating with the sweet songs that would become part of one of Israel's most precious legacies — *The Book of Tehillim*. No one knew that the love he would later lavish on his people was being nurtured in his care of helpless sheep. No one knew that the fearless warrior of the future was single-handedly slaying lions and bears, learning that only God is to be feared.

No one knew that the love David would later lavish on his people was being nurtured in his care of helpless sheep.

The moment of anointment came and Samuel asked that Jesse's sons come before him one by one. They were outstanding products of an outstanding family. The great prophet was impressed with Eliav, Jesse's first-born; he was sure that he was in the presence of God's chosen anointed — only to be told by God:

> Look not on his countenance nor on the height of his stature, because I have refused him: for it is not as a man sees, for a man looks on the outward appearance, but G-d looks on the heart.

So it was. One by one, each was rejected. Finally, Samuel asked Jesse if he had any more sons and Jesse answered strangely, *"There remains yet the youngest and he is tending the sheep."* Samuel ordered that he be brought. He was — and he was anointed David, King of Israel.

"There remains yet the youngest and he is tending the sheep."

As soon as he arrived, Samuel knew that they were in the presence of God's chosen. Samuel knew that this was to be no temporary, transitory king like

As soon as he arrived, Samuel knew that they were in the presence of God's chosen.

Saul. When Samuel picked up the horn of the holy oil, it began to bubble as though it could not wait to drop on the forehead of David. When Samuel anointed him, the oil hardened and glistened like pearls and precious stones, and the horn remained full (*Yalkut haMakiri Tehillim* 118).

But the taint on David's origin was a stubborn one:

וְכִרְאוֹת שָׁאוּל אֶת דָוִד יֹצֵא לִקְרַאת הַפְּלִשְׁתִּי
אָמַר אֶל אַבְנֵר שַׂר הַצָּבָא בֶּן מִי זֶה הַנַּעַר אַבְנֵר

— And when Saul saw David go out against the Philistine [Goliath] he said to Avner the captain of the host, Avner, whose son is this youth? (I Samuel 17:55).

Didn't Saul know who David was? The Talmud asks (*Yevamos* 76b), Scripture says (*I Samuel* 16:21) that Saul loved David very much and appointed him his personal armor-bearer — obviously Saul knew him well!

Saul became apprehensive and began to fear that David was more than a talented singer and devoted shepherd.

Saul became apprehensive and began to fear that David was more than a talented singer and devoted shepherd. When David volunteered to defend the honor of Israel by facing Goliath in combat, Saul offered the young man his own armor. David put it on and it fit — but Saul was head and shoulders above even the tallest of Israel and David was shorter than average! That the royal armor fit could well be a Divine indication that David was to be Saul's successor as king. He asked Avner which branch of Judah David was from. If he was from Zerach, then he would be illustrious, but no threat to Saul. But if he was from Peretz, then he was royalty, for it was from Peretz that the kings of Judah would descend.

Then, Doeg the Edomi stepped forward. Doeg was one of the greatest scholars of the age, head of the Sanhedrin, and a close friend and adviser to the king. Doeg said,

"Instead of asking whether or not he is worthy of kingship, ask whether or not he is fit to enter the congregation of God! He is descended from Ruth the Moabitess."

Avner defended David's legitimacy with the dictum expounded by the court of Boaz and reaffirmed by the court of Samuel.

Avner defended David's legitimacy with the dictum expounded by the court of Boaz and reaffirmed by the court of Samuel: A Moabite, but not a Moabitess, is forbidden to enter the congregation of God. Doeg fought back and, halachic great that he was, no one was able to refute his arguments against the fitness of David. Then Amassa, son of Yisra, arose and declared,

"Whoever refuses to acknowledge this law will be stabbed with my sword. This I have learned from the court of Samuel of Ramah — a Moabite, but not a Moabitess!"

These were the passions awakened by David. The greatest men of his generation questioned and agonized over his status. Finally it was only through a violent insistence upon the unshakable Jewish belief in its tradition as transmitted by the Torah greats that the royal house of David — embodiment of God's kingdom on earth — could come into being.

Finally it was only through a violent insistence upon the unshakable Jewish belief in its tradition as transmitted by the Torah greats that the royal house of David — embodiment of God's kingdom on earth — could come into being.

Doeg did not rest. Throughout the reign of Saul he was David's nemesis, inflaming Saul against the young Judean shepherd whose love for, and loyalty to the king were unmatched. He urged Saul to kill David as a rebel (see above Powers of the King) and he succeeded in having eighty-five priests of the city of Nob executed for having harbored David (I Samuel 22)

David endured patiently all the barbs slung at him throughout his lifetime. Yet even this patient, long-suffering model of righteousness lashed out at Doeg in a passionate, poignant appeal to conscience and decency:

'You, a powerful and wealthy man, head of the Sanhedrin — stoop to such a low level of evil and slander! Is it a show of strength to see someone teetering at the edge of an abyss and push him over? Or to see someone at the edge of a roof and throw him down? The true hero is the one who sees his fellow at the brink and pulls him back to safety! You saw how Saul

The true hero is the one who sees his fellow at the brink and pulls him back to safety!

*became angry with me and you attacked
me further — is this how one serves his
God? Do you think that if Achimelech
[High Priest of Nob] had not yet welcomed
me and given me a crust of bread that no
one in all Israel would have given me food?
A man who is occupied with God's
goodness, the study of Torah, has no right
to act this way. Why did you do this?'
(Midrash Shocher Tov).*

The Talmudic sages [*Sanhedrin 106b*] hold Doeg
up to rebuke as a person who made a mockery of his
learning. 'His learning was from the lips outward' —
it had no inner meaning. God asked him, "Wicked
one, why do you study My statutes — what will you
say when you come to the sections of the Torah that
forbid murder and slander?"

Brilliant man though he was, Doeg was condemned to prove by his own downfall that his tirades
against David were baseless. He forgot his learning
before his death and lost the respect of even his own
students. Scintillating Doeg, who held sway over the
great minds in Israel, died in disgrace as a ridiculed
caricature of a Torah scholar. Of him the Talmud
says: אַנְשֵׁי דָמִים וּמִרְמָה לֹא יֶחֱצוּ יְמֵיהֶם, *bloody and
deceitful men shall not live out their days (Psalms
55:24)* —Doeg died when he was only thirty-three.

*Not until then could
David hold up his
head without fear
that the canard
'Moabite' would be
slung at him.*

Not until then could David hold up his head
without fear that the canard 'Moabite' would be
slung at him.

But his days of adversity were not numbered; they
lasted throughout his life. War, betrayal, personal
tragedy, rebellion, abuse — all of these were his constant lot, but he responded with a life that became
אֲנִי תְפִלָּה, *I am prayer;* David became the very embodiment of prayer, his entire being became a song
of praise. In the end, David's greatness was
acknowledged. He was worthy of his people, but his
people were unworthy of him.

*In the end, David's
greatness was
acknowledged. He
was worthy of his
people, but his
people were
unworthy of him.*

*David asked God: 'Why can I not build
the Holy Temple?'*

> *God answered: 'Because if you build it, it will endure and never be destroyed'* (Yalkut Shimoni, II Samuel 145).

The Jewish people were not yet worthy of a Temple built by David. It would be too great, too permanent.

David was so great, so consistent, that any act of his had to endure forever. The Jewish people were not yet worthy of a Temple built by David. It would be too great, too permanent — because it would be his, and his people would not rise to such a level until the coming of *Mashiach (see Michtav me-Eliyahu II,* p. 275).

When he died, he left us with two treasures:

His *Tehillim,* the songs of praise and prayer that have sustained countless Jewish sparks amid constant storms and holocausts;

And his sacred seed, nurtured through millenia — just as the seed of Moab, Judah, Tamar, Boaz, and Ruth were nurtured — waiting for the time when it would explode into the flame of the seven days of creation; waiting for the day when a poor man will come riding on a donkey; possessing all talents and blessing, but ascribing nothing to himself and everything to God; leading all the world under the protective wings of Divine Presence when HASHEM will be King over the entire universe, on that day when HASHEM will be one and His Name will be one.

Waiting for the day when a poor man will come riding on a donkey; possessing all talents and blessing, but ascribing nothing to himself and everything to God.

Rabbi Nosson Scherman

מגילת רות

א וַיְהִי בִּימֵי שְׁפֹט הַשֹּׁפְטִים וַיְהִי רָעָב
בָּאָרֶץ וַיֵּלֶךְ אִישׁ מִבֵּית לֶחֶם יְהוּדָה לָגוּר
ב בִּשְׂדֵי מוֹאָב הוּא וְאִשְׁתּוֹ וּשְׁנֵי בָנָיו: וְשֵׁם
הָאִישׁ אֱלִימֶלֶךְ וְשֵׁם אִשְׁתּוֹ נָעֳמִי וְשֵׁם
שְׁנֵי־בָנָיו מַחְלוֹן וְכִלְיוֹן אֶפְרָתִים מִבֵּית

1. וַיְהִי *And it happened.* 'Wherever in the Bible we find the term וַיְהִי בִּימֵי, *And it happened in the days,* it indicates the approach of trouble. Thus, *And it came to pass in the days of Ahasuerus* — there was Haman. *And it came to pass when the Judges judged* — there was a famine' (*Megillah* 10b).

שְׁפֹט הַשֹּׁפְטִים — *When the Judges judged.* [Lit. 'in the days of the judgment of the Judges']. . .

The story of Ruth occurred before the reign of King Saul, when the Jews were governed by Judges. The Judge at the time was Ivtzan [*Jud. 12:8*] — whom the Sages identify as Boaz of *Megillas Ruth* [*Bava Basra* 91a] (*Rashi*).

According to *Seder Hadoros* and *Tzemach David,* the episode happened approximately in the year 2787 (973 B.C.E.)

The *Iggeres Shmuel* quotes *Rav Yosef ibn Yichiah* that Ivtzan was not *specifically* named in our verse in deference to his righteousness, for Scripture did not wish to implicate him in Elimelech's sin.

According to the *Malbim,* these events transpired during the days of the Judges, a period of which it was written [*Judges 21:25*]: בַּיָּמִים הָהֵם אֵין מֶלֶךְ בְּיִשְׂרָאֵל אִישׁ הַיָּשָׁר בְּעֵינָיו יַעֲשֶׂה, *In those days there was no king in Israel; every man did that which was right in his own eyes.* No specific Judge ruled at the time; it was during an interval *between* Judges, when no one individual exercised control over the Jews — that Elimelech came to leave the country — a time when power was seized by lesser men, unable to earn position through their personal merit, and everyone acted independently.

Some understand שְׁפֹט הַשֹּׁפְטִים as the period when 'God judged the Judges' — for they were the cause of the famine (*Ibn Ezra; Vilna Gaon*)..

'It was a generation which judged its Judges. If the judge said to a man: 'Take the splinter from between your teeth,' he would retort: 'Take the beam from between your eyes.' (*Bava Basra* 15b).

'Woe unto the generation whose Judges are judged,' bewails the *Midrash,* 'and woe to the generation whose Judges deserve to be judged.'

All the above interpretations are suggested by the use of the phrase בִּימֵי שְׁפֹט הַשֹּׁפְטִים, [lit. 'the days of the judgment of the Judges], instead of the more direct בִּימֵי הַשֹּׁפְטִים 'days of the Judges' (*Torah T'mimah*).

A different approach is taken by *Iggeres Shmuel:* The *Midrash* states that a famine comes only upon a strong and righteous people that can withstand the test. Therefore,

[Please note: *The source for every excerpt has been documented. Whenever the author has inserted a comment of his own it is inserted in square brackets.*]

And it happened in the days when the Judges judged, that there was a famine in the land, and a man went from Bethlehem in Judah to sojourn in the fields of Moab, he, his wife, and his two sons. ² The man's name was Elimelech, his wife's name was Naomi, and his two sons were named Machlon and

we can say that the generation was not lawless. On the contrary, it was a time when שְׁפֹט הַשֹּׁפְטִים — *the Judges judged* — and the people listened. It was to *this* generation that God, knowing they would withstand the test and not flee or be contumacious against the Desirable Land [i.e., Eretz Yisrael], brought a famine upon them. And it was so. No one left Eretz Yisrael — except for the single family mentioned by Scripture.

וַיְהִי רָעָב בָּאָרֶץ — *That there was a famine in the land.* ['The' land, *par excellence*; i.e., Eretz Yisrael].

[The judges in those days, say the commentaries, were devoid of Torah knowledge, and it was due to their laxity in rebuking the multitide who strayed from the Torah path that God punished the Jews with a famine.]

The word וַיְהִי is repeated twice in this verse to imply that there were two famines in the days of the Judges: a famine for bread and a famine for Torah. This teaches us that in any generation where there is a lack of Torah, famine must ensue *(Yalkut Shimoni; Mid Zuta).*

'At that moment the Holy One, blessed be He, said: 'My children are rebellious; yet to destroy them is impossible, to take them back to Egypt is impossible, exchange them for another people I cannot; what then shall I do to them? I will

punish them and purify them with famine' *(Midrash).*

וַיֵּלֶךְ אִישׁ — *A man went.* [The appelation אִישׁ, 'man,' throughout the Bible signifies prominence.] The *Targum* here translates גְּבְרָא רַבָּא' *a great man.*

Elimelech was very wealthy and the פַּרְנָס הַדּוֹר, provider of that generation, who left Eretz Yisrael because he was selfish and was afraid that all the impoverished people would come and knock at his door for help. For this he was punished *(Rashi).*

'He was punished because he struck despair into the hearts of Israel. When the famine came, he arose and fled' *(Midrash).*

Elimelech may have rationalized his departure by claiming that he could not bear to witness the corruption of the judges while powerless to correct the situation, or that he was not required to dispense more than a fifth of his resources to charity — hardly enough to feed all of the hungry *(Kol Yehuda).*

Ima Shel Malchus notes that in those days, the Jews had settled in Eretz Yisrael according to their tribal divisions, their families' and fathers' houses. An added insight into Elimelech's misdeed can be gained if we remember that all the inhabitants of Bethlehem were related to each other in some manner, and that now, in the days of trouble,

Elimelech's family had deserted its relatives and fled.'

[The *Midrash* notes that nothing is said about the wealth he took with him — surely he did not go empty-handed!] ...

And a certain man went — like a 'dead stump' [to which nothing is attached]! See how the Holy One, blessed be He, favors the entry into Eretz Yisrael over the departure *from* it! When the Jews returned from Babylon it is written: *Their horses ... their mules ... their camels,* etc. [*Ezra 2:66*]. But here the verse simply tells us: *and a certain man went* — like a mere stump. He left the country, and Scripture makes no mention of his property — as though he left empty-handed (*Midrash*).

The word וַיֵּלֶךְ, *went* [lit. *walked*], not וַיִּסַּע, *travelled*, is used. This indicates that he originally planned only a temporary stay (*Kol Yehuda*).

The phrase וַיֵּלֶךְ אִישׁ, *and a certain man went*, appears twice in Scripture: here, and in Exodus 2:1 [referring to Moses' father]. Esoterically speaking, just as there — וַיֵּלֶךְ אִישׁ מִבֵּית לֵוִי *'and a man of the house of Levi went'* resulted in the first Redeemer, Moses — so here, too, did וַיֵּלֶךְ אִישׁ מִבֵּית לֶחֶם יְהוּדָה *'a certain man from Bethlehem in Judah went'* resulted in the final Redeemer — the house of David (*Alshich; Baal haTurim*).

מִבֵּית לֶחֶם יְהוּדָה — *From Bethlehem in Judah.* [The verse could also be translated '*A man from Bethlehem in Judah went...*' i.e., that a man, who was a resident of Bethlehem, went, (the phrase being adjectival)]

[Bethlehem was one of the finest and most fruitful areas of Eretz Yisrael.]

[Perhaps יְהוּדָה, *in Judah*, is men-

tioned to distinguish it from the other Bethlehem in Zevulun (*Joshua 19:15*)].

Why is the phrase *'from Bethlehem in Judah to dwell in the fields of Moab'* inserted here [between '*a certain man*' and '*he, his wife, and his two sons*']? Grammatically, the verse should read: '*A certain man, along with his wife and two sons, went from Bethlehem in Judah to sojourn in the fields of Moab.*'...

This verse, structured as it is, seems to imply that leaving Eretz Yisrael at that time was his decision alone. וַיֵּלֶךְ אִישׁ, *A certain man went* — the decision to *leave* בֵּית לֶחֶם יְהוּדָה was his alone — and he compelled his wife and two sons to follow. Having unilaterally made the decision to leave, Elimelech asked his family where they wished to go. The ultimate choice — לָגוּר בִּשְׂדֵי מוֹאָב, *to sojourn in the fields of Moab* — was made with the unanimous consent of אִשְׁתּוֹ וּשְׁנֵי בָנָיו, *his wife and two sons (Iggeres Shmuel).*

לָגוּר בִּשְׂדֵי מוֹאָב — *To sojourn in the fields of Moab.* '*Fields*' are in plural because it was Elimelech's original intention to sojourn and wander about the many fields and cities — not to establish himself permanently in any one place in Moab (*Alshich*).

Elimelech's sin was compounded by his choice of a new homeland. Had he gone elsewhere, his sin would not have been so severe. Our verse specifically elaborates on his shameful act by telling us his destination: the detestable Moab of whom God cautioned us: לֹא יָבֹא עַמּוֹנִי וּמוֹאָבִי בִּקְהַל ה'...עַד־עוֹלָם *'An Ammonite or Moabite shall not enter into the assembly of HASHEM ... forever'* [*Deut. 23:4*], and also: לֹא תִדְרֹשׁ שְׁלֹמָם וְטוֹבָתָם כָּל יָמֶיךָ לְעוֹלָם, *'Thou shalt not seek their*

peace nor their prosperity all thy days forever' [Deut. 23:7]. And yet, Elimelech went to live among them, where he would greet them every morning with 'Shalom' or would at the very least respond to them, 'Shalom'! *(Iggeres Shmuel).*

Elimelech perhaps rationalized that it was better for him to dwell in open fields among Moabites, than to remain in Eretz Yisrael under the circumstances of lawlessness prevalent during the famine *(Pri Chaim).*

הוּא וְאִשְׁתּוֹ וּשְׁנֵי בָנָיו — *He, his wife, and his two sons.* 'He was the prime mover, his wife secondary to him, and his two sons secondary to both of them' *(Midrash).*

Elimelech's additional sin was that he took only his nearest kin — his wife and two sons along with him, not being concerned about anyone else *(Iggeres Shmuel).*

2. וְשֵׁם הָאִישׁ אֱלִימֶלֶךְ — *The man's name was Elimelech.* The *Midrash* explains that his name signified his arrogant attitude; he would boast: אֵלַי תָּבוֹא מַלְכוּת — 'to me shall kingship come. . .'

Being a member of the tribe of Judah and a descendant of Nachshon ben Aminadav, its prince, he reasoned that royalty would descend from him *(Torah T'mimah).*

Elimelech considered himself to be a prominent individual, always boasting 'to me shall kingship come.' Therefore, he should have considered the consequences of his desertion of the Land — and so, he deserved to be punished *(Kol Yehuda).*

[The holiness of Eretz Yisrael is such that a sin on its holy earth is more serious and more significant than a sin elsewhere. For this reason the punishment for sins committed in Eretz Yisrael is quicker in coming and more stringent. (See *Lev.* 18:25-28; and *Ramban* there.) In attempting to flee from divine judgment, Elimelech wanted to leave the Holy Land in the belief that if he were in a foreign, non-sacred land, his sins would be of lesser magnitude and less deserving of punishment.]

Elimelech wanted to flee from the Divine Decree — but was unsuccessful in escaping from it. This is implied in the words וַיֵּלֶךְ אִישׁ, *a certain man went,* i.e., anonymously, *incognito.* But מִדַּת הַדִּין — God's Attribute of Judgment recognized and identified him, as the verse continues: וְשֵׁם הָאִישׁ אֱלִימֶלֶךְ, *the man's name was Elimelech,* i.e., the prominent and famous Elimelech, leader of that generation, one who could have protested the injustices of the time but did not. Judgment was then visited upon him and his sons, and they died *(Zohar Chadash).*

וְשֵׁם אִשְׁתּוֹ נָעֳמִי — *his wife's name was Naomi.* 'For her actions were pleasant and sweet' [the translation of Naomi being 'pleasant'] *(Midrash).*

Not only was Elimelech well known, even his wife and two sons were אַנְשֵׁי שֵׁם — famous personages *(Malbim).*

שְׁנֵי בָנָיו — *His two sons.* 'Two' is mentioned because they were both equally great *(Rashba haLevi).*

מַחְלוֹן וְכִלְיוֹן — *Machlon and Kilion.* The *Midrash* says that their names indicate שֶׁנִּמְחוּ וְכָלוּ מִן הָעוֹלָם — 'they were blotted out and perished from the world.'

The *Talmud* enumerates them, along with Elimelech, as the leaders of that generation. They were all punished because they left Eretz Yisrael *(Bava Basra 91a).*

לֶחֶם יְהוּדָה וַיָּבֹאוּ שְׂדֵי־מוֹאָב וַיִּהְיוּ־שָׁם:

ג וַיָּמָת אֱלִימֶלֶךְ אִישׁ נָעֳמִי וַתִּשָּׁאֵר הִיא

ד וּשְׁנֵי בָנֶיהָ: וַיִּשְׂאוּ לָהֶם נָשִׁים מֹאֲבִיּוֹת שֵׁם הָאַחַת עָרְפָּה וְשֵׁם הַשֵּׁנִית רוּת

ה וַיֵּשְׁבוּ שָׁם כְּעֶשֶׂר שָׁנִים: וַיָּמֻתוּ גַם־

According to *Zohar Chadash*, he was called Machlon שֶׁמָּחַל לוֹ הקב״ה לְאַחַר זְמַן, — 'because the Holy One, blessed be He ultimately forgave him [posthumously, by allowing יִבּוּם, a levirate marriage, to take place with his widow Ruth] שֶׁהָיָה מוֹחֶה, because he protested the injustices of his father. Kilion was so named שֶׁנִּכְלָה מִן הָעוֹלָם, for he was utterly blotted out from the world.'

אֶפְרָתִים — *Ephrathites*. [This word, sometimes translated *'Ephraimite'* and sometimes *'Ephrathite,'* is variously interpreted by the Sages]—

The *Midrash* considers the word to be a title of honor, interpreting it to mean 'courtiers,' 'aristocrats.' It may be derived from the word אַפִּרְיוֹן — a *'crown'* i.e., one who possesses the 'crown' bequeathed by יַעֲקֹב אָבִינוּ, our Patriarch Jacob, at the time of his departure from the world. . .'

The word usually indicates a descendant of Ephraim, or a native of Ephrath, i.e., Bethlehem [see *Gen. 35:19, 48:7.*] The *Midrash* offers different interpretations because the word אֶפְרָתִים, *Ephrathites*, in our verse could not refer to the tribe of Ephraim since Elimelech and his sons were of the tribe of Judah. Also, the Sages did not define it as *Ephrathite* 'a native of Ephrath' because if Bethlehem is referred to as Ephrath by the author

of *Megillas Ruth*, then he should have used that name in verse 1 as well. Obviously, therefore, *'Ephrathite'* must be taken as a description of the family rather than as a reference to their city (*Torah T'mimah; Gishmei Bracha*).

The *Targum*, translating אֶפְרָתִים, adds the word רַבָּנִין 'masters.'

According to *Rashi*: אֶפְרָתִים means *distinguished persons* ... See how important they were! Eglon, the King of Moab married his daughter [Ruth] to Machlon, as the Master has expounded: Ruth was the daughter of Eglon.'

Bethlehem was originally called 'Ephrath,' and later given the name Bethlehem. Also, there was a very distinguished family in the tribe of Judah called אֶפְרָתִים, *Ephrathites*, because they descended from Ephrath [another name for Miriam, sister of Moses — (*Sotah 11a*)], the wife of Caleb [*I Chronicles 2:19*], a most distinguished lady (*Malbim*).

Pirkei d'Rabbi Eliezer notes that throughout the Bible 'every great man who arose in Israel had the title Ephrathite attached to his name.'

אֶפְרָתִים מִבֵּית לֶחֶם יְהוּדָה — *Ephrathites, from Bethlehem in Judah.* Bethlehem is repeated in this verse as if to say that the sons, as *Ephrathites*, distinguished persons, were also held responsible for the sin of Elimelech's departure from Bethlehem; they should have protested!

Kilion, Ephrathites of Bethlehem in Judah. They came to the field of Moab and there they remained.

³ *Elimelech, Naomi's husband, died; and she was left with her two sons.* ⁴ *They married Moabite women, one named Orpah, and the other Ruth, and they lived there about ten years.* ⁵ *The two of them,*

...They were the most prominent citizens of the most prominent city in Eretz Yisrael (*Pri Chaim; Malbim*).

וַיִּהְיוּ שָׁם — *And there they remained.* [Lit. 'and they were there.']

Although it was their original intention only to *sojourn temporarily* in the fields of Moab, nevertheless, once they arrived they decided to settle permanently (*Malbim*).

They felt themselves drawn to the Moabites whom they resembled. They were mean and ungenerous like the Moabites who '*did not meet Israel with bread and water on the way when they left Egypt*' [compare *Deut. 23:5*] (*Meishiv Nefesh* quoting *Ruth Zuta*).

The word וַיִּהְיוּ, 'they were,' rather than וַיֵּשְׁבוּ, 'they settled,' is used to imply that they achieved a new status [וַהֲוָיָה] there — they felt no remorse that they had departed from Eretz Yisrael ... and for this reason they died (*Rav Yosef Yavetz*).

The *Targum* translates וַיִּהְיוּ שָׁם as follows: וַהֲווֹ תַּמָּן רוּפִילִין 'they became officers there' [which, in the context of the traditional enmity between the Jews and Moab must be understood not as praise, but as condemnation, i.e., they stooped so low that they integrated themselves socially and militarily into the culture of Moab].

3. וַיָּמָת אֱלִימֶלֶךְ — *And Elimelech died.* An untimely death (*Midrash*). This punishment was inflicted upon the family 'because they should have begged for mercy for their generation and they did not do so' (*Bava Basra 91b*). Even though one could perhaps rationalize that their departure from the Holy Land was necessary under the conditions of famine and need, they were still not guiltless. It was they who were responsible for the hunger because they did not pray for their generation (*Nachlas Yosef*).

The *Talmud*, giving Elimelech's ancestry, states: 'Elimelech, Salmah, Ploni Almoni, and the father of Naomi were all descendants of Nachshon son of Aminadav [prince of the tribe of Judah]. This teaches us that even זְכוּת־אָבוֹת, the merit of ancestors, is of no avail when one leaves Eretz Yisrael for a foreign country (*Bava Basra 91a*).

אִישׁ נָעֳמִי — *Naomi's husband.* Naomi is mentioned here in conjunction with Elimelech's death, notes the *Talmud*, 'because the death of a man is felt by no one as keenly and as deeply as by his wife' (*Sanhedrin 22b*).

Elimelech, not Naomi, was punished, because, as the verse tells us, he was אִישׁ נָעֳמִי, *Naomi's husband*, and she was subject to his authority. Therefore, the onus of the sin was thrust upon him (*Rashi, Malbim*).

[This great man, this פַּרְנָס הַדּוֹר, (magnate of the generation), is described at his death merely as אִישׁ נָעֳמִי, 'Naomi's husband.' Only she grieved at his loss — to his people he had already died long before.]

וַתִּשָּׁאֵר הִיא וּשְׁנֵי בָנֶיהָ — *And she was left with her two sons.* 'She became like the שִׁיּוּרֵי מְנָחוֹת, remnants of the meal offerings' [i.e., of little importance, now that her husband was dead] (*Midrash*).

As translated with the additions of the *Targum*: 'And she was left' — a widow; 'and her two sons' — orphans.

Had Elimelech's sons sinned only in leaving the Holy Land, the punishment of being orphaned would have been retribution enough. But they sinned further by marrying Moabite women [see next verse] (*Pri Chaim*).

[Some commentators, however, understand וַתִּשָּׁאֵר in the sense of 'she remained' in a despised foreign land]: When her husband died, she should have seen it as a divine warning to return to Eretz Yisrael. Instead 'she remained there with her two sons' (*Malbim*), — as a result, her sons stayed on to marry Moabite women, and paid with their own lives (*Iggeres Shmuel*).

4. וַיִּשְׂאוּ לָהֶם נָשִׁים מֹאֲבִיּוֹת — *They married Moabite women,* [lit. 'and they married to themselves Moabite women'].

'Shouldn't the sons have learned a lesson from their father's death and returned to Eretz Yisrael? What did they do? They married Moabite women without even having their wives undergo ritual purification and conversion' (*Tanchuma, B'har*).

'עֲבֵירָה גּוֹרֶרֶת עֲבֵירָה' — 'One transgression leads to another' (*Simchas haRegel*).

It should be noted that only after their father's death did the sons marry women who were not of their people, an indication that Elimelech, for all his faults, would not have allowed them to stoop so low (*Alshich*).

The common expression וַיִּשְׂאוּ, 'married' is used rather than the legal term וַיִּקְחוּ, 'took,' — because the women were not ritually converted and were thus not legally married under Torah law (*Iggeres Shmuel; Malbim*).

The Torah's prohibition of marriage to a Moabite (even after ritual conversion) had within it the implication later expounded by the Sages that the ban extends only to a "Moabite but not to a Moabitess" [see *Deut. 23:4*]. Thus, their sin could be considered as of lesser magnitude. But Machlon and Kilion did not know that; in their own minds they *were* transgressing the law against Moabite marriage. Therefore their punishment was greater. (*Kol Yehudah*).

The word לָהֶם, 'to themselves' implies that they married these women not לְשֵׁם שָׁמַיִם, for the 'sake of heaven', but to satisfy their own selfish, sensual desires . . . and having married non-converted, Moabite women, whatever offspring would have resulted from these unions would have been considered non-Jewish (*Iggeres Shmuel*).

[There is an opinion (*Zohar Chadash* and *Ibn Ezra*), that Machlon and Kilion *did* subject their prospective brides to conversion and immersion, but the 'fear of their husbands was upon them.' (See *Introduction* for a detailed explanation of this view, and its ramifications.]

שֵׁם הָאַחַת עָרְפָּה — *One named Or-*

pah. She was named Orpah because she ultimately turned her back [עֹרֶף — *the nape of her neck*] on her mother-in-law *(Midrash)*.

וְשֵׁם הַשֵּׁנִית רוּת — *And the other Ruth.* [lit. 'and the name of the second, Ruth.] She was named Ruth because she 'saw' [רָאֲתָה — i.e. considered well] the words of her mother-in-law *(Midrash)*.

According to the *Talmud*: 'Rav Yochanan said: Why was she called Ruth? — Because there issued from her David who 'saturated' (רִוָּה) the Holy One, blessed be He with hymns and prayers *(Bava Basra 14b)*.

[The Torah contains 606 Commandments (in addition to the 7 Noachide Laws which are incumbent even upon non-Jews). The commentators note that this number, 606, is equal to the numerical value of the name רוּת, *Ruth*, the convert *par excellence*. This was the number of additional *mitzvos* she accepted upon her conversion.]

Esoterically speaking, the name Ruth [רוּת] is spelled with the letters of 'turtle-dove' [תּוֹר]. 'Just as the turtle-dove is fit for sacrifice on the altar, so was Ruth fit for inclusion in the Assembly of God' *(Zohar Chadash)*.

[The Sages tell us that Machlon and Kilion, wealthy and distinguished, rose to such prominence while living in Moab that Eglon, King of Moab, offered them his daughters' hands in marriage] —

'Ruth and Orpah were the daughters of Eglon, as it is written [Judges 3:19; (when Ehud came to Eglon to deliver God's message)] *". . . and Ehud said: I have a message from God to you. And [Eglon] arose from his throne."* The Holy One, blessed be He, said of him:

"You stood up from your throne in My honor, I will cause to emerge from you a descendent who will sit upon My throne" *(Midrash)*.

וַיֵּשְׁבוּ שָׁם כְּעֶשֶׂר שָׁנִים — *And they lived there about ten years.* [lit. they 'sat' (dwelt) there about ten years.]

This confirms the view that they had given up all thoughts of returning to Eretz Yisrael *(Malbim)*.

In verse 2 the verb וַיִּהְיוּ, *'and they were there'* is used; here, וַיֵּשְׁבוּ, *'and they lived there'* is used. Elimelech should have known better than to leave Eretz Yisrael. As soon as he 'was' there he was punished. But the sons were helpless in the matter and could not overrule their father. They were not punished until וַיֵּשְׁבוּ שָׁם, *they dwelt there,* and tarried for so long *(Iggeres Shmuel)*.

God waited all these years to give them the opportunity to repent. *(Midrash Zuta)*.

Having married princesses, they couldn't abandon them, nor could they return with them to Eretz Yisrael — they feared the Sages would have forced them to separate themselves from their Moabite wives, who, at the time, were still thought to be forbidden because the Sages had not yet ruled that a Moabitess was permitted. Therefore — divorce and return to Eretz Yisroel being impossible — God punished them with death. *(Simchas haRegel)*.

כְּעֶשֶׂר שָׁנִים — *About ten years.* [lit. *like ten years*]. The *Bach* explains why 'like' ten years is used. The *Midrash* (on verse 1) states that before the famine, the Jews in Eretz Yisrael had looked upon Elimelech as one who could provide their sustenance for ten years. They placed all their trust in him — rather than in God. When the famine

שְׁנֵיהֶם מַחְלוֹן וְכִלְיוֹן וַתִּשָּׁאֵר הָאִשָּׁה
מִשְּׁנֵי יְלָדֶיהָ וּמֵאִישָׁהּ: וַתָּקָם הִיא
וְכַלֹּתֶיהָ וַתָּשָׁב מִשְּׂדֵי מוֹאָב כִּי שָׁמְעָה

broke out, the miserly Elimelech left, and God caused his family to live away for a period *'like the ten years,'* a length of time equal to the ten years which the Jews had misplaced their trust in flesh and blood — until when these ten years were up, and the famine ended *(Meishiv Nefesh)*.

5. וַיָּמֻתוּ גַם־שְׁנֵיהֶם — *The two of them . . . also died.*

[God first punishes man, via warnings, depriving him of his property, and only after that, if man does not repent, does God smite him in his person.]

'The Merciful One never begins His retribution by taking a human life . . . And so it was with Machlon and Kilion also. First their horses, their asses, and their camels died, then Elimelech, and lastly the two sons' *(Midrash)*.

After being stripped of their money and cattle the two of them גַּם, *'also'* died *(Rashi)*.

The word גַּם, *also*, indicates that just as the death of their father was punishment for having remained outside of Eretz Yisrael, so was their death in punishment for that sin. *(Iggeres Shmuel)*.

[Just as the death of Elimelech — in verse 3 — follows as punishment for שָׁם וַיִּהְיוּ — *'and they remained there'*, so does the death of the sons follow as punishment for שָׁם וַיֵּשְׁבוּ — *'and they lived there']*

'Although [under certain conditions of great distress] one is permitted to emigrate, if one does, the act is not in conformity with the law

of righteousness. Remember Machlon and Kilion! They were the two great men of their generation and they left Eretz Yisrael at a time of great distress; nevertheless they incurred thereby the penalty of extinction' *(Rambam)*.

שְׁנֵיהֶם — *Both of them.* Because they were equally guilty *(Pri Chaim)*.

מַחְלוֹן וְכִלְיוֹן — *Machlon and Kilion.* Note that they are no longer referred to as *'Ephrathites,'* as above in verse 2 [see Comm. there], nor are they identified as the husbands of Ruth and Orpah. They are stripped of their prestige: they are simply *Machlon and Kilion. (Alschich)*.

The verse repeats their names to emphasize that not only did they die physically, but because they were childless, their very names — *Machlon and Kilion* — died with them *(Iggeres Shmuel)*..

וַתִּשָּׁאֵר הָאִשָּׁה מִשְּׁנֵי יְלָדֶיהָ וּמֵאִישָׁהּ — *And the woman was bereft of her two children and of her husband,* i.e., she was left alone without her children or her husband. Her children are mentioned first because when one recounts past events one usually mentions the most recent first; or because of the greater anguish associated with the death of her children who died young, whereas her husband died at an old age *(Ibn Ezra)*.

The *Midrash* notes that before punishing their persons, God first struck at their property, completely devastating and impoverishing them. Nevertheless, this verse tells

Machlon and Kilion, also died; and the woman was bereft of her two children and of her husband.

⁶ *She then arose along with her daughters-in-law to return from the fields of Moab, for she had heard*

us, Naomi did not anguish over the loss of her property, but over the loss of her children and husband (*Iggeres Shmuel*).

[After her husband's death Naomi was yet of some importance, but with her sons' death, that remaining prestige, too, left her] . . .

'Rav Chaninah said: She was left as the remnants of the remnants [of the meal offering; i.e., of no value whatsoever. See Comm. to verse 3 s.v. וַתִּשָּׁאֵר *'And she was left'*] (*Midrash*).

[Unlike verse 3 where they are called בָּנֶיהָ, her 'sons,' here Machlon and Kilion are called יְלָדֶיהָ, her 'children,' i.e., they died like young children without their own offspring].

An excellent insight is offered in *Ima Shel Malchus*:

Naomi had many times asked herself by what merit she had survived. Had she not sinned as much as they? ...Perhaps her sin was a greater one, and therefore her punishment, too was greater ... It was she — of the whole family — who was left, desolate, to bear the burden of sorrow of the entire family. ...

Naomi could not possibly have known, much less have dared to believe at the time, that she had been preserved through the kindness and compassion of HASHEM, who had allowed the spark of life of Elimelech's family to remain glowing in her ... leading to the birth of King David.

6. וַתָּקָם הִיא וְכַלֹּתֶיהָ — *She then arose along with her daughters-in-law.* The next verse tells us, in a seemingly redundant manner, וַתֵּצֵא מִן הַמָּקוֹם, *she left the place.* In this verse, therefore, וַתָּקָם, *she arose*, means: she 'resolved' to leave (*Iggeres Shmuel; Ibn Ezra; Vilna Gaon).*

The resolve to *leave this ill-fated place* was shared equally by them all, because they surmised that their evil fortune was bound up with their present luckless abode (*Malbim*).

She was afraid that if they stayed there one more day they would all die (*Alschich*).

The *Besuras Eliyahu* interprets וַתָּקָם as *'rising up from mourning'* i.e. as soon as the mourning period was over they resolved to leave.

The *Midrash* interprets וַתָּקָם in a spiritual sense: 'Fallen down, she now lifted herself up by returning to Eretz Yisrael' (*Lekach Tov*).

(According to *Rashi*, however, וַתָּקָם *'she arose'* in this verse implies *actual* departure, [see Comm. next verse]).

וַתָּשָׁב מִשְּׂדֵי מוֹאָב — *To return from the fields of Moab.* The word וַתָּשָׁב [lit. *'and she returned'*] is singular to imply that although the three of them unanimously agreed that they must leave their present luckless abode, at first it was Naomi alone who decided to leave Moab, her daughters-in-law concurring in that decision only later (*Malbim*).

פרק א
ז-ח

בִּשְׂדֵה מוֹאָב כִּי־פָקַד יהוה אֶת־עַמּוֹ
לָתֵת לָהֶם לָחֶם: וַתֵּצֵא מִן־הַמָּקוֹם אֲשֶׁר
הָיְתָה־שָּׁמָּה וּשְׁתֵּי כַלֹּתֶיהָ עִמָּהּ וַתֵּלַכְנָה
בַדֶּרֶךְ לָשׁוּב אֶל־אֶרֶץ יְהוּדָה: וַתֹּאמֶר
נָעֳמִי לִשְׁתֵּי כַלֹּתֶיהָ לֵכְנָה שֹּׁבְנָה אִשָּׁה

כִּי שָׁמְעָה בִּשְׂדֵי מוֹאָב — **For she had heard in the fields of Moab.** 'She heard from peddlers making their rounds from city to city,' says the *Midrash.* 'And what was it she heard? . . . כִּי־פָקַד ה' אֶת־עַמּוֹ לָתֵת לָהֶם לָחֶם, *That* HASHEM *had remembered His people by giving them food.'* Now that the famine was over, Jewish peddlers resumed their rounds in Moab selling the produce of Eretz Yisrael. It was from these peddlers that she heard the good news. The *Midrash* reasons that she heard it from Jewish peddlers because the Moabites would never have invoked the Name of HASHEM (the proper Name of God) as the Cause of the famine and its removal. Also, as the *Midrash* states, God ended the famine for the sake of עַמּוֹ, *His people;* she was reassured that the cause of the famine [i.e. the lawlessness of the times; see Comm. to verse 1] was remedied, the people having repented, and that the famine had permanently ended (*Malbim*).

Pri Chaim, on the other hand, analyzing the verse, comments that פָּקַד ה' אֶת עַמּוֹ 'HASHEM *has remembered His people'* — is an exact quotation of what the peddlers were going around saying; and since עַמּוֹ 'His people' is in the third person — implying that the speaker excluded himself — we must say that it was Moabite peddlers who were ac-

knowledging HASHEM's ending of the famine in Eretz Yisrael.

Nachlas Yosef stresses the word עַמּוֹ, *His people* — i.e. the word was out that the Jews once again became *God's people,* having fully repented from their evil ways.

It should be noted that Naomi did not resolve to return home until she had the assurance that the famine was finally over, and that God had ended it for the sake of עַמּוֹ *His people,* of which she, too, was part. For had He ended it for the sake of Eretz Yisrael, she could not be part of it, having forsaken the land. [The family's affront to the Land would have precluded their sharing in any prosperity granted for its sake. But 'a Jew remains a Jew even after having sinned' — thus Naomi could share in abundance given for the sake of the people] (*Alschich*).

According to the *Targum:* God gave the people food on account of the righteousness of the judge Ivtzan and the prayers of Boaz [who, according to the *Talmud* were the same person].

A homiletical interpretation is offered by *Kol Yehuda:* At first, Naomi was afraid to return home during the famine lest the Jews take revenge against her by not feeding her. She realized, however, that God, Who by warning against being vengeful, פָּקַד אֶת עַמּוֹ — *Had* (in effect) *commanded His people* [פָּקַד, 'remembered,' could also mean

in the fields of Moab that HASHEM had remembered His people by giving them food. 7 She left the place where she had been, accompanied by her two daughters-in-law, and they set out on the road to return to the land of Judah.

8 Then Naomi said to her two daughters-in-law:

'commanded']. לָתֵת לָהֶם לָחֶם to give them [i.e. Naomi and her family] bread just as Jews are commanded by the Torah to care for all unfortunates.

7. וַתֵּצֵא מִן־הַמָּקוֹם — *She left the place.* Rashi, who holds that וַתָּקָם, 'she arose', in the previous verse denotes actual departure rather than a resolve to leave, queries: Her return home is already mentioned in the preceding verse; why does this verse speak of her departure?...

[Her departure was particularly noticeable because]: 'The great person of a city is its brilliance, its distinction, its glory, and its praise. When he departs, its brilliance, its distinction, its glory, and its praise depart with him *(Midrash; Rashi).*

וּשְׁתֵּי כַלֹּתֶיהָ עִמָּהּ — *Accompanied by her two daughters-in-law.* [Lit. 'her two daughters-in-law with her']. The departure of the daughters-in-law was also particularly significant, as was Naomi's [see preceeding Comm.] *(Meishiv Nefesh).*

וַתֵּלַכְנָה — *And they set out,* [lit. 'they walked'] i.e. they discussed הִלְכוֹת גֵּרִים, the laws of proselytes. [This interpretation is suggested by the seemingly redundant use of the word וַתֵּלַכְנָה, they walked, which has the same root as הֲלָכָה, law.] *(Midrash).*

בַּדֶּרֶךְ — *On the road.* The Midrash offers this explanation for the

seemingly superfluous term בַּדֶּרֶךְ, *on the road*: The way was hard for them because they went barefoot. [i.e nothing cushioned their bare feet from the road — such was the degree of their poverty] *(Torah T'mimah).*

The words בַּדֶּרֶךְ לָשׁוּב 'on the road to return,' are superfluous; the verse could have read: 'And they set out to the land of Judah.' The verse, as structured, teaches us that when our intentions are good, God rewards us every step of the way *(Kol Yehudah).*

לָשׁוּב — *To return.* This can only refer to Naomi who was 'returning' to Eretz Yisrael. 'Returning,' in this context, could not refer to Ruth or Orpah who had never been in Eretz Yisrael *(Iggerres Shmuel).*

8. וַתֹּאמֶר נָעֳמִי — *Then Naomi said.* Naomi had assumed that her daughters-in-law were merely accompanying her to Judah out of respect and courtesy, with the intention of returning to Moab afterwards. She told them that this was unnecessary. Her maternal suggestion was that they should return to their mother's home, confident that God would reward them for having been good wives and dutiful daughters-in-law *(Malbim).*

לִשְׁתֵּי כַלֹּתֶיהָ. The verse mentions 'two' in order to make clear that Naomi showed no bias toward

לְבֵית אִמָּהּ יַעֲשֶׂה* יהוה עִמָּכֶם חֶסֶד כַּאֲשֶׁר עֲשִׂיתֶם עִם־הַמֵּתִים וְעִמָּדִי: יִתֵּן יהוה לָכֶם וּמְצֶאןָ מְנוּחָה אִשָּׁה בֵּית

*יַעַשׂ ק'

Ruth. Although she realized that Ruth's determination to convert was much stronger than Orpah's, she addressed them both in the same terms (Meishiv Nefesh).

Quite possibly, Naomi did not yet realize that Ruth's commitment was greater than Orpah's. She addressed them as equals in the hope that each would strengthen the other's resolve (Rav Yosef Yavetz; Pri Chaim).

לְכֵנָה שֹׁבְנָה — Go return. She asked them to return home because she did not want to be embarrassed [i.e. by returning to Eretz Yisrael with Moabite daughters-in-law] (Midrash Zuta). . .

[The Sages rule that one must attempt to dissuade a would-be convert three times; this was the first time — the others are in verses 11 and 12]. . .

If Naomi's only intention was to fulfill the halachic requirement that a potential proselyte be discouraged, then the word שֹׁבְנָה return, would have been sufficient. Since Naomi added לְכֵנָה, go, the Rabbis deduced that her intention was sincere, because she reflected that she, Elimelech's widow, was about to return to the Holy Land with non-Jewish daughters-in-law, and, as the Midrash tells us, she grew ashamed (Midrash Zuta).

According to Alshich, once they reached the 'road to return to the land of Judah,' Naomi realized that they had not escorted her as a mere courtesy, but that their intention was to remain with her in Judah.

She told them not to follow each other blindly, but, as individuals, to carefully consider the implications of conversion and to act out of a deep personal conviction. She said: "לְכֵנָה, 'go' along with me, or שֹׁבְנָה, 'return' to your mother's home, but, whatever course you choose, may God repay your goodness, and may you find husbands".

יַעֲשֶׂה ה' עִמָּכֶם חֶסֶד — May HASHEM deal kindly with you. The כְּתִיב — ksiv, [the traditional spelling] is יעשה, [the simple future tense], i.e. 'He will certainly deal kindly with you'] (Midrash).

[Our translation, of course, follows the קְרִי — kri, (the traditional reading) יַעַשׂ — the optative 'may He do' The juxtaposition of ksiv and kri indicate that, although Naomi said 'May He do' in the form of a prayer, she was fully confident that God would, indeed, reward their kindness].

'God does not withhold reward from any creature!' [i.e. God repays every good deed accordingly; what special implication did Naomi's blessing have?]. — Naomi's blessing must be understood as saying: Just as you both have gone beyond what is expected of you by doing חֶסֶד, kindness, so may HASHEM not only reward you in the usual manner, but may He go beyond the expected and do חֶסֶד, kindness, with you (Nachal Eshkol).

Naomi's intention was, 'Perhaps, my daughters-in-law, you do not part from me because you fear that if you desert me now — leaving

I

9

*'Go, return, each of you to her mother's house. May
HASHEM deal kindly with you, as you have dealt
kindly with the dead and with me! ⁹ May HASHEM
grant that you may find security, each in the home of*

me destitute — all your previous
kindness to me will be nullified; instead of being rewarded for the
good you have done for so many
years, you are afraid you will be
punished for the final lapse. Fear
not. You may return home to your
mothers and God will reward you
nonetheless *(Iggeres Shmuel).*

עִם הַמֵּתִים עֲשִׂיתֶם כַּאֲשֶׁר — *As you
have dealt kindly with the dead,* i.e.
by having been good to your husbands during their lifetimes, וְעִמָּדִי,
and to me (Malbim).

According to the *Midrash*: 'As
you have dealt with the dead' — in
that you [went beyond what is *required* of a wife and] busied yourselves with their shrouds; *'and with
me'* — in that you renounced the
marriage settlement to which you
were legally entitled ....
The *Midrash* thus understands
the verse as referring to *posthumous* kindness ['busying themselves with their shrouds']. Had
Naomi referred to kindness done
during the lifetimes of their husbands, she would have said *'with
your husbands'* instead of *'with the
dead' (Torah T'mimah).*

Perhaps this is why Naomi addressed them in the Hebrew
masculine gender [עֲשִׂיתֶם, עִמָּכֶם] as
if to say: Your posthumous
kindness to your husbands — in
preparing their shrouds and funeral
— was not a legal feminine obligation, but a masculine one
(Meishiv Nefesh).
The *Targum* translates: 'The

kindness you have done to your
husbands — *by refusing to remarry;* and to me, — *by feeding and
sustaining me.'*

9. [Naomi elaborates on her
blessing of the previous verse,
specifying that the 'kindness' for
which she prays is that God reward
them at long last with domestic con-
tentment].

לָכֶם ה' יִתֵּן — *May HASHEM grant
that you.* [Lit. 'May HASHEM give to
you], i.e. over and above what you
rightfully deserve *(Malbim).*
Ibn Ezra adds the word: בַּעַל, a
husband.

מְנוּחָה וּמְצֶאןָ — *That you may find
security,* [lit. 'rest']. The *k'siv* [tra-
ditional written form] of the word is
וּמְצֶאןָ, without the suffix, ה, i.e. in
singular. [Naomi foresaw that] 'only one of you will find rest; not
both' *(Midrash).*
Although Naomi foresaw that
only Ruth was destined to be blessed, she nevertheless addressed
them with the plural לָכֶם, *to you,*
out of respect for Orpah's feelings.
However the word וּמְצֶאןָ, *that you
may find,* is indistinguishable in its
spoken form from the singular to
the plural *(Iggeres Shmuel).*

אִישָׁה בֵּית אִשָּׁה — *Each in the home
of her husband.* [Lit. 'woman in the
home of her man']. From Naomi's
blessing 'we see that a woman has
no contentment except in her husband's house' *(Midrash).*
Witnessing the unhappiness of

אִישָׁה וַתִּשַּׁק לָהֶן וַתִּשֶּׂאנָה קוֹלָן
וַתִּבְכֶּינָה: וַתֹּאמַרְנָה־לָּהּ כִּי־אִתָּךְ נָשׁוּב
לְעַמֵּךְ: וַתֹּאמֶר נָעֳמִי שֹׁבְנָה בְנֹתַי לָמָּה
תֵלַכְנָה עִמִּי הַעוֹד־לִי בָנִים בְּמֵעַי וְהָיוּ
לָכֶם לַאֲנָשִׁים: שֹׁבְנָה בְנֹתַי לֵכְןָ כִּי
זָקַנְתִּי מִהְיוֹת לְאִישׁ כִּי אָמַרְתִּי יֶשׁ־לִי
תִקְוָה גַּם הָיִיתִי הַלַּיְלָה לְאִישׁ וְגַם יָלַדְתִּי

יא

יב

her daughters-in-law who became widowed after being barren for ten years, she wished them true domestic contentment in the future (Iggeres Shmuel).

וַתִּשַּׁק לָהֶן — *She kissed them.* A parting embrace (Malbim).

וַתִּבְכֶּינָה — *And they wept.* [The commentaries differ on whether the daughters-in-law cried on account of Naomi's imminent departure, or whether all three cried while reflecting on their sad state. The *Zohar Chadash* states that the spirits of their dead husbands stirred within them, evoking their tears].

10. וַתֹּאמַרְנָה לָּהּ — *And they said to her.* Now, they told her for the first time of their intention of returning with her (Malbim).

[The 'No!' in the translation is not in the Hebrew, but is implied in the context of the verse.]

לְעַמֵּךְ — *To your people.* At this point they expressed a desire not to accept the God of the Jews, but merely to settle among *'your people'* in Eretz Yisrael (Malbim).

According to *Alshich,* however, Naomi understood these words as an implicit declaration that they wished to convert. Otherwise their

statement would have been self-contradictory: one cannot join the Jewish nation without accepting its God.

11. שֹׁבְנָה בְנֹתַי — *Turn back, my daughters.* [This was the second of Naomi's three attempts to dissuade the would-be converts; see verses 8 and 12.]

הַעוֹד־לִי בָנִים בְּמֵעַי — *Have I more sons in my womb?* Naomi was not seriously suggesting that her daughters-in-law wait for unborn sons to grow up and become their husbands! Rather, her statement was metaphorical: 'Have I any grown-up sons whom I have been keeping hidden, out of your sight, in my womb, and whom I could instantly produce to become your husbands?' (Malbim).

וְהָיוּ לָכֶם לַאֲנָשִׁים — *'Who could become husbands to you?'* 'Could then a man marry the widow of his brother [who became widowed] before he was born? יִבּוּם, levirate marriage (see *Introduction*) would not apply to an as-yet unconceived child] (Midrash).

Since the law of levirate marriage could not apply, such a marriage would be forbidden by Torah law. Therefore, Naomi's words must be understood, not in the sense of יִבּוּם,

her husband.' She kissed them, and they raised their voice and wept. 10 And they said to her: 'No, we will return with you to your people.' 11 But Naomi said: 'Turn back, my daughters. Why should you come with me? Have I more sons in my womb who could become husbands to you? 12 Turn back, my daughters, go along, for I am too old to have a husband. Even if I were to say: there is hope for me, and even if I were to have a husband tonight — and even

levirate marriage, but rather as a loving gesture: 'Had I more sons in my womb, I would gladly give them to you in place of your dead husbands' (Ibn Ezra).

12. שֹׁבְנָה בְנֹתַי לֵכְןָ — *Turn back, my daughters, go along.* 'Three times is it written שֹׁבְנָה, 'turn back,' corresponding to the three times that a would be convert is dissuaded. If he still persists, he is accepted' (Midrash).

כִּי זָקַנְתִּי מִהְיוֹת לְאִישׁ — *For I am too old to have a husband.* i.e. to marry and bear children to be husbands to you (Rashi).

Naomi adds to her argument, 'Even if you agreed to wait until I remarry, have children and raise them to marriageable age, there are still two reasons why this is impossible — first, כִּי זָקַנְתִּי מִהְיוֹת לְאִישׁ, *I am too old to have a husband*; secondly, you could not bear to wait so long — הֲלָהֵן תְּשַׂבֵּרְנָה, *would you wait for them?* (Malbim).

כִּי אָמַרְתִּי יֶשׁ־לִי תִקְוָה — *Even if I were to say there is hope for me.* [The 'even' is not in the Hebrew, but the phrase is to be so understood according to the commentaries (e.g. Rashi)].

In a homiletic fashion Rav

Velvele Margolis interprets the verse as reflecting the social ills of society and the rationale for delaying marriage. Many people, wanting to climb the social ladder reject prospective suitors always hoping for someone better to come along. Thus, Naomi said: 'I am too old to have a husband because I wanted to become the wife of someone comparable to Elimelech, important and aristocratic; therefore I delayed remarriage כִּי אָמַרְתִּי יֶשׁ לִי תִקְוָה, because I always said: *There is hope for me*, I will find someone better, more suitable for me ' (Ginzei Malchus).

גַּם הָיִיתִי הַלַּיְלָה לְאִישׁ — *And even if I were to have a husband tonight.* The *Malbim* explains: According to our sages, Naomi said: 'If I had a husband tonight I might have borne sons' (Midrash). Now, according to the Sages, a woman who resigns herself to unmarried widowhood for ten years can no longer bear children afterward. Thus, the only two ways Naomi — ten years a widow — could have remained fruitful were if she had sustained the hope of remarriage throughout the period of widowhood; or if she would remarry *that very night*, the tenth anniversary of Elimelech's death.

בָנִים: הֲלָהֵן | תְּשַׂבֵּרְנָה עַד אֲשֶׁר יִגְדָּ֫לוּ
יג
הֲלָהֵן תֵּעָגֵ֫נָה לְבִלְתִּי הֱיוֹת לְאִישׁ אַל
בְּנֹתַי כִּי־מַר־לִי מְאֹד מִכֶּם כִּי־יָצְאָה בִי

Thus, we can translate the verse: *Turn back, my daughters, go along, for I am too old to have a husband,* i.e. having remained widowed ten years, I should, under normal circumstances, not be able to remarry and bear children. *But,* said Naomi, *I said there is hope for me* — i.e. I sustained the hope of remarrying throughout the ten years of my widowhood, thus enabling me to have children even after this period — or on the other hand *if I had a husband tonight,* specifically *tonight,* the last night of the ten year period, *I might have children.* ... and so I ask you: *Would you wait for them ... ? etc.*' (*Malbim*).

וְגַם יָלַדְתִּי בָנִים — *And even bear sons.* 'Or even if I had already given birth to children' (*Rashi*).

[*Rashi* apparently understands these words, not as the hypothetical result of *if I were to have a husband tonight,* but as an additional argument by Naomi, i.e. 'let us say I *had* given birth to sons ... *would you wait for them until they were grown?*'].

[The double use of גַם, *and* ('even'; 'furthermore') in this verse implies Naomi's resignation to an almost futile situation.]

13. הֲלָהֵן תְּשַׂבֵּרְנָה — *Would you wait for them?* i.e. for the hypothetical children to whom I might give birth? (*Iggeres Shmuel*).

הֲלָהֵן תֵּעָגֵנָה — *Would you tie yourselves down for them?* [The translation follows *Rashi* who holds that the root of תֵּעָגֵנָה is עוג, to en-

circle, to constrict. *Rashi* refutes those who translate the word as being related to עֲגוּנָה, *Agunah*, (a woman who is forbidden to marry because her husband is missing and she has no proof of his death.) The root of that word: עגן. Thus if תֵּעָגֵנָה stemmed from עגן (with the suffix נה, there would be a double נ in the word, or at the very least, the single נ with a *dagesh* (נּ) serving to take the place of the missing letter.)

In a lengthy grammatical discourse, the *Iggeres Shmuel* quotes the *Radak* as deriving the word from the root עגה, and translating it as 'delay'. The *Iggeres Shmuel* then refutes this translation, and insists that it is derived from עגן, as in עֲגוּנָה, *Agunah*, which the Sages always use when referring to a married woman living without her husband. Therefore, explains the *Iggeres Shmuel*, the ג, *gimmel,* is vocalized with a 'tzere,' (גֵ), for, were the word derived from the root עגה, the ג, *gimmel,* would be vocalized with a 'segol' (גֶ). ...

The *Iggeres Shmuel* thus translates: *Would you remain as Agunahs — in memory of your dead husbands?'*

The *Talmud* translates the word as coming from the Hebrew עֹגֶן, 'an anchor' — i.e. *would you remain anchored ... ?* (*Bava Basra 73a*).

לְבִלְתִּי הֱיוֹת לְאִישׁ — *And not marry anyone else?* [lit. *and not be to a man?*]. 'Would you delay and remain tied down, waiting for these children to grow up — with the end result that לְבִלְתִּי הֱיוֹת לְאִישׁ, *you*

bear sons — ¹³ *would you wait for them until they were grown up? would you tie yourselves down for them and not marry anyone else? No, my daughters! I am very embittered on account of you; for the hand*

will never marry anyone because you will be too old to have husbands? No, my daughters!... (*Iggeres Shmuel*).

אַל בְּנוֹתַי — *No, my daughters!* i.e. do not come with me (*Ibn Ezra*).

The *Midrash* quotes Naomi as saying, אַלְלַי בְּנוֹתַי, *'woe is to me, my daughters . . .* [Had she meant an absolute negation, an order that they not accompany her based on the irrefutable logic cited earlier, she would have said לֹא. The word אַל, on the other hand, indicates an entreaty (*Torah T'mimah*)].

כִּי־מַר־לִי מְאֹד מִכֶּם — *I am very embittered on account of you.* [The translation follows the majority of the commentaries and the *Midrash*, which renders: *'on account of you.'*]

Naomi blamed her bitterness and the tragedies of her sons' death on their marriage to gentile women, rather than to their leaving Eretz Yisrael because that had been done at the command of their father (*Binyan Ariel*).

Although she had attempted to discourage them by insisting that there were no more unborn sons in her womb, she made it clear that she would not have allowed her children to marry Ruth and Orpah in any case (*Simchas haRegel*).

The *Chidah*, in his above-mentioned *Simchas haRegel*, offers an alternate interpretation of מִכֶּם: Naomi felt that her sons had been placed in an impossible situation by their marriages to the Moabite

princesses. Machlon and Kilion could not divorce or desert them because of the political repercussions. They could not return to Eretz Yisrael with Moabite wives. Naomi reasoned that her sons had no alternative but to remain in Moab *'because of them.'* As a result, God had punished her sons.

Other commentaries interpret מִכֶּם — *'more than you'* i.e. *'I am more embittered than you* [for I have suffered more tragedies than you]' (*Rav Arama; Iggeres Shmuel; Malbim*).

The *Vilna Gaon* interprets the phrase: 'I am greatly distressed witnessing your plight, כִּי יָצְאָה בִי יַד ה׳, *although the hand of God has gone forth against me*, I am more concerned with your anguish.'

According to the *Bach*, מִכֶּם is not 'additive' but 'causitive' i.e. *'I am embittered for your sake* — seeing your bereavement, and remembering that because of you my sons died.'

כִּי־יָצְאָה בִי יַד ה׳ — *for the hand of HASHEM has gone forth against me.* 'Against me, against my sons, and against my husband' (*Midrash*).

Whatever God could possibly have done to me, He has already done (*Malbim*).

יָצְאָה — *Gone forth* [lit. *'went out'*] is used because God's wrath was so severe in this case that it *'went out'* beyond the bounds of its usual temperance (*Iggeres Shmuel*).

יַד ה׳ — *The hand of God,* i.e. *affliction.* The reference to 'hand' is an-

יד יַד־יהוה: וַתִּשֶּׂנָה קוֹלָן וַתִּבְכֶּינָה עוֹד
וַתִּשַּׁק עָרְפָּה לַחֲמוֹתָהּ וְרוּת דָּבְקָה בָּהּ:
טו וַתֹּאמֶר הִנֵּה שָׁבָה יְבִמְתֵּךְ אֶל־עַמָּהּ
וְאֶל־אֱלֹהֶיהָ שׁוּבִי אַחֲרֵי יְבִמְתֵּךְ:
טז וַתֹּאמֶר רוּת אַל־תִּפְגְּעִי־בִי לְעָזְבֵךְ לָשׁוּב

thropomorphic; speaking in human terms (Ibn Ezra.)

The Iggeres Shmuel offers a novel interpretation: Naomi told her daughters-in-law not to think that she blamed them for her sons' death; 'אַל בְּנֹתַי', no my daughters, do not think that my bitterness is because of you. Definitely not! The hand of G-d has gone forth against me — in retribution for my own sins.'

14. The Alshich paraphrases verses 11-14:

Naomi, realizing that they wanted to convert and go to Eretz Yisrael, called them בְּנֹתַי my daughters, — and said: 'If you desire to serve HASHEM, you can do that in Moab. If you wonder whom you could marry in Moab — all of them being idol worshipers — then realize that no Jew will marry you, because you are Moabites [and the law permitting marriage to female Moabites was not yet promulgated]). Don't rely on me for husbands; I am too old for marriage. Even if I were to marry, even tonight, who can say that I will give birth. If I do give birth, I might bear only daughters! And even if I were to have sons, would you wait for them?

'You might reply that you are content to accompany me to Eretz Yisrael with no thought of remarriage. No, my daughters: My state of bitterness is for you — I cannot bear to see you in such a troubled state, for the hand of God has gone forth against me; you are sinless. It was for my sins that God has been punishing me, and you have been bearing my iniquity.

When Orpah and Ruth heard this, they cried. Orpah kissed her mother-in-law, but in Ruth's clinging to her; Naomi realized a רוּחַ קְדוּשָׁה, a spirit of holiness (Alshich)

וַתִּשֶּׂנָה קוֹלָן וַתִּבְכֶּינָה עוֹד — They raised up their voice and wept again. There is an א, aleph, missing [from ותשנה] teaching that תָּשַׁשׁ כֹּחָן, their strength diminished, as, weeping, they went on their way (Midrash)...

(i.e. the word וַתִּשֶּׂאנָה — with an א aleph, as in verse 9 — means and they raised up. Here, since וַתִּשֶּׂנָה omits the א, aleph, the Midrash homiletically links the word to תשש, 'to be weak.' The verse indicates that they wept continuously throughout their conversation with Naomi until even their strength to cry was weakened (Iggeres Shmuel).

וַתִּשַּׁק עָרְפָּה לַחֲמוֹתָהּ — Orpah kissed her mother-in-law. [The kiss was their parting. No words. Only a kiss. Scripture divulges no more, but the pain was intense. As Naomi watched Orpah walk towards Moab, she knew that the last vestige of her son Kilion was lost to her forever].

of HASHEM has gone forth against me.

14 *They raised up their voice and wept again. Orpah kissed her mother-in-law, but Ruth clung to her.*
15 *So she said: 'Look, your sister-in-law has returned
to her people and to her god; go follow your sister-
in-law.'* 16 *But Ruth said: 'Do not urge me to leave*

ןִרוּת דָּבְקָה־בָּה — *But Ruth clung to
her.* Ruth, too, remained silent. Her
eyes showed her devotion to Naomi
— her eyes and her refusal to go. But
Naomi could not understand:
wasn't Orpah right? *(Ima Shel
Malchus).*

'Ruth and Orpah were of royal
lineage, descended from Eglon king
of Moab *(Nazir 23b)*; it was a heroic
sacrifice to forsake their country to
accompany the impoverished
Naomi. There, on a country road in
the fields of Moab, *was enacted one
of the great scenes of history.* Three
times did Naomi urge Ruth and Orpah to desist from their kindliness
and turn back. They refused to
yield, but on the third time, Orpah
weakened and returned to her land
and her people. Ruth persisted in
her resolve to go with Naomi...
Generations later, David the
descendant of Ruth, faced Goliath,
the descendant of Orpah, on the
battlefield' *(Behold a People).*

15. הִנֵּה שָׁבָה יְבִמְתֵּךְ — *Look, your
sister-in-law has returned.* [Orpah's
departure is not stated, but it is inferred from her 'farewell' kiss in the
previous verse.]

The accent in Hebrew, notes
Rashi, is under the שׁ of שָׁבָה, indicating that it is simple past tense,
i.e. *she returned*, unlike the same
word [in *Esther 2:14*] where there
the accent is under the ב and the
tense is imperfect: בָּעֶרֶב הִיא שָׁבָה,
'*in the evening she would return'.*

אֶל־עַמָּהּ וְאֶל־אֱלֹהֶיהָ — *To her people
and to her god.* Rashba haLevi
understands לְעַמֵּךְ, *to your people,'*
in verse 10 as indicating their desire to convert. In contrast, he
notes, the expression *'returned to
her people and her god'* in this verse
reveals that she renounced her
previous intention to embrace
Judaism.

[The *Ibn Ezra* and *Zohar
Chadash*, in keeping with their
interpretation that Ruth and Orpah
had already converted when they
got married, (see *Comm.* to v.4);
deduce from this verse that Orpah
now *'returned'* to her old faith. (See
Introduction for full exposition of
this interpretation)].

שׁוּבִי אַחֲרֵי יְבִמְתֵּךְ — *Follow your
sister-in-law.* [i.e. *'return after your
sister-in-law'*]. Naomi said: Your
sister-in-law accompanied me
because she was ashamed to leave.
Now she finally succumbed and returned home. I grant you the same
opportunity to depart gracefully
and follow her *(Iggeres Shmuel).*

Naomi simply said, 'follow your
sister-in-law; she carefully refrained from adding 'to her god'
(Alshich).

16. אַל־תִּפְגְּעִי־בִי — *Do not urge me.*
'Do not persist so diligently in trying to dissuade me from joining
you. Don't offer me excuses לְעָזְבֵךְ,
to leave you, לָשׁוּב מֵאַחֲרָיִךְ, *and not
follow you* in your return to

מֵאַחֲרָיִךְ כִּי אֶל־אֲשֶׁר תֵּלְכִי אֵלֵךְ וּבַאֲשֶׁר
תָּלִינִי אָלִין עַמֵּךְ עַמִּי וֵאלֹהַיִךְ אֱלֹהָי:
יז בַּאֲשֶׁר תָּמוּתִי אָמוּת וְשָׁם אֶקָּבֵר כֹּה
יַעֲשֶׂה יהוה לִי וְכֹה יוֹסִיף כִּי הַמָּוֶת
יח יַפְרִיד בֵּינִי וּבֵינֵךְ. וַתֵּרֶא כִּי־מִתְאַמֶּצֶת

Judaism — for no matter what, I am determined to convert' (Iggeres Shmuel).

'Better that my conversion should be at your hands than at those of another' (Midrash).

The Midrash [understanding תִּפְגְעִי as a form of פגע, 'misfortune'] translates 'Do not turn your misfortune against me' — i.e. do not seek to turn me away by reciting your misfortunes to me (Yefe Anaf); — do not court misfortune through me, by repulsing me (Anaf Yosef); — do not sin and incur punishment by dissuading me from converting (Torah T'mimah).

כִּי אֶל־אֲשֶׁר תֵּלְכִי אֵלֵךְ — For wherever you go, I will go. [From this, the Sages infer,] 'If one desired to become a proselyte, he is acquainted with the various punishments [for neglect of the Commandments], so that if he wishes to withdraw, let him do so [Yevamos 47b]. (Or, following the approach of the Zohar Chadash/Ibn Ezra — that Ruth and Orpah had already converted upon marrying Machlon and Kilion [see Introduction] — Naomi was testing Ruth's resolve and commitment, now that her husband was dead, by acquainting her with the additional commandments.) From Ruth's responses we can deduce what Naomi must have told her ...

Naomi said: 'We are forbidden [to move on the Sabbath beyond the 2,000 cubits in each direction from one's town or resting place known as] תְּחוּם שַׁבָּת, the Sabbath boundaries!' — [to which Ruth replied] Wherever you go, I will go (Yevamos 47b).

When Naomi heard Ruth's absolute resolve to convert, she began to unfold the laws to her, saying: 'My daughter, Jewish girls do not go to gentile theaters and circuses' [which had a well-deserved reputation for lewdness]; to which she replied: 'Wherever you go, I will go' (Midrash). ...

Do not ascribe to me a motive different from your own. It is my desire, also, to live in Eretz Yisrael so that I may fulfill the mitzvos that the Torah associates with that land (Malbim).

וּבַאֲשֶׁר תָּלִינִי אָלִין — Where you lodge, I will lodge. 'We are forbidden יִחוּד, seclusion between man and woman!' — 'Where you lodge,' Ruth responded, 'I will lodge' (Yevamos 47b).

'My daughter, Jewish girls do not live in a house which has no mezuzah,' — to which Ruth responded: 'Where you lodge, I will lodge' (Midrash).'I do not expect luxuries; I am prepared to be a mere lodger because there is only one object in my going' [as follows:] (Malbim).

עַמֵּךְ עַמִּי — Your people are my people. 'I will never forsake the Torah

you, to turn back and not follow you. For wherever you go, I will go; where you lodge, I will lodge; your people are my people, and your God is my God; 17 *where you die, I will die, and there I will be buried. Thus may HASHEM do to me — and more! — if anything but death separates me from you.'*

18 *When she saw she was determined to go with*

---

of the Jews and the Oneness of G-d' (*Ibn Ezra*).

[Naomi said]: 'We have been given 613 Commandments!' Ruth answered, '*Thy people shall be my people*' [i.e. I am now part of your people and I accept the *mitzvos*] (*Yevamos 47b*).

וֵאלֹהַיִךְ אֱלֹהָי — *Your God is my God*. 'We are forbidden idolatry!' Said Ruth. '*Your God is my God*' (*Yevamos 47b*).

This refers to the acceptance of all the *mitzvos* for, by accepting the sovereignty of God, one accepts all of His commandments. ... Another interpretation: '*Your God is my God* ... who will repay me the reward of my labor' (*Midrash*).

17. בַּאֲשֶׁר תָּמוּתִי אָמוּת — *Where you die, I will die*. [According to the *Talmud* and *Midrash*, Naomi enumerated the four forms of capital punishment to which Ruth responded; By *whatever mode you die, I will die*; i.e. I am prepared to face death for capital offenses; *and there be buried*].

She expressed her innermost desire to die, the same מוֹת יְשָׁרִים, *death of the upright* as would Naomi (*Malbim*).

'I want to die in Eretz Yisrael,' Ruth declared (*Zos Nechemasi*)

וְשָׁם אֶקָּבֵר — *And there I will be buried*. For our sages tell us that he

who is buried in Eretz Yisrael is likened to one who is buried under the altar (*Zos Nechemasi*).

כֹּה יַעֲשֶׂה ה' לִי וְכֹה יוֹסִיף — *Thus may HASHEM do to me — and more*. [Ruth emphasized her loyalty to the Jews by invoking God's name, in this formula of an oath which is common in the Bible. Usually, however, the name אֱלֹקִים — *God of Judgment* is used in such a context.]

Ruth insisted that she would willingly follow Naomi in her beliefs, where she went, and where she slept. But death is out of one's hands. She prayed, therefore, that she would die near enough to Naomi to be buried alongside her (*Iggeres Shmuel*).

This was the crux of Ruth's plea: 'My main reason for following you was I realized that as close as we are in life, if I remain in my heathen state we will be separated in death — you will return to HASHEM, and I will wallow amidst idolators' (*Malbim*).

18. מִתְאַמֶּצֶת הִיא לָלֶכֶת — *She was determined to go*. The verb אמץ suggests moral strength and determination — (*Malbim*).

[Once Ruth's genuine convictions were demonstrated beyond any doubt, Naomi stopped dissuading her].

According to *Zos Nechemasi*, this

הִיא לָלֶכֶת אִתָּהּ וַתֶּחְדַּל לְדַבֵּר אֵלֶיהָ:
וַתֵּלַכְנָה שְׁתֵּיהֶם עַד־בֹּאָנָה בֵּית לָחֶם
וַיְהִי כְּבֹאָנָה בֵּית לֶחֶם וַתֵּהֹם כָּל־הָעִיר
עֲלֵיהֶן וַתֹּאמַרְנָה הֲזֹאת נָעֳמִי: וַתֹּאמֶר
אֲלֵיהֶן אַל־תִּקְרֶאנָה לִי נָעֳמִי קְרֶאןָ לִי
מָרָא* כִּי־הֵמַר שַׁדַּי לִי מְאֹד: אֲנִי מְלֵאָה

*י״א במקום ה׳   כא

verse refers to Naomi: i.e. when Naomi perceived that God had not stricken her down like her husband and children, she realized that she was endowed with a special strength לָלֶכֶת אִתָּהּ, to accompany her [i.e. Ruth] and that she should be the instrument for bringing Ruth into the fold. Everything that God had wrought was in preparation for this event; Naomi then stopped arguing with Ruth.

וַתֶּחְדַּל לְדַבֵּר אֵלֶיהָ — She stopped arguing with her.[lit. she stopped 'talking' to her].

From this verse the Rabbis (Yevamos 47b) deduced that 'A convert is not to be persuaded or dissuaded too much' (Rashi).

19. וַתֵּלַכְנָה שְׁתֵּיהֶם — And the two of them went on. [lit. 'And they went, the two of them'].

See how precious proselytes are to God! Once she decided to convert, Scriptures ranked her equally with Naomi (Midrash; Rashi).

שְׁתֵּיהֶם, 'the two of them' is mentioned to stress the determination of Ruth, who, although she was leaving her home, birthplace and kindred, marched on with the same strength of soul and purpose as Naomi. Also, they went, the two of them; just the two of them alone. They didn't even wait for a caravan (Iggeres Shmuel).

The Alshich deduces from the fact that שְׁתֵּיהֶם, the two of them ends with the masculine ם instead of the feminine ן, — that the two were afraid to travel the dangerous roads of Moab alone — and they disguised themselves as men — עַד בֹּאָנָה בֵּית לֶחֶם, until they reached Bethlehem at which time they discarded their disguises.

עַד־בֹּאָנָה בֵּית לָחֶם — Until they came to Bethlehem. [The journey to Bethlehem was a profound emotional experience for Naomi. She recalled the scenery and paths that had once been her own and which she and Elimelech had renounced ten years earlier.]

וַתֵּהֹם כָּל הָעִיר עֲלֵיהֶן — the entire city was tumultuous over them. The fact that 'the entire city' learned of their return so quickly, notes the Iggeres Shmuel, indicates that the townsfolk were gathered together. The Midrash offers several reasons for such an assembly:

That day was the reaping of the Omer [the measure of the barley which was offered on the second day of Passover], and all the inhabitants of the surrounding towns assembled to watch the ceremony; the wife of Boaz died on that day, and a multitude of Jews assembled to pay their respects. Just then Ruth entered with Naomi — Thus, one

her, she stopped arguing with her, ¹⁹ *and the two of*
them went on until they came to Bethlehem.

And it came to pass, when they arrived in
Bethlehem, the whole city was tumultuous over
them, and the women said: 'Could this be Naomi?'
²⁰ *'Do not call me Naomi [pleasant one],' she replied,*
'call me Mara [embittered one], for the Almighty has
dealt very bitterly with me. ²¹ *I was full when I went*

Call me
embittered'

[the wife of Boaz] was taken and the other [Ruth] entered (Midrash).

Naomi had always gone about surrounded with servants, and now, when the townsfolk gathered together to see two women — alone, hungry and barefoot — the pitiful sight threw all the citizens into a state of tumult and flurry (Malbim).

וַתֹּאמַרְנָה הֲזֹאת נָעֳמִי — And the women said, 'Could this be Naomi?' ["The women' is not explicit in the Hebrew but it is, to be inferred because תֹּאמַרְנָה, they said, is in the feminine form.]

The afflicted Naomi had so changed in appearance from her past glory that her former neighbors could hardly recognize her (Alshich).

When they first appeared, the *whole city was tumultuous* at their very arrival, but upon closer scrutiny of Naomi's appearance, it was *the women* who addressed her (Gishmei Brachah).

'Is this the one whose actions were fitting and נְעִימִים , pleasant? In the past, she used to go in a covered carriage, and now she walks barefoot; in the past, she wore a cloak of fine wool, and now she is clothed in rags; in the past, her appearance was full from food and drink, now it is shrunken from

hunger — *could this be Naomi?'* (Midrash).

Did you see what befell her for Leaving Eretz Yisrael? (Rashi).

20. אַל תִּקְרֶאנָה לִי נָעֳמִי ... מָרָא —*Do not call me Naomi . . . call me Mara.* Naomi said, 'Don't think that I was righteous and my deed pleasant, and that God punished me unjustly; No! *call me 'Embittered One'* because my deeds were bitter, and *God justly dealt bitterly with me'* (Alshich).

Also, by calling me 'Naomi' you are reminding me of my former glory and thus making my pain even worse (Pri Chaim).

מָרָא —*Mara* ends with an *aleph* א instead of the usual *he* ה to accentuate the extent of her bitterness. There are two other instances of words usually ending in a *he* that are spelled with an *aleph*, in both cases to strengthen the connotation: *Numbers 11:20* זָרָא for זָרָה — 'very loathsome; and *Daniel 11:44* חֵמָא for חֵמָה — 'great anger' (Rabbeinu Bachyai).

21. אֲנִי מְלֵאָה הָלַכְתִּי — *I was full when I went away* — 'I went out full with sons and daughters! Another interpretation: 'I was pregnant' (Midrash).

הָלַכְתִּי וְרֵיקָם הֱשִׁיבַנִי יהוה לָמָּה
תִקְרֶאנָה לִי נָעֳמִי וַיהוה עָנָה בִי וְשַׁדַּי
כב הֵרַע־לִי: וַתָּשָׁב נָעֳמִי וְרוּת הַמּוֹאֲבִיָּה
כַלָּתָהּ עִמָּהּ הַשָּׁבָה מִשְּׂדֵי מוֹאָב וְהֵמָּה
בָּאוּ בֵּית לֶחֶם בִּתְחִלַּת קְצִיר שְׂעֹרִים:

פרק ב א וּלְנָעֳמִי מיֻדַּע לְאִישָׁהּ אִישׁ גִּבּוֹר חַיִל
א־ב ב מִמִּשְׁפַּחַת אֱלִימֶלֶךְ וּשְׁמוֹ בֹּעַז: וַתֹּאמֶר
*מוֹדַע ק'

'Full' — with wealth and children
(Rashi; Ibn Ezra).

וְרֵיקָם הֱשִׁיבַנִי ה' — And empty has
HASHEM brought me back' [Wid-
owed, childless, and poverty-
stricken].

לָמָּה תִקְרֶאנָה לִי נָעֳמִי —How can you
call me Naomi: [lit. why do you call
me Naomi]. How can you call me a
name describing good fortune — a
name which in retrospect, I was
never really entitled to — seeing
how afflicted I have become!
(Malbim).

עָנָה בִי ה' — HASHEM has testified
against me. [lit. 'and HASHEM
answered in me'].

He testified against me that I sinned against Him (Rashi).

'You see from the gravity of my
punishment how severely I sinned
against God, for the punishment
bears witness to the extent of my
evil ways. To you, my sin was leaving Eretz Yisrael during a famine —
an action which might be justified.
But HASHEM, Who knows our innermost intentions, knew that we
left to avoid feeding the poor and

that we stayed overlong in Moab'
(Rashba haLevi).

וְשַׁדַּי הֵרַע־לִי — the Almighty has
brought misfortune upon me! [lit.
'And the Almighty did bad to me.']

Here Naomi refers to God as שַׁדַּי,
(Shaddai) Almighty God, the name
which indicates that, despite His
infinite power, He is the God
שֶׁאוֹמֵר לְצָרוֹתַי דַּי Who says 'enough
[דַּי] of my suffering.' Although He
took my husband and sons, He
stopped short of taking my life,
limiting His punishment to having
הֵרַע לִי, brought misfortune upon
me (Alshich).

22. הַשָּׁבָה מִשְּׂדֵי מוֹאָב — Who
returned from the fields of Moab.

The subject of 'who returned' is
not clear: According to Ibn Ezra it
refers to Naomi; Iggeres Shmuel
comments that it refers to Ruth
despite the fact that she could not
have 'returned', having never been
in Eretz Yisrael. Ruth entered Eretz
Yisrael with the same burning
desire as did Naomi, so Scriptures
describes it as 'she returned' — as if
she had lived there before and it had

away, but HASHEM has brought me back empty. How can you call me Naomi — HASHEM has testified against me, the Almighty has brought misfortune upon me!'

²² *And so it was that Naomi returned, and Ruth the Moabite, her daughter-in-law, with her — who returned from the fields of Moab. They came to Bethlehem at the beginning of the barley harvest.*

II
1

Naomi had a relative through her husband, a man of substance, from the family of Elimelech, whose name was Boaz.

been her birthplace.

'People pointed to her (Ruth) saying: This is the first one who returned from the fields of Moab' (*Yerushalmi, Yevamos 8:3*) i.e., she is the first Moabite woman who שָׁבָה,'repented', and converted to Judaism. With her the law of 'Moabite not Moabitess' [see *Introduction*] was promulgated (*Torah T'mimah*).

Quite possibly no other Moabite woman had ever converted before, because it would have been her impression that she would not be permitted to marry a Jew; Ruth's sincerity was so great, however, that she converted without caring if she could ever remarry (*Iggeres Shmuel*).

[The *Midrash* seems to imply that the subject is Naomi: *This is the one who returned from the fields of Moab!* (i.e. people pointed a finger at Naomi, identifying her as the one who returned from Moab — (*Iggeres Shmuel*)].

בְּתְחִלַּת קְצִיר שְׂעֹרִים — *In the beginning of barley harvest.* The verse refers to the *Omer* harvest [i.e. Passover] (*Midrash; Rashi*).

This chronological detail serves as an introduction to the next chapter; it tells us that it was already the harvest season and too late to plant new crops in the fields belonging to the family of Elimelech. Hence they were poverty-stricken (*Malbim*).

II

1. וּלְנָעֳמִי מוֹדָע — *Naomi had a relative* [Moda]. The word 'moda' means 'kinsman,' 'relative' (*Midrash*) — a familiar relative (*Ibn Ezra*).

He was the son of Elimelech's brother (*Rashi*).

Although Boaz was a close relative, Naomi avoided him even in her dire need. She did not ask him for

רוּת הַמּוֹאֲבִיָּה אֶל־נָעֳמִי אֵלְכָה־נָּא
הַשָּׂדֶה֙ וַאֲלַקֳטָה בַשִּׁבֳּלִים אַחַ֗ר אֲשֶׁ֤ר
אֶמְצָא־חֵן֙ בְּעֵינָ֔יו וַתֹּ֥אמֶר לָ֖הּ לְכִ֥י בִתִּֽי:
ג וַתֵּ֤לֶךְ וַתָּבוֹא֙ וַתְּלַקֵּט֙ בַּשָּׂדֶ֔ה אַחֲרֵ֖י

---

support because she still felt shame at having deserted her people during the famine, while Boaz stayed on and supported them. In addition, she was aware that Boaz was angry that she had brought a Moabite girl back with her. He avoided them both until God brought Ruth to his fields [verse 3] and he realized how virtuous she was (*Alshich*).

Scripture tells us of the strength of these two women. Even though she had a rich relative she did not thrust herself upon him — and Ruth, the daughter of the King of Moab was not too proud to shoulder the burden of support for herself and her mother-in-law (*Alkabetz*).

On the other hand, it should be mentioned that according to the Sages, Boaz's wife died on the day that Naomi and Ruth returned to Bethlehem (see Comm. 1:19 s.v. וַתֵּהֹם). Boaz, involved with the funeral and mourning, could not give them a proper welcome. When Ruth chanced upon his field, on the day he returned from mourning, he recognized her rare qualities. Seeing her glean, he assumed that she would not avail herself of charity, preferring to maintain herself with her own hands. Also, as a widower, he did not want to be suspected of ulterior motives regarding Ruth, so he refrained from overt acts of kindness toward her. As a result of his restraint in regard to Ruth, Naomi also did not benefit of his

beneficence (*Rav Arama; Iggeres Shmuel*).

אִישׁ גִּבּוֹר חַיִל — A mighty man of substance [usually translated '*a mighty man of valor.*' Our translation follows *Rashi* in *Exodus* 18:21: 'men of substance, who need not flatter or show partiality'].

— A man endowed with the highest human qualities including magnanimity and dislike of ill-gotten gains (*Malbim*).

וּשְׁמוֹ בֹּעַז — *And his name was Boaz.*

In the case of wicked men, their names are given before the word שֵׁם, '*name*', as it says: גָּלְיָת שְׁמוֹ, *Goliath was his name;* נָבָל שְׁמוֹ, *Nabal was his hame;* שֶׁבַע בֶּן בִּכְרִי שְׁמוֹ, *Sheva son of Bichri was his name.* But the names of the righteous are preceded by the word שֵׁם, '*name*', as it says: וּשְׁמוֹ קִישׁ, *his name was Kish;* וּשְׁמוֹ שָׁאוּל, *his name was Saul;* וּשְׁמוֹ יִשַׁי, *his name was Jesse;* וּשְׁמוֹ מָרְדְּכַי, *and his name was Mordechai;* וּשְׁמוֹ אֶלְקָנָה, *and his name was Elkanah;* וּשְׁמוֹ בֹּעַז, *and his name was Boaz.* They thus resemble their Creator of whom it is written וּשְׁמִי ה', '*But by My Name* HASHEM *I made Me not known to them* [*Ex.* 6:2] (*Midrash*).

Our Sages said [*Bava Basra 91a*] that Boaz was the judge Ivtzan [see *Comm.* to 1:1] (*Ibn Ezra*).

2. וַתֹּאמֶר רוּת הַמּוֹאֲבִיָּה — *Ruth the Moabite said.* Scripture praises the righteousness of Ruth, who according to the Sages, was the

2 *Ruth the Moabite said to Naomi: 'Let me go out to the field, and glean among the ears of grain behind someone in whose eyes I shall find favor.' 'Go ahead, my daughter,' she said to her.*

3 *So off she went. She came and gleaned in the field*

daughter of Eglon, King of Moab. The verse stresses the noble character of this princess who offered to glean like a common pauper to spare her mother-in-law the indignity of *her* going out and being subject to the humiliating gaze of those who knew her in her former affluence (*Malbim*).

אֵלְכָה־נָּא הַשָּׂדֶה — *Let me go out to the field* i.e. to the safety of the field; not to vineyards where poor people must be concerned with the danger of climbing trees in order to glean forgotten fruits (*Malbim*).

וַאֲלַקְטָה בַשִׁבֳּלִים — *And glean among the ears of grain* i.e. she limited herself to לֶקֶט, *gleaning* [the ears of grain that *fell* from the hands of harvesters to which the poor were entitled — *Lev. 19:9; 13:22; Deut. 29:19*] — because fields for *gleaning* were plentiful and she would not have to compete fiercely with the other poor, unlike the competition for פֵּאָה, *Pe'ah* [see ibid.] which was much more severe (*Malbim*).

אַחַר אֲשֶׁר אֶמְצָא־חֵן בְּעֵינָיו — *Behind someone in whose eyes I shall find favor.* i.e. where the owner will permit me to glean and not scold me (*Rashi*).

אַחַר, 'After I find favor in his eyes' (*Targum*), i.e. 'I will not glean in a field until I am sure the owner allows it and that I won't be embarassed by the other gleaners (*Malbim*).

She stressed that she will glean

אַחַר, 'after,' i.e. 'in back of,' as a gesture of modesty (*Simchas ha-Regel*).

לְכִי בִתִּי — *Go ahead, my daughter.* 'It is not that I hold you in low esteem that I permit you to so degrade yourself by gleaning like a common pauper — I permit you only because of the circumstances and our dire needs which demand it' (*Iggeres Shmuel*).

'Even had you been בִּתִּי, *my own daughter*, I would have let you go (*Alshich*).

[Naomi obviously consented very reluctantly, remembering only too painfully her former wealth and the circumstances which brought her to such depths, and which now forced her daughter-in-law to descend to pauperdom by gleaning to provide for their basic sustenance].

The term בִּתִּי, *'my daughter'* in this particular instance is not necessarily an indication of Ruth's youth. According to Rabbinic tradition, she was then forty years of age (*Midrash*).

3. וַתֵּלֶךְ וַתָּבוֹא — *So off she went; she came.* [lit. 'and she went and she came.']. 'She repeatedly went and came until she found decent people to accompany.' (*Shabbos 113b*).

The *Midrash* interprets this to mean that she went back and forth to 'mark off', i.e. familiarize herself, with the country lanes, so as not to lose her way on her return (*Rashi*).

According to *Malbim*, the prox-

הַקֹּצְרִים וַיִּקֶר מִקְרֶהָ חֶלְקַת הַשָּׂדֶה
ד לְבֹעַז אֲשֶׁר מִמִּשְׁפַּחַת אֱלִימֶלֶךְ: וְהִנֵּה־
בֹעַז בָּא מִבֵּית לֶחֶם וַיֹּאמֶר לַקּוֹצְרִים
יהוה עִמָּכֶם וַיֹּאמְרוּ לוֹ יְבָרֶכְךָ יהוה:
ה וַיֹּאמֶר בֹּעַז לְנַעֲרוֹ הַנִּצָּב עַל־הַקּוֹצְרִים
ו לְמִי הַנַּעֲרָה הַזֹּאת: וַיַּעַן הַנַּעַר הַנִּצָּב עַל־

imity of these verbs suggest that as soon as she left she arrived — i.e. the field of Boaz to which she went was very near her home.

Rav Alkabetz sees in these words what must have been a brief account of her daily schedule: i.e. 'she would go and return daily until the harvest was over.'

Rav Arama interprets it simply: *'she went'* — i.e. she left her home, *'and she came'* — i.e. she arrived at the field.

וַתְּלַקֵּט בַּשָּׂדֶה אַחֲרֵי הַקֹּצְרִים — *And [she] gleaned in the field behind the harvesters.* Although it was morning, the time when other poor people were involved in the more productive gathering of פֵּאָה, *Pe'ah* [see *Leviticus* 19:9-10; *Deut.* 24:19], Ruth limited herself to לֶקֶט [leket] *gleaning,* and she was directly *'behind the harvesters,'* because there was no one else *gleaning* at the time (*Malbim*).

She limited her gleaning to the grain the harvesters left *behind* them — i.e. that which they definitely and undoubtedly discarded; also, she stayed in back of them out of modesty, so no one would glance at her (*Rav Gakkun*).

וַיִּקֶר מִקְרֶהָ — *her fate made her happen.* [This translation is in consonance with the profound philosophy of *Rav S.R. Hirsch* as expressed in his *Commentary* on Genesis 24:12]: 'Nothing is farther from the Jewish concept of 'מִקְרֶה' ['*happening*'] than the idea of '*chance,*' with which it is associated. Rather, it refers to those moments of one's life that he himself did not direct but which directed him; they were only events which were not expected, not reckoned on, not intended, but which, all the more, could be the most intentional messages sent by the One Who directs and brings about all things.'

The *Malbim* notes that the fact that she was gleaning in the field of Boaz would seem to be nothing more than coincidence. The verse stresses, however, that it was מִקְרֶהָ, *'her' fate* i.e. the apparent coincidence was divinely arranged with *her* benefit in mind. By *'chancing'* upon the field of Boaz, she was implementing the heavenly plan to build the royal house of Israel.

אֲשֶׁר מִמִּשְׁפַּחַת אֱלִימֶלֶךְ—*Who was of the family of Elimelech,* who—prophetically—would prove ready to exercise his right as גּוֹאֵל, *redeemer,* and would יַבְּמָה, *marry her,* and ultimately father the Davidic dynasty (*Malbim*).

4. וְהִנֵּה־בֹעַז בָּא — *Behold, Boaz had arrived.* He had returned to his field after completion of the mourning

behind the harvesters, and her fate made her happen upon a parcel of land belonging to Boaz, who was of the family of Elimelech.

⁴ Behold, Boaz arrived from Bethlehem. He greeted the harvesters, 'HASHEM be with you!' And they answered him: 'May HASHEM bless you!' ⁵ Boaz then said to his servant who was overseeing the harvesters: 'To whom does that young woman

---

period for his wife *(Iggeres Shmuel)*.

The word וְהִנֵּה, 'behold,' suggests something unusual. Boaz's coming to the field was unusual, and it was the guiding hand of Divine Providence that led him there on that particular day in order to meet Ruth. Also, Boaz is credited by the Sages with originating the custom of greeting one's neighbor in the Name of HASHEM so as to instill into the hearts of that lawless generation [see Comm. 1:1] the all-pervading presence of God as the Source of mankind's welfare. The custom was introduced that day with the sanction of the Sages in Bethlehem *(Malbim)*, and with the intimated approval of the Heavenly Beth Din *(Midrash)*.

יְבָרֶכְךָ ה' — *May HASHEM bless you.* 'May He bless you with an abundant harvest!' *(Ibn Ezra)*.

Boaz had just been widowed and the Sages consider הַשָּׁרוּי בְּלֹא אִשָּׁה — one who dwells without a wife, as שָׁרוּי בְּלֹא בְּרָכָה — one who dwells without 'blessing'. They greeted him, therefore, יְבָרֶכְךָ ה' — 'may HASHEM 'bless' you with a worthy wife' *(Iggeres Shmuel)*.

Rav Alkabetz observes that the workers did not *initiate* the greeting because one does not greet a

mourner; he greeted first and they responded.

5. לְמִי הַנַּעֲרָה הַזֹּאת — *To whom does that young woman belong?* i.e. 'is she fit to enter the Assembly of HASHEM?'

The *Talmud* asks: 'Was it then Boaz's practice to inquire about young girls? [Surely he didn't inquire about *every* girl gleaning in the fields!] — Rav Eleazar answered: Her [*halachic*] knowledge and exemplary conduct caught his attention. She would glean two ears [of grain that fell from the harvesters' hands] but she would not glean three [in accordance with the law in *Mishnah Pe'ah 6:5*] *(Shabbos 113b)*.

'When he noticed her modesty, he inquired about her. She would stand while gleaning the standing ears and sit while gleaning the fallen ears; the other women hitched up their skirts, and she kept hers down; the other women jested with the harvesters, while she remained reserved; the other women gathered from *between* the sheaves, while she gathered only from that which was definitely abandoned' *(Midrash)*.

According to the *Malbim* who commented [verse 3] that Ruth was the only woman gleaning in the

הַקּוֹצְרִים וַיֹּאמֶר נַעֲרָה מוֹאֲבִיָּה֙ הִיא
הַשָּׁבָה עִם־נָעֳמִי מִשְּׂדֵי מוֹאָב: וַתֹּאמֶר ז
אֲלַקֳטָה־נָּא֙ וְאָסַפְתִּי בָעֳמָרִים אַחֲרֵי
הַקּוֹצְרִים וַתָּבוֹא וַתַּעֲמוֹד מֵאָז הַבֹּקֶר֙
וְעַד־עַתָּה זֶה שִׁבְתָּהּ הַבַּיִת מְעָט: וַיֹּאמֶר֙ ח

---

field at the time, her presence was obvious and Boaz readily noticed her. He assumed that she was related to one of the harvesters who had cleared the field of the other paupers so she could glean alone. This aroused his curiosity and he inquired about her identity.

Some commentators feel that Boaz was interested in finding out if she was married or single, but he was ashamed to pose the question explicitly lest he be suspected of harboring unseemly thoughts about her. Instead he asked seemingly innocent questions about the identity of a stranger who was obviously new to Bethlehem, confident that the reply would supply the information he sought (*Iggeres Shmuel*).

The *Dubna Maggid* points out that just as Ruth's 'coincidental choice' of Boaz's field [verse 3] and Boaz's unusual visit to his field on that particular day were acts of Divine Providence, so, too, was his notice of her and his inquiry about her upon his arrival — *immediately after he greeted his men and before even asking about the progress of the harvest* — also an act of Divine Providence.

6. וַיַּעַן הַנַּעַר הַנִּצָּב עַל־הַקּוֹצְרִים — *The servant who was overseeing the harvesters replied.* His position as overseer and trusted employee is repeated to emphasize that he responded to Boaz's inquiry in a most

familiar and intimate manner [see *Midrash* further] (*Nachal Eshkol*).

נַעֲרָה מוֹאֲבִיָּה הִיא — 'She is a Moabite girl' — 'and yet you say her conduct is praiseworthy and modest? Her mother-in-law instructed her well' (*Midrash*). i.e. 'her good manners are not her own,' the overseer responded. 'Her seemingly modest behavior was drilled into her by her mother-in-law' (*Torah T'mimah*).

The overseer tried, by many means to dissuade Boaz from showing interest in the girl. He replied that she is a נַעֲרָה, *a young woman* and was too young for Boaz [who was eighty years old at the time! Despite the fact that, according to the *Midrash*, she was forty years old, her beauty was that of a young girl.] Additionally, she was מוֹאֲבִיָּה, *a Moabite*, and as such not permitted in marriage (for the law of 'Moabite not Moabitess' was not yet widely known [see *Introduction*]). The overseer also suggested that she was still *a Moabite* at heart: her conversion had not been sincerely motivated out of love of God or desire to 'find shelter under His wings,' but rather out of love for Naomi (*Iggeres Shmuel*).

'Also,' the overseer added, 'her luck is bad — she buried her husband and is destitute' (*Zos Nechemasi*).

The overseer said: 'Furthermore

belong?' 6 'She is a Moabite girl,' the servant who was overseeing the harvesters replied, ' — the one that returned with Naomi from the fields of Moab; 7 and she had said: "Please let me glean, and gather among the sheaves behind the harvesters." So she came, and has been on her feet since the morning until now; except for her resting a little in the hut.'

(even if her marriage to a Jew were permitted), are there no *Jewish* girls for someone as important as Boaz to marry? — Girls *not* brought up amidst the miserliness of the Moabites?' (*Rashba haLevi*).

Alshich notes that the overseer probably did not dare verbalize these jibes at Ruth to his master; the propriety of the master-servant relationship would not have allowed it. Rather, from the wording and tone of the overseer's response Boaz inferred his displeasure.

הַשָּׁבָה עִם נָעֳמִי מִשְּׂדֵי מוֹאָב — *The one that returned with Naomi from the fields of Moab.* According to the *Malbim's* interpretation of the episode, the overseer responded: 'Don't wonder why I allow a foreign Moabite woman to glean in your field. *She is the one that returned with Naomi*; she converted, and as a Jew is entitled to glean.'

The *Iggeres Shmuel* stresses the positive in the overseer's response: 'She is a young Moabite woman,' — she is young and capable of child-bearing; 'a Moabitess' — female, and thus not under the ban of 'Moabite'; 'the one who returned with Naomi,' — the sincerity of her conversion is beyond reproach, for she returned with an impoverished Naomi, leaving her country and royal ancestry behind.

7. וַתֹּאמֶר — *And she had said.* [This is a continuation of the overseer's response to Boaz.] . . .

אֲלַקֳטָה־נָא — *Please let me glean.* i.e. the *leket* [gleaning] of the sheaves (*Rashi*).

Note how even though gleaning was a legal right granted by the Torah to the impoverished, for which no permission is required, Ruth nevertheless displayed good manners and modesty by first asking permission (*Iggeres Shmuel*).

וְאָסַפְתִּי בָעֳמָרִים אַחֲרֵי הַקּוֹצְרִים — *And [I will] gather among the sheaves 'forgotten' stalks after the harvesters,* i.e. the שִׁכְחָה, i.e. a stalk overlooked or 'forgotten' by the harvesters (*Rashi*).

A different interpretation: 'I don't want charity; I'll even pay you for the privilege of gleaning by *helping the harvesters gather the sheaves*' (*Iggeres Shmuel*).

וַתָּבוֹא וַתַּעֲמוֹד — *So she came and has been on her feet.* — Diligently involved with her needs (*Ibn Ezra*).

'She has been working all along until this very moment, just prior to your arrival' (*Malbim*).

זֶה שִׁבְתָּה הַבַּיִת מְעָט — *Except for her resting a little in the hut.* [The translation of the very obscure Hebrew follows *Ibn Ezra* and *Malbim*].

According to the *Midrash*: 'She gathered a quantity — barely

בֹּעַז אֶל־רוּת הֲלוֹא שָׁמַעַתְּ בִּתִּי אַל־
תֵּלְכִי לִלְקֹט בְּשָׂדֶה אַחֵר וְגַם לֹא־
תַעֲבוּרִי מִזֶּה וְכֹה תִדְבָּקִין עִם־נַעֲרֹתָי:
עֵינַיִךְ בַּשָּׂדֶה אֲשֶׁר־יִקְצֹרוּן וְהָלַכְתְּ
אַחֲרֵיהֶן הֲלוֹא צִוִּיתִי אֶת־הַנְּעָרִים
לְבִלְתִּי נָגְעֵךְ וְצָמִת וְהָלַכְתְּ אֶל־הַכֵּלִים

ט

enough for two — for her who was in the house [Naomi] since she was waiting for it.' [The language of the *Midrash*, too, is obscure. The above rendering follows *Mattanos Kehunah*.] The *Torah T'mimah* comments that according to the *Midrash*, the overseer misunderstood the question, and feared that Boaz was angry with him for allowing this stranger to enter the field. He defended himself by saying that she gleaned only a small amount and gave it to Naomi who had remained home, and for whom there was no other form of sustenance.

8. וַיֹּאמֶר בֹּעַז — *Then Boaz said.* [Having heard that the girl is Naomi's daughter-in-law, he displayed special interest in her, but apparently did not reveal that he was a relative].

הֲלוֹא שָׁמַעַתְּ בִּתִּי — *Hear me well, my daughter.* [Lit. 'have you not heard, my daughter?'].

Boaz said: You heard me discussing you with my overseer. Don't think I inquired about you because of any displeasure at your being here. To the contrary! I insist that you stay on and glean in my fields exclusively ...' *(Iggeres Shmuel).*

According to Pri Chaim (who holds that the overseer spoke positively about Ruth): 'You have surely heard, my daughter, what the overseer said about you and how, impressed with your modest ways, he allowed you to glean here.'

בִּתִּי — *My daughter.* [A natural way for an elderly man to address a woman much younger than he. It also suggests that he would now treat her in a paternal fashion. (See *comment* end of verse 2, s.v. בִּתִּי]

A question arises:

Is this the same righteous Boaz lauded by the Sages? Ruth and Naomi were his closest kin; he should have offered them his home and supported them in dignity and comfort rather than just allowing Ruth the 'privilege' of exercising a pauper's legal right to glean the harvest!

—As soon as Boaz met Ruth he was told of her modest behavior and he was greatly impressed. But she was a foreigner and he wanted to assure himself, first hand, of her integrity, so he put her to the test. Had her conversion been insincere and had it been motivated by the knowledge that her relative, Boaz, would treat her royally, her reaction to his offer would have revealed her as a fraud. Instead she reacted superbly — like the righteous person she truly was [See also Commentary on 2:1] *(Rav Arama).*

אַל־תֵּלְכִי לִלְקֹט בְּשָׂדֶה אַחֵר — *Do not*

8 *Then Boaz said to Ruth: 'Hear me well, my daughter. Do not go to glean in another field, and don't leave here, but stay here close to my maidens.* 9 *Keep your eyes on the field which they are harvesting and follow them. I have ordered the young men not to molest you. Should you get thirsty,*

go to glean in another field.' 'You may not be welcome by the owner' (*Malbim*).

Boaz said: 'A poor person leaves one field for another for two reasons: the crop is exhausted; or the inhospitality of the owner forces him to leave. Neither reason applies here, therefore: *Do not go to glean in another field ...'* (*Pri Chaim*).

The *Midrash*, interpreting the verse on a more lofty plane explains 'field' allegorically: '*Do not go to glean in another 'spiritual' field* — 'Thou shalt have no other gods before Me' [*Exodus 20:3*].

וְגַם לֹא־תַעֲבוּרִי מִזֶּה — *Also, don't leave here.* 'Even to another one of my own fields' (*Malbim*).

'Reside here and don't return home until the harvest is over' (*Rav Arama*).

וְכֹה תִדְבָּקִי עִם־נַעֲרֹתָי — *Stay here close to my maidens.* [Lit. 'and right here shall you cleave to my maidens']. 'Stay on the side of my field where the girls are working; not on the other side with the men' (*Malbim*).

9. עֵינַיִךְ בַּשָּׂדֶה — *Keep your eyes on the field.* [Lit. 'your eyes on the field!']—Keep your eyes on the field that the girls are harvesting (*Malbim*).

Boaz recognized Ruth as a צִדְקָנִית, a righteous woman whose עַיִן טוֹב, 'generous eye' [antonym of

עַיִן הָרַע, 'evil eye'] will cause blessing to descend upon the object of her generosity as scripture says: טוֹב עַיִן הוּא יְבֹרָךְ, *He that has a generous eye shall bring blessing* [lit. 'shall be blessed'] (*Proverbs 22:9*). Knowing that Ruth would be a source of blessing to whatever field provided her sustenance, Boaz asked her to '*keep her eyes on the field during the harvest*' so that a blessing would descend on the crop (*Iggeres Shmuel*).

'*Keep your eyes on the field* — and as soon as it is harvested be the first to glean.' Boaz was planning to tell his men to deliberately discard sheaves for Ruth to glean [verse 16], and he wanted to make sure that she would benefit from his largesse by being on the scene first (*Kol Yaakov*).

וְהָלַכְתְּ אַחֲרֵיהֶן — *And follow them* [אַחֲרֵיהֶן — is feminine] i.e. '*follow the maidens.*' [They will harvest, and you will glean after them] (*Malbim*).

לְבִלְתִּי נָגְעֵךְ — *Not to molest you.* Even if you are all alone in the field (*Rashba haLevi*).

[נָגְעֵךְ, 'molest you,' can also be understood in the more simple sense: 'not to interfere with you'].

— 'They have been so commanded by the Torah: וְאָהַבְתֶּם אֶת הַגֵּר, '*love the stranger*' [*Deut. 10:19*] (*Midrash Lekach Tov*)

The *Midrash*, which has been

פרק ב
י-יא

י וְשָׁתִית מֵאֲשֶׁר יִשְׁאֲבוּן הַנְּעָרִים: וַתִּפֹּל
עַל־פָּנֶיהָ וַתִּשְׁתַּחוּ אָרְצָה וַתֹּאמֶר אֵלָיו
מַדּוּעַ מָצָאתִי חֵן בְּעֵינֶיךָ לְהַכִּירֵנִי וְאָנֹכִי
יא נָכְרִיָּה: וַיַּעַן בֹּעַז וַיֹּאמֶר לָהּ הֻגֵּד הֻגַּד לִי
כֹּל אֲשֶׁר־עָשִׂית אֶת־חֲמוֹתֵךְ אַחֲרֵי מוֹת
אִישֵׁךְ וַתַּעַזְבִי אָבִיךְ וְאִמֵּךְ וְאֶרֶץ
מוֹלַדְתֵּךְ וַתֵּלְכִי אֶל־עַם אֲשֶׁר לֹא־יָדַעַתְּ

allegorically explaining this verse as
an admonition by Boaz for Ruth to
be faithful to her new religion [see
Comm. end of verse 8], translates
לְבִלְתִּי נְגָעֵךְ — 'they will not discourage you.'

וְהָלַכְתְּ אֶל־הַכֵּלִים —Go to the jugs. 'If
you get thirsty, don't hesitate to
drink from the jugs of water fetched
by the young men' (Rashi).

'Go yourself, and don't have the
young men bring it to you. The less
you associate with them, the better
(Rav Yavetz).

מֵאֲשֶׁר יִשְׁאֲבוּן הַנְּעָרִים — From what
the young men have drawn. 'And
don't worry that the men might be
angry; I already warned them לְבִלְתִּי
נְגָעֵךְ not to bother you' (Iggeres
Shmuel).

The well with the good drinking
water was far from the fields and
laborious to fetch from. Therefore,
the men who brought the water
would keep it for themselves. The
poor would have to drink inferior
water drawn from closer wells. Boaz
told Ruth that if she became thirsty
she should not hesitate to drink
from the men's jugs, as they had
been instructed by him personally
not to interfere with her (Malbim).

10. וַתִּפֹּל עַל־פָּנֶיהָ — Then she fell

on her face ... bowing to the ground.
In humble gratitude for his
graciousness and cordiality towards
her (Alshich).

At the same time she bowed
down and praised God for His
beneficence (Meishiv Nefesh).

מַדּוּעַ...וְאָנֹכִי נָכְרִיָּה Why ... though I
am a foreigner. 'What did you see in
me that made you take special
notice and inquire about me though
I am a נָכְרִיָּה, an ordinary stranger.
Many other women who glean here
also are strangers, but no one pays
any special attention to them' (Iggeres Shmuel).

According to Pri Chaim, Ruth
was not aware that Boaz was a
relative. Her question was
prompted by the fact that she
thought it unusual for a stranger to
be showered with such attention.

The Targum translates: 'How is it
that I have found favor in your
eyes? — I am of a foreign nation, a
daughter of Moab, a nation not fit
to enter into קְהַל ה', the Assembly
of Hashem.'

11. [Boaz responds that he has
heard of her extraordinary and
magnanimous deeds in the exemplary way she treated her
mother-in-law, and her leaving

go to the jugs and drink from what the young men have drawn.'

¹⁰ *Then she fell on her face, bowing down to the ground, and said to him: 'Why have I found favor in your eyes that you should take special note of me though I am a foreigner?'*

¹¹ *Boaz replied and said to her: 'I have been fully* Boaz's *informed of all that you have done for your mother-* generosity *in-law after the death of your husband; how you left your father and mother and the land of your birth and went to a people you had never known before.*

home and family to embrace Judaism.]

הֻגַּד הֻגַּד לִי — *I have been fully told.* The verb הגד is doubled for emphasis. 'Your deeds are so widely discussed that *I have been hearing about them in the house and in the fields* i.e from all sides' (*Midrash*).

Ruth considered herself unworthy of Boaz's attention and she sincerely wanted him to explain the reason for his unexpected kindness; therefore, she posed the question to him. He responded that she — for her goodness — deserves much more kindness than he is capable of performing for her, and that whatever he did for her was miniscule compared to the rewards which would be bestowed upon her from God [see next verse] (*Alshich; Rashba haLevi*).

כֹּל אֲשֶׁר-עָשִׂית אֶת-חֲמוֹתֵךְ — *All that you have done for your mother-in-law.* Boaz told Ruth that his favorable attitude to her was a result of two things: Firstly, despite the fact that a woman usually has ill feelings toward her mother-in-law, Ruth treated Naomi in an exemplary manner — especially after

Naomi became widowed and forlorn — thus demonstrating a rare nobility of character; and secondly, for having left her parents and homeland to convert, etc. (*Malbim*).

אַחֲרֵי מוֹת אִישֵׁךְ — *After the death of your husband* — 'and certainly during his lifetime' (*Midrash*)

וַתַּעַזְבִי אָבִיךְ וְאִמֵּךְ וְאֶרֶץ מוֹלַדְתֵּךְ — *How you left your father and mother and the land of your birth.* i.e. 'Your conversion is remarkable because, in the face of coercion to remain in Moab, you freely left your parents' home and the country of your birth and, with no material considerations, you came to a strange country (*Alshich*).

אֲשֶׁר לֹא-יָדַעַתְּ תְּמוֹל שִׁלְשֹׁם — *Which you have never known before* [lit. 'which you have not known yesterday and the day before']. Boaz said; 'the law permitting female Moabite converts to marry Jews was popularized only in the last few days, and you could not possibly have been aware of it when you converted. Therefore, you could only have been motivated by the purest religious motivations with no ulterior motives' (*Rashba haLevi*).

יב תְּמוֹל שִׁלְשֹׁם: יְשַׁלֵּם יהוה פָּעֳלֵךְ וּתְהִי
מַשְׂכֻּרְתֵּךְ שְׁלֵמָה מֵעִם יהוה אֱלֹהֵי
יִשְׂרָאֵל אֲשֶׁר־בָּאת לַחֲסוֹת תַּחַת־כְּנָפָיו:
יג וַתֹּאמֶר אֶמְצָא־חֵן בְּעֵינֶיךָ אֲדֹנִי כִּי
נִחַמְתָּנִי וְכִי דִבַּרְתָּ עַל־לֵב שִׁפְחָתֶךָ

12. יְשַׁלֵּם ה' פָּעֳלֵךְ — *May HASHEM reward your actions.* [lit. *HASHEM will repay your actions*] The verse may be interpreted either as a prayer for divine reward or as a promise of it. One who performs acts of חֶסֶד, *kindliness*, with the poor is likened to one who lends money to God, and He assuredly repays all His debts (*Iggeres Shmuel*).

The *Malbim* differentiates between פּוֹעֵל, an artisan who is paid for a specific project, e.g. a tailor for a garment; and שׂוֹכֵר, a salaried employee who is paid for a period of time regardless of actual production. . .

Thus Boaz said: 'For the kindness you have shown your mother-in-law, *HASHEM will reward your actions* [פָּעֳלֵךְ] as an artisan is rewarded for whatever handiwork he has actually produced. But for accepting the Torah and the service of God as a שׂוֹכֵר, an employee, of HASHEM, so to speak, you have come under God's wings — under His perpetual protection and care — you will be paid your 'salary' [מַשְׂכֻּרְתֵּךְ] fully and regularly' (*Malbim*).

Only God can reward you, for no human act is capable of rewarding you commensurate with your deed (*Rav Arama*).

וּתְהִי מַשְׂכֻּרְתֵּךְ שְׁלֵמָה — *And may your payment be full* [lit. *and your payment will be full*]. The *Iggeres Shmuel* interprets this verse as follows: *HASHEM will definitely reward your actions* in this world; *and your payment will be full*, boundless, *from HASHEM, the God of Israel*, in the world to come when you will bask directly in His radiance. And all of this will be *in reward for* having converted with a sincere heart, *to seek shelter under His wings*. . .

The *Iggeres Shmuel* further comments that Ruth's merits might be greater than those of Abraham. Of Abraham's merits, the Sages sometimes note that תָּמָה זְכוּת אָבוֹת, the merit of the Patriarchs [which act as a shield] is exhausted (*Shabbos 55a*); but of Ruth's merit Boaz blessed her that it be שְׁלֵמָה, *full*, i.e. eternally undiminishable. Abraham left his father's house only in response to God's call, לֶךְ לְךָ, *'Get thee out'* [Gen. 1:1] but Ruth left on her own initiative — without a divine call, and despite the dissuasion of her mother-in-law, — in order to come under the wings of HASHEM.

אֲשֶׁר־בָּאת לַחֲסוֹת תַּחַת־כְּנָפָיו — *Under whose wings you have come to seek refuge.* [Commenting on the anthropomorphic reference to the 'wings' of God, the Midrash enumerates the many anthropomorphic references to 'wings' in תנ"ך, the Scriptures]:

¹² *May HASHEM reward your actions, and may your payment be full from HASHEM, the God of Israel, under whose wings you have come to seek refuge.'*
¹³ *Then she said: 'May I continue to find favor in your eyes, my lord, because you have comforted me, and because you have spoken to the heart of your*

Rav Abin said, We gather from Scriptures that there are wings to the earth (Isaiah 24:16); wings to the sun (Malachi 3:20); wings to the חַיּוֹת, *celestial beings* (Ezekiel 3:13); wings to the כְּרוּבִים, *cherubim* (I Kings 8:7); wings to the שְׂרָפִים, *seraphim* (Isaiah 6:2) . . .

'Come and see how great is the power of צַדִּיקִים, the righteous, and the power of צְדָקָה, righteousness, and charity, and how great the power of גּוֹמְלֵי חֶסֶד, those who do kindly deeds, for they find shelter neither in the shadow of the morning, nor of the sun, the *chayos*, the *cherubim*, or the *seraphim*, but *under the wings of Him at whose word the world was created'* (*Midrash*).

Boaz wished her that she should never have to rely on flesh and blood for sustenance, but on HASHEM alone (*Zos Nechemasi*).

The *Dubna Maggid* elaborates, in his *Kol Yaakov*, on the concept of reward for performing *mitzvos*, and sums up that the highest reward for any *mitzvah* is the satisfaction of the performance of that mitzvah which is a reward and incentive unto itself. Thus, Boaz told Ruth: Have no fear, my daughter, HASHEM will repay your actions: but may you reach a level of righteousness sufficient to appreciate that the most 'complete payment' from HASHEM, *the God of Israel,* is the very fact *that you have*

been inspired to seek shelter under His wings.'(Also *Vilna Gaon*)

Boaz's blessing was that in addition to rewarding Ruth for the performance of every *mitzvah* she would perform, God should also additionally reward her for the crucial decision upon which all her future good deeds ultimately hinged — the decision to 'come under His wings' (*Chidah*, quoting *his father*).

13. אֶמְצָא־חֵן בְּעֵינֶיךָ אֲדֹנִי — *May I continue to find favor in your eyes.* [The word *'continue'* is not in the Hebrew but is so understood by the commentators].

After he told her his reasons for favoring her, she expressed hope that she will continue to find favor in his sight (*Malbim*).

כִּי נִחַמְתָּנִי —*Because you have comforted me* — by your promise of care and divine compassion (*Vilna Gaon; Malbim*).

The *Targum* adds, 'and declared me fit to enter the congregation of HASHEM.'

Even if Boaz were to do nothing for her, his words of comfort were sufficient to win her gratitude (*Alshich*).

וְכִי דִבַּרְתָּ עַל־לֵב שִׁפְחָתֶךָ — *And because you have spoken to the heart of your maid-servant,* i.e. 'words which are receptive to the heart' (*Rashi* on Gen. 50:21).

Not merely אֶל לֵב, *to the heart,*

וְאָנֹכִי לֹא אֶהְיֶה כְּאַחַת שִׁפְחֹתֶךָ: וַיֹּאמֶר
לָהּ בֹּעַז לְעֵת הָאֹכֶל גֹּשִׁי הֲלֹם וְאָכַלְתְּ
מִן־הַלֶּחֶם וְטָבַלְתְּ פִּתֵּךְ בַּחֹמֶץ וַתֵּשֶׁב
מִצַּד הַקֹּצְרִים וַיִּצְבָּט־לָהּ קָלִי וַתֹּאכַל
וַתִּשְׂבַּע וַתֹּתַר: וַתָּקָם לְלַקֵּט וַיְצַו בֹּעַז
אֶת־נְעָרָיו לֵאמֹר גַּם בֵּין הָעֳמָרִים תְּלַקֵּט

but עַל לֵב, [lit. 'upon the heart'], i.e.
that your words prevailed over my
feelings (Rav S.R. Hirsch, ibid).

שִׁפְחֹתֶךָ — your maid-servant. [A
deferential term used in Scriptures
by women when addressing gentlemen (comp. עַבְדְּךָ, 'your servant'
used by men.)]

וְאָנֹכִי לֹא אֶהְיֶה כְּאַחַת שִׁפְחֹתֶךָ —
Though I am not as worthy as one
of your maid-servants. [This translation follows Rashi, and Malbim.
Literally the words mean: 'And I
will not be as one of your maid-
servants.']

Ibn Ezra seems to translate: I am
not even worthy enough to be as
one of your maidservants.

You have indeed comforted me
by your kind words, for I have
never considered myself, to be as
worthy in your eyes as one of your
maid-servants (Iggeres Shmuel).

A different aproach is taken by
Mashal Umelitza: Ruth heard
Boaz's promise to her of divine
reward for her good actions. She
answered him: Thank you, my
lord, for your attempt to comfort
me with promises of reward, but it
is unnecessary, I am not like one of
your maid-servants who perform
good deeds for the sake of reward;
my intentions are only לְשֵׁם שָׁמַיִם
"for the sake of Heaven."

14. לְעֵת הָאֹכֶל — At mealtime. By

this time their conversation had
stretched so long that dinner was
being served (Alschich).

He did not invite her earlier
because he was afraid she would
demur; he waited until everyone except her was eating, and then he invited her (Iggeres Shmuel).

גֹּשִׁי הֲלֹם — Come over here. i.e. to
Boaz's table (Pri Chaim).

According to the Midrash: 'Approach to royalty.' [prophetically
intimating to her the kings who
would one day descend from her]
(Midrash).

וְאָכַלְתְּ מִן־הַלֶּחֶם — And partake of
the bread. i.e. the bread of the
harvesters (Midrash). Share our
meal with us (Alshich).

וְטָבַלְתְּ פִּתֵּךְ בַּחֹמֶץ — And dip your
morsel in the vinegar. To refresh
yourself from the heat (Ibn Ezra).

Harvesters use vinegar to allay
the thirst, cool the body, and
stimulate the digestive system. Boaz
was afraid that, as a princess, Ruth
was not accustomed to spending so
many hours in the sun. He suggested vinegar to avoid sunstroke
(Rav Alkabetz).

וַתֵּשֶׁב מִצַּד הַקֹּצְרִים — So she sat
beside the reapers. Not in front of
them, so they should not glance at
her; not in back of them so she
should not watch them; but
alongside them (Alshich; Midrash).

maid-servant—though I am not even as worthy as one of your maid-servants.'

¹⁴ *At mealtime, Boaz said to her, 'Come over here and partake of the bread, and dip your morsel in the vinegar.' So she sat beside the harvesters. He handed her parched grain, and she ate and was satisfied, and had some left over.*

¹⁵ *Then she got up to glean, and Boaz ordered his young men, saying: 'Let her glean even among the*

Boaz invited her to גֹּשִׁי הֲלֹם, *come over here*, and sit with him at the head of the table, but obviously she modestly preferred to station herself *beside the reapers (Malbim).*

וַיִּצְבָּט־לָהּ קָלִי — *He handed her parched grain.* [i.e. Boaz to Ruth] This is the only place in Scripture where this word (וַיִּצְבָּט, *and he handed*) occurs (Rashi; Ibn Ezra).

Seeing that she was *sitting beside the reapers* and that she modestly refrained from taking any food, Boaz himself handed the food to her like a gracious host *(Iggeres Shmuel).*

'The verse teaches us that if a man is about to perform a good deed, he should do it with all his heart. For had Boaz known that Scripture would record of him *'he handed her parched grain,'* he would have fed her fatted calves...

'In the past when a man performed a good deed the prophet recorded it, but nowadays when a man performs a good deed who records it? — Elijah records it and the Messiah and the Holy One blessed be He affix His seal to it *(Midrash).*

וַתֹּאכַל וַתִּשְׂבַּע וַתֹּתַר — *And she ate and was satisfied and had some left over.*

According to the *Midrash* [connecting the word קָלִי, *'parched grain'* with קָלִיל, *'a little'*] Boaz gave her just a 'pinch of parched grain between his two fingers', and Ruth's stomach was blessed for she was satisfied with such a small morsel and even had some left over.

Other commentaries, [*Ralbag, Malbim, Rav Alkabetz*], however, interpret this verse that Boaz displayed unusual generosity: he graciously prepared her a portion so abundant that she ate her fill and still had a great deal left over.

Alshich notes that this was the first filling meal she had eaten in a long while.

15. וַתָּקָם לְלַקֵּט — *Then she got up to glean.* Having eaten, she returned to her task with increased vigor *(Alshich.)*

וַיְצַו בֹּעַז אֶת־נְעָרָיו — *Boaz gave orders to his young men.* Boaz's invitation to Ruth was meant as a signal to her that he was ready to support her at his table. He assumed that she would no longer wish to demean herself by gleaning in the fields like a common pauper. But when he saw that she was determined to continue gleaning, he acquiesced to her wishes. Simultaneously, however, he informed his employees that he

טז וְלֹא תַכְלִימוּהָ: וְגַם שֹׁל־תָּשֹׁלוּ לָהּ מִן־
הַצְּבָתִים וַעֲזַבְתֶּם וְלִקְּטָה וְלֹא תִגְעֲרוּ־
בָהּ: יז וַתְּלַקֵּט בַּשָּׂדֶה עַד־הָעָרֶב וַתַּחְבֹּט
אֵת אֲשֶׁר־לִקֵּטָה וַיְהִי כְּאֵיפָה שְׂעֹרִים:
יח וַתִּשָּׂא וַתָּבוֹא הָעִיר וַתֵּרֶא חֲמוֹתָהּ אֵת
אֲשֶׁר־לִקֵּטָה וַתּוֹצֵא וַתִּתֶּן־לָהּ אֵת אֲשֶׁר־
הוֹתִרָה מִשָּׂבְעָהּ: יט וַתֹּאמֶר לָהּ חֲמוֹתָהּ
אֵיפֹה לִקַּטְתְּ הַיּוֹם וְאָנָה עָשִׂית יְהִי

expected them to treat her especially well (*Pri Chaim*).

גַם בֵּין הָעֲמָרִים תְּלַקֵּט — *Let her glean even among the sheaves.* [i.e. give her a completely free hand]. '*Even if she gleaned from between the sheaves* — which the poor are not legally entitled to — *nevertheless*,' Boaz ordered, '*do not embarrass her*' (*Ralbag*).

וְלֹא תַכְלִימוּהָ — *Do not embarrass her* [Quietly encourage her, and be sympathetic to her situation].

16. שֹׁל־תָּשֹׁלוּ לָהּ מִן־הַצְּבָתִים — *And even deliberately pull out some for her from the heaps.* Pretend you forgot them (*Rashi*) [He knew that her pride would not permit her to take charity] — 'Rav Yochanan used to deliberately drop coins in order that Rav Shimon bar Abba (who was extremely poor) might 'find' them. Rav Yehudah used to leave lentils about in order that Rav Shimon ben Chalafta might acquire them' (*Midrash*).

Rav Alkebetz stresses the word לָהּ , *for her*, to indicate that Boaz made it clear that when they deliberately pulled out stalks and 'forgot' them, the stalks should be dropped where Ruth could reach them before anyone else.

וְלֹא תִגְעֲרוּ בָהּ — *And don't rebuke her*. [Even though you might not understand my intent, and my request causes you extra work, don't vent your anger at her].

With this Boaz explicitly stated his noble intention to fully sustain her (*Malbim*).

She is a convert — and thus deserving of our compassion (*Nachal Eshkol*).

17. וַתְּלַקֵּט בַּשָּׂדֶה עַד הָעָרֶב — *So she gleaned in the field until evening.*

The verse stresses '*gleaned*' because although the harvesters were deliberately dropping large amounts for her as Boaz ordered, Ruth limited herself to the meager gleanings she was entitled to by law [i.e. a maximum of two stalks at a time], and avoided Boaz's charity. Nevertheless, the verse tells us, her efforts were greatly blessed, because she worked hard and managed to gather over an *ephah* of barley (*Iggeres Shmuel*).

For this reason she had to glean '*until evening*'; had she availed herself of Boaz's charity she could have finished much earlier (*Ibn Yachya*).

sheaves; do not embarrass her. ¹⁶ *And even deliberately pull out some for her from the heaps and leave them for her to glean; don't rebuke her.'*

¹⁷ *So she gleaned in the field until evening, and she beat out what she had gleaned — it came to about an ephah of barley.* ¹⁸ *She carried it and came to the city. Her mother-in-law saw what she had gleaned, and she took out and gave her what she had left over after eating her fill.*

¹⁹ *'Where did you glean today?' her mother-in-law asked her. 'Where did you work? May the one that*

וַתַּחְבֹּט אֵת אֲשֶׁר לִקֵּטָה — *And she beat out what she had gleaned* — to make it easier to carry. The burden of carrying home the ears still attached to the stalks would have been too much for her *(Midrash Lekach Tov).*

The *Iggeres Shmuel* also suggests that Ruth was afraid to travel the roads alone. Had she not beaten the stalks into flour, she would have had to make two or three trips carrying stalks. This she wanted to avoid.

וַיְהִי כְּאֵיפָה שְׂעֹרִים — *And it came to about an ephah of barley.* Very heavy to carry *(Ibn Ezra).*

An *ephah* equals three *seahs* [see Exodus 17:36 where an *ephah* equals ten *omers.* (An omer is a day's food for one person). Thus, Ruth's yield from her first day of gleaning was sufficient to feed Naomi and herself for five days — a rather impressive amount].

18. וַתִּשָּׂא וַתָּבוֹא הָעִיר — *She carried it and came to the city.* She went directly home without stopping or detouring *(Midrash Lekach Tov).*

She went to Naomi that day to ask permission to accept Boaz' invitation and remain henceforth with his maidens *(Rav Arama).*

וַתֵּרֶא חֲמוֹתָהּ אֵת אֲשֶׁר לִקֵּטָה — *Her mother-in-law saw what she had gleaned.* Ruth had worked so quickly, that darkness had not yet descended, and Naomi was still able to see Ruth approaching by daylight *(Iggeres Shmuel).*

Ruth did not go about pompously displaying her gleanings; her mother-in-law looked into her packages to see *(Rav Alkebetz).*

אֵת אֲשֶׁר הוֹתִרָה מִשָּׂבְעָהּ — *what she had left over after eating her fill.* Iggeres Shmuel stresses 'her' fill — i.e. someone else might have eaten more; Ruth purposely left food for her mother-in-law.

19. אֵיפֹה לִקַּטְתְּ הַיּוֹם — *Where did you glean today?* Seeing such an abundant load, Naomi knew that the gleaning had to have been done in the field of a particularly friendly owner *(Alkabetz).*

וְאָנָה עָשִׂית — *And where did you work?* Besides the gleanings, Ruth

מַכִּירֵךְ בָּרוּךְ וַתַּגֵּד לַחֲמוֹתָהּ אֵת אֲשֶׁר־
עָשְׂתָה עִמּוֹ וַתֹּאמֶר שֵׁם הָאִישׁ אֲשֶׁר
עָשִׂיתִי עִמּוֹ הַיּוֹם בֹּעַז: וַתֹּאמֶר נָעֳמִי
לְכַלָּתָהּ בָּרוּךְ הוּא לַיהוֹה אֲשֶׁר לֹא־עָזַב
חַסְדּוֹ אֶת־הַחַיִּים וְאֶת־הַמֵּתִים וַתֹּאמֶר

פרק ב
ב

also brought back leftovers from the afternoon meal to which Boaz had invited her. Naomi therefore asked *'where did you glean today, yielding such a large produce; and where did you work*, even bringing back left-over food?' (*Iggeres Shmuel*).

The quality of the leftovers made it obvious that Ruth could not have merely spent the day gleaning, but must have performed some extra work to have earned so sumptuous a meal; on the other hand, the sheer abundance of her gleanings bespoke a full day of toil in the field. Therefore, in bewilderment, Naomi asked her both questions: *'where did you glean today and where did you work? —* a kind person must have befriended you' (*Malbim*).

The *Iggeres Shmuel* notes that it was unusual for the gleaners to beat the stalks while still in the field; usually the landowner would not allow it, and they would have to carry the stalks home and beat it there. Seeing Ruth coming home with beaten grain, Naomi was prompted to ask her: *'Where did you work?* Which owner was kind enough to allow you to beat the stalks in his field?'

יְהִי מַכִּירֵךְ בָּרוּךְ — *May the one that gave you such generous notice be blessed.* [Lit. 'May he that recognized you be blessed']. 'May blessing alight upon the head of the

field-owner who so generously permitted you to glean in his field!' (*Rashi*).

'I hope that this man's intentions are blessed and that it was not lust which prompted him to be so extraordinarily kind to you' (*Iggeres Shmuel*).

An alternate interpretation: Naomi said: The large amount you gleaned in one day is quite impressive; how did you manage it? יְהִי מַכִּירֵךְ בָּרוּךְ! — I am certain that the *'man who will come to know you'* some day as his wife *'will indeed be blessed'* — having such an industrious wife as you! (*Vilna Gaon*)

Ruth modestly *'told her mother-in-law all that had occurred'* — that it was not her zeal which allowed her to glean so much; but the kindness of Boaz (*Alshich*)

וַתַּגֵּד לַחֲמוֹתָהּ — *And she told her mother-in-law.* וַתַּגֵּד, *'told'* has a harsher connotation than וַתֹּאמֶר, *said.* Ruth was angered by Naomi's suggestion that the land-owner's intentions were not honorable, so she detailed all that had happened and revealed his name (*Iggeres Shmuel*).

Ruth explained that the special kindness was not for any labor performed by her, but rather because the landowner was impressed with the stories circulating about her (*Malbim*).

שֵׁם הָאִישׁ ... בֹּעַז — *The name of the man with whom I worked is Boaz.*

took such generous notice of you be blessed.' So she told her mother-in-law whom she had worked by, and said: 'The name of the man by whom I worked today is Boaz.'

²⁰ *Naomi said to her daughter-in-law: 'Blessed be he of HASHEM, for not failing in his kindness to the living or to the dead! 'The man is closely related to*

'As the judge of Israel, Boaz was greatly impressed with the rumors about my special relationship with you and my conversion, so he rewarded me with extra food (*Malbim*).

[Apparently, Ruth was making a simple revelation, still not aware that Boaz was related to them. Naomi, however, was especially delighted at hearing Boaz's name. She felt that Boaz, as a cousin and as a recent widower, might feel obligated to enter into a levirate marriage with Ruth thus perpetuating the name of Machlon.]

אֲשֶׁר עָשִׂיתִי עִמּוֹ — *By whom I worked*. [Lit. 'with whom I wrought']. The *Midrash* comments in a homiletical fashion: The verse does not read אֲשֶׁר עָשָׂה עִמָּדִי, *who has wrought for me*; but אֲשֶׁר עָשִׂיתִי עִמּוֹ, *I have wrought for him*. This teaches us that יוֹתֵר מֵאֲשֶׁר בַּעַל הַבַּיִת עוֹשֶׂה עִם הֶעָנִי, more than the householder does for the poor man, עוֹשֶׂה הֶעָנִי עִם בַּעַל הַבַּיִת, the poor man does for the householder [i.e. the householder benefits more — spiritually — from the charity he dispenses, than the poor man gains — temporally — from the charity he receives from the householder.]

20. בָּרוּךְ הוּא לַה׳ — *Blessed be he of HASHEM.* When Naomi heard that the man was Boaz she said: This

righteous man has no need of *my* blessing. בָּרוּךְ הוּא לַה׳ *He is blessed of HASHEM.*

[In the preceding verse she merely blessed him. Now that he was identified as Boaz, she blessed him in God's Name].

אֲשֶׁר לֹא עָזַב חַסְדּוֹ אֶת הַחַיִּים וְאֶת הַמֵּתִים — *For not failing in his kindness to the living or to the dead.* [There is a difference of opinion among the commentators whether the subject of this ambiguous phrase is God or Boaz. The translation follows *Ibn Ezra* and the majority of the commentators according to whom the subject is Boaz].

Naomi blessed Boaz who always sought to do kindness with the living and the dead. The kindness he did with the living (Ruth and Naomi) is obvious; the *kindness he did with the dead* is the gratification that the dead receive beyond the grave when benefits are bestowed upon their living relatives (*Iggeres Shmuel*).

'To the living' — by sustaining us; and *to the dead* — for he will ultimately perform יִבּוּם, *levirate marriage*, with you and he will thus do kindness to the memory of your dead husband' (*Alshich; Pri Chaim*).

According to *Rav Arama*, Naomi said: 'I have been wondering all

פרק ב כא לָהּ נָעֳמִי קָרוֹב לָנוּ הָאִישׁ מִגֹּאֲלֵנוּ הוּא:
כב וַתֹּאמֶר רוּת הַמּוֹאֲבִיָּה גַּם כִּי־אָמַר אֵלַי
עִם־הַנְּעָרִים אֲשֶׁר־לִי תִּדְבָּקִין עַד אִם־
כָּלּוּ אֵת כָּל־הַקָּצִיר אֲשֶׁר־לִי: וַתֹּאמֶר
נָעֳמִי אֶל־רוּת כַּלָּתָהּ טוֹב בִּתִּי כִּי תֵצְאִי

along how this man, famous for his kindness, has ignored us so since our arrival here. But now, seeing *that he has not failed in his kindness to us, the living, or to the memory of our dead husbands, I truly bless him.'*

The subject of the phrase, *'who has not failed in his kindness,* may be God. Thus, Naomi blessed him: *May he be blessed of HASHEM who has not failed in His kindness to the living* — in this world; *or to the dead* — in the world to come (*Iggeres Shmuel*).

קָרוֹב לָנוּ הָאִישׁ מִגֹּאֲלֵנוּ הוּא — *This man is closely related to us, he is one of our redeeming kinsmen.* The גֹּאֵל, *redeemer,* is the next of kin who is obligated to redeem the property which his impoverished relative was compelled to sell (see *Leviticus 25:25*).

'I no longer question this man's motives — he is our close relative and he is fulfilling the verse — מִבְּשָׂרְךָ לֹא תִתְעַלָּם, *'do not hide yourself from your own flesh'* [*Isaiah 58:7*] (*Ibn Yachya*).

The *Iggeres Shmuel* quotes a homiletic interpretation: מִגֹּאֲלֵנוּ הוּא — from him will eventually descend our Redeemer, a reference to the Messiah.

21. גַּם כִּי־אָמַר אֵלַי — *What's more, he even said to me.* 'You blessed him for what he did on my behalf.

He deserves your additional blessing for having also invited me to *'stay close to his workers'* (*Rav Yavetz*).

Rav Yehudah Ibn Shushan notes that at first Ruth did not mention Boaz's offer for her to stay with his maidens for fear that Naomi might suspect Boaz of dishonorable, ulterior motives. Once Naomi revealed that Boaz was a close kinsman, however, Ruth was reassured that Boaz was sincere so she confidently related his additional kind offer.

עִם־הַנְּעָרִים אֲשֶׁר־לִי תִּדְבָּקִין *Stay close to my workers* [lit. *'cleave to my young men.'* Our translation follows *Rav Alkabetz;* see below].

[There is a great discrepancy here between Boaz's actual words (*'stay here close to my maidens* — verse 8), and Ruth's version (*stay close to my young men').* Various interpretation are offered:

The *Midrash,* noting that in this verse her title *'Moabite'* was restored, comments, 'In truth she was still *'a Moabite,'* for Boaz said to her *'stay here close to my maidens,'* while she said, 'to my young men...'

The *Torah T'mimah* explains the *Midrash* in two possible ways: *'She was still a Moabite'* — and still imbued with the immorality of her upbringing. At the very least, it was very indelicate of her to describe

us,' Naomi then said to her; 'he is one of our redeeming kinsmen.'

²¹ And Ruth the Moabite said: 'What's more, he even said to me: Stay close to my workers, until they have finished all my harvest.' ²² Naomi said to her daughter-in-law Ruth: 'It is fine, my daughter, that you go out with his young women, so that you will

Boaz as asking her to keep company with his young *men.* Scripture refers to her as a Moabite, as an implied rebuke as if to say, "Spoken like a descendent of the nation that was born in incest." Or, as a Moabite, Ruth was not intimately familiar with the Hebrew differentiation between the masculine and feminine forms. In the Moabite language, like English, most nouns do not have separate male and female forms. Ruth mistakenly used the masculine form without intending to be suggestive, because, as the *Midrash* interprets, "*she was a Moabite!*" Naomi tactfully corrected her mistake [next verse].

Rav Alkabetz feels that Ruth simply used נְעָרִים as a general term for *'workers'* without making a distinction between male and female workers.

The *Simchas haRegel* suggests that Ruth had become aware of the recently publicized law permitting her, as a female Moabite to 'enter the Assembly of God.' She was, of course, anxious to tell this to her mother-in-law, but, out of modesty, she alluded to it by hinting that Boaz told her she could now *'cleave to one of his young men'* i.e. is henceforth permitted to marry an Israelite. [See comment of *Simchas haRegel* next verse].

The *Besuras Eliyahu* notes, that in any case, the phrase גַּם כִּי־אָמַר אֵלַי *'what's more, he said to me'* is obscure. He suggests that Ruth's intention was to convey the idea to Naomi that she held Boaz and his men in such high esteem that she remarked, 'I would listen to him, גַּם כִּי אָמַר אֵלִי, *even if her were to tell me* עִם הַנְּעָרִים אֲשֶׁר לִי תִּדְבָּקִין, *'stay close to my young men.'*

22. .. אֶל־רוּת כַּלָּתָהּ טוֹב בִּתִּי — *To Ruth, her daughter-in-law ... fine, my daughter.* [Note how Naomi's motherly response is accented in this verse by the contrasting use of *'mother-in-law'* and *'daughter'*].

According to the interpretation of *Simchas haRegel* [see his comm. end of previous verse], Naomi answered: 'Fine, I am overjoyed to learn that you are now permitted to marry within the fold. As for the practical matter of how to respond to Boaz, yes, you may dwell with his maidens.'

כִּי תֵצְאִי עִם נַעֲרוֹתָיו — *That you go out with his young women.* 'I am sure that if Boaz invited you to associate with his young men he knows them well and they are צַדִּיקִים, righteous, and above reproach. Nevertheless, my motherly advice is *'go out with his young women'* (Rashba haLevi).

פרק ב עִם־נַעֲרוֹתָיו וְלֹא יִפְגְּעוּ־בָךְ בְּשָׂדֶה אַחֵר:

כג וַתִּדְבַּק בְּנַעֲרוֹת בֹּעַז לְלַקֵּט עַד־כְּלוֹת קְצִיר הַשְּׂעֹרִים וּקְצִיר הַחִטִּים וַתֵּשֶׁב אֶת־חֲמוֹתָהּ:

פרק ג א וַתֹּאמֶר לָהּ נָעֳמִי חֲמוֹתָהּ בִּתִּי הֲלֹא

א־ב אֲבַקֶּשׁ־לָךְ מָנוֹחַ אֲשֶׁר יִיטַב־לָךְ: וְעַתָּה הֲלֹא בֹעַז מֹדַעְתָּנוּ אֲשֶׁר הָיִית אֶת־

וְלֹא יִפְגְּעוּ־בָךְ בְּשָׂדֶה אַחֵר — *So that you will not be annoyed in another field.* [lit. 'and they will not annoy you in another field'].

[Boaz had cautioned his men against molesting her in any way (verse 16) and Ruth was thus safe in Boaz's fields; she had no such assurances in other fields.].

[It is perhaps possible to translate וַיִּפְגַּע — 'be met,' i.e. 'so that you will not be met in another field and appear to be כְּפוּיָה טוֹב, ungracious of his hospitality].

The *Malbim* adds: 'and come under suspicion.'

23. וַתִּדְבַּק בְּנַעֲרוֹת בֹּעַז לְלַקֵּט — *So she stayed close to Boaz's young women to glean.* Most commentators feel that she spent the entire harvest period with Boaz's young women away from Naomi.

According to *Iggeres Shmuel*, the verse specifies 'to glean' — only during gleaning time, i.e. Ruth stayed close to the young women only during the day, when she gleaned. She did not sleep away from Naomi for the duration of the harvest; she went home every night so as not to leave her mother-in-law alone.

עַד־כְּלוֹת קְצִיר הַשְּׂעֹרִים וּקְצִיר הַחִטִּים — *Until the end of the barley harvest and of the wheat harvest.* A total period of three months (*Midrash*).

The *Malbim* notes that this period of time is equal to the יְמֵי הַבְּחָנָה, the ninety day waiting-period a new convert must wait before she can marry. After this period was up, she began considering יִבּוּם, levirate remarriage .

וַתֵּשֶׁב אֶת־חֲמוֹתָהּ — *She stayed* [lit. 'sat'] *with her mother-in-law.* Although the verse mentions that Ruth *cleaved* [וַתִּדְבַּק], to the young women, nevertheless, her deep love for and 'cleaving' to [compare 1:14] Naomi never subsided. As soon as the harvest was over she resumed living with her mother-in-law, because Ruth's love for Naomi surpassed all other considerations (*Iggeres Shmuel; Malbim*).

Also, the verse ends with וַתֵּשֶׁב אֶת־חֲמוֹתָהּ, 'she stayed with her mother-in-law,' to emphasize that although Ruth was away in the fields gleaning, her thoughts were with Naomi *as if she were living with her* (*Iggeres Shmuel*).

not be annoyed in another field.'

²³ *So she stayed close to Boaz' young women to glean, until the end of the barley harvest and of the wheat harvest. Then she stayed (at home) with her mother-in-law.*

Naomi, her mother-in-law, said to her: 'My daughter, I must seek security for you, that it may go well with you. ² Now, Boaz, our relative, with

III
Prefatory Remarks

[When reading this chapter, we must attempt to approach it by comprehending fully the purity and innocence with which the Sages — in the context of Biblical times — understood the episode as being fully לְשֵׁם שָׁמַיִם, for the sake of Heaven. 'Two women sacrificed themselves for the sake of the tribe of Judah,' — declares the Yalkut Shimoni, — 'Tamar and Ruth.'

During the harvest, while Ruth spent her time gleaning in Boaz's field and had at least limited access to him, Naomi dreamt and hoped that Boaz would bestir himself and 'redeem' Ruth, thus perpetuating Machlon's memory.

But now the harvest was over and Boaz had made no such move. The future prospect of Ruth's meeting Boaz was remote, and Naomi feared that since Boaz had not taken the initiative when Ruth was so at hand, he could hardly be expected to respond to more conventional suggestions of marriage when Ruth was out of sight. For all they knew, Boaz might even be offended at the mere suggestion of his marrying Ruth. After all, Naomi was destitute, Ruth was of foreign, Moabite stock, and Boaz was a man of substance, the Judge and leader of the generation. Could she expect to approach him and simply ask him to redeem and marry this girl?

Naomi became convinced that the condition of stalemate could not continue. Things had to be brought to a head one way or the other.

It must be remembered that the prohibition of יִחוּד פְּנוּיָה, the seclusion of a man with an unmarried woman — later forbidden by the court of King David — had not yet been proclaimed. Naomi therefore decided that the best course of action — however daring and unconventional — was for Ruth herself to approach Boaz under the most intimate and personal circumstances and remind him of his responsibility to the family of his dead uncle, Elimelech. In a personal confrontation — convinced that her motives were sincere — his compassion for her bitter plight might be evoked. (See Introduction.) — M.Z.]

1. וַתֹּאמֶר לָהּ נָעֳמִי חֲמוֹתָהּ — *Naomi, her mother-in-law, said to her.* Naomi and Ruth both interpreted Boaz's actions towards Ruth in his field as if he was considering marriage with her. They waited until the harvest was over and Boaz was free of business worries. Still, he made no move in that direction. Naomi therefore sought out ways to

expedite the matter. She was convinced that a direct action was needed (Kol Yehuda; Akeidas Yitzchak).

בְּתִּי — *My daughter.* [The word בְּתִּי, 'my daughter,' is treated differently throughout the Book, according to its context; see Comm. on 2:2; 2:8; and 2:22.] In this case, the Com-

mentaries observe, *'my daughter,'* is stressed because human nature is such that when one's daughter-in-law is left widowed, the mother-in-law begrudges her remarriage. However, when a daughter is widowed, her mother encourages quick remarriage. Therefore, Naomi addressed Ruth as follows:

'Although I am your mother-in-law, I feel as if you are my own daughter, and I seek only the very best security in marriage for you, that it may go well with you. If you counter: Boaz is an old man [he was 80 at the time! — (Midrash)] and how 'good' could such a marriage be?' — Yes! Earthly pleasures might not be plentiful, but the Heavenly reward for being married to such a צַדִּיק, *righteous man, as he — and the righteous children that would result from such a marriage — is abundant! (Nachal Eshkol; Iggeres Shmuel).*

הֲלֹא אֲבַקֶּשׁ־לָךְ מָנוֹחַ — *I must seek security for you* [lit. 'shall I not find 'rest' for you?']. A woman has no security ['rest'] until she marries *(Rashi)* — [compare Naomi's blessing in 1:9 וּמְצֶאןָ מְנוּחָה, *'that you may find security'*].

On an esoteric level, the *Zohar Chadash* explains the use of the term *'rest'* as a synonym for marriage: The first husband's 'spirit' continues to stir within his widow's body until she remarries and replaces it with a new spirit. Naomi, therefore, suggested to Ruth that she must seek to quiet the spiritual turmoil within herself — the rem-

nants of Machlon — by marriage, to as near a kin as possible and thereby find *'rest'*.

אֲשֶׁר יִיטַב לָךְ — *That it may go well with you.* 'I am not concerned with the memory of my son; your welfare is foremost in my mind' *(Meishiv Nefesh).*

[The phrase may also be interpreted in the spiritual sense: 'Your marriage to this צַדִּיק, righteous man, though he is old, will bring you spiritual happiness.' As the *Talmud* interprets לְמַעַן יִיטַב לָךְ, *that it may go well with you* [*Deut. 5:16*] — 'in the world to come *(Kiddushin 39b)*].

[The word יִיטַב which we have translated *'it' may go well,* can also be translated *'he' may do good.* The *'he'* could conceivably apply to the new husband who will *'treat you well'*].

2. הֲלֹא בֹעַז מֹדַעְתָּנוּ אֲשֶׁר הָיִית אֶת־נַעֲרוֹתָיו — *Now, Boaz, our relative, with whose maidens you have been.* Naomi, afraid that Ruth would possibly have a negative attitude towards marrying this octogenarian, enumerates his qualities: 'His name *Boaz* is known and familiar to all; *he is our relative,* from the same aristocratic family as your late husband, and he is a "redeemer" of ours; you are personally familiar with his righteousness and kindnesses *having been with his maidens ...' (Iggeres Shmuel).*

אֲשֶׁר הָיִית אֶת־נַעֲרוֹתָיו — *With whose maidens you have been.* [A

*whose maidens you have been, will be winnowing
barley tonight on the threshing floor. ³ Therefore,
bathe and annoint yourself, don your finery, and go
down to the threshing floor, but do not make*

reference to verses 22 and 23 of the preceding chapter.]

הַלַּיְלָה — *Tonight.* [Naomi was certain that Boaz would spend the night there because] 'the generation was crime-ridden, and he would sleep on the threshing floor to guard his grain from thieves' *(Rashi).*

Now that the harvest was over, and it was the most productive one in many years, Naomi knew that Boaz would certainly be well-disposed toward taking a new wife to share his good fortune *(Meishiv Nefesh).*

The *Malbim* comments that there must have been workers at the threshing floor during working hours. If any of them were to see Ruth going to the threshing floor that particular night, they would assume she was going to visit the girls with whom she had worked previously, and to rejoice with her relative Boaz over his abundant harvest.

3. וְרָחַצְתְּ — *Bathe* [lit. 'wash']. Since the verse does not specify hands or face, but simply 'bathe,' in a general sense, and since Naomi would not have to instruct Ruth to do such a basic thing, the *Midrash* interprets this verse in the spiritual sense: וְרָחַצְתְּ, *wash yourself,* 'clean yourself from your idolatry,' [i.e. take a ritual bath] *(Torah T'mimah).*

The *Bach* quotes a *Midrash haNe'elam* that a convert is not free of the remnant of his impurity until

three months following conversion. The three months were now ended [see *Comm.* to verse 1], and Naomi thus instructed her to take a ritual bath and cleanse herself entirely.

Rav Breuer notes that Naomi specified these Sabbath-like preparations to ready Ruth for her holy mission because she was preparing for a solemn, holy occasion.

וְסַכְתְּ — *And anoint yourself.* With perfume — as was the custom of Jewish nobility, both men and women *(Ibn Ezra).*

The *Midrash* interprets anoint yourself 'with good deeds and righteous conduct.'

וְשַׂמְתְּ שִׂמְלֹתַיִךְ עָלָיִךְ — *Don your finery.* [Lit. 'place your dress upon yourself'].

'Was she then naked? — It must refer to Sabbath garments. It was from this verse that Rav Chaninah said: A man should have two sets of garments, one for weekdays and one for Sabbath *(Yerushalmi: Pe'ah 8:6)*

According to the *Akeidas Yitzchak* and *Malbim,* Naomi did not advise Ruth to go down to the threshing floor *wearing* her Sabbath finery. The verse says וְשַׂמְתְּ, *place,* not וְלָבַשְׁתְּ, *wear, dress.* Rather, Naomi advised Ruth to *place her dress* on her, i.e. take along her Sabbath clothes and change into them at the threshing floor after everyone else was gone and she was in hiding.

The *k'siv* [traditional spelling] of the word is in first person: ושמתי, *'I*

ד לָאִישׁ עַד כַּלֹּתוֹ לֶאֱכֹל וְלִשְׁתּוֹת: וַיְהִי
בְשָׁכְבוֹ וְיָדַעַתְּ אֶת־הַמָּקוֹם אֲשֶׁר יִשְׁכַּב־
שָׁם וּבָאת וְגִלִּית מַרְגְּלֹתָיו וְשָׁכָבְתִּי*

ה וְהוּא יַגִּיד לָךְ אֵת אֲשֶׁר תַּעֲשִׂין: וַתֹּאמֶר
אֵלֶיהָ כֹּל אֲשֶׁר־תֹּאמְרִי * אֶעֱשֶׂה. וַתֵּרֶד

ו הַגֹּרֶן וַתַּעַשׂ כְּכֹל אֲשֶׁר־צִוַּתָּה חֲמוֹתָהּ:

ז וַיֹּאכַל בֹּעַז וַיֵּשְׁתְּ וַיִּיטַב לִבּוֹ וַיָּבֹא

*וְשָׁכַבְתְּ ק'

*אֵלַי קרי ולא כתיב

---

will dress you,' to imply that Naomi
intimated 'my זְכֻיּוֹת, merits, will
enhance your appearance' (*Shoresh
Yishai*).

וְיָרַדְתְּ הַגֹּרֶן — *And go down to the
threshing floor.* [The *k'siv* is first
person: וירדתי, *'I will go down,'*
which the *Midrash* interprets: 'my
merits will descend with you.'— i.e.
'through my merits the plan will
work, and Boaz will not be angry
with you' (*Nachal Eshkol*).

'Go down' is used, because the
threshing floor was situated below
the city (*Midrash*).

אַל־תִּוָּדְעִי לָאִישׁ — *Do not make
yourself known to the man.* 'The'
man — i.e. to Boaz (*Rashi*).

Remain hidden (*Ralbag*), and the
workers will assume that you left
before them (*Malbim*).

4. וַיְהִי בְשָׁכְבוֹ — *And when he lies
down,* i.e. when you see him preparing to retire, note his sleeping
place. Then later, in the dark of
night when he is fast asleep, you
can easily locate him (*Targum; Iggeres Shmuel*).

וְגִלִּית מַרְגְּלֹתָיו — *Uncover his feet.*
The *Malbim* suggests that Naomi
was proposing a method of
reminding Boaz, as a redeemer, of
his moral obligation to marry Ruth.

A brother who refuses to enter into
יִבּוּם, *a levirate marriage,* undergoes
a ceremony of *chalitzah* which in-
volves the removal of his shoe [see
Deut. 25:5-10]. For Naomi to
directly suggest that Boaz marry
Ruth would have been a gross impropriety. Therefore she asked
Ruth to *'uncover his feet,'* a gesture
reminiscent of *chalitzah,* in the
hope that it would make Boaz aware
of his moral obligation to her.

וְשָׁכָבְתְּ — *And lie down.* [Here, too,
the *ksiv* [traditional spelling] of the
imperative verb 'lie down' is written
as if it were a first person verb—
וְשָׁכַבְתִּי, *I will lie down,* as if to say
that Naomi's merit will accompany
her (see preceding verse) and Naomi
thus identified herself with the
deed].

וְהוּא יַגִּיד לָךְ... — *He will tell you
what you are to do.* Whether you or
he should undertake to approach a
closer redeemer (*Malbim*).

The *Besuras Eliyahu* takes הוּא,
'he' to refer to God, i.e. Naomi said:
'I can't possibly know what Boaz
will say or how you should respond.
Follow my directions and God will
inspire you to say the right thing.'

5. כֹּל אֲשֶׁר־תֹּאמְרִי [אֵלַי] אֶעֱשֶׂה — *All
that you say to me I will do.* The

*yourself known to the man until he has finished
eating and drinking. ⁴ And when he lies down, note
the place where he lies, and go over, uncover his feet,
and lie down. He will tell you what you are to do.'
⁵ She replied, 'All that you say to me I will do.'
⁶ So she went down to the threshing floor and did
everything as her mother-in-law instructed her.
⁷ Boaz ate and drank and his heart was merry. He*

word אֵלַי *'to me'* is read, but it does
not appear in the written Hebrew
text. This, and all textual readings,
as transmitted by the Soferim, are
Halachah from Moses at Sinai
(Nedarim 37b). [i.e. the 'contradiction' between the written and
read versions is apparent but not
real. Each is valid; the discrepancy
is to teach us the deeper meaning
implied in the text. The Commentaries offer serveral interpreta-
tions]:

The absence of אֵלַי, *'to me'*, in the
Hebrew, suggests that Ruth cast her
whole dependence upon Naomi,
and removed *'herself'* for all decision making. Ruth vowed to do not
only what Naomi had *specifically
instructed her* to do, but even what
she only *alluded* to, indirectly
through others. Moreover, 'even
those instructions which were not
אֵלַי, *"to me,"* i.e. for my own
benefit, I will still do' (*Iggeres
Shmuel*).

According to *Akeidas Yitzchak*,
אֵלַי, *to me*, is read but not written to
convey that although the advice
seemed improper *'to her,'* nevertheless Ruth would obey because
Naomi had given it.

M'lo ha'Omer suggests that the
omitted אֵלַי demonstrates the extent
to which Ruth left matters בִּידֵי
שָׁמַיִם, in the hands of Heaven — as

if she excluded *herself*, and had no
personal stake in their resolution;
she left everything to God's beneficence.

'Although you tell me that Boaz
will instruct me, I will first consult
you, and *all that you say to me I will
do* (*Alshich; Malbim*).

6. וַתֵּרֶד הַגֹּרֶן וַתַּעַשׂ... — *So she went
down to the threshing floor and did
everything her mother-in-law told
her*. Ruth didn't follow her bidding
in every detail. She feared that by
going to the threshing floor per-
fumed and festively attired she
would attract curious glances making it impossible to carry out her
mission discreetly. Therefore, the
verse tells us first וַתֵּרֶד הַגֹּרֶן, *she
went down to the threshing floor* —
and then *did everything her
mother-in-law told her* Only after
arriving at the threshing floor did
Ruth follow Naomi's bidding by
perfuming and dressing in her best
finery (*Rashi; Malbim*).

אֲשֶׁר־צִוַּתָּה חֲמוֹתָהּ — *As her mother-
in-law instructed her.* Although
Ruth didn't quite understand or fully agree with the plan, she did it
blindly and respectfully, *because
her mother-in-law instructed her*
(*Besuras Eliyahu*).

7. וַיִּיטַב לִבּוֹ — *And his heart was
merry.* Having recited the grace

פרק ג

ח־ט

ח לִשְׁכַּב בְּקָצֶה הָעֲרֵמָה וַתָּבֹא בַלָּט וַתְּגַל
מַרְגְּלֹתָיו וַתִּשְׁכָּב: וַיְהִי בַּחֲצִי הַלַּיְלָה
וַיֶּחֱרַד הָאִישׁ וַיִּלָּפֵת וְהִנֵּה אִשָּׁה שֹׁכֶבֶת
ט מַרְגְּלֹתָיו: וַיֹּאמֶר מִי־אָתְּ וַתֹּאמֶר אָנֹכִי
רוּת אֲמָתֶךָ וּפָרַשְׂתָּ כְנָפֶךָ עַל־אֲמָתְךָ כִּי

after meals (Midrash) and having added a special prayer thanking God for heeding his prayers and putting an end to the famine [see Comm. 1:6] (Targum).

His heart was merry — because he studied Torah (Rashi).

The Sages note the difference between a צַדִּיק, righteous man, and a רָשָׁע, wicked man. Boaz' *heart was merry*, and the presence of a pure, beautiful and festively attired woman was a great temptation. Nevertheless, he mastered his impulses and did nothing in the least immoral. Of the wicked Ahasuerus, on the other hand, we find that when 'his heart was merry' [Esther 1:10] he ordered his queen to appear before his guests unclothed (Iggeres Shmuel).

בְּקָצֶה הָעֲרֵמָה — At the end of the grain pile. To guard his grain from that immoral generation (Midrash) [see Comm. verse 2, s. v. הַלַּיְלָה, 'tonight']. Also because they are so scrupulous about earning their money honestly, the righteous are zealous about their property (Sotah 12a).

וַתָּבֹא בַלָּט — And she came stealthily 'בְּנַחַת, quietly' (Rashi). Radak derives the word from לוט, wrapped, and translates: 'She came with her face covered.

8. בַּחֲצִי הַלַּיְלָה — In the middle of the night when he got up to study Torah. . . (Iggeres Shmuel)

וַיֶּחֱרַד הָאִישׁ — The man was startled. 'He could easily have cursed her but God put it in his heart to bless her, as it is said [verse 10] בְּרוּכָה אַתְּ לַה', Be blessed of HASHEM' (Midrash)

וַיִּלָּפֵת — And turned about. [So Ibn Ezra; according to Rashi]: He thought she was a demon and he wanted to scream so she 'placated' him.

The Talmud, deriving the word from לֶפֶת, turnip, translates: 'His skin hardened like a turnip' [from fright] (Sanhedrin 19b)

וְהִנֵּה אִשָּׁה — A woman. 'Purest of women' (Midrash).

He touched her head and realized it was a woman (Rashi)

Perhaps she whispered: 'Don't be afraid!' and he recognized it as a woman's voice, or he distinguished a womanly form by the light of the moon (Ibn Ezra).

'How few words are used to express the 'fear' Boaz must have felt during this incident! The leader of that generation, involved all his life in elevating the morals of his people, spends a night in his threshing floor to guard against robbers in that lawless generation, wakes up in the middle of the night and finds a woman lying at his feet! What audacity she must have had; how embarrasing for him, what an awkward position to be put in to!

Under normal circumstances he should have cursed her and

went to lie down at the end of the grain pile, and she came stealthily, uncovered his feet, and lay down. ⁸ In the middle of the night the man was startled, and turned about — there was a woman lying at his feet!

⁹ 'Who are you?' he asked. And she answered: 'I am your handmaid, Ruth. Spread your robe over your handmaid; for you are a redeemer.'

banished her for her unseemly act. But the sincerity of Ruth and the determination of Naomi caused Providence to inspire Boaz with a compassion for Ruth. Recognizing her sincerity, he did not curse her — instead he blessed her. This is but another one of the many miracles wrought for the Jews in the middle of the night throughout their history.

As interpreted by the Sages, this is the incident King David referred to when generations later he would get up at midnight and recount all the miracles wrought for the Jews throughout history: חֲצוֹת לַיְלָה — *'At midnight I rise to thank You for Your righteous judgments. (Psalms 119;62)* And among the miracles he recounted was the miracle wrought for his great-grandparents, that midnight on the threshing floor. As the *Midrash* states: *'And the righteousness which you have wrought for my great-grandfather and great-grandmother,* for had Boaz hastily cursed her but once, from where would I have come?' *(Nachalas Yosef)*

9. וַיֹּאמֶר מִי־אָתְּ — *'Who are you?' he said. 'A woman,'* she answered. 'Married or unmarried?' She answered, 'unmarried.' *(Midrash).*

וּפָרַשְׂתָּ כְנָפֶךָ עַל־אֲמָתְךָ — *Spread your robe over your handmaid.*

[כְּנָפֶיךָ can be understood as *'your wings'*; i.e. 'protection'.]

The 'wing' is a metaphor borrowed from birds — who shield each other with their wings during mating. Therefore it is used as a symbol of marriage *(Malbim).*

Most commentators, however, understand the word in the sense of 'corner' of a garment, i.e. *'place the corner of your garment over me as a token of marriage'* *(Rashi).*

'Take me as your wife, with a proper wedding ceremony' *(Iggeres Shmuel).*

'Cursed be the wicked' says the *Midrash* [noting the difference between the behavior of Ruth and others]. In the case of Potiphar's wife and Joseph it is said [Gen. 312] *'Lie with me',* but here Ruth said: *'Spread your robe over your handmaid'*

כִּי גֹאֵל אָתָּה — *For you are a redeemer,* and, as such, it is incumbent upon you to redeem the estate of my husband in accordance with Lev. 25. Ruth explained to Boaz that she and her mother-in-law are forced to sell their inheritance, and as a redeemer, it is his obligation to buy the property so that it would remain in the family. She then made an additional request: 'Take possession of me, too, so that the name of the deceased will be perpetuated on his property. If you marry me, peo-

גֹאֵל אָתָּה: וַיֹּאמֶר בְּרוּכָה אַתְּ לַיהוה יֹ
בִּתִּי הֵיטַבְתְּ חַסְדֵּךְ הָאַחֲרוֹן מִן-הָרִאשׁוֹן
לְבִלְתִּי-לֶכֶת אַחֲרֵי הַבַּחוּרִים אִם-דַּל
וְאִם-עָשִׁיר: וְעַתָּה בִּתִּי אַל-תִּירְאִי כֹּל יֹא
אֲשֶׁר-תֹּאמְרִי אֶעֱשֶׂה-לָּךְ כִּי יוֹדֵעַ כָּל-
שַׁעַר עַמִּי כִּי אֵשֶׁת חַיִל אָתְּ: וְעַתָּה כִּי יֹב
אָמְנָם כִּי אִם* גֹאֵל אָנֹכִי וְגַם יֵשׁ גֹאֵל

*כתיב ולא קרי

ple will say: She was the wife of Machlon' whenever I visit the field (Rashi).

'And it is your duty to 'redeem' the soul of Machlon and marry me...' (Alshich)

The Bach states, esoterically, that she hinted: 'Only from both of us together will the Davidic dynasty descend, not from only one of us.'

10. בְּרוּכָה אַתְּ לַה׳ בִּתִּי — 'Be blessed of HASHEM, my daughter. [The Sages stress Boaz's righteousness and superhuman self control. He recognized her mission as a difficult one and wholly devoted לְשֵׁם שָׁמַיִם, for the sake of Heaven. No evil thoughts came to his mind. He was moved, and he blessed her.]

'He might easily have cursed her, but God put it in his heart to bless her' (Midrash).

Boaz compared this incident in his mind with the incidents of Lot's daughters and Judah and Tamar. He said, 'You, my daughter, are more blessed than Lot's daughters and Tamar, because your actions do not involve serious prohibitions such as theirs did (Kol Yehuda).

הֵיטַבְתְּ חַסְדֵּךְ הָאַחֲרוֹן מִן-הָרִאשׁוֹן — You have made your latest act of kindness greater than the first. For a woman in the prime of life to give up the opportunity to marry a young man in favor of marrying a very old one is a great sacrifice. Yet you are prepared to do this solely to perpetuate the name of your late husband. This, your latest act of kindness, is even greater than your earlier kindness to your mother-in-law. [According to Bach it is also greater than the kindness you did your soul by embracing Judaism...] (Ralbag; Rav Arama; Iggeres Shmuel; Alshich)

לְבִלְתִּי-לֶכֶת אַחֲרֵי הַבַּחוּרִים — In that you have not gone after the young men. With your beauty you could have whoever you want, and yet you honor your husband's memory by choosing me, though I am old, because I am a close relative (Ibn Ezra; Malbim).

אִם-דַּל וְאִם-עָשִׁיר — Be they poor or rich. 'Rav Shmuel b. Isaac said. A woman usually prefers a poor young man to an old rich man' (Midrash).

11. כֹּל אֲשֶׁר-תֹּאמְרִי אֶעֱשֶׂה-לָּךְ — Whatever you say I will do for you! Boaz reassured her that he was not merely putting her off with soothing words (Meishiv Nefesh).

'I will even do anything you request of me in the future, but at the

¹⁰ *And he said: Be blessed of HASHEM, my
daughter; you have made your latest act of kindness
greater than the first, in that you have not gone after
the younger men, be they poor or rich. ¹¹ And now,
my daughter, do not fear; whatever you say, I will do
for you; for all the men in the gate of my people
know that you are a worthy woman. ¹² Now while it
is true that I am a redeemer; there is also another*

moment we face an obstacle: there
is a redeemer closer than I' *(Iggeres
Shmuel).*

Knowing he could not marry her
immediately, he reassured her in
this way because he did not want
her to be discouraged for having approached him *(Alshich).*

כִּי יוֹדֵעַ כָּל־שַׁעַר עַמִּי — *For all the men
in the gate of my people know.* [Lit.
'the gate of my people knows — i.e.
those who assemble at the gate, the
gathering point of the city.]

'Those who sit at the gate of the
Great Sanhedrin' *(Targum).*

It now became manifestly clear to
Boaz why the law of 'Moabite not
Moabitess' 'happened' to be the
topic of discussion of the Sanhedrin
and was 'revealed' to them immediately prior to Ruth's arrival
(Nachal Eshkol).

Boaz said: My intentions are
compatible with yours. But don't
worry, even though you think that
the wise men at the gate will try to
dissuade me, saying it is below my
dignity to marry a Moabite girl,
have no fear. 'The people at the gate
know you are a worthy woman'
(Malbim).

The *Iggeres Shmuel* offers a different interpretation of these
verses: '*Do not fear, my daughter; I
want to marry you. And things will*

probably work out. '*I*' *will be the
one to do whatever you say. Only I
and the people of my gate [i.e.
Sanhedrin] are aware that as a
female Moabite you are now permitted to me — everyone else thinks
you are still prohibited. The other
redeemer definitely does not know
the law and he will demur, but, in
the event he does decide to redeem
you, then it is for the best. I promise
you, however, that if he does not
accept the responsibility of redeeming you with a good heart, I
myself will redeem you.*

כִּי אֵשֶׁת חַיִל אָתְּ — *That you are a
worthy woman* — and fit for a גִּבּוֹר
חַיִל, '*man of substance*' [2:1, i.e.
Boaz] *(Midrash Lekach Tov).*

12. כִּי גֹאֵל אָנֹכִי — *I am a redeemer.*
The written text has כִּי אִם גֹאֵל אָנֹכִי
— '*For if I am a redeemer;* but ac-
cording to the *Masorah* the word אִם
if, is כְּתִיב וְלֹא קְרִי, '*written but not
read*': This occurs several times in
Scripture and is a *halachah* from
Moses at Sinai *(Nedarim 37b)* [see
Comm. beginning of verse 5].

The word אִם is not read because
it implies uncertainty, while in fact
there *was* definitely another גּוֹאֵל
(Midrash Lekach Tov; Rashi).

Commenting on why the אִם is
written, *Rav Alkabetz* suggests that

יג קָרוֹב מִמֶּנִּי: לִינִי|הַלַּיְלָה וְהָיָה בַבֹּקֶר
אִם־יִגְאָלֵךְ טוֹב יִגְאָל וְאִם־לֹא יַחְפֹּץ
לְגָאֳלֵךְ וּגְאַלְתִּיךְ אָנֹכִי חַי־יהוה שִׁכְבִי
עַד־הַבֹּקֶר: וַתִּשְׁכַּב מַרְגְּלוֹתָו עַד־הַבֹּקֶר
וַתָּקָם בְּטֶרֶם יַכִּיר אִישׁ אֶת־רֵעֵהוּ
טו וַיֹּאמֶר אַל־יִוָּדַע כִּי־בָאָה הָאִשָּׁה הַגֹּרֶן:
וַיֹּאמֶר הָבִי הַמִּטְפַּחַת אֲשֶׁר־עָלַיִךְ

it implies a doubt that Boaz left un-stated. Boaz was impressed by Ruth's noble act and was flattered at the suggestion that he 'redeem' Ruth and raise up the memory of her husband but he was doubtful whether he could function in that capacity and have children due to his advanced age [he was eighty!].

וְגַם יֵשׁ גֹּאֵל קָרוֹב מִמֶּנִּי — *There is also another redeemer closer than I.* A brother of Elimelech; whereas Boaz was only a nephew. [see Comm. next verse] *(Rashi).*

[Boaz did not believe that the closer redeemer would exercise his right, but he was obliged to first consult him and give him the op-portunity of so doing.]

13. לִינִי הַלַּיְלָה — *Stay the night.* Without a husband *(Rashi).*

'This night you will spend without a husband, but you will not be without a husband for another night' *(Midrash).*

When Ruth heard, now for the first time, that there was a redeemer closer than Boaz, she grew dis-couraged and got up to leave. Boaz then asked her not to lose heart, but to remain the night, and then he swore to her that he is quite ready to

marry her if the other redeemer would not *(Rav Alkabetz).*

*[The *Minchas Shai* observes that in some texts the ל, *lamed* of לִינִי is enlarged, in some the נ, *nun* is enlarged, and in many manuscripts none are enlarged.]

אִם־יִגְאָלֵךְ טוֹב יִגְאָל — *If he will redeem you, fine! let him redeem.*

The *Midrash* states that Salmon, Tov, and Elimelech were brothers. Many commentators [e.g. *Alshich; Bach, Rav Arama, Malbim)* main-tain therefore that the word טוֹב, *Tov,* is the name of the closer redeemer, the '*Ploni Almoni*' refer-red to later. According to their in-terpretation, the verse translates thus: אִם־יִגְאָלֵךְ טוֹב, *if Tov will redeem you,* יִגְאָל, *let him redeem...'*

Ibn Ezra, however, disagrees: If Scripture, here identifies the redeemer as Tov, why should he be referred to as '*Ploni Almoni*' later? Rather the meaning is: *If he will redeem you fine,* he is a good man, etc.

The redeemer was not learned, and Boaz knew that if, by some chance, he would agree to redeem, it would be the result of shame, not of conviction. Therefore, the transla-tion is 'If he will redeem you from the goodness of his heart, let him

redeemer closer than I. **13** *Stay the night, then in the morning, if he will redeem you, fine! let him redeem. But if he does not want to redeem you, then I will redeem you "Chai HASHEM"! Lie down until the morning.'*

14 *So she lay at his feet until the morning and she arose before one man could recognize another, for he said: 'Let it not be known that the woman came to the threshing floor.'* **15** *And he said, 'Hold out the shawl you are wearing and grasp it.' She held it, and he*

---

redeem; if he does not so desire, then I will redeem' *(Shoresh Yishai).*

חַי־ה' — *Chai HASHEM!* [Lit. *'As HASHEM lives!* A Biblical form of oath]. Ruth accused him of paying lip-service to her request, so he jumped up and swore to her that he was sincere. Some Sages say he was addressing his יֵצֶר הָרַע, evil inclination *(Rashi).*

שִׁכְבִי עַד־הַבֹּקֶר — *lie down until the morning,* i.e., early in the morning, so you can leave at the crack of dawn and not be discovered *(Iggeres Shmuel).*

14. וַתִּשְׁכַּב מַרְגְּלוֹתָו עַד־הַבֹּקֶר — *So she lay at his feet until the morning.* [Some commentators see in the fact that מַרְגְּלוֹתָו is spelled defectively חסר, (it should be spelled מַרְגְּלוֹתָיו with a *yud*) that she did not lay close to his feet. Instead, out of modesty, she moved away].

בְּטֶרֶם יַכִּיר אִישׁ אֶת־רֵעֵהוּ — *Before one man could recognize another.* [רֵעֵהוּ, lit. *'his friend'*] The word בְּטֶרֶם, *before,* is spelled here with a

superfluous ו, *vav,* teaching that she spent six hours with him, the numerical equivalent of the letter ו, *vav. (Midrash);* and we can further appreciate from this length of time the extent of their self control *(Torah T'minah).*

וַיֹּאמֶר אַל־יִוָּדַע כִּי־בָאָה הָאִשָּׁה הַגֹּרֶן — *And he said, let it not be known that the woman came to the threshing floor.* The *Midrash* comments that he was addressing himself to God: "All that night Boaz lay stretched out upon his face and prayed, 'Lord of the Universe, it is revealed and known to you that I did not touch her; so may it be Your will that it not be known that the woman came *into* the threshing-floor, that the name of Heaven be not profaned through me.'"

He wasn't concerned for his own reputation; he was known as a צַדִּיק, *a righteous man,* and he was old — he would not be accused of unbecoming conduct. It was Ruth's reputation he was concerned with; after all *she* went out in the middle of the night! He therefore specified that it not be known that the woman *came to the threshing-floor (Alshich).*

וָאֶחֱזִי־בָהּ וַתֹּאחֶז בָּהּ וַיָּמָד שֵׁשׁ־שְׂעֹרִים טו
וַיָּשֶׁת עָלֶיהָ וַיָּבֹא הָעִיר: וַתָּבוֹא אֶל־
חֲמוֹתָהּ וַתֹּאמֶר מִי־אַתְּ בִּתִּי וַתַּגֶּד־לָהּ
אֵת כָּל־אֲשֶׁר עָשָׂה־לָהּ הָאִישׁ: וַתֹּאמֶר יז
שֵׁשׁ־הַשְּׂעֹרִים הָאֵלֶּה נָתַן לִי כִּי אָמַר
אֵלַי* רֵיקָם אֶל־חֲמוֹתֵךְ:
וַתֹּאמֶר שְׁבִי בִתִּי עַד אֲשֶׁר תֵּדְעִין אֵיךְ יח

15. וַיָּמָד שֵׁשׁ־שְׂעֹרִים — *And he measured out six measures of barley* [lit. *'and he measured six barleys'*]. The exact measure is not stated. The Talmud discusses this: 'What are *'six barleys'* Shall we translate it literally [i.e. six grains of barley] — But would [the magnanimous] Boaz give only six grains? On the other hand, if it means six se'ah's [the measure usually used on the field and in the threshing-floor (*Rashi*)], a woman cannot carry such a heavy weight! — Rather he symbolically alluded to her [by giving her a token six barley grains] that six righteous men each possessing six outstanding virtues, are destined to descend from this marriage: David, the Messiah, Daniel, Hananiah, Mishael and Azariah' (*Sanhedrin 93a-b*).

Rav Einhorn, in his Commentary to the Midrash points at that since it says *'measured'* and later וַיָּשֶׁת עָלֶיהָ, *he laid it on her*, it must refer to a quantity larger than six grains! He resolves the apparent contradiction by suggesting that first he gave her the symbolic six grains, then he measured out a larger quantity which she carried home.

The *Malbim* maintains that שֵׁשׁ does not mean *'six'* in this verse but

that *'Shesh'* was a standard measure, one-sixth of a *se'ah*. Half a *shesh* is considered enough for one meal for one person. Thus, Boaz gave her enough to provide a meal for herself and Naomi. The implication of this gesture was that by the time that meal was finished she would be 'redeemed' and won't have to worry about the next meal.

According to *Rav Alkabetz*, the reason he gave her the barley [in addition to having given it as a gift for Naomi as Ruth states in the verse 17], was so that if anyone would see her leaving the threshing floor early in the morning, he would assume that she was carrying home barley gleanings.

וַיָּבֹא הָעִיר — *Then he went into the city.* 'Surely it should have stated that *she* went into the city, yet it says, *'he went to the city'?* — it teaches that he accompanied her lest she be molested (*Midrash*)

16. וַתָּבוֹא אֶל־חֲמוֹתָהּ — *She came to her mother-in-law.* [Imagine the anxiety Naomi must have experienced through the night, waiting for Ruth and wondering whether her hazardous plan had succeeded].

measured out six measures of barley, and set it on her; then he went into the city.

16 *She came to her mother-in-law who said: 'How do things stand with you, my daughter?' So she told her all that the man had done for her,* **17** *and she said: 'He gave me these six measures of barley for he said to me, Do not go empty-handed to your mother-in-law.'*

18 *Then she said, 'Sit patiently, my daughter, until*

מִי־אַתְּ בִּתִּי — *How do things stand with you my daughter?* [lit. 'who are you, my daughter?'] The translation follows the *Midrash:* Did she then not recognize her? — Yes, but she meant: 'Are you still a maiden or a married woman?' She answered, 'A maiden', *and she told her all that the man had done for her. Midrash Lekach Tov* offers the above commentary, and also suggests that perhaps it was still dark and Naomi did not recognize her.

אֵת כָּל־אֲשֶׁר עָשָׂה־לָהּ הָאִישׁ — *All that the man had done for her.* The question demanded more than a 'yes' or 'no' answer. Ruth went into elaborate detail so Naomi would know exactly where matters stood *(Alshich).*

17. כִּי אָמַר [אֵלַי] — *For he said to me.* [The word אֵלַי 'to me' is read, but it does not appear in the written Hebrew text. This is *Halachah* from Moses at Sinai *(Nedarim 37b);* see *Comm.* on 2:5]

By omitting אֵלַי, *to me,* Ruth intimated that Boaz in his modesty, did not even look directly at her during their conversation *(Iggeres Shmuel).*

אַל־תָּבוֹאִי רֵיקָם אֶל־חֲמוֹתֵךְ — *Do not go empty-handed to your mother-in-law.* It is not recorded that Boaz actually told her this. However, the large amount of grain he had given her, could not have been intended for Ruth alone, so Ruth 'stretched the truth' a bit for the sake of שָׁלוֹם בַּיִת *domestic tranquility,* and to flatter her lonely, widowed mother-in-law. Perhaps this is why אֵלַי, is not written, because in actuality Boaz had not said it; she, in her wisdom, added it on her own *(Iggeres Shmuel).*

Ruth also wanted to impress upon her mother-in-law that the barley was intended for her, and not as a gift to Ruth for loose conduct on the threshing floor *(Rav Alkabetz).* Nor did she want Naomi to think that it was a farewell gift and that Boaz had forsaken them *(Ibn Shushan).*

18. וַתֹּאמֶר שְׁבִי בִתִּי — *Sit patiently, my daughter.* i.e. Be prepared *(Alshich).*

We can do nothing but wait. We have done ours, God will now do His *(Zos Nechemasi).*

אֵיךְ יִפֹּל דָּבָר — *How the matter will*

פֶּרֶק ג   יִפֹּל דָּבָר כִּי לֹא יִשְׁקֹט הָאִישׁ כִּי אִם־
כִּלָּה הַדָּבָר הַיּוֹם:

פֶּרֶק ד   א   וּבֹעַז עָלָה הַשַּׁעַר וַיֵּשֶׁב שָׁם וְהִנֵּה הַגֹּאֵל
א־ב   עֹבֵר אֲשֶׁר דִּבֶּר־בֹּעַז וַיֹּאמֶר סוּרָה שְׁבָה־
ב   פֹּה פְּלֹנִי אַלְמֹנִי וַיָּסַר וַיֵּשֵׁב: וַיִּקַּח עֲשָׂרָה
אֲנָשִׁים מִזִּקְנֵי הָעִיר וַיֹּאמֶר שְׁבוּ־פֹה

turn out. If your destined husband
is Boaz or Tov (Zos Nechemasi).

Since all decrees issue from
Heaven (Ibn Ezra).

כִּי אִם־כִּלָּה הַדָּבָר הַיּוֹם — Unless he
settles the matter today. Rav Huna
said in the name of Rav Shmuel b.
Yitzchak: The yes of the righteous
is yes, and their no, no.' (Midrash).
[If Boaz said he will act on the matter, rest assured he will not delay].

IV

1. וּבֹעַז עָלָה הַשַּׁעַר — Boaz,
meanwhile, had gone up to the gate.
To fulfill his promise to Ruth [3:13]
(Zos Nechemasi).

Boaz was the head of the
Sanhedrin, and in that capacity he
stationed himself there (Iggeres
Shmuel).

[The gate, like the gates around
the Old City of Jerusalem today,
was a fairly large edifice. The
Sanhedrin convened there, Torah
was taught, and disputes settled.]

וַיֵּשֶׁב שָׁם — And sat down there.
Knowing that there was nothing
more he could do, and confident
that God would arrange something
for him (Iggeres Shmuel).

וְהִנֵּה הַגֹּאֵל עֹבֵר — Just then, the
redeemer passed by. The Midrash,
noting the striking coincidence of
the redeemer's passing by just at
that very moment, asks: 'Was he
waiting behind the gate? — Rav
Shmuel bar Nachman answered,
Had he been at the opposite end of
the earth God would have caused
him to fly, so to speak, to be there,
in order to relieve the righteous
Boaz of the anxiety of waiting ...'

The Midrash continues: 'Boaz
played his part, Ruth played hers,
Naomi played hers, whereupon the
Holy One, blessed be He, said: I,
too, must play Mine.'

The word וְהִנֵּה, just then, suggests something unusual [see
Comm. of Malbim on 2:4]. The redeemer did not usually pass by the

רות   [120]

you know how the matter will turn out, for the man will not rest unless he settles the matter today.'

IV
1-2

oaz, meanwhile, had gone up to the gate, and sat down there. Just then, the redeemer of whom Boaz had spoken passed by. He said, 'come over, sit down here, 'Ploni Almoni,' and he came over and sat down. ² He then took ten men of the elders of the

gate. Divine Providence guided him that day אֲשֶׁר דִּבֶּר בֹּעַז, *as Boaz had spoken,* i.e. to enable the righteous Boaz to fulfill his promise to Ruth *(Malbim).*

סוּרָה שְׁבָה־פֹּה — *Come over, sit down here.* [Lit. *'turn away'*] from your planned destination and sit here *(Malbim).*

פְּלֹנִי אַלְמֹנִי — *Ploni Almoni.* —[A pseudonym. Sometimes translated *'So and so'*. Compare *I Samuel 21:3,* and *II Kings 6:8*].

His real name was withheld because he did not discharge his duty as redeemer. The meaning of *Ploni* is 'hidden;' *Almoni* — 'nameless.' Another interpretation: *Almoni* — mute and devoid of Torah. He should have known the law of 'Moabite not Moabitess' but instead he asserted *'lest I imperil my own inheritance'* [verse 6] *(Rashi; Midrash).*

Rav Shmariah Halkriti explains the word אַלְמֹנִי — 'fit for an אַלְמָנָה, [widow].

Boaz probably addressed him by his real name, Tov; it is Scripture

that disguised his name to avoid his embarrassment *(Rav Alkabetz).*

According to *Ima Shel Malchus,* it was only proper that he was not called by his real name, Tov; he did not deserve to be called *Tov* — 'good', because he ignored his familial obligation.

וַיֵּשֶׁב — *And he sat.* Even though *Ploni Almoni* was Boaz's uncle [see Comm. 2:17 s.v. אִם יִגְאָלֵךְ], he did not take a seat until told to do so by Boaz, who was the head of the Sanhedrin.

He sat and waited, because Boaz did not tell him why he wanted him until the quorum of ten assembled *(Alshich).*

2. וַיִּקַּח עֲשָׂרָה אֲנָשִׁים מִזִּקְנֵי הָעִיר — *He then took ten men of the elders of the city.* 'Rav Eleazar ben Rav Yose said: From here we learn that the blessing of the bridegroom [i.e. a wedding ceremony] requires a מִנְיָן, quorum of ten. Rav Yuden ben Pazzi said: Not only the marriage of a bachelor to a maiden, but even the marriage of a widower to a widow

ג וַיֵּשֵׁבוּ: וַיֹּאמֶר לַגֹּאֵל חֶלְקַת הַשָּׂדֶה אֲשֶׁר
לְאָחִינוּ לֶאֱלִימֶלֶךְ מָכְרָה נָעֳמִי הַשָּׁבָה
ד מִשְּׂדֵה מוֹאָב: וַאֲנִי אָמַרְתִּי אֶגְלֶה אָזְנְךָ
לֵאמֹר קְנֵה נֶגֶד הַיֹּשְׁבִים וְנֶגֶד זִקְנֵי עַמִּי
אִם־תִּגְאַל גְּאָל וְאִם־לֹא יִגְאַל הַגִּידָה לִּי

[as Boaz and Ruth] requires a quorum of ten (Midrash).

According to others in the Talmud, the presence of ten elders was required to publicly confirm the halachah permitting a female Moabite into the community of Israel. [This auspicious public gathering made the law clear to all, and thus Boaz could marry Ruth the Moabite] (Kesubos 7b).

According to the Malbim, Boaz wanted to make sure he would not be subject to accusations of partiality toward Ruth in promulgating the law allowing her to enter the Assembly of God. He therefore expounded the law while the responsibility of redemption still lay upon Ploni Almoni.

וַיֵּשְׁבוּ פֹּה שְׁבוּ — 'Sit here,' and they sat down. Boaz was head of the Sanhedrin, and though they were older than he, they did not sit until he asked them to because 'an inferior has no right to take a seat until his superior grants him permission' (Midrash; Zos Nechemasi).

He bid them to remain there and be present for a wedding ceremony which, regardless of who the redeemer turned out to be, was sure to take place (Malbim).

3. חֶלְקַת הַשָּׂדֶה — The parcel [lit. 'portion] of land. Possibly, there was a large field, a part of which belonged to Elimelech (Ibn Ezra).

Perhaps the reason[*] why it is referred to as חֶלְקַת הַשָּׂדֶה, the part of the land is that the three brothers:Elimelech, Tov and Salmon inherited a large field from their father and divided it among themselves. Boaz inherited a portion of land from his father, Salmon [see 2:3], Tov had his, and Naomi was administering her late husband's portion. Boaz had therefore advised the kinsman that he should purchase the piece adjacent to both their properties so that a non-relative should not intrude on the family property (Iggeres Shmuel).

לְאָחִינוּ לֶאֱלִימֶלֶךְ — To our brother, Elimelech. [The Talmud and Midrash note that Elimelech was not Boaz's brother, but his uncle — the brother of Boaz's father, Salmon — but he called him 'brother' in a general sense, as the Midrash puts it, 'because one does not refrain from calling his uncle 'brother'.]

מָכְרָה נָעֳמִי — Is being offered for sale by Naomi. [The literal translation of the Hebrew is 'Naomi has sold,'but the context of the verse, according to most of the commentators demands our translation, because Naomi had not in fact sold the field, as it appears from verse 5. Rather, מָכְרָה נָעֳמִי here means 'Naomi was determined to sell.' The commentators discuss the halachic status of such a sale and suggest that in a

city, and said: 'Sit here,' and they sat down.

³ Then he said to the redeemer: 'The parcel of land which belonged to our brother, Elimelech, is being offered for sale by Naomi who has returned from the fields of Moab. ⁴ I resolved that I should inform you to this effect: Buy it in the presence of those sitting here and in the presence of the elders of my people. If you are willing to redeem, redeem! But if it will not be

classic sense 'redemption' would imply that the field had *already* been either sold or was in the process of being sold to someone else, and it is the duty of the near-of-kin to 'redeem' its sale. In the strict *halachic* sense, however, had the property already been sold to another, there would have to be a two-year waiting period between sale and redemption (which certainly was not the case here). Therefore, in the final analysis, most commentators (*Rashi, Ramban, Ibn Ezra, Alkabetz, Alshich*) agree that in this case, a prior sale had not taken place.]

הַשָּׁבָה מִשְּׂדֵה מוֹאָב — *Who has returned from the field of Moab.* Destitute, hungry and barefoot (*Iggeres Shmuel*).

4. וָאֲנִי אָמַרְתִּי — *I resolved* [lit. *'I said'*]. Since I wanted to avoid having the field fall into the hands of strangers — and you precede me — I decided to give you the first option to act as redeemer (*Malbim*).

אֶגְלֶה אָזְנְךָ לֵאמֹר — *I should inform you to this effect.* I personally, not via an intermediary (*Midrash Lekach Tov*).

קְנֵה נֶגֶד הַיֹּשְׁבִים... — *Buy it in the presence of those sitting here ...*

Note that here Boaz uses the word קָנֵה, *buy*, and later in the verse גָאַל, *redeem. There is a difference: One who buys looks for a bargain, and tries to purchase at the lowest possible price. A* גָאַל, *redeemer, however, is more magnanimous; to keep his family estate intact he will graciously pay more. Boaz, therefore, said: 'In the presence of the elders, etc., I officially advise you to 'buy'; but, between ourselves, my advice is 'redeem it' i.e. act more magnanimously, because if you won't, I will'* (Iggeres Shmuel).

Boaz was apprehensive that before their departure to Moab, Machlon and Kilion might have sold their estates. He therefore insisted that this transaction take place *'in the presence of those sitting here and in the presence of the elders of my people', i.e. in public,* to prevent the possibility of an unknown purchaser arising later and laying claim to the field (*Meishiv Nefesh*).

אִם־תִּגְאַל גְּאָל — *If you are willing to redeem, redeem.* 'Immediately, and without delay' (*Alshich*) [as it is your primary right and obligation to do according to *Leviticus 25:25*].

וְאִם־לֹא יִגְאַל — *But if it will not be redeemed.* [The phrase literally

ה

ו

וְאֵֽדְעָ֗* כִּ֣י אֵ֤ין זֽוּלָֽתְךָ֙ לִגְא֔וֹל וְאָנֹכִ֖י אַחֲרֶ֑יךָ
וַיֹּ֖אמֶר אָנֹכִ֥י אֶגְאָֽל: וַיֹּ֣אמֶר בֹּ֗עַז בְּיוֹם־
קְנוֹתְךָ֥ הַשָּׂדֶ֖ה מִיַּ֣ד נָעֳמִ֑י וּ֠מֵאֵ֠ת ר֣וּת
הַמּֽוֹאֲבִיָּ֞ה אֵֽשֶׁת־הַמֵּת֙ קָנִ֔יתִי* לְהָקִ֥ים
שֵׁם־הַמֵּ֖ת עַל־נַחֲלָת֑וֹ: וַיֹּ֣אמֶר הַגֹּאֵ֗ל לֹ֤א
אוּכַל֙ לִגְאָל־לִ֔י פֶּן־אַשְׁחִ֖ית אֶת־נַחֲלָתִ֑י

*וְאֵֽדְעָה ק'

*קָנִ֫יתָ

*יָתִיר ו'

means: 'But if he will not redeem' According to the Midrash, Boaz said this phrase directly to the elders.]

כִּי אֵין זוּלָתְךָ לִגְאוֹל — *For there is no one else to redeem it but you. i.e. no one else from among our relatives (Rashi). — just the two of us (Alshich).*

And according to the Torah, you, as the closest relative, are given the first option (Akeidas Yitzchak).

וַיֹּאמֶר אָנֹכִי אֶגְאָל — *And he said, I am willing to redeem.* He consented because he was aware only of his obligation to redeem Naomi's field. — At that time, he knew nothing of Ruth (Malbim).

According to the Midrash, he assumed that he had no obligation vis-a-vis Ruth's portion of the estate (Yefe Anaf).

5. בְּיוֹם־קְנוֹתְךָ הַשָּׂדֶה מִיַּד נָעֳמִי — *The day you buy the field from Naomi.* When Boaz heard the kinsman was accepting his obligation, he told him of the condition attached to the redemption: he must also, at the same time, marry Ruth (Midrash Lekach Tov).

'When you buy Naomi's field, don't think you thereby have fulfilled your obligation. Naomi owns only half the estate; [according to the Zohar Chadash (that Ruth con-

verted when she married Machlon) — see Introduction] the other half belongs to Ruth — and it is absolutely essential that when you redeem Naomi's portion you must also redeem Ruth's (Pri Chaim).

וּמֵאֵת רוּת הַמּוֹאֲבִיָּה אֵשֶׁת־הַמֵּת קָנִיתָ — *You must also buy from Ruth the Moabite, the wife of the deceased.* [The translation of this obscure Hebrew phrase follows Rashi, who continues: 'and she is not willing [to sell] unless you marry her'].

'And just as we cannot leave the redemption of the field to an outsider, so can we not allow a righteous woman like Ruth to be married to an outsider'(Zos Nechemasi).

The Iggeres Shmuel notes that Boaz stressed מוֹאֲבִיָּה, the Moabite [even though female Moabites had already been officially permitted] and he also mentioned אֵשֶׁת־הַמֵּת, wife of the deceased, invoking the memory of the dead, in a further attempt to discourage the kinsman. Boaz hoped to keep the mitzvah of the redemption for himself.

[My father, Harav Aron Zlotowitz שליט״א, pointed out that the Shaarei Teshuvah on Orach Chaim 484:1, quotes this Iggeres Shmuel to support a halachah: Although misleading someone is prohibited —

IV
5-6

redeemed, tell me, that I may know; for there is no one else to redeem it but you, and I after you.' And he said: 'I am willing to redeem it.'

⁵ Then Boaz said: 'The day you buy the field from Naomi, you must also buy it from Ruth the Moabite, wife of the deceased, to perpetuate the name of the deceased on his inheritance.' ⁶ The redeemer said, 'Then I cannot redeem it for myself, lest I imperil my

in financial matters — however in matters pertaining to the performance of a *mitzvah*, in a case where no one has *specifically* been appointed to perform that particular *mitzvah*, that *mitzvah* is considered open to all who wish to fulfill it. One should strive as much as possible, by whatever means, to perfect his soul and acquire that *mitzvah* for himself.]

The כְּתִיב, traditional spelling is קָנִיתִי, 'I bought,' because Boaz prophetically foresaw that it was *he* who would ultimately consummate the transaction *(Torah T'mimah)*.

לְהָקִים שֵׁם־הַמֵּת עַל נַחֲלָתוֹ — *To perpetuate the name of the deceased on his inheritance.* Boaz made clear that the main purpose of this entire transaction was *'to perpetuate the name of the deceased on his inheritance;* acquisition of the field itself was secondary *(Vilna Gaon)*.

6. לֹא אוּכַל לִגְאָל־לִי — *'Then I cannot redeem it for myself.'* 'Machlon and Kilion died only because they took them [Ruth and Orpah — Moabite women] as wives; shall *I* then go and take her?' *(Midrash)*.

I cannot allow myself to take on a second wife and destroy the harmony of my home *(Targum)*.

The *Iggeres Shmuel* stresses לֹא אוּכַל as meaning 'I am unable' — i.e. 'my merits are insufficient to effect a redemption of Machlon's soul; his sin was great and he needs זְכֻיּוֹת merits, like yours, Boaz, to effect true redemption.' The *Malbim* stressing לִי, *for myself*, translates: 'I cannot redeem because it will not remain לִי, *in my name*, but rather in the name of the deceased, and *I will thus destroy my own inheritance.'*

פֶּן אַשְׁחִית אֶת נַחֲלָתִי — *Lest I imperil my own inheritance.* [The *Midrash* takes נַחֲלָה to mean *'children'* (comp. *Psalms 127:3*, נַחֲלַת ה' בָּנִים, 'the heritage of God is children').]

'Heaven forfend that I should take her; I will not contaminate my seed — even if I myself will not die for the sin [of marrying a Moabite woman], my children may suffer. I will not cause my children to become disqualified." But, the *Midrash* continues, he was unaware of the law newly publicized 'Moabite but not Moabitess' [see *Introduction*].

The *Chidah* discusses this *Midrash* and asks the obvious question: If he was unaware, why didn't they tell it to him? Furthermore, they had just finished confirming it [see Comm. to 4:2], Didn't he hear? — Rather, he was unlearned in Torah and could not comprehend

גָּאַל־לָךְ אַתָּה אֶת־גְּאֻלָּתִי כִּי לֹא־אוּכַל
לִגְאֹל: וְזֹאת לְפָנִים בְּיִשְׂרָאֵל עַל־
הַגְּאֻלָּה וְעַל־הַתְּמוּרָה לְקַיֵּם כָּל־דָּבָר
שָׁלַף אִישׁ נַעֲלוֹ וְנָתַן לְרֵעֵהוּ וְזֹאת

how the law could have been unknown for so long until it was just
now repromulgated. He thought
they were mistaken in their ruling —
therefore he used the uncertain term
פֶּן, 'lest.' He was uncertain himself,
and he refused to put his progeny in
jeopardy, hence he 'made himself
unaware.'

The *Bach* questions how the
kinsman could have been so brazen
as to disagree with a ruling of the
Sanhedrin, an act which is rebellious and, under some circumstances, punishable by death! Also,
if according to the kinsman the ruling permitting a female Moabite
was improper, how dare he suggest
that Boaz take her? — Rather, he
acknowledged the ruling as valid,
but he considered himself insignificant to execute it, for were the ruling ever disputed [as it was when
Doeg later attempted to disqualify
David!; see *Introduction*] — his seed
would be disqualified, and he would
have been of insignificant stature to
combat the slur. Therefore he stressed לִי, *for myself*, i.e. I, a commoner
cannot take this awesome responsibility upon myself. He felt that
such a precedent-setting act must
be done by a great man, a leader and
judge such as Boaz himself. גָּאַל־לָךְ
אַתָּה, 'You redeem for yourself' he
said to Boaz, 'because as a man of
great stature *your* deeds are less
prone to be disputed.

According to *Rav Velvele Brisker*
[pointed out to me by my friend
Harav David Cohen] *Ploni Almoni*
mistakenly thought that this law
was *interpreted* by the Sanhedrin —
and as such, open to possible later
reinterpretation. He was not aware
that it was a never-before-invoked
*tradition from Moses at Sinai, and
hence uncontestable.*

גָּאַל־לָךְ אַתָּה אֶת־גְּאֻלָּתִי — *Take over
my right of redemption for
yourself.* [Lit. 'Redeem for yourself
my redemption']. 'Boaz, you are a
man of merits; you accept the
responsibility' (*Iggeres Shmuel*).

'You don't have a wife and
children; you do it!' (*Alshich*).

'I feel a female Moabite is
prohibited and I don't want to contaminate my seed thereby. If you
permit it *take over my right of
redemption yourself,* because under
the circumstances *I am unable to
redeem* (*Pri Chaim*).

The greater the selfishness of the
egoist, the more generous the
measure of altruism he allows to
others' (*Rav Breuer*).

7. וְזֹאת לְפָנִים בְּיִשְׂרָאֵל — *Now this
was formerly done in Israel* — i.e. in
ancient times (*Ibn Ezra*).

Since the next verse goes on to
tell us that Boaz removed his shoe to
consummate the transaction. This
verse introduces the custom, explaining that, although it is not
Biblical in origin, it is nevertheless
an ancient and well founded one
(*Iggeres Shmuel*).

own inheritance. Take over my redemption responsibility on yourself for I am unable to redeem.'

⁷ Formerly this was done in Israel in cases of redemption and exchange transactions to validate all matters: one would draw off his shoe, and give it to

Rav Alkabetz notes that this ancient form of acquisition, once very much in mode, fell into disuse for some time, and Boaz reinstituted it on that occasion. Therefore the author found it appropriate to explain the custom as being old, and וְזֹאת הַתְּעוּדָה בְּיִשְׂרָאֵל, *having the strength of Torah-law* עֵדוּת, *testimony, ratification.*

עַל־הַגְּאוּלָה וְעַל־הַתְּמוּרָה — *In cases of redemption and exchange transactions.* 'Redemption' — i.e. sales; 'exchange transactions' — 'חֲלִיפִין' (Rashi).

[This verse parenthetically discusses קִנְיָן , the mode of acquisition of property which was in vogue at that time. According to *halachah*, whenever a transaction occurs, the transaction may be consummated — even before money changes hands — by a symbolic barter, an example of which is חֲלִיפִין, *'exchange'*. In our times it is called קִנְיָן סוּדָר, lit. *'acquisition of a scarf'* during which a garment is symbolically grasped by both parties to the transaction.]

[According to the *Rambam*: 'Real estate ... may be acquired by symbolic barter. This act is called *Kinyan.* The fundamental principal of this mode of acquisition is that the transferee should give the transferor an article of some utility no matter how small its value and say to him, "Acquire this article in exchange for the yard ... you sold me for so much and so much." If

this is done, then the moment the vendor lifts the article and takes possession of it, the purchaser acquires title to the land ... though he has not paid its price. Then neither party may renege.']

שָׁלַף אִישׁ נַעֲלוֹ וְנָתַן לְרֵעֵהוּ — *One would draw off his shoe and give it to the other.* A shoe was used because it was always convenient and available; a shirt or other necessary garment could not very well be removed leaving the purchaser bare! (*Ibn Ezra*).

The *Targum*, without further elucidation translates נַעַל, *'shoe'* as *'glove.'*

[It must be made clear that the transference of a shoe described in this verse is not to be confused with the act of *chalitzah* (*Deut. 29:9*) where a similar symbolic action takes place. *Chalitzah* is applicable only in the case of a sister-in-law, where the brother of the deceased does not want to perform יִבּוּם, *levirate marriage.* Thus procedure 'frees her to marry whomsoever' she desires. Note, also, that in reference to *chalitzah* (*Deut.,* ibid.) the Torah uses the word חָלַץ for 'removal' instead of its synonym שָׁלַף used in this verse, suggesting a different procedure]. Therefore, the verse describes this procedure as one accompanying *every* exchange and sales transaction, so as not to confuse it with *chalitzah* (*Meishiv Nefesh*).

פֶּרֶק ד

ח הַתְּעוּדָה בְּיִשְׂרָאֵל: וַיֹּאמֶר הַגֹּאֵל לְבֹעַז
ט קְנֵה־לָךְ וַיִּשְׁלֹף נַעֲלוֹ: וַיֹּאמֶר בֹּעַז
לַזְּקֵנִים וְכָל־הָעָם עֵדִים אַתֶּם הַיּוֹם כִּי
קָנִיתִי אֶת־כָּל־אֲשֶׁר לֶאֱלִימֶלֶךְ וְאֵת כָּל־
י אֲשֶׁר לְכִלְיוֹן וּמַחְלוֹן מִיַּד נָעֳמִי: וְגַם אֶת־
רוּת הַמֹּאֲבִיָּה אֵשֶׁת מַחְלוֹן קָנִיתִי לִי
לְאִשָּׁה לְהָקִים שֵׁם־הַמֵּת עַל־נַחֲלָתוֹ
וְלֹא־יִכָּרֵת שֵׁם־הַמֵּת מֵעִם אֶחָיו וּמִשַּׁעַר

וְזֹאת הַתְּעוּדָה בְּיִשְׂרָאֵל — *This was the process of ratification in Israel.* תְּעוּדָה stems from עֵדוּת, 'testimony' (*Ibn Ezra*); and the transference of the shoe, once completed, was 'testimony' hallowed by Biblical tradition, that the transaction was complete and irrevocable (*Ralbag; Alshich*).

[The *halachos* stemming from this verse are fully treated in *Choshen Mishpat* 195].

8. קְנֵה־לָךְ — *Buy it for yourself.* The *Bach* observes that (in verse 6) the kinsman renounced his right of redemption, but Boaz did not immediately respond. He was apprehensive that the kinsman would later regret it and lay claim to the redemption. Only after the kinsman, noting Boaz's silence specifically said *'buy it for yourself'* — before the elders and the entire community — did Boaz formalize his acceptance by drawing off his shoe.

וַיִּשְׁלֹף נַעֲלוֹ — *He drew off his shoe.* 'Whose shoe, Boaz's or the kinsman? — It is more likely Boaz's shoe, for according to the established *halachah*, it is the purchaser who gives the pledge

(*Bava Metzia* 47a; *Midrash*). The Talmud [*Bava Metzia* 47a] records a minority opinion that it was the kinsman who drew off his shoe and gave it to Boaz as if to say 'As I hand you the shoe, I hand over the rights of redemption' (*Ibn Ezra*).

9, וְכָל־הָעָם — *And all the people* [Obviously, a crowd had assembled by this time, to witness the events.]

עֵדִים אַתֶּם הַיּוֹם — *You are witnesses this day.* This phrase is repeated twice (in this and the next verse). The *Malbim* explains that he summoned two groups of witnesses: one for the purchase of the land, and the other for the marriage of Ruth.

Boaz thus took every possible precaution to ensure the legality of the proceeding (*Nachlas Yosef*).

לְכִלְיוֹן וּמַחְלוֹן — *Kilion and Machlon.* Their names are recorded here in seemingly reverse order from the other places where they are mentioned. They are listed in this verse in the order of their death and the succession of their inheritance (*Vilna Gaon; Bach; Iggeres Shmuel*).

According to *Alshich*, Boaz men-

רות [128]

*the other. This was the process of ratification in
Israel. ⁸ So, when the redeemer said to Boaz: 'Buy it
for yourself,' he drew off his shoe.*

*⁹ And Boaz said to the elders, and to all the people:
'You are witness this day, that I have bought all that
was Elimelech's and all that was Kilion's and
Machlon's from Naomi.*

*¹⁰ And, what it more important, I have also 'ac-
quired' the wife of Machlon as my wife, to
perpetuate name of the deceased on his inheritance,
that the name of the deceased not be cut off from*

---

tioned Kilion first to stress that his property had also been redeemed so that no descendent of his widow Orpah would ever be able to dispute Boaz's absolute right of ownership. One must be concerned with the inferior members of the family. Hence he mentioned him first (*Zos Nechemasi*).

מִיַּד נָעֳמִי — *from the hand of Naomi.* i.e. with Naomi's consent (*Zos Nechemasi*).

These commentators point out that according to *halachah*, the estates of Machlon and Kilion would not have reverted to Naomi. What then is the significance of מִיַּד נָעֳמִי *from the hand of Naomi?* — Several explanations are given. According to the *Bach* it was given back to Naomi as a gift; the *Chidah* suggests that it remained part of the marriage settlement in her care.

10. וְגַם אֶת־רוּת הַמֹּאֲבִיָּה.. קָנִיתִי לִי לְאִשָּׁה — *And, what is more, I have also 'acquired' Ruth the Moabite wife of Machlon.* The act of taking Ruth as his wife was separate from the redemption of the field. For this

event he enlisted them as separate witnesses (*Malbim*).

[Boaz mentions the 'acquisition' of Ruth with great delicacy. The acquisition of a wife and property are referred to with the same legalisms, but there the similarity ends. A Jewish wife is a respected and beloved partner in the sacred text of building a home. Therefore, Boaz mentions his marriage separately to make it clear that he does not lump Ruth with his newly acquired land.]

He referred to her as מֹאֲבִיָּה, *the Moabite,* to stress to the populace — who might not as yet have heard the ruling permitting female Moabites — that although she was a Moabite, she was nevertheless permitted to him (*Shaar Bas Rabim*).

אֵשֶׁת מַחְלוֹן — *wife of Machlon.* She is still considered Machlon's 'wife' because as the *Zohar* states her husbands 'spirit' still stirred within her [see Comm. on 3:1] (*Malbim*).

לְהָקִים שֵׁם־הַמֵּת — *And thereby perpetuate the name of the deceased.* [Here again Boaz emphasizes the sincerity with which he embarked on this transaction. His purpose

יא מְקוֹמוֹ עֵדִים אַתֶּם הַיּוֹם: וַיֹּאמְרוּ כָּל־
הָעָם אֲשֶׁר־בַּשַּׁעַר וְהַזְּקֵנִים עֵדִים יִתֵּן
יהוה אֶת־הָאִשָּׁה הַבָּאָה אֶל־בֵּיתֶךָ כְּרָחֵל|
וּכְלֵאָה אֲשֶׁר בָּנוּ שְׁתֵּיהֶם אֶת־בֵּית
יִשְׂרָאֵל וַעֲשֵׂה־חַיִל בְּאֶפְרָתָה וּקְרָא שֵׁם
בְּבֵית לָחֶם: וִיהִי בֵיתְךָ כְּבֵית פֶּרֶץ אֲשֶׁר־
יב יָלְדָה תָמָר לִיהוּדָה מִן־הַזֶּרַע אֲשֶׁר יִתֵּן
יג יהוה לְךָ מִן־הַנַּעֲרָה הַזֹּאת: וַיִּקַּח בֹּעַז
אֶת־רוּת וַתְּהִי־לוֹ לְאִשָּׁה וַיָּבֹא אֵלֶיהָ

was not selfish, but to 'perpetuate Machlon's memory — not with *actual* levirate marriage, for that did not apply here, but symbolically]. . .

'By his wife going about the field doing her business all who see her will say, she was the wife of Machlon. His name is thereby perpetuated because of her' (*Rashi*).

11. כָּל־הָעָם — *All* [The blessing was a spontaneous response offered in unison by all present].

They witnessed the proceedings and also blessed him in three ways: a. הָאִשָּׁה, *the woman* — despite the fact that she is of foreign stock and upbringing, by virtue of her *coming into your house*, the house of a righteous man like yourself, she will become like *Rachel and Leah* — also foreigners, daughters of Laban the Aramean, who married Jacob and *built up the House of Israel*. So will Ruth, too, merit righteous and royal descendants; b. *Boaz* himself should *prosper as an Ephrathite*, i.e. his distinguished family name, bringing further glory to his family, [see Comm. 1:2 s.v. אֶפְרָתִים) *and be famous in Bethlehem*, i.e. may your own accomplishments bring such

praise to Bethlehem that all will say 'The great man Boaz was born here!'; and c. [next verse] *your house* i.e. the children you will have from this marriage may be considered as if they were the children of Machlon because you are taking Ruth in the spirit of levirate marriage (see Introduction), nevertheless, just *as the home of Peretz whom Tamar bore* [Gen. Chapter 38] was ascribed to *Judah*; so may your 'house' be honored and distinguished through the offspring which HASHEM will give *you* by this young woman' (*Malbim*).

וַעֲשֵׂה־חַיִל בְּאֶפְרָתָה — *And be famous in Bethlehem.* The *Alshich* offers: May she no longer be called 'Ruth the Moabite' but 'Ruth of Bethlehem.'

כְּרָחֵל וּכְלֵאָה — *like Rachel and like Leah.* Although those present were of the tribe of Judah, descendent of Leah, they agreed that Rachel was the mainstay of the house, and they mentioned Rachel first (*Rashi*).

The *Gishmei Brachah* suggests that the people compared Ruth to Rachael and Leah because they too came from non-righteous parents.

among his brethren, and from the gate of his place.
You are witnesses today.'

11 *Then all the people who were at the gate, and the*
elders, said: 'We are witnesses! May HASHEM make
the woman who is coming into your house like
Rachel and like Leah, both of whom built up the
House of Israel. May you prosper in Ephrath and be
famous in Bethlehem; 12 *and may your house be like*
the house of Peretz, whom Tamar bore to Judah,
through the offspring which HASHEM will give you
by this young woman.'

Holy
seeds
unite

13 *And so, Boaz took Ruth and she became his*
wife; and he came to her. HASHEM let her conceive,

Sarah and Rivka were not mentioned because each of them had one evil son — Yishmael and Esav — whereas Rachel and Leah had only righteous children; also Ruth, like Rachel and Leah deserted their parents' home to cleave to God and a righteous husband.

12. וִיהִי בֵיתְךָ כְּבֵית פֶּרֶץ — *May your house be like the home of Peretz whom Tamar bore unto Judah.* By evoking Tamar's memory, they meant to allay any guilt Boaz might have felt about the propriety of the circumstances leading to his marriage to Ruth (*Gishmei Brachah*).

13. בֹּעַז אֶת־רוּת — *And so, Boaz took Ruth and she became his wife.* This was not a true levirate marriage. Boaz first 'took' her as his wife, formally, with קִידוּשִׁין, 'sanctification', and only *then* וַיָּבֹא אֵלֶיהָ, *did he consummate the marriage* (*Malbim*). [see *Rambam*: 'According to *Scriptural Law*, there need be no marriage ceremony for

Levirate marriage, since she is his wife already, married to him by Heaven'] The verse makes it clear that Boaz did not act in accordance with the custom [see *Rambam*] of יִבּוּם, levirate marriage.

On that very night, Boaz died (*Yalkut Shimoni*).

[With Ruth's marriage and the birth of her child, her place in Jewish history is secure. Ruth's name is no longer mentioned in the *Megillah*. The Sages maintain she enjoyed unusual longevity. She lived to see her royal descendent Solomon on the throne (*Bava Basra 91b*).]

וַיִּתֵּן ה' לָהּ הֵרָיוֹן — *HASHEM let her conceive* [lit. HASHEM gave her conception]. God, in His Providence allowed her to conceive immediately, although with her first husband — who had been a young man — she never conceived (*Malbim*).

The numerical value of הֵרָיוֹן, conception, equals 271; the amount of days which, according to the Sages [*Niddah, 38b*], a pregnant woman carries (*Nachal Eshkol*).

יד וַיִּתֵּן יהוה לָהּ הֵרָיוֹן וַתֵּלֶד בֵּן: וַתֹּאמַרְנָה הַנָּשִׁים אֶל־נָעֳמִי בָּרוּךְ יהוה אֲשֶׁר לֹא הִשְׁבִּית לָךְ גֹּאֵל הַיּוֹם וְיִקָּרֵא שְׁמוֹ בְּיִשְׂרָאֵל: טו וְהָיָה לָךְ לְמֵשִׁיב נֶפֶשׁ וּלְכַלְכֵּל אֶת־שֵׂיבָתֵךְ כִּי כַלָּתֵךְ אֲשֶׁר־אֲהֵבַתֶךְ יְלָדַתּוּ אֲשֶׁר־הִיא טוֹבָה לָךְ מִשִּׁבְעָה בָּנִים: טז וַתִּקַּח נָעֳמִי אֶת־הַיֶּלֶד וַתְּשִׁתֵהוּ בְחֵיקָהּ וַתְּהִי־לוֹ לְאֹמֶנֶת: יז וַתִּקְרֶאנָה לוֹ הַשְּׁכֵנוֹת שֵׁם לֵאמֹר יֻלַּד־בֵּן לְנָעֳמִי וַתִּקְרֶאנָה שְׁמוֹ עוֹבֵד הוּא אֲבִי־יִשַׁי אֲבִי

וַתֵּלֶד בֵּן — *and she bore a son.* Rav Alkabetz comments that 'unto him' is not mentioned because Boaz was already dead when the child was born.

14. אֲשֶׁר לֹא הִשְׁבִּית לָךְ גֹּאֵל — *who has not left you without a redeemer.* i.e. the child will 'redeem' you from dying childless as he carries the soul of your son Machlon. Also, since Boaz died on the night of his marriage, had the child not been conceived that very night, Naomi would truly have been cut off completely (*Alshich*).

הַיּוֹם — *Today.* This phrase is seemingly superfluous, and the *Midrash* interprets it as an additional blessing: 'Just as the day [i.e. the sun] holds dominion in the skies, so may your seed produce one [the Messiah from the House of David] who will hold sway over Israel forever. . .

Rav Chunya said: 'It was the result of the blessings of these women that the line of David was not cut off entirely in the days of

Ataliah [see *II Kings*]' (*Midrash*).

וְיִקָּרֵא שְׁמוֹ בְּיִשְׂרָאֵל — *And may his name be famous in Israel.* (lit. 'may his name be called in Israel) He will be righteous, and people will name their children after him (*Iggeres Shmuel*).

Pri Chaim observes that had this child been born during Machlon's lifetime — before Ruth's conversion [according to those who maintain that Ruth's conversion took place after her husband's death (see *Introduction*)] — the child would have been considered a non-Jew following the nationality of his mother; now, after Machlon's death and Ruth's conversion, 'his name is called' in Israel i.e. he is a full-fledged Jew.

15. וְהָיָה לָךְ לְמֵשִׁיב נֶפֶשׁ — *He will become your life-restorer* [lit. 'as one who refreshes the soul']. [i.e. a comforter, after so many years of trials and suffering].

The *Malbim* explains that his birth, in a sense, 'revived' the soul of her son Machlon.

and she bore a son. **14** *And the women said to Naomi,
'Blessed be HASHEM who has not left you without a
redeemer today! May his name be famous in Israel.
15 He will become your life-restorer, and sustain your
old age; for your daughter-in-law, who loves you,
has borne him, and she is better to you than seven
sons.'*

16 *Naomi took the child, and held it in her bosom,
and she became his nurse.* **17** *The neighborhood*

*women gave him a name, saying: 'A son is born to
Naomi.' They named him Oved; he was the father of*

וּלְכַלְכֵּל אֶת־שֵׂיבָתֵךְ — *And sustain
your old age.* As a son of Ruth, who
so selflessly sustained you in her
youth, he will certainly sustain you
in your old age (*Alshich*).

He will sustain you in your old
age with delicacies (*Targum*).

אֲשֶׁר־הִיא טוֹבָה לָךְ מִשִּׁבְעָה בָּנִים — *and
she is better to you than seven sons.*
The *Midrash* differs on whether this
refers to the seven sons of Jesse
(enumerated in I *Chron.* 2:13) or to
the seven generations listed in
verses 18-21).

16. וַתְּהִי־לוֹ לְאֹמֶנֶת — *And became
his nurse.* The *Alshich* explains that
Naomi was miraculously enabled to
nurse the child. It became manifestly clear to all that Machlon's
memory had been perpetuated
through the child and, in a spiritual
sense, *a child had truly been born to
Naomi.'*

17. וַתִּקְרֶאנָה לוֹ הַשְּׁכֵנוֹת שֵׁם — *The
neighborhood women gave him a
name.* Seeing the miracle God
wrought for Naomi, allowing her to
nurse the child, they realized that a
continuity of Machlon's soul had
been implanted in the child; it was

truly Naomi's child (*Zos
Nechemasi*).

יֻלַּד־בֵּן לְנָעֳמִי — *A son is born to
Naomi.* The *Talmud* remarks: 'Was
it then Naomi who bore him? Surely it was Ruth who bore him! — But
Ruth bore and Naomi brought him
up; hence he was called after
Naomi's name' (*Sanhedrin 19b*).

It was through her counsel that
the marriage came about, and so it
was proper that the child should be
called after her (*Nachlas Yosef*).

'The neighbors described the
child as a son born to Naomi,' with
reference to the legitimacy of the
child, which some questioned, for
he had been born from a Moabitess.
That is to say, it is not the name of
the Moabite mother which is called
on this child, but the name of
Naomi — a granddaughter of
Nachshon son of Aminadov, a
prince among his people. And Ruth
had also become to Naomi like her
own child from birth — how dare
anyone slur this noble child! (*Sefer
haToda'ah*)

וַתִּקְרֶאנָה שְׁמוֹ עוֹבֵד — *They called his
name Oved.* i.e. as a blessing that
this child will 'serve [עוֹבֵד] God

יח דָּוִד: וְאֵ֫לֶּה תּוֹלְד֣וֹת פָּ֔רֶץ פֶּ֫רֶץ הוֹלִ֥יד

יט אֶת־חֶצְר֑וֹן: וְחֶצְרוֹן֙ הוֹלִ֣יד אֶת־רָ֔ם וְרָ֖ם

כ הוֹלִ֥יד אֶת־עַמִּֽינָדָ֑ב: וְעַמִּֽינָדָב֙ הוֹלִ֣יד

אֶת־נַחְשׁ֔וֹן וְנַחְשׁ֖וֹן הוֹלִ֥יד אֶת־שַׂלְמָֽה:

כא וְשַׂלְמוֹן֙ הוֹלִ֣יד אֶת־בֹּ֔עַז וּבֹ֖עַז הוֹלִ֥יד אֶת־

כב עוֹבֵֽד: וְעֹבֵד֙ הוֹלִ֣יד אֶת־יִשַׁ֔י וְיִשַׁ֖י הוֹלִ֥יד

אֶת־דָּוִֽד:

with a full heart (*Iggeres Shmuel*).

אֲבִי דָוִד — *The father of David*. According to *Iggeres Shmuel* this phrase refers back to Oved, i.e. it was not merely by the merit of Jesse that David was born; by the merit of Oved were Jesse and David born. He was the '*father of Jesse*' and the '*father of David.*'

'This story was the cause of severe harassment to the house of David. "How long," said David to God, "will they speak angrily and say: Is he not of unworthy lineage? Is he not descended from Ruth the Moabite? (*Ruth Rabbah* 8:1)...A man-made story would have attributed the privilege of David's birth to an aristocratic Israelite mother, in accordance with the dignity of Boaz, the descendant of the illustrious Nachshon ben Aminadov. The gentile monarchs had their lineage traced to gods or celestial bodies (the sun or the stars), and this was taught to the people as a religious principle. But this is another monument to the truthfulness of the prophetic books, *wherein the voice of prophecy spoke without fear of man*. It was only because of the prestige of prophecy in Israel that this narrative was able to be told and was preserved' (*Behold A People*).

18. Having detailed David's descent from Ruth the Moabite, the author now traces his lineage to Judah (*Rashi*).

וְאֵלֶּה תּוֹלְדוֹת פָּרֶץ — *Now these are the generations of Peretz:* [The son of Judah]. Judah was avoided here, and the listing of generations begins with Peretz to avoid evoking the memory of the Judah-Tamar incident which is embarrasing to many (*Iggeres Shmuel; Meishiv Nefesh*). [See *Comm.* of *Gishmei Bracha* on verse 12.].

IV

Jesse, the father of David.

18-22   ¹⁸ *Now these are the generations of Peretz: Peretz begot Chetzron;* ¹⁹*and Chetzron begot Ram, and Ram begot Aminadav;* ²⁰ *and Aminadav begot Nahshon, and Nahshon begot Salmah;* ²¹ *and Salmah begot Boaz, and Boaz begot Oved;* ²² *and Oved begot Jesse, and Jesse begot David.*

חֶצְרוֹן — *Chetzron.* [Mentioned, in *Gen.* 46:12].

19. וְחֶצְרוֹן הוֹלִיד אֶת־רָם — *Chetzron begot Ram.* The *Midrash* points out that Yerachmiel, not Ram, was the elder son. Having married a Canaanite woman *(I Chron. 11:26)*, Yerachmiel was unworthy to be an ancestor of the house of David.

[Ram is not mentioned in the Torah. In I Chron. 2:9 he is identified as the second son of Chetzron].

עַמִּינָדָב — *Aminadav.* [One of the greatest personalities of the tribe of Judah during the slavery in Egypt. His daughter, Elisheva was the wife of Aaron the *Kohen (Exodus 6:23).]*

20. נַחְשׁוֹן — *Nachshon* [the leader of the tribe of Judah. The Sages credit him with being the first one to plunge into the Red Sea. According to *Seder Olam Rabba* he died in the second year in the Desert.]

שַׂלְמָה — *Salmah.* [Sometimes called *Salmon.* He was the brother of Elimelech and Tov].

21. וּבֹעַז הוֹלִיד אֶת עוֹבֵד — *And Boaz begot Oved.* 'Who served [עָבַד, *(avad)*] the Master of the Universe with a perfect heart *(Targum).*

22. וְיִשַׁי הוֹלִיד אֶת דָּוִד — *And Jesse begot David.*

So said the Holy One blessed be He to David: 'What need have I to record the geneology of Peretz, Hezron, Ram, Aminadav, Nachshon, Salmon, Boaz, Oved, Jesse? Only on account of you; מָצָאתִי דָּוִד עַבְדִּי, *I have found my servant David'* [*(Psalms 89:21)*] *(Midrash).*

תם ונשלם שבח לאל בורא עולם

Bibliography—
Biographical Sketches

Bibliography
of Authorities Cited in the Commentary

Italics are used to denote the name of a work. **Bold italics** *within the biography indicate the specific book of that particular author cited in the commentary.*

An asterisk (*) precedes the names of contemporary figures

Alkabetz, Rav Shlomo haLevi:

[b. 1505-Salonica; d. 1576 Safed]
One of the greatest Kabbalists and mystical poets of his day. Author of the Piyyut 'L'cha Dodi' recited every Friday evening. He was a contemporary and friend of Rav Yosef Karo, author of *Shulchan Aruch.*

His commentary on Ruth, **Shoresh Yishai,** published in 1561 is quoted by nearly every commentator on Ruth after him.

He is cited constantly in *Iggeres Shmuel,* who refers to him in various ways: '*Rashba haLevi*'; *Rav Shlomo haLevi;*' *Harav ibn Alkabetz haLevi*'.

He wrote commentaries on most of the Bible, the Passover Hagaddah, on *Kabbalah,* and was a noted Paytan.

In his Piyyut, '*L'cha Dodi,*' he speaks of the sufferings of the Jewish people and their aspirations for Redemption. Probably no other Piyyut has reached the popularity of '*L'cha Dodi*'; it is recited every Friday evening by all Jewish congregations throughout the world.

Alshich, Rav Moshe:

[Also spelled Alshekh]

Rav, Posek and Bible Commentator. Born in Andrionople in 1508; studied Torah there in Yeshiva of Rav Yosef Karo. Settled in Safed where he spent most of his life and was ordained there by Rav Karo with the full *Semichah* reintroduced by Rav Yaakov Berav. Among his pupils was Rav Chaim Vital, whom he ordained in 1590.

He died in Damascus, where he was travelling, before 1600.

He wrote Commentaries on most of the Bible, and published a collection of 140 of his *halachic* Responsa.

His **Eynei Moshe** on *Ruth* was published in 1615.

Alter, Rav Yitzchak Meir

(1789-1866)

Gerrer Rebbe; founder of the Gerrer Chassidic dynasty. Rav Yitzchak Meir was a disciple of the Maggid of Koznitz, and later of Rav Simcha Bunem of Pshyscha, and of Rav Menachem Mendel of Kotzk.

After the Kotzker's death in 1859, Rav Yitzchak Meir was acknowledged Rebbe by the majority of Kotzk Chassidim

His influence was far-reaching. Although his leadership lasted only seven years, he had a formative influence on the development of Chassidus in Poland. Gerrer Chassidus became a powerful element in Orthodox Polish Jewry.

He is most famous for *Chiddushei haRim,* novellae on the Talmud and *Shulchan Aruch,* and was frequently referred to by the name of his work, "The Chiddushei haRim."

Alter, Rav Yehudah Aryeh Leib:

(1847-1903)

Gerrer; known by his work 'Sefas Emes'.

His father, Rav Avraham Mordechai, a great but chronically ill man, died when Yehudah Leib was only 12 years old. His upbringing fell to his grandfather, the illustrious Chidushei haRim. Yehudah Aryeh would study eighteen hours a day as a youth. It became widely known

that a fitting successor was being groomed for the Chiddushei haRim.

He was 19 years old when his grandfather died and, despite the pleas of the chassidim, insisted he was unworthy to become Gerrer Rebbe. Several years later, after the death of Rav Henach of Alexandrow, he acceded to their wishes and molded Ger into the largest chassidus in Poland.

A prodigious and diligent scholar, he nevertheless found time to counsel tens of thousands of disciples every year and to become an effective leader in Torah causes. His discourses were distinguished for profundity and originality.

Although he never wrote for publication, his writings were posthumously published as **Sefas Emes**, separate volumes of novellae on Talmud, and chassidic discourses on Torah and festivals.

Anaf Yosef

see *Rav Chanoch Zundel ben Yosef.*

Arama, Rav Yitzchak b. Moshe:
(1420-1494)

Spanish Rav, philospher and preacher. He was Rav of Calatayud where he wrote most of his works. After the expulsion of the Jews from Spain in 1492, he settled in Naples where he died.

He is best known for his book **Akeidas Yitzchak**, a collection of allegorical commentaries on the Torah. First published in 1522, it has been reprinted many times and has exercised great influence on Jewish thought.

Because of this work he is often referred to as the 'Baal Akeidah' ['author of the Akeidah.]

He also wrote a **Commentary on the Five Megillos** which was printed together with his *Commentary to the Torah* in Salonica, 1573.

He wrote *Yad Avshalom*, a commentary on *Proverbs*, in memory of his son-in-law Avshalom, who died shortly after his marriage.

Ashkenazi, Rav Shmuel Jaffe:
16th Century Rav in Constantinople.

Not being satisfied with any commentary to the *Midrash*, Rav Shmuel devoted himself to writing a comprehensive commentary to *Midrash Rabba* and to the *Aggados* in the *Talmud.*

His first published work was *Yefe Mar'eh* on the *Aggados* in the Jerusalem *Talmud* (1597); *Yefe To'ar* to *Midrash Rabba: Genesis, Exodus, and Leviticus* (1606); **Yefe Anaf** to *Ruth, Esther,* and *Lamentations* (1691); and *Yefe Kol* to *Song of Songs* (1739).

His commentary to *Ecclesiastes*, and his *halachic* writing are still in manuscript form.

Avodah Zarah

Talmudic tractate on *Seder Nezikin.*

Azulai, Rav Chaim Yosef David:
Known by his Hebrew acronym CHIDA.

Born in Jerusalem in 1724; died in Leghorn in 1806. Halachist, Kabbalist, and bibliographer-historian, he possessed great intellectual powers and many-faceted talents.

He went abroad as an emissary and he would send large sums of money back to Israel. He ended his mission in 1778 in Leghorn where he spent the rest of his life.

His fame as a *halachist* rests on his glosses to *Shulchan Aruch,* contained in his *Birkei Yosef,* a work constantly cited by later authorities.

He was the author of the famous bibliographic work Shem haGedolim. Among his many works was the homiletical **Nachal Eshkol** on the *Five Megillos,* and **Simchas haRegel** on *Ruth.*

Baal haTurim:

see *Rav Yaakov ben Asher.*

Bach:

see *Sirkes, Rav Yoel.*

Bachrach, Rav Yehoshua.

Contemporary Bible scholar on Israeli scene.

Educated in Lithuanian Yeshivos, the first of which was the Yeshivah of Rav Shimon Shkop in Grodno.

He is senior lecturer in *Neviim Rishonim* at the Jerusalem College for Women (Michlalah). He published a monumental study of David and Saul; a book on Jonah and Elijah; and a commentary on *Esther*. His commentary on Ruth, *Ima Shel Malchus* ("Mother of Royalty"), is a poetically profound synthesis of *p'shat* (plain meaning) and *d'rash* (homiletical interpretation).

Bamidbar Rabba:

The *Midrash Rabba* to *Numbers*. See *Midrash Rabba*.

Bava Basra:

Talmudic tractate in *Seder Nezikin*.

Bava Kamma:

Talmudic tractate in *Seder Nezikin*.

Behold a People:

see **Miller, Rav Avigdor*.

Besuras Eliyahu:

see *Rav Eliyahu Shlomo Avraham ha-Kohen*.

Binyan Ariel:

see *Rav Shaul ben Aryeh Leib of Amsterdam*.

Breuer, Rav Raphael:

(1881-1932)

Grandson of Rav S.R. Hirsch; son of Rav Shlomo Breuer; and late brother of Rav Joseph Breuer, shlita, of Washington Heights.

Rav Breuer was born in Papa, Hungary. He was district Rabbi at Aschaffenburg, Bavaria.

He published a commentary (in German) on many books of the Bible. His *Commentary on Ruth* was published as part of his commentary to the *Five Megillos* between the years 1908-12.

Rav Chanoch Zundel Ben Yosef

(d. 1867).

Rav Chanoch lived in Bialystock, Poland, where he devoted his life to writing commentaries on the *Midrash* and the *Ein Yaakov*.

He published two commentaries which appear side-by-side in the large editions of the *Midrash Rabba* and *Ein Yaakov*: *Eitz Yosef,* in which he strives to give the plain meaning of the text; and *Anaf Yosef* which is largely homiletical.

Rav Chanoch also published a commentary to *Pirkei Avos,* but his commentaries to *Yalkut Shim'oni* and the *Mechilta* are still in manuscript.

Chidah:

See *Azulai, Rav Chaim Yosef David*.

Chidushei haRim:

see *Alter, Rav Yitzchak Meir*.

Chafetz Chaim:

See *Rav Yisrael Meir haKohen*.

Rav Yehudah Leib Chasman:

(1869-1935)

Born in Lithuania, he studied in Slobodka, Volozhin, and Kelm. He was strongly influenced by three of the *Mussar* giants of the era: Rav Simcha Zisel Ziev of Kelm; Rav Yitzchak Lazar of St. Petersburg — both of whom were among the foremost disciples of Rav Yisrael Salanter; and Rabbi Nosson Zvi Finkel of Slobodka.

Rav Chasman held several positions as Rav and lecturer of Talmud. He found his place in Shtutzin, Lithuania, where, after assuming the rabbinate in 1909, he established a Yeshivah that grew to 300 students. However, the destruction and

dislocation brought about by World War I, destroyed the Torah life of the city.

After the War, Rav Chasman was a vital activist in rebuilding Torah life in Europe.

The call to become 'Mashgiach' (Spiritual Guide) of the Hebron Yeshivah in Eretz Yisrael, gave him the opportunity to become a seminal figure in the development of the Torah Yishuv.

Ohr Yohel, published posthumously by his students, is a collection of his lectures and writings.

Chayes, Rav Zvi Hirsch:

(1807-1856).

Born in the Galician region of Poland. Even at the age of 5 he was known as a prodigy, having mastered the entire T'nach by heart.

He was ordained at 21 by Rav Ephraim Zalman Margolias of Brody. Rav Chayes's most famous rabbinical position was Kalisch. He wrote extensively and originally in addition to glosses on the Talmud and halachic responsa. Noteworthy was his *M'vo haTalmud* (Introduction to the Talmud), printed in most editions of the Talmud; Responsa; *Imre Binah; Darkei Horaah.*

Among his most basic writings were a series of monographs called **Toras haNevi'im**, in which he dealt with and clarified many obscure topics in the Torah and post-Biblical tradition.

Derech Hashem:

see *Luzatto, Rav Moshe Chaim*

Dessler, Rav Eliyahu Eliezer:

(1891-1954).

One of the outstanding personalities of the Mussar movement. He was born in Homel, Russia.

In 1929 he settled in London. He excercised a profound influence on the teaching of Mussar, not only because of the profundity of his ideas, but also on

account of his personal, ethical conduct.

In 1941 he became director of the Kollel of Gateshead Yeshiva in London.

In 1947, at the invitation of Rav Yosef Kahaneman, he became Mashgiach of Ponovez Yeshiva in Bnei Brak, Israel, and there remained until his death.

His teachings reflect a harmonious mixture of Mussar, Kaballah, and Chassidus. Some of his ideas were published by his pupils in **Michtav me-Eliyahu** (3 vols. 1955-64).

Dubna Maggid:

See *Kranz, Rav Yaakov.*

Eidels, Rav Shmuel Eliezer ben Yehuda haLevi:

1555-1631.

(Known as Maharsha — Moreinu ha-Rav Shmuel Eliezer.)

One of the foremost Talmud commentators, whose **commentary** is included in almost every edition of the Talmud.

Born in Cracow, he moved to Posen in his youth. In 1614 he became Rav of Lublin, and in 1625 of Ostrog, where he founded a large Yeshivah.

Einhorn, Rav Zev Wolf:

Rav in Vilna, end of 19th century.

Author of **Peirush Maharzu,** comprehensive and well-detailed commentary to *Midrash Rabba* appearing in the Romm edition.

Rav Eleazar b. Yehudah of Worms:

[*Heb.* Eleazar of Germizah.] Also known as *Baal haRokeach*].

1160-1237.

Scholar in the field of Halachah, Kaballah, and Paytan in medieval Germany. Student of Rav Yehudah haChassid the author of *Sefer Chassidim.*

Rav Eleazar is known primarily for his authoritative halachic work **Sefer**

Rokeach, which is quoted extensively in the *Shulchan Aruch.*

His students were many, among them Rav Yitzchak of Vienna, author of *Or Zarua.* Among his exegetical works are **Shaarei Binah.**

Rav Eliyahu Shlomo Avraham haKohen:

(d. 1729).

Born in Smyrna, he spent most of his life there as *Dayyan* and *Rav.*

His most famous works are *Shevet Mussar* on Ethics and homiletics; *Midrash halttamari,* a homiletical work on ethical subjects. Because of this work, he became known as 'Rav Eliyahu halttamari'. He also wrote *Midrash Talpiyos,* novellae on various subjects arranged alphabetically; and *D'na Pashra* [abbreviated: *Perush SHir Hashirim, Ruth, Esther]* commentary on three *Megillos:* — *Song of Songs, Ruth* and *Esther.*

The commentary on *Ruth* is entitled **B'suras Eliyahu.**

Rav Eliyahu ben Shlomo Zalman of Vilna [Vilna Gaon]:

Also known by his acronym haGRA = haGaon Rav Eliyahu.

(Born, first day Passover 1720; died third day of Chol haMoed Sukkos 1797).

One of the greatest spiritual leaders of Jewry in modern times. A child prodigy and man of phenomenal genius, his knowledge of every facet of Torah learning was without equal. His glosses and commentaries encompassed nearly every one of the important classical writings.

The GRA also familiarized himself with astronomy, algebra, and geography in order to better understand certain Talmudic laws and discussions.

According to his sons, he did not sleep more than two hours a night, and never for more than half an hour at a time. He would often study with his feet in cold water to prevent himself from falling asleep.

More than 70 of his works and commentaries have been published. His **Commentary to Ruth** has been reprinted several times.

His influence was immense. According to the testimony of one of his contemporaries, 'without his knowledge, no important activity can be carried out.'

Epstein, Rav Baruch haLevi:

(1860-1940).

Born in Bobruisk, Russia. He received his early education from his father, Rav Yechiel Michel Epstein, author of *Aruch haShulchan.*

Rav Baruch later studied under his uncle, Rav Naftali Zvi Yehudah Berlin [the 'Netziv'].

He was the author of several works, but he is best known for a brilliant commentary to Chumash **Torah T'mimah,** in which he quotes and explains the Halachic and Aggadic passages on the various verses. He also wrote **Gishmei Bracha** on the Five *Megillos.*

Eshkol haKofer:

See *Sava, Rav Avraham ben Yaakov.*

*Feinstein, Rav Moshe:

Contemporary Posek and Rosh Yeshivah, Harav Feinstein is considered by many to be the *Gadol Hador* — Torah leader of the generation.

Born in Russia in 1895, Harav Feinstein was known as a child prodigy. He came to America in 1937 and became Dean of Mesivtha Tiferet Jerusalem on New York's lower East side. Harav Feinstein responds to Halachic inquiries from around the world daily. Author of 'Igrose Moshe' — 5 volumes of his Halachic responsa; and an ongoing series of *Dibrose Moshe* — his novellae on Talmud.

Gans, Rav David.

(1541-1516).

Chronicler and mathematician.

Rav David was a student of the RAMA (Rav Moshe Isserles) and the MAHARAL of Prague (Rav Yehudah Loew), where he mastered his Talmudic studies.

He spent most of his life in Prague where he wrote many works, most of which have been lost.

Encouraged by the RAMA, Rav David published the historical work for which he is most famous: *Tzemach David*. The book is in two parts: one part deals with Jewish history; the other with general history.

This work has become a standard reference work for later chroniclers.

Gishmei Brachah:

see *Epstein, Rav Baruch haLevi.*

halkriti:

see *Rav Shemariah ben Eliyahu halkriti.*

Heilprin, Rav Yechiel b. Shlomo:

(1660-1746).

Lithuanian Rav, Kabbalist and historian.

He was a descendant of RASHAL (Rav Shlomo Luria), and traced his ancestry back through Rashi to the Tanna, Rav Yochanan haSandlar.

He was Rav and Rosh Yeshivah at Minsk, where he studied Kabbalah and published several works.

He is most known for his **Seder haDoros**, a history from Creation down to his own time.

He based his work on *Sefer haYuchsin* of Rav Avraham Zacuto; *Shalsheles haKaballah* of Rav Gedaliah ibn Yachya; and *Tzemach David* of Rav David Gans, as well as on an abundance of Talmudic and Midrashic references.

Hirsch, Rav Shamshon Raphael:

(1808-1888).

The father of modern German Orthodoxy. He was a fiery leader, brilliant writer, and profound educator. His greatness as a Talmudic scholar was obsured by his other monumental accomplishments. After becoming chief Rabbi and member of Parliament in Bohemia and Moravia, he left to revitalize Torah Judaism in Frankfort-am-Main which he transformed into a Torah bastion.

His best known works are the classic six-volume **Commentary on Chumash** noted for its profound and brilliant philosophical approach to Biblical commentary; and *Horeb,* a philosophical analysis of the mitzvos.

Ibn Ezra, Rav Avraham:

(Born 1089 in Toledo; died 1164).

Famous poet, philosopher, grammarian, astronomer — and above all — Biblical commentator. He also wrote a **Commentary on the Megillos** — including Ruth.

In all his Bible commentaries he strived for the plain, literal meaning of the verse. His aim was to explain the etymology of difficult words within their grammatical context. Next to Rashi, his commentary on the Torah is most widely studied, and appears in almost all large editions of the Bible.

In France, he met Rav Yaakov Tam ['Rabbeinu Tam'] — grandson of Rashi], and a deep friendship between the two followed.

According to some, he married the daughter of Rav Yehudah haLevi, and had five sons.

Legend has it that he once met the Rambam and dedicated a poem to him on the day of his death.

Ibn Shushan, Rav Yehudah

Rav in Magnesia, about 1500.

Member of illustrious Ibn Shushan Spanish family of Toledo, which can be traced back to the 12th century.

Little is known about Rav Yehudah. He is the author of a **Commentary on Ruth,** and is quoted extensively in many *halachic* works, and by *Iggeres Shmuel.*

Ibn Yachya, Rav Yosef.

Bible commentator; member of the famous Ibn Yachya family of which many scholars were descendants.

He was born in Florence, Italy in 1494, his parents having fled to that country from Portugal.

He relates in his preface to his *Torah Or* that in her first month of pregnancy with him, his mother, under threat of being ravaged, had thrown herself off a roof in Pisa, in order to preserve her modesty, and she was miraculously saved.

She then fled to Florence where he was born.

He published his **Commentary to the Five Megillos.** Two of his other works: *Derech Chaim* and *Ner Mitzvah* were consigned to flames at the burning of the Talmud in Padua in 1554.

Rav Yosef had three sons, one of whom was Gedaliah, the author of *Shalsheles haKabbalah.*

Rav Yosef died in 1534. Ten years after his death his remains were brought to Eretz Yisrael. Rav Yosef Caro arranged for his burial in Safed.

Iggeres Shmuel:

See *Uzeda, Rav Shmuel de.*

Ima Shel Malchus:

see *Bachrach, Rav Yehoshua.*

Josephus, Flavius

[Hebrew: Yosef ben Gorion haKohen].

Jewish, Roman general and historian (born in 37 or 38; died after 100).

He boasted of belonging to the Hasmonim dynasty on his mother's side. As a boy he was distinguished by his profound memory.

During the great Jewish war in 66, he was entrusted by the Sanhedrin with the defense of the Galilee.

Captured in the war and led before Vespasian, he prophecised that Vespasian would become Emperor (just as Rav Yochanan ben Zakkai had also done) — and Vespasian released him, rewarding him with a command in the Roman army.

He spent the rest of his life writing a history and 'apology' of the Jews — which is a classic, eye-witness account of the period. The accuracy, however, of the religious sections is questionable. He was generally despised as a traitor and turncoat by the Jews.

It is said that a statue of him was erected in Rome after his death.

Kimchi, Rav David:

French grammarian; known by his acronym 'RADAK'.

Born in Narbonne, 1160; died there in 1235.

His father, Rav Yosef, also a grammarian died when Rav David was a child, and he studied under his brother, Rav Moshe, who had also published several volumes on grammar.

Radak's commentary on Bible is profound, and is included in most large editions of the Bible.

Many have applied to him the saying from *Pirkei Avos*: 'Without *kemach* ['flour' i.e. 'Kimchi'] no Torah; such was his great influence.

His main work was the **Michlol,** the second edition of which came to be known independantly as *the Sefer ha-Sharashim.*

In his commentary, he stressed the *derech ha'peshat*, the plain sense, wherever possible, striving for clarity and readibility, rather than the com-

pression and obscurity of some of his contemporary commentators.

His **Commentary to Ruth** was published in Paris, 1563.

Kitov, Rav Eliyahu.

Israeli scholar and author; died, 1976.

Famous for his *Ish uBeiso* ('The Jew and His Home'); **Sefer haTodaah** ('The Book of our Heritage'), both of which have been translated into English by Rav Nathan Bulman; and his series of *Sefer haParshios* on the Five Books of the Bible.

Kol Yaakov:

See *Kranz, Rav Yaakov.*

Kol Yehuda:

Kabbalistic and philosophical commentary to **Ruth,** *Lamentations,* and *Esther,* by Rav Yehudah Leib ben Eliezer published in 1727.

Rav Yaakov Kranz:

(1741-1804).

Known as the 'Dubna Maggid.'

Born near Vilna; Rav Yaakov demonstrated his skill as a preacher at an early age, and was barely 20 years old when he became *darshan* in his city. He later became *darshan* in several cities, but he achieved his fame as preacher in Dubna where he served for 18 years.

He came into frequent contact with the Vilna Gaon, who, it is said, enjoyed his homiletical interpretations, stories, and parables.

The Dubna Maggid's works were printed posthumously by his son Yitzchak, and his pupil Baer Flahm. Among these works were: *Ohel Yaakov* on *Chumash;* **Kol Yaakov** on the *Five Megillos;* Commentary on the Passover *Haggadah;* and *Mishlei Yaakov,* a collection of his parables.

Rav Levi ben Gershom:

(Acronym: RALBAG).

Born in Bangols, France in 1288; died 1344.

One of the most important Bible commentators of his time, he was also a mathematician, astonomer, philosopher, and physician.

He wrote commentaries to *Job, Song of Songs, Ecclesiastes;* **Ruth;** *Esther;* the Five Books of the Torah; Former Prophets; *Proverbs; Daniel; Nechemiah;* and *Proverbs.*

His commentary to *Job* was one of the first books printed in Hebrew (Ferrara, 1477).

Lipowitz, Rav Yosef:

Noted Israeli Bible scholar and lecturer of the last generation.

Rav Lipowitz was one of the outstanding pupils of Rav Nosson Finkel *(der Alter)* of Slobodka.

He published several works on Bible, among them the very philosophical **Nachalas Yosef**, his commentary on *Ruth.* Written in poetic Hebrew, the author appears to be lecturing, as it were, weaving the various Midrashim and philosophical *ha-hkafos* [perspective] into a flowing, lucid commentary.

Luria, Rav David:

(1798-1855; Known as RADAL).

Lithuanian Rav and *posek.* Student of Rav Shaul Katzenellenbogen of Vilna.

After the death of his mentor, the Vilna Gaon, Radal was considered one of the Torah leaders of is generations. His scholarly writings embrace almost all of Torah literature. Among his works is his commentary to the Midrash, **Chidushei Radal**, printed in the Romm edition of the *Midrash Rabba.*

Luzatto, Rav Moshe Chaim

(1707-1746)

Kabbalist; author of Mussar ethical works; and poet.

Born in Padua, Italy, Rav Moshe Chaim was regarded as a genius from child-

hood, having mastered *T'nach, Midrash* and *Talmud* at an early age. He later went on to delve into Kabbalistic and ethical studies.

He is most famous for his profound ethical treatise, *Mesilas Yesharim* ('The Path of the Upright') which has, alongside the *Chovos haLevavos* of Rav Bachya ibn Paquda, became the standard ethical-Mussar work.

Among his Kabbalistic works were: Razin Genizin, **Megillas Sesarim;** *Maamar haGeulah;* **Derech Hashem.**

In 1743, he emigrated to Eretz Yisrael. He lived a short time in Acre, and died there, with his family, in a plague.

Maharal:

see *Rav Yehudah Loewe ben Bezalel.*

Maharsha:

see *Eidels, Rav Shmuel Eliezer ben Yehudah haLevi.*

Malbim, Rav Meir Leibush:

(1809-1879).

Rav, preacher and Biblical commentator.

The name Malbim is an acronym of 'Meir Leibush ben Yechiel Michel.'

The Malbim was also known as the 'ilui [prodigy] from Volhynia.' He was Rav in several cities, but he suffered much persecution on account of his uncompromising stand against Reform, leading to his short-term imprisonment on a false accusation. He wandered much of his life, serving as Rav in various cities for several years at a time.

His fame and immense popularity rests upon his commentary to the Bible which was widely esteemed. His first published commentary was on *Megillas Esther* (1845). His commentary to the remaining books of the Bible were published between then and 1876. His commentary to *Ruth* is entitled **Geza Yishai.**

Margolios, Rav Chaim Mordechai.

Polish Rav and *Posek;* died in 1818.

Rav Chaim was Rav in Great Dubna, where he operated a printing office.

Together with his brother Rav Ephraim [author of *Bais Ephraim* and *Mattei Ephraim*], he published **Shaarei Teshuvah**, a digest of the Responsa literature dealing with the laws of the *Shulchan Aruch Orach Chaim*, from the time of Rav Yosef Karo until his day.

This work was continued on the three remaining sections of *Shulchan Aruch* by Rav Tzvi Hirsch Eisenstadt and published under the name *Pis'chei Teshuvah.*

Mashal Umelitzah

Collection of homiletic interpretations on the Torah by Rav Avraham Naftali Galanti. Published in New York City during the last generation.

Matanos Kehunah:

see *Rav Yissachar Berman haKohen.*

Megilas Sesarim:

see *Luzatto, Rav Moshe Chaim.*

Michtav me-Eliyahu:

see *Dessler, Rav Eliyahu Eliezer.*

Michlol:

see *Kimchi, Rav David.*

Meishiv Nefesh:

see *Sirkes, Rav Yoel.*

Midrash:

see *Midrash Rabbah.*

Midrash haNe'elam:

see *Zohar Chadash.*

Midrash Lekach Tov:

Early Midrash on various Books of the Bible. This *Midrash* has been published at separate times on the various books of the Bible as the manuscripts have

been discovered. *Ruth* was published in 1867.

Midrash Rabbah:

[Lit. 'The Great Midrash'].

The oldest Amoraic classical *Midrash* on the *Five Books of the Bible and the Megillos.*

[Note: Throughout the commentary of this Book, whenever 'Midrash' alone is shown as the source, the reference is to Midrash Ruth Rabba.]

Midrash Tanchuma:

The ancient *Midrash* on the Torah which has come down to us in two versions.

One of the versions is the oldest collections of *Midrashim* known.

Midrash Zuta.

Also called *Ruth Zuta* ('Minor Ruth'). This *Midrash* was probably compiled before the 10th century. It is quoted by the author of *Midrash Lekach Tov* which was written in the 11th century.

It was published by Buber from a Parma manuscript in 1894.

*Miller, Rav Avigdor:

Contemporary Rav, noted lecturer and author. A major force on the American Orthodox scene. Rav in Brooklyn, New York. Author of *Rejoice O Youth!; Sing You Righteous; Torah Nation; Behold A People.*

Minchas Shay:

see *Rav Yedidiah Shlomo of Norzi.*

M'lo haOmer:

see *Zeunz, Rav Aryeh Leib.*

Rav Moshe ben Maimon:

Known by his acronym: RAMBAM; Maimonides.

(1135-1204).

One of the most illustrious figures in Judaism in the post-Talmudic era, and among the greatest of all time. He was a rabbinic authority, codifier, philosopher, and royal physician. According to some, he was a descendant of Rav Yehudah haNasi.

Born in Cordoba; Moved to Eretz Yisrael and then to Fostat, the old city of Cairo, Egypt.

At the age of 23 he began his commentary on the *Mishnah,* which he authored all through his wanderings. His main work was *Mishneh-Torah Yad-haChazakah,* his codification of the spectrum of *Halachah* until his day. This was the only book he wrote in Hebrew, all his other works having been written in Arabic, a fact he regretted later in life.

He is also known for his *Moreh Nevuchim ('Guide for the Perplexed'),* and for his many works in the field of medicine, hygiene, astronomy, etc.

Truly it may be said 'from Moshe to Moshe there arose none like Moshe.'

Rav Moshe ben Nachman:

Known by his acronym: RAMBAN; Nachmanides.

(1194-1270)

One of the leading Torah scholars and authors of Talmudic literature during the generation following Rambam; also a renowned philosopher, biblical commentator, poet and physician .

Born in Gerona, to a famous rabbinic family. He is sometimes referred to, after his native town, as Rabbenu Moshe Gerondi, where he spent most of his life, supporting himself as a physician. He exercised extensive influence over Jewish life. Even King James I consulted him on occasion.

Already at the age of 16 he had published works on Talmud and Halachah.

Among his works were: *Milchemes Hashem,* in defense of the Rif against the 'hasagos' of Rav Zerachiah haLevi in his Sefer haMaor; *Sefer haZechus,* in response to the 'hasagos' of the Ravad on the Rif; *Sefer haMitzvos; Iggeres*

haRamban; Iggeres haKodesh; and his profound and encyclopedic **Commentary on the Torah,** which is printed in all large editions of the Bible.

in 1263 he was coerced by King Jame I into holding a public disputation with the apostate Pablo Christiani which led to a victory for the Ramban, but which aroused the anger of the of the church and resulted in his barely secceeding to escape from Spain. He then emigrated to Eretz Yisrael. In 1268 he became Rav in Acco, successor to Rav Yechiel of Paris.

He died in 1276; his burial site has not been definitely ascertained.

Nachalas Yosef:

see *Lipowitz, Rav Yosef.*

Nachal Eshkol:

see *Azulai, Rav Chaim Yosef David.*

Niddah:

Talmudic tractate in *Seder Nashim.*

Ohr Yohel:

See *Chasman, Rav Yehudah Leib.*

Pirkei Avos:

"Chapters" or *"Ethics"* of the Fathers. A Talmudic tractate in *Seder Nezikin.* Read in the Synagogue on Shabbos afternoons from Passover to Rosh Hashanah.

Pirkei d'Rabbi Eliezer:

Ancient aggadic work attributed to the first century *Tanna,* Rabbi Eliezer ben Hyrcanos.

Pri Chaim:

Commentary to the *Five Megillos* by Rav Chaim Knoller, published in Premyshla, Poland c 1903.

The **Commentary on Ruth** is based on the approach of the *Malbim* whom the author quotes extensively and upon whom he elaborates in a most original manner.

Also by the same author is *Kavod Chachamim* in which he explains what may seem to be discrepencies between the *aggados* of the Talmud and quoted verses in the Bible, as well as Masoretic differences.

Pri Tzaddik:

See next entry.

Rabinowitz, Rav Tzadok haKohen:

(1823-1900)

Born in Kreisburg, Latvia, young Tzadok attracted attention as a phenomenal genius. Orphaned at the age of six, he was raised by his uncle near Bialystock. Such was the child's reputation, that Rav Yitzchak Elchanan Spektor of Kovno made a point of testing him when he happened to be near by.He prophesied that 'the boy will light a great torch of knowledge in Israel.

In later years, Rav Tzadok lived in Lublin where he became acquainted with Rav Leibele Eiger, a disciple of Rav Mordechai Yosef of Izbica. Rav Tzadok became their disciple, and, with their passing, became Rebbe of the Chassidim of Izbica. He became known far and wide as the 'Kohen of Lublin'. The breadth and depth of his thought were astonishing. Many considered him the greatest Torah scholar in all of Poland.

Pri Tzaddik, is a collection of his discourses on the weekly portion, and festivals. He was a very prolific writer. Although much of his works have been published, he left many unpublished manuscripts that were destroyed during World War II.

Among his other works are Responsa *Tiferes Zvi; Meishiv Tzaddik;* and *Resisei Layla.*

Radak:

see *Kimchi, Rav David.*

Ralbag:

see *Rav Levi ben Gershom.*

Rambam:

see *Rav Moshe ben Maimon.*

Ramban:

See *Rav Moshe ben Nachman.*

Rashba haLevi:

see *Alkabetz, Rav Shlomo haLevi.*

Rashi:

see *Rav Shlomo ben Yitzchak.*

Saba, Rav Avraham ben Yaakov.

15-16th Century Kabbalist, Bible commentator and Darshan.

Rav Avraham was among those expelled from Spain in 1492. He moved to Portugal where he wrote his commentary **Eshkol haKofer** to the *Chumash,* the *Five Megillos,* and *Pirkei Avos.*

In his youth, many of his works were lost, and he was forced to rewrite them later in life from memory.

His commentary to the *Chumash* was entitled *Tzror haMor.*

According to the *Shem haGedolim,* he died on board a ship on Erev Yom Kippur 1508.

Sanhedrin:

Talmudic tractate in *Seder Nezikin.*

Seder haDoros:

see *Heilprin, Rav Yechiel b. Shlomo.*

Seder Olam:

Early Midrashic-chronological work. *Seder Olam* is mentioned in the Talmud (*Shab. 88a; Yev. 82b et al.*) and is ascribed to the *Tanna* Rav Yose ben Chalafta.

Sefas Emes:

See *Alter, Rav Yehudah Aryeh Leib.*

Shaar Bas Rabim:

Scholarly and erudite anthology of commentaries on the Torah and *Megil-*

los by Rav Chaim Aryeh Leib Yedvav-nah; late 19th century.

Sefer haTodaah:

see *Kitov, Rav Eliyahu.*

Shaarei Binah:

see *Rav Eleazar ben Yehudah of Worms.*

Shaarei Teshuvah:

see *Margolios, Rav Chaim Mordechai.*

Rav Shaul ben Aryeh Leib of Amsterdam:

Born 1717 in Risha; died in Amsterdam, 1790.

Member of famous rabbinical family.

Served as Rav in many important cities, and upon the death of his father he replaced him as Rav of the prestigious Ashkenazi community of Amsterdam, where he served until his death.

He published many works on Bible, Talmud and Halachah, most famous of which was **Binyan Ariel.**

When the Chidah visited Amsterdam, he stayed at the home of Rav Shaul and was so awed by his erudition and righteousness, that he praised him most flourishingly in his *Shem haGedolim.*

Rav Shemariah ben Eliyahu haIkriti:

(1275-1355).

Italian Bible commentator and philosopher. When he was a child, his family moved to Crete where his father was appointed Rabbi; hence his surname 'haIkriti' ['the Cretan'] or, as he is also known, 'haYevani', ['the Greek'].

Until the age of thirty he studied Bible almost exclusively; then he immersed himself in Talmud and philosophy. His reputation as a Bible scholar was so great that he was invited to the court of King Robert of Naples, a patron of Jewish learning, where he devoted himself to his studies, and published *Philosophical Commentaries* on the Bible, of which his commentary to *Song of Songs* is still extant.

He is quoted extensively by the early commentators, among them: *Rav Alkabetz; Alshich;* and *Iggeres Shmuel.*

Among his other works were *Elef haMagen,* a commentary on the Aggadah in tractate *Megillah;* and *Piyyutim.*

He tried to reconcile the Rabbanites and Karaites, and because of this certain zealots leveled accusations against him, and he died in prison.

Shem haGedolim:

see *Azulai, Rav Chaim Yosef David.*

Rav Shlomo ben Yitzchok:

(RASHI)

Leading commentator on the Bible and Talmud.

He was born in Troyes, France in 1040 — the year in which Rabbeinu Gershom M'or haGolah died. According to tradition, Rashi's ancestry goes back to Rav Yochanan haSandlar and to King David.

The summit of Rashi's commentaries was his commentary on the Talmud — an encyclopaedic and brillian undertaking. Nothing can be compared to the impact this commentary has had upon all who study the Talmud. Rashi's commentary has opened to all what otherwise would have been a sealed book. Without his commentary, no one would dare navigate the 'Sea of Talmud.' Every word is precise and laden with inner meaning. Rashi's corrections of the Talmud text were, for the most part, introduced into the standard editions and became the accepted text.

Rashi's **Commentary to the Bible**, too, made a similar impact — and virtually every printed Bible contains his commentary which is distinguished by its conciseness and clarity.

Many Halachic works from the 'School of Rashi' have come down to us: *Sefer haOrah; Sefer haPardes; Machzor Vitry; Siddur Rashi;* and responsa.

Rashi died on Tammuz 29, 1105. His burial place is not known.

Shabbos:

Talmudic tractate in *Seder Moed.*

Shoresh Yishai:

See *Alkabetz, Rav Shlomo haLevi.*

Sirkes, Rav Yoel:

(known as 'BACH' from his work 'Bayis Chashash')

Polish *Rav, Posek* and Commentator. Born in Lublin in 1561.

Student of Rav Shlomo, Rav of the City, he then studied in the Yeshiva of Brisk under Rav Meshullam Feivish (later Rav of Cracow), and Rav Zvi Hirsh Shur, a student of the RAMA.

Rav Sirkes was Rabbi in many cities, among them Lublin, Brisk and Cracow.

His most famous works are *Bayis Chadash* [BACH] on the *Tur, Hagahos HaBach* on the *Talmud,* and his Responsa.

He published an analytical commentary of *Ruth* entitled **Meishiv Nefesh** along with his super-commentary on *Rashi, Be'er Mayim.*

In his old age he wanted to emigrate to Eretz Yisrael, but he never did. He died in Cracow at the age of 79 in 1640.

Soloveichik, Rav Yitzchak Zev haLevi

(1889-1960)

Known as Rav Velvele Brisker.

Son of Rav Chaim Brisker, Rav Velvele was regarded by many to be the supreme *Talmudic* authority of his day.

Born in Volozhin, he was the student of his father Rav Chaim, who was his only teacher.

His erudition and acumen were evident in his early youth, and upon the death of his father, he succeeded him as Rav in Brisk where he became a central figure in the Torah world. During World War II his wife and four children were murdered in Brisk; he fled to Vilna with his surviving five sons and two daughters, and managed to flee from

there to Eretz Yisrael.

He settled in Jerusalem, where he founded a kollel for a group of select young men. Later a yeshiva was founded which was administered by his Rav Yosef Dov.

He confined himself to his studies, and was considered the spiritual heir of the Chazon Ish (Rav Yeshaya Karelitz).

He exercised a great influence over extensive circles in the Torah world.

Sotah

Talmudic tractate in *Seder Nashim*.

Tanchuma

See *Midrash Tanchuma*.

Targum

The ancient, authoritative translation of the Bible into Aramaic.

Toldos Am Olam:

See *Rottenberg, Rav Shlomo*.

Torah Nation

See *Miller, Rav Avigdor*.

Torah T'mimah

See Epstein, *Rav Baruch haLevi*.

Tzemach David

See Gans, *Rav David*.

Uzeda, Rav Shmuel de

Born in Safed c. 1540.

He studied Kabbalah with Rav Yitzchak Luria [ARI zal] and Rav Chaim Vital.

In 1557 he traveled to Constantinople where he published his commentary, an encyclopedic super-commentary on Ruth, **Iggeres Shmuel,** which has been reprinted many times and appears in large editions of the Bible.

His most famous work is *Midrash Shmuel,* a detailed commentary on *Pirkei Avos* with reference to many connecting sources such as Rabbenu Yona of Gerondi, Meiri, Rav Yosef Ibn

Shushan, and Rashbam, which were at that time in manuscript, but have since been printed.

Rav Velvele Brisker

See *Soloveichik, Rav Yitzchak Zev haLevi*.

Vilna Gaon

See *Rav Eliyahu ben Shlomo Zalma of Vilna*.

Rav Yaakov ben Asher

(1270-1340)

Posek and codifier.

Son of Rav Asher ben Yechiel (the 'ROSH') under whom he studied. He was born in Germany, and in 1303 he accompanied his father to Toledo, where he lived in great poverty, and devoted his life to Torah.

Rav Yaakov's enduring fame rests on his encyclopaedic Halachic codification *Arbaah Turim,* which is the forerunner of our Shulchan Aruch today, and as a result of which he is referred to as the "Baal haTurim."

The arrangement and wealth of content made it a basic work in halachah and it was disseminated greatly through the Jewish world. It became so widely accepted, that when Rav Yosef Caro wrote his major work, *Bais Yosef,* , he decided to "base it upon the *Turim* "because it contains most of its views of the *Poskim*."

Rav Yaakov also wrote a comprehensive commentary on the Chumash anthologizing the literal explanations *(p'shat)* by earlier Bible commentators. To the beginning of each section he added "as a little appetizer, *gemmatrios* and explanations of the *Masorah,* in order to attract the mind." Ironically the whole work was printed only twice. It was just these "appetizers" that were popularly published alongside most editions of the Bible under the title **Ba'al HaTurim.**

Among Rav Yaakov's students was Rav David Abudarham.

According to *Shem haGedolim* Rav Yaakov died en route to Eretz Yisrael.

Yalkut Shimoni

The best known and most comprehensive Midrashic anthology covering the entire Bible.

It is attributed to Rav Shimon ha-Darshan of Frankfort who lived in the 13th century.

The author collected *Midrashim* from more than 50 works, arranging them into more than 10,000 statements of *Aggadah Halachah* according to the verses of the Bible.

Yavetz, Rav Yitzchak ben Shlomo

Turkish Bible commentator in the second half of the sixteenth century.

He published commentaries on *Pirkei Avos* and most of the Bible.

His commentary on *Ruth* is called *Tzemach Tzaddik*. He is quoted extensively by *Iggeres Shmuel*.

Rav Yedidiah Shlomo of Norzi

Rav and Commentator.

Born in Mantua 1560; died in 1626. Became Rav in Mantua in 1585.

Rav Yedidiah consecrated the greater part of his life to studying the *Masorah* of the Bible — and by studying every previously printed *Masorah* text, comparing the various readings scattered through *Talmudic* and *Midrashic* literature, as well as in published and unpublished manuscripts.

The resulting work was entitled *Poretz Geder* but was published under the name *Minchas Shai*.

This work, which was as perfect as thorough learning and conscientious industry could make it, has become the most accepted work in establishing the *Masorah*. The *Minchas Shai* is printed in the back of all large Bibles.

Rav Yehudah Loewe ben Bezalel.

Known as the MAHARAL of Prague.

One of the seminal figures in the last 500 years of Jewish thought, Rav Yehudah was born c. 1512 and died in Prague in 1609. His genealogy can be traced to King David.

Although he was universally acknowledged as one of the rabbinic greats of the era, while his life was not an easy one. He delayed his marriage for 20 years due to financial difficulties. He was Chief Rabbi of Moravia, residing in Nikolsburg, for 20 years. Then, in 1573, he transferred his yeshiva to Prague, the Torah metropolis of Europe. Upon two different occasions, he accepted the rabbinate of Posen in order to settle communal strife.

He was elected Chief Rabbi of Prague in 1597 as a very old man. It appears that the position had been denied him up to then because of his outspokenness in attacking social evils and religious laxity.

Though commonly known as a folk hero and miracle worker, his greatest contribution was his formulation of a self-contained system of Jewish thought. His many books and lengthy sermons formed the basis for much of the significant writing of succeeding centuries.

Among his many erudite works were: *Novellae* on *Shulchan Aruch Yoreh Deah; Gur Aryeh* on the Torah; *Be'er haGolah* on the Passover *Hagaddah; Derech Chaim; Netzach Yisrael; Nesivos Olam,* etc. Many of his works are extant and were recently republished in an 18-volume set: *Sifrei Maharal.*

Yefe Anaf

See *Ashkenazi, Rav Shmuel Jaffe.*

Yerushalmi, Peah

Tractate *Peah* in the Jerusalem Talmud.

Yevamos

Talmudic tractate in *Seder Nashim.*

Rav Yissachar Berman haKohen

Known as Berman Ashkenazi.

16-17th Century commentator on the Midrash.

Very little is known about him except that he was born in Sczebrzesyn, Poland, and that he was a student of the Rama (Rav Moshe Isserles).

He is the author of the famous commentary to the Midrash Rabba, *Matanos Kehuna,* first published in 1584, and appearing subsequently in nearly every edition of the Midrash.

Rav Yissachar makes it very clear in his introduction that he was very concerned with establishing the correct text for the *Midrashim,* basing his text upon all the various printed editions up to his time and on various manuscripts.

Zohar Chadash

A part of the *Zohar* which was printed slightly later than the main body of the text. Incorporated within the *Zohar Chadash* is the **Midrash haNe'elam** on the Torah and **Midrash Ruth haNe'elam. Midrash Ruth haNe'elam** as also appeared as a separate work called *Tapuchei Zahav.*

Zos Nechemasi

Commentary on *Ruth* by Rav Shlomo ben Chaim Chaykl Yanovsky of Warsaw; early 19th Century.

Zuenz, Rav Aryeh Leib

(1773-1833)

Polish Rav and Kabbalist. At a young age his genius was recognized and he became known as Leib Charif ('sharp-witted').

For a time he was Rav of Prague, then Warsaw, then he became Rosh Yeshiva in Praga, a suburb of Warsaw.

He was the author of many works, and on his deathbed he promised to intercede in Heaven on behalf of anyone who published his works, with the result that many Jews came forward to publish them.

He is known for his *Get Mekushar* and *Geresh Yerachim.* His commentary on Ruth is called **M'lo ha'Omer.**

kids' baking

THE AUSTRALIAN
Women's Weekly

contents

Baking with your children is a wonderful experience and a great excuse to spend time together. I love baking with my two granddaughters. Don't forget, children need help when starting out in the kitchen — an adult must be supervising at all times. Check out the helpful hints and safety tips in the front of this book, to make sure your junior chefs turn into brilliant bakers.
Editorial & Food Director

Australian cup and spoon measurements are metric. A conversion chart appears on page 77.

When you're cooking there should always be an adult with you, especially when using knives, a hot stove, boiling water, electrical appliances and the oven. Be careful when opening and closing a hot oven, and always use oven mitts when taking baking dishes, oven trays or cake pans out of the oven.

CHECKING EGGS

Always check eggs before you use them in a recipe. If you crack an egg straight in with the other ingredients you run the risk of having egg shell in your finished recipe. Or if the egg has gone bad, you will have to throw the whole bowl of ingredients away and start again. Use the back of a butter knife to gently crack the egg then pull the shell apart letting the egg white and yolk drop into a small clean bowl. Check egg for freshness and remove any bits of shell before using it in the recipe.

SOFT PEAKS

To whip cream until soft peaks form, use an electric mixer or a whisk to whip air into the cream until it begins to thicken. When you lift the beaters out of the cream, the tips of the cream peaks should droop and fall over – the cream will just hold its shape when dropped from a spoon. This is the same for beating egg whites. Egg whites must be beaten in a clean, dry bowl and make sure there are no bits of egg yolk or the egg whites will not beat up at all.

MEASURING

To use a measuring cup or tablespoon properly for dry ingredients, shake the ingredient loosely into the cup, don't pack it in (unless the recipe tells you to). Level off the surface with the back of a knife or metal spatula. For wet ingredients, use a measuring jug with the measures clearly labelled on the side. Pour the wet ingredient into the jug, bend down so your eyes are the same level as the top surface of the liquid and check the right amount of liquid is in the jug.

baking tips & safety

CREAMING
Have all the ingredients at room temperature. Most butter cakes begin with the creaming process in which the butter and sugar are beaten until light and fluffy. This process puts air into the mixture and helps the sugar start to dissolve (it continues to dissolve in the oven). It is best to do this with a benchtop electric mixer or hand-held mixer – a food processor won't get enough air into the mixture. Rinse the bowl and beaters under hot water and dry well before mixing ingredients.

TURNING OUT A CAKE
Using oven mitts, carefully remove the cake pan from the oven and sit it on a heatproof mat or wooden board. Push a metal or wooden skewer into the cake then pull it back out. If there is no cake mixture stuck to the skewer, the cake is cooked. Turn the cake pan upside-down onto a wire rack; remove the pan then lining paper. Put another rack over cake bottom and, holding the two racks like a sandwich, turn the cake over so it's top-side up.

MELTING CHOCOLATE
Break chocolate pieces into a microwave-safe bowl and leave it uncovered; put it in a microwave oven on medium (55%) for 1 minute. Stir chocolate with a plastic spatula or metal spoon (not a wooden spoon). If it hasn't melted completely, repeat the microwave method, in shorter bursts, until chocolate is smooth. Or, place chocolate pieces in a heatproof bowl over a saucepan of barely simmering water (the water must not touch base of the bowl). Stir chocolate until it is melted and smooth.

cakes

Try making a simple cake, like a cinnamon tea cake, perfect
for an afternoon tea with grandma. Or what about the ultimate
cool cake — the raspberry swirl? You will love how easy and fun
these recipes are for beginner cake-bakers.

tip Un-iced cake can be
frozen for up to 3 months.
Wrap in plastic wrap, then foil.

marble cake

- **250g (8 ounces) butter, softened**
- **1 teaspoon vanilla extract**
- **1¼ cups (275g) caster (superfine) sugar**
- **3 eggs**
- **2¼ cups (335g) self-raising flour**
- **¾ cup (180ml) milk**
- **pink food colouring**
- **2 tablespoons cocoa powder**
- **2 tablespoons milk, extra**

butter frosting

- **90g (3 ounces) butter, softened**
- **1 cup (160g) icing (confectioners') sugar**
- **1 tablespoon milk**

serves 12
prep + cook time 1 hour 40 minutes **nutritional count per serve** 25g total fat (15.9g saturated fat); 1980kJ (473 cal); 57.9g carbohydrate; 5.7g protein; 1.4g fibre

1 Preheat oven to 180°C/350°F. Grease a deep 22cm (9-inch) round or 19cm (8-inch) square cake pan; line base with baking paper.

2 Beat butter, extract and sugar in a medium bowl with an electric mixer until light and fluffy. Beat in eggs, one at a time. Stir in sifted flour and milk, in two batches.

3 Divide mixture between three bowls; tint one mixture pink. Combine sifted cocoa with extra milk in a cup; stir into second mixture; leave remaining mixture plain. Drop alternate spoonfuls of mixtures into pan. Pull a skewer backwards and forwards through cake mixture to create a marbled effect.

4 Bake cake about 1 hour. Stand cake in pan 5 minutes before turning, top-side up, onto a wire rack to cool.

5 Make butter frosting. Spread frosting over top of cake.

butter frosting Beat butter in a small bowl with an electric mixer until light and fluffy; beat in sifted icing sugar and milk, in two batches.

candy cupcakes

- 80g (2½ ounces) butter, softened
- ¼ teaspoon vanilla extract
- ⅓ cup (75g) caster (superfine) sugar
- 2 eggs
- 1 cup (150g) self-raising flour
- 2 tablespoons milk
- 2 x 40g (1½-ounce) jars mini boiled lollies

1 Preheat oven to 180°C/350°F. Line a 12-hole (2-tablespoon/40ml) flat-based patty pan with paper cases.
2 Combine butter, extract, sugar, eggs, sifted flour and milk in a small bowl; beat with an electric mixer on low speed until ingredients are combined. Increase speed to medium; beat for about 2 minutes or until mixture is smooth and paler in colour.

3 Divide mixture into paper cases; bake for 15 minutes. Remove cakes from the oven; sprinkle lollies over cakes. Bake a further 5 minutes or until lollies melt, taking care not to touch the hot melted candy. Stand cakes in pan 5 minutes before turning, top-side up, onto a wire rack to cool.

makes 12 prep + cook time 35 minutes **nutritional count per serve** 6.4g total fat (3.8g saturated fat); 628kJ (150 cal); 20.9g carbohydrate; 2.6g protein; 0.5g fibre

tips Un-iced cake can be frozen for up to 3 months; wrap in plastic wrap, then foil. Cake can be made a day ahead, and iced on the day of serving; store in an airtight container.

raspberry swirl cake

- 250g (8 ounces) butter, softened
- 1 teaspoon vanilla extract
- 1¼ cups (275g) caster (superfine) sugar
- 3 eggs
- 2¼ cups (335g) self-raising flour
- ¾ cup (180ml) milk
- 150g (4½ ounces) frozen raspberries, partly thawed

butter frosting

- 100g (3 ounces) butter, softened
- 1 cup (160g) icing (confectioners') sugar
- 1 tablespoon milk
- pink food colouring

serves 12
prep + cook time 1 hour 30 minutes
nutritional count per serve 26.1g total fat (16.7g saturated fat); 2032kJ (485 cal); 58.4g carbohydrate; 5.6g protein; 1.8g fibre

1 Preheat oven to 180°C/350°F. Grease a deep 22cm (9-inch) round cake pan; line base and side with baking paper.

2 Beat butter, extract and sugar in a medium bowl with an electric mixer until light and fluffy. Beat in eggs, one at a time. Stir in sifted flour and milk, in two batches.

3 Divide mixture between two small bowls. Lightly crush raspberries in another small bowl with a fork; gently stir crushed raspberries into one bowl of cake mixture. Drop alternate spoonfuls of mixtures into pan. Pull a skewer back and forth through cake mixture to create a marbled effect.

4 Bake cake for about 1 hour. Stand cake in the pan for 5 minutes before turning, top-side up, onto a wire rack to cool.

5 Meanwhile, make butter frosting. Spread plain frosting over cake; dollop cake with spoonfuls of pink frosting, swirl frosting for a marbled effect.

butter frosting Beat butter in a small bowl with an electric mixer until as white as possible; beat in sifted icing sugar and milk, in two batches. Divide frosting between two small bowls; tint one bowl of frosting pink.

- 250g (8 ounces) butter, softened
- 1 teaspoon vanilla extract
- 1¼ cups (275g) caster (superfine) sugar
- 3 eggs
- 2¼ cups (335g) self-raising flour
- ¾ cup (180ml) milk

1 Preheat oven to 180°C/350°F. Grease a deep 22cm (9-inch) round or 19cm (8-inch) square cake pan; line base with baking paper.
2 Beat butter, extract and sugar in a medium bowl with an electric mixer until light and fluffy. Beat in eggs, one at a time. Stir in sifted flour and milk, in two batches.
3 Spread mixture into pan; bake 1 hour. Stand cake in pan 5 minutes before turning, top-side up, onto a wire rack to cool.

basic butter cake

tips Cake is best made on the day of serving. Cake can be frozen for up to 3 months; wrap in plastic wrap, then foil.

serves 12
prep + cook time 1 hour 30 minutes
nutritional count per serve
19.2g total fat (12.1g saturated fat);
1531kJ (366 cal); 44g carbohydrate;
5.3g protein; 1.1g fibre

serves 10
prep + cook time 50 minutes
nutritional count per serve
6.7g total fat (4.2g saturated fat);
759kJ (181 cal); 28.1g carbohydrate;
2.6g protein; 0.7g fibre

cinnamon tea cake

- 60g (2 ounces) butter, softened
- 1 teaspoon vanilla extract
- ⅔ cup (150g) caster (superfine) sugar
- 1 egg
- 1 cup (150g) self-raising flour
- ⅓ cup (80ml) milk
- 10g (½ ounce) butter, extra, melted
- 1 teaspoon ground cinnamon
- 1 tablespoon caster (superfine) sugar, extra

1 Preheat oven to 180°C/350°F. Grease a deep 20cm (8-inch) round cake pan; line base with baking paper.
2 Beat butter, extract, sugar and egg in a small bowl with an electric mixer until light and fluffy. Stir in sifted flour and milk.
3 Spread mixture into pan; bake about 30 minutes. Stand cake in pan 5 minutes before turning, top-side up, onto a wire rack. Brush top of cake with melted butter; sprinkle with combined cinnamon and extra sugar. Serve warm with whipped cream or butter, if you like.

serves 16
prep + cook time
50 minutes (+ cooling)
nutritional count
per serve 10.8g total fat
(6.5g saturated fat); 1089kJ
(260 cal); 40g carbohydrate;
2.2g protein; 0.3g fibre

tips Use a serrated or electric knife to split and cut the sponge. This cake is best made on the day of serving.

raspberry cream sponge

- 4 eggs
- ¾ cup (165g) caster (superfine) sugar
- ⅔ cup (100g) wheaten cornflour (cornstarch)
- ¼ cup (30g) custard powder (instant pudding mix)
- 1 teaspoon cream of tartar
- ½ teaspoon bicarbonate of soda (baking soda)
- ¾ cup (240g) raspberry jam (conserve)
- 1½ cups (375ml) thickened (heavy) cream, whipped

raspberry glacé icing

- 45g (1½ ounces) fresh raspberries
- 2 cups (320g) icing (confectioners') sugar
- 15g (½ ounce) butter, softened
- 2 teaspoons hot water, approximately

1 Preheat oven to 180°C/350°F. Grease a deep 22cm (9-inch) square cake pan with butter.

2 Beat eggs and sugar in a small bowl with an electric mixer for about 10 minutes or until thick and creamy and sugar has dissolved; transfer to a large bowl.

3 Sift dry ingredients twice, then sift over egg mixture; fold to combine. Spread mixture into pan.

4 Bake sponge for about 25 minutes. Turn sponge immediately onto a baking paper-covered wire rack, then turn top-side up to cool.

5 Meanwhile, make raspberry glacé icing.

6 Split sponge in half. Sandwich with jam and cream. Spread sponge with icing, sprinkle with fresh rose petals, if you like.

raspberry glacé icing Push raspberries through a fine sieve into a small heatproof bowl; discard solids. Sift icing sugar into same bowl; stir in butter and enough of the water to make a thick paste. Place bowl over a small saucepan of simmering water; stir until icing is spreadable.

carrot & orange cupcakes

- ⅔ cup (160ml) vegetable oil
- ¾ cup (165g) firmly packed brown sugar
- 2 eggs
- 1 teaspoon finely grated orange rind
- 1½ cups (210g) firmly packed coarsely grated carrot
- 1¾ cups (260g) self-raising flour
- ¼ teaspoon bicarbonate of soda (baking soda)
- 1 teaspoon mixed spice

orange glacé icing
- 2 cups (320g) icing sugar
- 20g butter, melted
- 2 tablespoons orange juice, approximately

1 Preheat oven to 180°C/350°F. Line a 12-hole (⅓-cup/80ml) muffin pan with paper cases.

2 Beat oil, sugar, eggs and rind in a small bowl with an electric mixer until thick and creamy. Transfer mixture to a large bowl; stir in carrot, then sifted dry ingredients.

3 Divide mixture into paper cases; bake about 30 minutes. Stand cakes in pan 5 minutes, before turning, top-side up, onto a wire rack to cool.

4 Meanwhile, make orange glacé icing. Spread cakes with icing.

orange glacé icing
Sift icing sugar into a small heatproof bowl; stir in butter and enough juice to make a firm paste. Stir over a small saucepan of simmering water until spreadable.

makes 12
prep + cook time 50 minutes **nutritional count per serve** 14.7g total fat (2.7g saturated fat); 1545kJ (369 cal); 56.9g carbohydrate; 3.6g protein; 1.4g fibre

tips You need about two medium carrots (240g) to get the amount of grated carrot required for this recipe. Oranges and carrots are a great flavour combination, and the orange icing gives just the right finish to these delicious little cupcakes.

makes 20
prep + cook time
1 hour (+ refrigeration)
**nutritional count per
serve** 9.7g total fat
(6.5g saturated fat);
737kJ (176 cal);
18.6g carbohydrate;
3.6g protein; 1.4g fibre

pineapple jelly cakes

- 6 eggs
- ⅔ cup (150g) caster (superfine) sugar
- ⅓ cup (50g) cornflour (cornstarch)
- ½ cup (75g) plain (all-purpose) flour
- ⅓ cup (50g) self-raising flour
- 80g (2½ ounces) packet pineapple jelly crystals
- 1 cup (80g) desiccated coconut
- 1 cup (75g) shredded coconut
- ⅔ cup (160ml) thickened (heavy) cream

1 Preheat oven to 180°C/350°F. Grease a 19cm x 30cm (8-inch x 12-inch) lamington pan; line base and long sides with baking paper, extending paper 5cm (2 inches) over sides.

2 Beat eggs in a large bowl with an electric mixer for 10 minutes or until thick and creamy; gradually add sugar, beating until dissolved between additions. Fold in triple-sifted flours. Spread mixture into pan.

3 Bake about 30 minutes. Turn cake onto a baking paper-covered wire rack to cool.

4 Meanwhile, make jelly according to packet instructions; refrigerate about 2 hours or until jelly is set to the consistency of unbeaten egg white.

5 Trim and discard edges from cake; cut cake into 20 squares. Dip each square into jelly; toss in combined coconuts. Place on a tray, refrigerate 30 minutes.

6 Meanwhile, beat cream in a small bowl with an electric mixer until firm peaks form. Cut cakes in half; sandwich with cream.

biscuits & slices

Biscuits and slices are the best things to cook with kids — they're simple and quick to make, and are the perfect after-school snack. Whichever recipe you choose, they'll be gobbled up in no time.

tip Store cookies in an airtight container.

peanut butter & cornflake cookies

- 395g (12½ ounces) canned sweetened condensed milk
- ½ cup (140g) crunchy peanut butter
- 3 cups (120g) Crunchy Nut cornflakes
- 80g (2½ ounces) white chocolate Melts

makes 26
prep + cook time
45 minutes (+ standing)
nutritional count per cookie 4.7g total fat
(1.6g saturated fat);
468kJ (112 cal);
14.3g carbohydrate;
3.4g protein; 0.8g fibre

1 Preheat oven to 200°C/400°F. Grease and line two oven trays with baking paper.

2 Combine condensed milk, peanut butter and cornflakes in a large bowl. Drop level tablespoons of mixture, 5cm (2 inches) apart, onto oven trays. Bake about 12 minutes; cool on trays.

3 Melt chocolate in a small heatproof bowl over a small saucepan of simmering water (don't let water touch base of bowl). Drizzle cookies with chocolate; stand at room temperature until chocolate sets.

banana, date & rolled oat cookies

- 125g (4 ounces) butter, softened
- 1 teaspoon finely grated lemon rind
- 1 cup (220g) firmly packed brown sugar
- 1 egg yolk
- ⅓ cup mashed banana
- 1½ cups (225g) plain (all-purpose) flour
- ½ teaspoon bicarbonate of soda (baking soda)
- 1 cup (90g) rolled oats
- ½ cup (75g) finely chopped dried dates
- ⅔ cup (60g) rolled oats, extra
- 4 dried dates (35g), seeded, chopped coarsely, extra

1 Preheat oven to 180°C/350°F. Grease two oven trays; line with baking paper.

2 Beat butter, rind, sugar and egg yolk in a small bowl with an electric mixer until combined; stir in banana then sifted flour and soda, oats and dates.

3 Roll level tablespoons of mixture into balls; roll each ball in the extra oats then place on trays 5cm apart. Press a piece of coarsely chopped date into the centre of each ball. Bake 15 minutes. Cool cookies on trays.

tips You need one medium overripe banana (230g) for this recipe. Rolled oats are flattened oat grains rolled into flakes; commonly used for porridge. Use traditional oats for baking.

makes 28
prep + cook time
35 minutes
**nutritional count per
cookie** 4.4g total fat
(2.6g saturated fat);
539kJ (129 cal);
19.9g carbohydrate;
1.7g protein; 1.7g fibre

makes 26
prep + cook time
35 minutes
nutritional count per
cookie 6.8g total fat
(2.8g saturated fat);
497kJ (119 cal);
12.8g carbohydrate;
1.9g protein; 0.7g fibre

jammy flower cookies

- **125g (4 ounces) butter, softened**
- **½ teaspoon vanilla extract**
- **½ cup (110g) caster (superfine) sugar**
- **1 cup (120g) ground almonds**
- **1 egg**
- **1 cup (150g) plain (all-purpose) flour**
- **1 teaspoon finely grated lemon rind**
- **⅓ cup (110g) raspberry jam (conserve)**
- **2 tablespoons apricot jam (conserve)**

1 Preheat oven to 180°C/350°F. Grease oven trays; line with baking paper.

2 Beat butter, extract, sugar and almonds in a small bowl with an electric mixer until light and fluffy. Add egg, beat until combined; stir in sifted flour.

3 Divide rind between both jams; mix well.

4 Roll level tablespoons of cookie mixture into balls; place balls about 5cm (2 inches) apart on oven trays, flatten slightly. Using the end of a wooden spoon, press a flower shape (about 1cm/1 inch deep) into the dough; fill each hole with a little jam, using apricot jam for centres of flowers.

5 Bake about 15 minutes. Cool on trays.

teddy bear biscuits

- 200g (6½ ounces) unsalted butter, softened
- 1 teaspoon vanilla extract
- ¾ cup (165g) caster (superfine) sugar
- 1 egg
- 40g (1½ ounces) dark eating (semi-sweet) chocolate, grated finely
- 1¼ cups (175g) plain (all-purpose) flour
- 2 tablespoons cocoa powder
- 24 mini M&M's
- 12 dark chocolate Melts

1 Preheat oven to 180°C/350°F. Grease three oven trays; line with baking paper.

2 Beat butter, extract, sugar and egg in a small bowl with an electric mixer until just changed to a paler colour; do not overbeat. Stir in chocolate, sifted flour and cocoa. Refrigerate 15 minutes.

3 Roll 24 level teaspoons of the mixture into balls. Roll remaining mixture into 12 larger balls for teddy faces. On each tray, flatten four large balls with the palm of your hand to form an 8cm (3¼-inch) diameter circle. Position two small balls on top of each circle for ears.

Flatten ears with the palm of your hand. Slide one paddle-pop stick two-thirds of the way into the dough of each face.

4 Position M&M's into dough for eyes and a Melt for noses.

5 Bake biscuits about 12 minutes or until browned lightly. Cool on trays.

makes 12
prep + cook time
50 minutes (+ refrigeration)
nutritional count per
biscuit 16g total fat
(10.4g saturated fat);
1134kJ (272 cal);
29.4g carbohydrate;
2.3g protein; 0.7g fibre

tip Store double chocolate freckles in an airtight container for up to 1 week.

double chocolate freckles

- 125g (4 ounces) butter, softened
- ¾ cup (165g) firmly packed brown sugar
- 1 egg
- 1½ cups (225g) plain (all-purpose) flour
- ¼ cup (35g) self-raising flour
- ¼ cup (35g) cocoa powder
- 200g (6½ ounces) dark eating (semi-sweet) chocolate, melted
- ⅓ cup (85g) hundreds and thousands

makes 42
prep + cook time 40 minutes
(+ refrigeration & standing)
nutritional count per
freckle 4.1g total fat
(2.5g saturated fat); 398kJ
(95 cal); 13.5g carbohydrate;
1.3g protein; 0.5g fibre

1 Beat butter, sugar and egg in a small bowl with an electric mixer until combined. Stir in sifted dry ingredients, in two batches.

2 Knead dough on a floured surface until smooth; roll between sheets of baking paper until 5mm (¼ inch) thick. Cover; refrigerate 30 minutes.

3 Preheat oven to 180°C/350°F. Grease three oven trays; line with baking paper.

4 Using a 3cm (1¼-inch), 5cm (2-inch) and 6.5cm (2¾-inch) round cutters, cut 14 rounds from dough using each cutter. Place 3cm rounds on one oven tray; place remainder on other oven trays.

5 Bake small cookies about 10 minutes; bake larger cookies about 12 minutes. Cool on wire racks.

6 Melt chocolate in a small bowl over a small saucepan of simmering water (don't let water touch base of bowl). Spread tops of cookies with chocolate; sprinkle with hundreds and thousands. Set at room temperature.

chocolate caramel slice

- ¾ cup (110g) plain (all-purpose) flour
- ⅓ cup (25g) desiccated coconut
- ⅓ cup (75g) firmly packed brown sugar
- 90g (3 ounces) butter, melted
- 395g (12½ ounces) canned sweetened condensed milk
- 60g (2 ounces) butter, extra
- 2 tablespoons maple syrup
- 200g (6½ ounces) dark eating (semi-sweet) chocolate, chopped coarsely
- 2 teaspoons vegetable oil

1 Preheat oven to 160°C/325°F. Grease a shallow 22cm (9-inch) square cake pan; line base and sides with baking paper, extending paper 5cm (2 inches) above edges.

2 Combine sifted flour, coconut, sugar and butter in a medium bowl; press mixture firmly over base of pan. Bake about 15 minutes or until browned lightly; cool.

3 Meanwhile, combine condensed milk, extra butter and syrup in a small saucepan; stir over medium heat until smooth, pour over base. Return to oven; bake 30 minutes. Cool.

4 Combine chocolate and oil in a small saucepan; stir over low heat until smooth. Pour chocolate over caramel, tilt pan to spread chocolate evenly. Refrigerate slice about 3 hours or until set before cutting into squares.

serves 16
prep + cook time
45 minutes (+ refrigeration)
nutritional count
per piece 15.6g total fat
(9.8g saturated fat);
1251kJ (299 cal);
37.1g carbohydrate;
4.2g protein; 0.7g fibre

tip Store slice in an airtight container in the fridge for up to 4 days.

makes 32
prep + cook time
50 minutes (+ standing)
**nutritional count per
piece** 5.4g total fat
(3.3g saturated fat);
426kJ (102 cal);
12.5g carbohydrate;
1.3g protein; 0.3g fibre

mini chocolate brownies

- 125g (4 ounces) butter, chopped
- 200g (6½ ounces) dark eating (semi-sweet) chocolate, chopped coarsely
- ¾ cup (165g) caster (superfine) sugar
- 1 teaspoon vanilla extract
- 2 eggs, beaten lightly
- 1 cup (150g) plain (all-purpose) flour

1 Preheat oven to 180°C/350°F. Grease a deep 19cm (8-inch) square cake pan; line base and two sides with baking paper, extending paper 2cm (¾ inch) above edges of pan.

2 Stir butter and chocolate in a medium heatproof bowl over a medium saucepan of simmering water until smooth. Remove from heat; stir in sugar and extract then egg and flour. Pour mixture into pan; bake about 30 minutes or until just firm. Cool in pan.

3 Turn brownie onto a board; cut into 16 squares then halve squares to form triangles.

tips For an easy sour cream frosting, melt 100g (3 ounces) dark eating chocolate and fold it into ¼ cup sour cream. Store brownies in an airtight container for up to 4 days. To freeze, wrap in plastic then foil; freeze for up to 3 months.

nutty cornflake slice

- **125g (4 ounces) butter, chopped coarsely**
- **½ cup (110g) caster (superfine) sugar**
- **⅓ cup (80ml) light corn syrup**
- **⅓ cup (95g) crunchy peanut butter**
- **4 cups (160g) corn flakes**
- **350g (11 ounces) milk eating chocolate**

1 Grease a 20cm x 30cm (8-inch x 12-inch) rectangular pan; line base and long sides with baking paper, extending paper 5cm (2 inches) over sides.

2 Stir butter, sugar, syrup and peanut butter in a large saucepan over low heat until sugar dissolves. Bring to the boil. Reduce heat; simmer, uncovered, without stirring, 5 minutes.

3 Gently stir in corn flakes. Spread mixture into pan; press firmly. Refrigerate about 30 minutes or until set.

4 Melt chocolate in a small bowl over a small saucepan of simmering water (don't let water touch base of bowl) until smooth. Spread chocolate over slice; stand at room temperature until set, before cutting.

makes 24 pieces
prep + cook time
25 minutes (+ refrigeration)
nutritional count
per piece 10.6g total fat
(5.8g saturated fat);
791kJ (189 cal);
23.1g carbohydrate;
2.8g protein; 0.7g fibre

tip Store slice in an airtight container for up to three days.

tip Slice can be stored in an airtight container for up to a week.

double chocolate slice

- **125g (4 ounces) butter, chopped coarsely**
- **1 cup (220g) firmly packed dark brown sugar**
- **185g (6 ounces) dark eating (semi-sweet) chocolate**
- **1¼ cups (110g) rolled oats**
- **¾ cup (75g) coarsely chopped walnuts**
- **1 egg**
- **¾ cup (110g) plain (all-purpose) flour**
- **¼ cup (35g) self-raising flour**
- **½ teaspoon bicarbonate of soda (baking soda)**
- **⅔ cup (130g) dark Choc Bits**

1 Preheat oven to 160°C/325°F. Grease 20cm x 30cm (8-inch x 12-inch) rectangular pan; line base and long sides with baking paper, extending paper 5cm (2 inches) over sides.

2 Melt butter in a medium saucepan over low heat. Remove from heat; stir in sugar until smooth.

3 Coarsely chop half the chocolate.

4 Stir oats and nuts into butter mixture, then egg, sifted dry ingredients, chopped chocolate and Choc Bits.

5 Spread mixture into pan. Bake about 30 minutes. Cover hot slice with foil; cool.

6 Melt remaining chocolate. Turn slice, top-side-up, onto a wire rack; drizzle with chocolate. Stand at room temperature until set, before cutting.

makes 24 pieces
prep + cook time
50 minutes (+ cooling)
nutritional count per piece 10.8g total fat
(5.3g saturated fat);
849kJ (203 cal);
24.1g carbohydrate;
2.6g protein; 1g fibre

muffins, scones & bread

Aside from its lunchbox snack ideas, this chapter lets your little ones learn how to knead dough, make scones and handle muffin mixture — all great kitchen skills to have.

café-style banana bread

- 1 cup mashed banana
- 1 cup (220g) firmly packed dark brown sugar
- 2 eggs
- 40g (1½ ounces) butter, melted
- ½ cup (125ml) buttermilk
- ¼ cup (90g) treacle
- 1½ cups (225g) plain (all-purpose) flour
- 1 cup (150g) self-raising flour
- 2 teaspoons mixed spice
- 1 teaspoon bicarbonate of soda (baking soda)

1 Preheat oven to 180°C/350°F. Grease 14cm x 21cm (5½-inch x 8½-inch) loaf pan; line base with baking paper, extending paper 5cm (2 inches) over sides.
2 Combine banana, sugar, eggs, butter, buttermilk and treacle in a large bowl; stir in sifted dry ingredients. Spoon mixture into pan.
3 Bake bread about 1 hour. Stand bread in pan 10 minutes; turn, top-side up, onto a wire rack to cool.

tips You will need 2 large (460g) overripe bananas to get the cup of mashed banana needed for this recipe. Dark brown sugar, though not essential to the bread's success, does improve the bread's flavour and colour. You can use golden syrup or honey instead of the treacle. Don't overmix the batter; lumpy is good in this case. Serve the bread as it is, or toasted with butter.

serves 10
prep + cook time 1¼ hours
nutritional count per serve
5g total fat (2.6g saturated fat);
1298kJ (310 cal);
59.6g carbohydrate;
6.5g protein; 2.2g fibre

- 1¼ cups (175g) self-raising flour
- 90g (3 ounces) butter, melted
- 2 eggs, beaten lightly
- 2 x 125g (4-ounce) cans creamed corn
- ½ cup (50g) pizza cheese
- 2 tablespoons finely chopped fresh chives

1 Preheat oven to 200°C/400°F. Oil two 12-hole (1-tablespoon/20ml) mini muffin pans.

2 Sift flour into a medium bowl; stir in butter, eggs, corn, cheese and chives. Divide mixture into pan holes.

3 Bake muffins about 15 minutes. Stand muffins in pan 5 minutes; turn onto a wire rack to cool.

mini corn muffins

tip The muffins can be stored, refrigerated in an airtight container, for up to 2 days or frozen for 1 month. You can substitute gluten-free self raising flour for the self raising flour.

makes 24
prep + cook time
30 minutes
nutritional count per
muffin 3.9g total fat
(2.4g saturated fat); 310kJ
(74 cal); 8g carbohydrate;
1.5g protein; 0.4g fibre

makes 12
prep + cook time 40 minutes
nutritional count per pinwheel 8.5g total fat (5.4g saturated fat); 761kJ (182 cal); 19g carbohydrate; 6.8g protein; 0.9g fibre

vegemite pinwheels

- **2 cups (300g) self-raising flour**
- **1 tablespoon caster (superfine) sugar**
- **50g (1½ ounce) butter, chopped**
- **¾ cup (180ml) milk**
- **2 tablespoons Vegemite**
- **1¼ cups (150g) coarsely grated cheddar cheese**

1 Preheat oven to 200°C/400°F. Oil a 20cm x 30cm (8-inch x 12-inch) slice pan.
2 Combine sifted flour and caster sugar in a medium bowl; rub in butter. Stir in milk, mix to a soft sticky dough.

3 Turn dough onto a floured surface; knead lightly until smooth. Roll dough out between two sheets of floured baking paper to a 28cm x 40cm (11-inch x 16-inch) rectangle. Spread Vegemite over dough; sprinkle with cheese. Starting from a long side, roll dough up firmly; trim ends. Using an oiled serrated knife, cut roll into 12 slices; place pinwheels, cut-side up, in a single layer, in pan. Bake about 30 minutes. Serve pinwheels warm.

yoghurt, berry & white chocolate muffins

- 1½ cups (225g) wholemeal self-raising flour
- ½ cup (110g) caster (superfine) sugar
- 2 tablespoons vegetable oil
- 2 eggs, beaten lightly
- 1 cup (280g) low-fat yoghurt
- 1 cup (150g) frozen mixed berries
- 100g (3 ounces) white eating chocolate, chopped coarsely

1 Preheat oven to 180°C/350°F. Grease a 12-hole (⅓-cup/80ml) muffin pan.
2 Combine flour and sugar in a large bowl. Add remaining ingredients; mix batter until just combined. Divide batter between pan holes. Bake about 30 minutes. Stand muffins 5 minutes before serving, dusted with sifted icing sugar, if you like.

tips You can use milk or dark chocolate instead of white for the muffins and still get the same melt-in-the-mouth result. These muffins are best served warm.

makes 12
prep + cooking time 50 minutes
nutritional count per muffin 7.2g total fat (2.5g saturated fat); 807kJ (193 cal); 25.3g carbohydrate; 5.6g protein; 2.4g fibre

tip Unbaked scones can be frozen for up to a month. Bake them from the freezer, adding about 10 minutes to the baking time.

spinach & cheese monster scones

- 250g (8 ounces) packet finely chopped frozen spinach, thawed
- 2½ cups (375g) self-raising flour
- 1 tablespoon caster (superfine) sugar
- 50g (1½ ounces) butter, chopped
- ½ cup (60g) coarsely grated cheddar cheese
- ¾ cup (180ml) milk

1 Preheat oven to 240°C/475°F. Oil a deep 20cm (8-inch) square cake pan.

2 Squeeze out excess liquid from spinach. Combine sifted flour and sugar into a medium bowl; rub in butter. Stir in cheese and the spinach then stir in milk to make a soft sticky dough. Turn dough onto a floured surface; knead lightly until smooth.

3 Press dough out to a 2cm (¾-inch) thickness. Cut 16 x 4.5cm (1¾-inch) rounds from dough. Place scones, just touching, in pan. Bake about 20 minutes. Serve warm.

makes 16
prep + cook time 30 minutes
nutritional count per scone 4.6g total fat (2.8g saturated fat); 535kJ (128 cal); 17.2g carbohydrate; 3.8g protein; 1.2g fibre

- 3 cups (450g) self-raising flour
- 30g (1 ounce) butter
- ½ cup (125ml) milk
- 1 cup (250ml) water, approximately

1 Preheat oven to 180°C/350°F. Grease an oven tray.
2 Sift flour into a bowl; rub in butter. Make a well in centre, add milk and enough water to mix to a soft sticky dough. Knead on a floured surface until smooth.
3 Press dough into a 15cm (6-inch) circle, place on tray. Cut a cross through dough, about 1cm (½-inch) deep. Brush top with a little extra milk or water; dust with a little extra flour.
4 Bake 30 minutes or until damper sounds hollow when tapped.

damper

tip Serve damper warm with butter.

serves 6
prep + cook time 45 minutes
nutritional count per
serving 5.8g total fat
(3.4g saturated fat); 1292kJ
(309 cal); 53.9g carbohydrate;
8.1g protein; 2.9g fibre

makes 12
prep + cook time 30 minutes
nutritional count per muffin
10.9g total fat (6.7g saturated fat);
1331kJ (318 cal); 49g carbohydrate;
5.6g protein; 1.2g fibre

tips Muffins can be stored in an airtight container for up to 2 days. To freeze, wrap in plastic then foil, freeze for up to 3 months.

choc-chip jaffa muffins

- 2½ cups (375g) self-raising flour
- 100g (3 ounces) cold butter, chopped finely
- 1 cup (220g) caster (superfine) sugar
- 1¼ cups (310ml) buttermilk
- 1 egg
- ¾ cup (135g) dark Choc Bits
- 2 teaspoons finely grated orange rind

1 Preheat oven to 200°C/400°F. Grease a 12-hole (⅓-cup/80ml) muffin pan.
2 Sift flour into a large bowl; rub in butter. Stir in sugar, buttermilk and egg. Do not overmix; mixture should be lumpy. Stir in Choc Bits and rind.
3 Divide mixture into pan holes; bake about 20 minutes. Stand muffins in pan for 5 minutes before turning, top-side up, onto a wire rack to cool.

vanilla bean scones

- **2½ cups (375g) self-raising flour**
- **1 tablespoon caster (superfine) sugar**
- **30g (1 ounce) cold butter, chopped**
- **¾ cup (180ml) milk**
- **½ cup (125ml) water**
- **1 vanilla bean**
- **300ml (½ pint) thickened (heavy) cream**
- **2 tablespoons icing (confectioners') sugar**
- **¾ cup (240g) strawberry jam (conserve)**
- **250g (8 ounces) strawberries, sliced thinly**

makes 16
prep + cook time 40 minutes
nutritional count per
scone 9.2g total fat
(5.9g saturated fat); 915kJ
(219 cal); 30.4g carbohydrate;
3.4g protein; 1.4g fibre

1 Preheat oven to 220°C/425°F. Spray a deep 22cm (9-inch) square cake pan with cooking oil.

2 Sift the flour and caster sugar into a large bowl; rub in butter.

3 Combine milk and the water in a medium jug. Split the vanilla bean open lengthways, scrape the vanilla bean seeds into the milk mixture; throw away the bean.

4 Make a well in the centre of the flour mixture; pour in the milk mixture. Use a flat-bladed knife to slice through the flour mixture, mix to make a soft sticky dough. Knead dough gently on a lightly floured surface until just smooth.

5 Press and shape the dough into a 20cm (8-inch) square. Dip a sharp knife into some flour; cut the dough into 16 squares. Place the squares in the pan so they are just touching. Brush the scones with a little extra milk. Bake 20 minutes. Turn the scones out of the pan onto a wire rack to cool slightly.

6 Meanwhile, beat cream and half the sifted icing sugar in a small bow with an electric mixer until soft peaks form.

7 Sandwich scones with jam, strawberries and cream. Sprinkle with remaining icing sugar.

tips Cooked scones can be kept in the freezer for up to three months. When you're ready to serve them, take scones out of the freezer, wrap them in foil, and heat in a warm oven.

allergy-friendly

Baked goodies often contain common allergens. This
chapter includes some great dairy-free, gluten-free, nut-free
and egg-free recipes, so your child won't have to miss out.

butter cake

- 200g (6½ ounces) butter, softened
- 2¼ cups (300g) gluten-free self-raising flour
- 1 cup (220g) caster (superfine) sugar
- ½ cup (125ml) milk
- 2 eggs
- 2 egg whites
- 3 x 10g (½ ounce) packets gluten-free edible sugar roses

fluffy frosting
- 1 cup (220g) caster (superfine) sugar
- ½ cup (125ml) water
- 2 egg whites
- green and pink food colouring

serves 12
prep + cook time
1 hour 15 minutes
nutritional count per
serving 15.1g total fat
(9.5g saturated fat);
1359kJ (325 cal);
61.4g carbohydrate;
3.1g protein; 0.4g fibre

1 Preheat oven to 180°C/350°F. Grease and line a deep 25cm (10-inch) heart-shaped cake pan.

2 Beat butter in a medium bowl with an electric mixer until changed to a paler colour. Sift flour and ¼ cup of the sugar together. Beat flour mixture and milk into the butter, in two batches, until just combined.

3 Beat eggs and egg whites in a small bowl with an electric mixer until thick and creamy. Gradually add remaining sugar, one tablespoon at a time, beating until sugar dissolves between additions. With motor operating on low speed, gradually pour egg mixture into flour mixture; beat until just combined.

4 Spread mixture into pan; bake 50 minutes. Stand cake 10 minutes; turn, top-side up, onto a wire rack to cool.

5 Make fluffy frosting. Spread top and sides of cake with pink fluffy frosting; decorate cake with roses. Spoon green fluffy frosting into a small piping bag with a small plain nozzle; pipe leaves onto cake.

fluffy frosting Stir sugar and the water in a small saucepan over high heat, without boiling, until sugar is dissolved. Boil, uncovered, without stirring, about 5 minutes or until syrup reaches 116°C on a candy thermometer (syrup should be thick but not coloured). Remove from heat; allow bubbles to subside. Beat egg whites in a small bowl with an electric mixer until soft peaks form. While mixer is operating, add hot syrup in a thin stream; beat on high speed for about 10 minutes, or until mixture is thick and cool. Reserve 2 tablespoons of the frosting in a small bowl; tint this green. Tint remaining frosting pink.

tip This recipe is gluten-free and nut-free. Make sure a grown-up helps with the hot syrup for the fluffy frosting. This cake can be baked in a deep 23cm (9-inch) square cake pan for about the same time as the heart-shaped cake.

chocolate cupcakes

- 200g (6½ ounces) butter, softened
- 2¼ cups (300g) gluten-free self-raising flour
- ¼ cup (25g) cocoa powder
- 1 cup (220g) caster (superfine) sugar
- ¾ cup (180ml) milk
- 2 eggs
- 2 egg whites

chocolate icing

- 1 cup (160g) pure icing (confectioners') sugar
- 1 tablespoon cocoa powder
- 2 tablespoons water

makes 24
prep + cook time
40 minutes (+ cooling)
**nutritional count
per cake** 7.8g total fat
(4.9g saturated fat);
635kJ (152 cal);
27.4g carbohydrate;
1.6g protein; 0.2g fibre

1 Preheat oven to 180°C/350°F. Line two 12-hole (⅓-cup/80ml) muffin pans with paper cases.

2 Beat butter in a large bowl with an electric mixer until pale. Beat sifted flour, cocoa and ¼ cup of the caster sugar alternately with milk into butter, in two batches, until combined.

3 Beat eggs and egg whites in a small bowl with an electric mixer until thick and creamy. Gradually add remaining caster sugar, one tablespoon at a time, beating until sugar dissolves between additions. Gradually beat egg mixture into flour mixture until combined.

4 Drop 2½ tablespoons mixture into each paper case; bake cakes about 20 minutes. Turn, top-side up, onto a wire rack to cool.

5 Meanwhile, make chocolate icing. Spread cold cakes with icing.
chocolate icing Sift sugar and cocoa into a small bowl; stir in water.

- 125g (4 ounces) butter, softened
- ½ cup (80g) icing (confectioners') sugar
- 1 vanilla bean
- 1¼ cups (85g) plain (all-purpose) flour

1 Place butter and sifted icing sugar in a small bowl. Split vanilla bean; scrape seeds into bowl. Beat with an electric mixer until light and fluffy; stir in sifted flour, in batches.

2 Knead dough on a floured surface until smooth. Shape dough into a 25cm (10-inch) rectangular log. Enclose log in plastic wrap; refrigerate about 30 minutes or until firm.

3 Preheat oven to 180°C/350°F. Grease oven trays; line with baking paper.

4 Cut log into 1cm (½-inch) slices; place slices about 2cm (¾-inch) apart on trays. Bake about 12 minutes. Cool on trays.

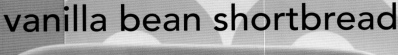

vanilla bean shortbread

tip This recipe is egg-free and nut-free. Store shortbread in an airtight container for 1 week.

makes 22
prep + cook time
30 minutes (+ refrigeration)
nutritional count per biscuit 4.5g total fat (2.9g saturated fat); 284kJ (68 cal); 6.4g carbohydrate; 0.5g protein; 0.1g fibre

makes 30
prep + cook time
55 minutes (+ cooling)
**nutritional count per
meringue** 0g total fat
(0g saturated fat); 79kJ
(19 cal); 4.8g carbohydrate;
0.2g protein; 0g fibre

tip This recipe is gluten-free
and nut-free. Store meringues in an
airtight container for up to 1 week.

rainbow meringues

- **2 egg whites**
- **½ cup (110g) caster (superfine) sugar**
- **pink, yellow and green food colouring**
- **¼ cup (50g) mixed glacé cherries,
  chopped coarsely**

1 Preheat oven to 120°C/250°F. Grease
and line two oven trays.
2 Beat egg whites in a small bowl with an
electric mixer until soft peaks form.
Gradually add sugar, beating until dissolved
between additions.

3 Divide mixture into 3 separate bowls; tint
with food colourings.
4 Spoon mixture into a piping bag fitted
with 5mm (¼-inch) fluted tube. Pipe
meringues onto trays 2cm (¾-inch) apart;
top each meringue with a cherry piece.
(Use a clean piping bag and tube for each
different coloured meringue).
5 Bake meringues about 45 minutes. Cool
in oven with door ajar.

allergy-friendly **63**

saucy caramel pudding

- 1 cup (135g) gluten-free self-raising flour
- ⅓ cup (75g) firmly packed brown sugar
- 20g (¾ ounce) butter, melted
- ½ cup (125ml) milk

caramel sauce

- 1⅓ cups (330ml) water
- ⅓ cup (75g) firmly packed brown sugar
- 30g (1 ounce) butter

1 Preheat oven to 180°C/350°F. Grease a deep 1-litre (4-cup) ovenproof dish.
2 Combine sifted flour, sugar, butter and milk in a medium bowl. Pour mixture into dish.
3 Make caramel sauce.
4 Pour sauce slowly, over the back of a spoon, evenly onto mixture in dish. Bake pudding about 50 minutes. Stand for 10 minutes before serving.

caramel sauce Combine ingredients in a small saucepan; stir over medium heat, without boiling, until smooth.

serves 4
prep + cook time 1 hour 10 minutes
nutritional count per serving 11.7g total fat (7.6g saturated fat); 1208kJ (289 cal); 67.1g carbohydrate; 1.7g protein; 0.5g fibre

tips This recipe is wheat-free, gluten-free, nut-free and egg-free. It's best made just before serving.

tips This recipe is wheat-free, gluten-free and egg-free. Stewed apple and pastry can be prepared 2 days ahead; keep covered in the fridge. Turnovers can be made two days ahead, keep in an airtight container at room temperature. Turnovers are not suitable to freeze.

apple turnovers

- **2 medium apples (300g), peeled, chopped finely**
- **1 teaspoon caster (superfine) sugar**
- **2 tablespoons water**
- **1 teaspoon pure icing (confectioners') sugar**

gluten-free pastry
- **1¼ cups (225g) rice flour**
- **¼ cup (35g) cornflour (100% corn)**
- **¼ cup (30g) soy flour**
- **⅓ cup (75g) caster (superfine) sugar**
- **150g (4½ ounces) cold butter, chopped coarsely**
- **2 tablespoons cold water, approximately**

makes 18
prep + cook time
40 minutes
nutritional count per turnover 7.2g total fat
(4.6g saturated fat);
631kJ (151 cal);
19.6g carbohydrate;
1.7g protein; 0.7g fibre

1 Preheat oven to 200°C/400°F. Grease and line two oven trays with baking paper.
2 Make gluten-free pastry.
3 Combine apple, sugar and the water in a small saucepan; bring to the boil. Reduce heat; simmer, covered, about 5 minutes or until apple is tender. Cool.
4 Roll pastry lightly between sheets of baking paper until 5mm (¼-inch) thick; cut 18 x 8cm (3¼-inch) rounds from pastry. Drop heaped teaspoons of apple mixture into the centre of each round; fold to enclose filling, pinching edges to seal. Place turnovers on tray.

5 Bake turnovers in the oven for about 15 minutes; cool on trays. Serve dusted with sifted icing sugar.
gluten-free pastry
Process flours, sugar and butter until crumbly. Add enough of the water to make ingredients come together. Knead dough gently and lightly on a floured surface until smooth.

potato scones

- **125g (4 ounces) butter, softened**
- **⅓ cup (55g) pure icing (confectioners') sugar**
- **2 egg yolks**
- **1 cup (230g) cold mashed sieved cooked potato**
- **2 cups (270g) gluten-free self-raising flour**
- **2 teaspoons gluten-free baking powder**
- **2 teaspoons milk, approximately**
- **¼ cup (80g) raspberry jam**
- **¼ cup (60ml) double thick cream**

1 Preheat oven to 220°C/425°F. Grease an oven tray.
2 Beat butter, sifted sugar and egg yolks in a small bowl with an electric mixer until light and fluffy. Transfer to a large bowl; stir in mashed potato.
3 Stir in sifted flour and baking powder; mix to a soft dough. Knead dough lightly on a floured surface until just smooth.

4 Press dough out to a 2.5cm (1-inch) thickness. Dip a 5cm (2-inch) round cutter into flour; cut as many rounds as possible from the dough. Place scones 3cm (1¼-inch) apart on tray. Gently knead scraps of dough together; repeat process.
5 Brush tops of scones with milk; bake about 25 minutes or until scones sound hollow when tapped firmly on the top. Serve with jam and cream.

makes 12
prep + cook time
40 minutes
**nutritional count per
scone** 11.5g total fat
(7.2g saturated fat);
732kJ (175 cal);
31.5g carbohydrate;
1.6g protein; 0.8g fibre

pancetta & cheese muffins

- 1 teaspoon olive oil
- 200g (6½ ounces) gluten-free pancetta, chopped finely
- 4 green onions (scallions), sliced thinly
- 1¼ cups (175g) gluten-free self-raising flour
- ⅓ cup (55g) polenta
- ¾ cup (75g) pizza cheese
- ⅔ cup (160ml) milk
- 2 eggs
- 60g (2 ounces) butter, melted

1 Preheat oven to 200°C/400°F. Line a 12-hole (⅓-cup/80ml) muffin pan with paper cases.

2 Heat oil in a medium frying pan over high heat; cook pancetta, stirring, about 3 minutes or until browned lightly. Add onion; cook, stirring, until soft. Cool.

3 Combine flour, polenta and ½ cup of the cheese in a medium bowl; stir in combined milk and eggs, melted butter and pancetta mixture.

4 Divide mixture between paper cases; sprinkle with remaining cheese. Bake about 20 minutes. Stand muffins in pan 5 minutes before turning, top-side up, onto a wire rack to cool.

tips This recipe is gluten-free and nut-free. Muffins are best made on day of serving. Polenta is both ground corn and the dish made from it. It comes in coarse and fine textures, and can be used in cakes and muffins, or fried and topped with char-grilled vegies.

makes 12
prep + cook time 35 minutes
**nutritional count per
muffin** 9.7g total fat
(5.1g saturated fat); 598kJ
(143 cal); 16.7g carbohydrate;
7.2g protein; 0.4g fibre

pizza pinwheels

- 125g (4 ounces) butter, softened
- 1 tablespoon pure icing (confectioners') sugar
- 2 egg yolks
- 1 cup (220g) cooked mashed potato, sieved
- 1 cup (150g) potato flour
- ½ cup (80g) brown rice flour
- 1 tablespoon gluten-free baking powder
- ⅓ cup (90g) tomato paste
- 125g (4 ounces) gluten-free shaved ham, chopped finely
- 30g (1 ounce) baby spinach leaves
- 1½ cups (150g) pizza cheese

1 Preheat oven to 220°C/425°F. Oil a 20cm x 30cm (8-inch x 12-inch) slice pan.

2 Beat butter, sifted icing sugar and yolks in a small bowl with an electric mixer until light and fluffy. Transfer mixture to a large bowl; stir in mashed potato.

3 Add sifted dry ingredients; stir to make a soft dough. Knead dough lightly on a floured surface until smooth. Roll dough between sheets of floured baking paper to a 20cm x 30cm (8-inch x 12-inch) rectangle shape.

4 Spread tomato paste over dough; sprinkle with ham, spinach and 1 cup of the cheese.

5 Starting from a long side, roll dough up firmly using paper as a guide; trim ends. Using an oiled serrated knife, cut roll into 12 slices; place pinwheels, cut-side up, in a single layer, in the pan. Bake 20 minutes. Remove pinwheels from the oven, sprinkle with remaining cheese; bake a further 10 minutes.

makes 12
prep + cook time
50 minutes
nutritional count per
pinwheel 13.4g total fat
(8g saturated fat);
961kJ (230 cal);
19.7g carbohydrate;
7.4g protein; 1.1g fibre

ALMOND a flat, pointy-ended nut with a creamy white kernel that is covered by a brown skin.

meal also known as finely ground almonds; powdered to a flour-like texture and used in baking or as a thickening agent.

BAKING POWDER a raising agent consisting of two parts cream of tartar to one part bicarbonate of soda. The acid and alkaline combination, when moistened and heated, gives off carbon dioxide, which aerates and lightens the mixture during baking. Available gluten-free.

BICARBONATE OF SODA also known as baking or carb soda; a mild alkali used as a leavening agent in baking.

BISCUITS also called cookies.

butternut snap a crunchy biscuit made with golden syrup, oats and coconut.

chocolate-chip cookies plain biscuits with pieces (or chips) of chocolate.

plain chocolate a crisp sweet biscuit with added cocoa powder but no icing or filling.

BUTTER use salted or unsalted (sweet) butter; 125g is equal to one stick (4 ounces).

unsalted butter has no added salt, and is often called 'sweet' butter. The salt content of regular salted butter is sometimes discernable in a sweet recipe, especially with chocolate. You can use regular butter in most cakes and baking, but it's advisable to stick to unsalted butter when it's specified in delicate toppings, icings and so on.

BUTTERMILK originally the term given to the slightly sour liquid left after butter was churned from cream, today it is commercially made similarly to yoghurt. Sold alongside all fresh milk products in supermarkets; despite the implication of its name, it's low in fat.

CAPSICUM also known as bell pepper or, simply, pepper. Be sure to discard seeds and membranes before use. Roasted capsicum is also available, bottled in oil or brine, from most supermarkets and delicatessens.

CARAMEL TOP 'N' FILL a delicious caramel filling made from milk and cane sugar. It can be used straight from the can for slices, tarts and cheesecakes. Has similar qualities to sweetened condensed milk.

CHEESE

cream commonly known as Philly or Philadelphia, a soft, cow's-milk cheese. Also available as a spreadable light cream cheese, which is a blend of cottage and cream cheeses.

parmesan also known as parmigiano, a hard, grainy, cows-milk cheese.

pizza a blend of grated mozzarella, cheddar and parmesan cheeses.

ricotta a sweet, moist, white, cow's-milk cheese with a slightly grainy texture. Its name roughly translates as 'cooked again'. Made from whey, a by-product of other cheese-making, to which fresh milk and acid are added.

CHIVES related to the onion and leek; have a subtle onion flavour.

CHOCOLATE

Choc Bits also known as chocolate chips and chocolate morsels; available in milk, white and dark chocolate. These hold their shape in baking and are ideal for decorating.

chocolate Melts discs of compound dark, milk or white chocolate ideal for melting and moulding.

dark eating also known as semi-sweet or luxury chocolate; made from a high percentage of cocoa liquor and cocoa butter, and a little added sugar.

milk eating most popular eating chocolate; mild and very sweet.

white eating contains no cocoa solids but derives its sweet flavour from cocoa butter. Very sensitive to heat so watch carefully if melting.

COCOA POWDER also known as cocoa; dried, unsweetened, roasted then ground cocoa beans.

CONFECTIONERY

boiled lollies a thick syrup of boiled sugar and water, to which colour and flavourings are added before the mixture

glossary

is rolled and cut into pieces and hardened. Also known as rock candy, humbugs and bullseyes.

CORNFLOUR known as cornstarch; used as a thickening agent in all types of cooking.

wheaten cornflour made from wheat rather than corn – gives sponge cakes a lighter texture (due to the fact wheaten cornflour has some gluten).

CRANBERRIES, DRIED have the same slightly sour, succulent flavour as fresh cranberries. Available in most supermarkets and health-food stores.

CREAM we use fresh cream, also known as pure cream and pouring cream, unless otherwise stated. Minimum fat content 35%.

sour a thick, cultured soured cream. Minimum fat content 35%.

thickened whipping cream containing a thickener. Minimum fat content 35%.

CREAM OF TARTAR acid ingredient in baking powder; added to confectionery mixtures to help prevent sugar from crystallising. Keeps frostings creamy and improves volume when beating egg whites.

CURRANTS, DRIED tiny, almost black raisins so-named after a grape variety that originated in Corinth, Greece.

CUSTARD POWDER instant mixture used to make pouring custard; similar to North American instant pudding mixes.

DAIRY-FREE SPREAD also known as dairy-free margarine. We used Diet Becel, a commercial product with a fat content of 2.4g per 5g of spread.

FLOUR

plain an all-purpose flour made from wheat.

potato made from cooked potatoes that have been dried and ground.

rice a very fine flour made from ground white rice.

self-raising plain flour sifted with baking powder in the proportion of 1 cup flour to 2 teaspoons baking powder. Also available gluten-free from most supermarkets.

soy made from ground soy beans.

wholemeal also known as whole wheat flour. Flour milled from the whole wheat grain (bran and germ).

FOOD COLOURING a digestible substance used to give colour to food, can be made from vegetable dyes and is available in liquid or powdered form.

GINGER also called green or root ginger; the thick root of a tropical plant.

ground also known as powdered ginger; used as a flavouring in cakes, pies and puddings but cannot be substituted for fresh ginger.

GLACÉ FRUIT fruit that has been preserved in a sugar syrup.

GOLDEN SYRUP a by-product of refined sugar cane; pure maple syrup or honey can be substituted.

HAZELNUTS also known as filberts; plump, grape-sized, rich, sweet nut with a brown inedible skin that is removed by rubbing heated nuts together vigorously in a tea towel.

meal also known as ground hazelnuts.

JAM also known as preserve or conserve.

JELLY CRYSTALS a powdered mixture of gelatine, sweetener and artificial fruit flavouring that's used to make a moulded, translucent, quivering dessert. Also known as jello.

LEMON CURD a smooth spread, usually made from lemons, butter and eggs.

LOLLIES confectionery; also known as sweets or candy.

MAPLE SYRUP a thin syrup distilled from the sap of the maple tree. Maple-flavoured syrup or pancake syrup is not an adequate substitute for the real thing.

MARMALADE a preserve, usually based on citrus fruit.

MIXED SPICE a blend of spices that is generally used in sweet dishes such as fruit cakes, shortbread biscuits and fruit pies.

MUESLI also known as granola; a combination of grains (mainly oats), nuts and dried fruits.

OATS, ROLLED flattened oat grain rolled into flakes; traditionally used for porridge. Use traditional oats for baking.

OIL

cooking spray we use a cholesterol-free cooking spray made from canola oil.

olive made from ripened olives. Extra virgin and virgin are the first and second press, respectively, of the olives and are therefore considered the best; the "extra light" or "light" name on other types refers to taste not fat levels.

peanut pressed from ground peanuts; the most commonly used oil in Asian cooking because of its high smoke point (capacity to handle high heat without burning).

vegetable any of a number of oils sourced from plant rather than animal fats.

ONIONS, GREEN also known as scallions or, incorrectly, shallots; an immature onion picked before the bulb has formed, with a long, bright-green edible stalk.

PARSLEY, FLAT-LEAF also known as continental or italian parsley.

PEPITAS dried pumpkin seeds.

PISTACHIOS pale green, delicately flavoured nuts inside hard off-white shells. To peel, soak shelled nuts in boiling water for about 5 minutes; drain, then pat dry with absorbent paper. Rub skins with a cloth to remove skins.

PROSCIUTTO a kind of unsmoked Italian ham; salted, air-cured and aged, it is usually eaten uncooked.

QUINCE yellow-skinned fruit with a hard texture and astringent, tart taste; eaten cooked or as a preserve. Quince paste is available from specialist food stores and some delicatessens.

RAISINS dried sweet grapes.

RHUBARB has thick, celery-like stalks that can reach up to 60cm long; the stalks are the only edible portion of the plant — the leaves contain a toxic substance. Though generally eaten as a fruit, rhubarb is a vegetable.

SAUCE, BARBECUE a spicy, tomato-based sauce used to marinate, or as a condiment.

SPINACH also known as english spinach and, incorrectly, silver beet.

SUGAR

brown a soft, finely granulated sugar retaining molasses (a thick dark syrup produced from sugar cane) for its characteristic colour and flavour.

caster also known as superfine or finely granulated table sugar.

dark brown a moist sugar with a rich distinctive full flavour that comes from natural molasses syrup. It is ideal for sweetening fruits, puddings and fruit cakes, gingerbread or chocolate cakes, adding both colour and flavour.

icing also known as confectioners' sugar or powdered sugar; granulated sugar crushed with a small amount of cornflour added.

icing, pure also known as confectioners' sugar or powdered sugar. Has no added cornflour.

SULTANAS dried grapes, also known as golden raisins.

SWEETENED CONDENSED MILK a canned milk product consisting of milk with more than half the water content removed and sugar added to the remaining milk.

TOMATO

cherry also known as tiny tim or tom thumb; a small, round tomato.

paste triple-concentrated tomato purée used to flavour soups, sauces and casseroles.

pasta sauce a prepared sauce made from tomatoes, herbs and spices.

TREACLE a concentrated syrup with a distinctive flavour and dark black colour; a by-product of sugar refining.

VANILLA

bean dried long, thin pod from a tropical golden orchid; the tiny black seeds impart a luscious vanilla flavour in baking and desserts.

extract vanilla beans that have been submerged in alcohol. Vanilla essence is not a suitable substitute.

VEGEMITE Australia's favourite sandwich spread — made from brewers' yeast extract, substitute with Marmite.

conversion chart

measures

One Australian metric measuring cup holds approximately 250ml, one Australian metric tablespoon holds 20ml, one Australian metric teaspoon holds 5ml. The difference between one country's measuring cups and another's is within a 2- or 3-teaspoon variance, and will not affect your cooking results. North America, New Zealand and the United Kingdom use a 15ml tablespoon. All cup and spoon measurements are level. The most accurate way of measuring dry ingredients is to weigh them. When measuring liquids, use a clear glass or plastic jug with metric markings. We use large eggs with an average weight of 60g.

dry measures

METRIC	IMPERIAL
15g	½oz
30g	1oz
60g	2oz
90g	3oz
125g	4oz (¼lb)
155g	5oz
185g	6oz
220g	7oz
250g	8oz (½lb)
280g	9oz
315g	10oz
345g	11oz
375g	12oz (¾lb)
410g	13oz
440g	14oz
470g	15oz
500g	16oz (1lb)
750g	24oz (1½lb)
1kg	32oz (2lb)

liquid measures

METRIC	IMPERIAL
30ml	1 fluid oz
60ml	2 fluid oz
100ml	3 fluid oz
125ml	4 fluid oz
150ml	5 fluid oz
190ml	6 fluid oz
250ml	8 fluid oz
300ml	10 fluid oz
500ml	16 fluid oz
600ml	20 fluid oz
1000ml (1 litre)	1¾ pints

length measures

METRIC	IMPERIAL
3mm	⅛in
6mm	¼in
1cm	½in
2cm	¾in
2.5cm	1in
5cm	2in
6cm	2½in
8cm	3in
10cm	4in
13cm	5in
15cm	6in
18cm	7in
20cm	8in
23cm	9in
25cm	10in
28cm	11in
30cm	12in (1ft)

oven temperatures

These oven temperatures are only a guide for conventional ovens. For fan-forced ovens, check the manufacturer's manual.

	°C (CELSIUS)	°F (FAHRENHEIT)
Very slow	120	250
Slow	150	275-300
Moderately slow	160	325
Moderate	180	350-375
Moderately hot	200	400
Hot	220	425-450
Very hot	240	475

The imperial measurements used in these recipes are approximate only. Measurements for cake pans are approximate only. Using same-shaped cake pans of a similar size should not affect the outcome of your baking. We measure the inside top of the cake pan to determine sizes.

index

Published in 2013 by Bauer Media Books, Sydney
Bauer Media Books are published by Bauer Media Limited
54 Park St, Sydney
GPO Box 4088, Sydney, NSW 2001.
phone (02) 9282 8618; fax (02) 9126 3702
www.awwcookbooks.com.au

MEDIA GROUP

BAUER MEDIA BOOKS
Publishing Director - Gerry Reynolds
Publisher - Sally Wright
Director of Sales, Marketing & Rights - Brian Cearnes
Editorial & Food Director - Pamela Clark
Creative Director - Hieu Chi Nguyen
Food Concept Director - Sophia Young

Published and Distributed in the United Kingdom by Octopus Publishing Group
Endeavour House
189 Shaftesbury Avenue
London WC2H 8JY
United Kingdom
phone (+44)(0)207 632 5400; fax (+44)(0)207 632 5405
info@octopus-publishing.co.uk;
www.octopusbooks.co.uk

Printed in China

International foreign language rights, Brian Cearnes, Bauer Media Books
bcearnes@bauer-media.com.au

A catalogue record for this book is available from the British Library.
ISBN 978-1-74245-356-9
© Bauer Media Limited 2013
ABN 18 053 273 546